Modernizing Marriage

Gender and Globalization
Susan S. Wadley, *Series Editor*

Other titles in the Gender and Globalization series

*Bodies That Remember: Women's Indigenous Knowledge
and Cosmopolitanism in South Asian Poetry*
    Anita Anantharam

Family, Gender, and Law in a Globalizing Middle East and South Asia
    Kenneth M. Cuno and Manisha Desai, eds.

*Imperial Citizen: Marriage and Citizenship
in the Ottoman Frontier Provinces of Iraq*
    Karen M. Kern

Jamaat-e-Islami Women in Pakistan: Vanguard of a New Modernity?
    Amina Jamal

Lines in Water: Religious Boundaries in South Asia
    Eliza F. Kent and Tazim R. Kassam, eds.

The Moroccan Women's Rights Movement
    Amy Young Evrard

Policing Egyptian Women: Sex, Law, and Medicine in Khedival Egypt
    Liat Kozma

Women, Islam, and Identity: Public Life in Private Spaces in Uzbekistan
    Svetlana Peshkova

Modernizing Marriage

Family, Ideology, and Law in Nineteenth-
and Early Twentieth-Century Egypt

Kenneth M. Cuno

Syracuse University Press

Copyright © 2015 by Syracuse University Press
Syracuse, New York 13244-5290

All Rights Reserved

First Edition 2015

15 16 17 18 19 20   6 5 4 3 2 1

∞ The paper used in this publication meets the minimum requirements of the American National Standard for Information Sciences—Permanence of Paper for Printed Library Materials, ANSI Z39.48-1992.

For a listing of books published and distributed by Syracuse University Press, visit www.SyracuseUniversityPress.syr.edu.

ISBN: 978-0-8156-3392-1 (cloth)   978-0-8156-5316-5 (e-book)

Library of Congress Cataloging-in-Publication Data

Cuno, Kenneth M., 1950–
  Modernizing marriage : family, ideology, and law in nineteenth and early twentieth century Egypt / Kenneth M. Cuno.
    pages cm. — (Gender and globalization series)
  Includes bibliographical references and index.
  ISBN 978-0-8156-3392-1 (cloth : alk. paper) — ISBN 978-0-8156-5316-5 (e-book)
  1. Marriage—Egypt—19th century. 2. Marriage—Egypt—20th century. I. Title.
  HQ691.7.A14 2015
  306.81096209'034—dc23   2014046526

Manufactured in the United States of America

For Marilyn, Paul, and Carrie

Kenneth M. Cuno is an associate professor of history at the University of Illinois at Urbana–Champaign. His recent books are *Race and Slavery in Nineteenth-Century Egypt, Sudan, and the Ottoman Mediterranean: Histories of Trans-Saharan Africans*, co-edited with Terence Walz (2010); and *Family, Gender, and Law in a Globalizing Middle East and South Asia*, co-edited with Manisha Desai (2009). He also authored the chapter "Egypt to c. 1919" in vol. 5 of *The New Cambridge History of Islam* (2010).

Contents

List of Illustrations · ix
List of Tables · xi
Transliteration, Names, and Citations · xiii
Preface and Acknowledgments · xv
Abbreviations · xxi

Introduction · 1

1. Marriage in Politics: *The Obsolescence of Household Government and the Shift to Monogamy in the Khedival Family* · 19

2. Marriage in Practice: *The Changing System of Marriage and Household Formation* · 45

3. Marriage Reformed: *Modernist Intellectuals and the New Family Ideology* · 77

4. Marriage in Law: *Transformations in the Law Applied* · 123

5. Marriage Codified: *The Invention of Egyptian Personal Status Law* · 158

6. Marriage Modernized? *The Curious History of "House of Obedience"* · 185

Conclusion and Epilogue · 205

Notes · 219
Select Bibliography · 267
Index · 291

Illustrations

1. Khedive Tawfiq and Khediva Amina Hanimeffendi and their children · *40*
2. Iskandar Abdelmalek and Liza Henein, their daughter Margueritte, and their son Amin · *55*
3. An unidentified couple posing in wedding attire · *69*
4. "Fallah Family of Sakha," in al-Gharbiyya province · *73*
5. Al-Tahtawi's promise of monogamy · *136*
6. Chapter on the Marriage Guardian in a juridical text · *168*
7. Introduction and beginning of Qadri's personal status code · *170*

Tables

1. The First Marriages of the Children of Khedive Ismail · *37*
2. Proportion of Household Types in the Four Villages and Cairo, 1847–48 · *62*
3. Proportion of Household Types in the Four Villages, 1868 · *63*
4. Married Men by Age in Cairo and the Four Villages, 1847–48 · *64*
5. Married Women by Age in Old Cairo and the Four Villages, 1847–48 · *65*
6. Married Men and Women by Age in the Four Villages, 1868 · *66*
7. Polygynous Married Muslim Men in the Four Villages · *71*

Transliteration, Names, and Citations

There are several systems for transliteration of Arabic into Roman characters in the United States and Europe. Transliteration involves choosing and sometimes compromising between faithfulness to the Arabic orthography and the way words are actually pronounced. The gap between the classical and modern literary forms of Arabic and the spoken vernaculars in syntax, vocabulary, and pronunciation adds another complicated set of issues. Moreover, in most Arab histories there are terms and names, especially before the twentieth century, that come from Ottoman Turkish, which can be rendered in modern Turkish orthography or in transliteration as either Ottoman or Arabic.

My approach is guided by the goal of communication with those unfamiliar with Middle Eastern languages, some of whom I hope will read this book out of an interest in comparative family history, women and gender history, and legal history. I use a simplified version of the transliteration system of the *International Journal of Middle East Studies*, minus the diacritical marks, and using symbols for the ayn (') and hamza (') only when they occur in the middle or at the end of a word. I have left these symbols entirely out of familiar names and terms like "Ismail" and "ulama." I use Arabic plurals like "ulama" that are part of the English lexicon, but otherwise I Anglicize plurals (hadiths instead of *ahadith*), and I use the equivalent English terms in place of Arabic or Turkish whenever possible ("judge" instead of *qadi*).

I Romanize terms and names to match the orthography of standard Arabic except when there is a different conventional spelling in English, when a Turkish name has no Arabic equivalent, or when a family has expressed a preference to me. This system is inconsistent, but it reflects modern Egyptian usage.

In the interval since I began this project some archival materials have been relocated and reorganized. I began my research in the provincial Sharia Court records in the Public Record Office (Dar al-Mahfuzat), but they have since been moved to the National Archives (Dar al-Watha'iq). For the sake of consistency I cite them according to their present location. Another change that overtook my research was the partial computerization of the holdings of the National Archives, and as a result some but not all of my citations to archival materials include an archival code.

Preface and Acknowledgments

Khedive Ismail had multiple wives and concubines, as befitted the head of the ruling dynasty of Egypt. That style of conjugality displayed his grandeur and masculinity. However, his grandson Khedive Abbas II practiced polygyny surreptitiously, like a man with a mistress in a legally monogamous society, even though polygyny remains legal in Egypt to this day. The concern of Abbas to maintain a monogamous image in public was a consequence of the development of a conjugal family ideal during the late nineteenth and early twentieth centuries. This book discusses the formation of that ideal—how the family and marriage were (re)imagined—as well as sociodemographic and legal changes affecting marriage in those decades.

I began this project serendipitously some two decades ago, during a trip to Cairo to research questions of Islamic jurisprudence in the Ottoman era. Having some free time I decided to explore the new materials that had been collected and cataloged in the National Archives since my previous work there. I was curious about the registers of the census of 1848, and when I saw the detail they contained I thought they had the potential to complement qualitative sources like Sharia Court records and fatwas, which often dealt with family matters. Research in late nineteenth-century Sharia Court records convinced me of the important effects of changes in legal procedure prior to the codification of Muslim family law beginning in the 1920s, something that is overlooked in extant legal histories. And the legal sources led me to the writings of nineteenth-century modernist intellectuals, two of whom, Muhammad Abduh and Qasim Amin, were judges. The writings of Egyptian modernist intellectuals, women as well as men, had previously been examined for evidence of the influence of

Enlightenment ideas, the development of national identity, and nascent feminism, but not for their ideas about the family and marriage. In the end I decided to begin my discussion with two chapters that address the changing political, social, and demographic factors that influenced patterns of marriage and family formation from the mid-nineteenth century to the early twentieth century. The third chapter examines the new family ideology promoted by modernist intellectuals and popularized in the periodical press. The final three chapters analyze changes in the legal system that affected marriage and marital relations. An epilog and conclusion briefly discuss the legislation of the 1920s governing marriage and divorce and subsequent developments.

Over the years I have accumulated many debts of gratitude to institutions, colleagues, and friends that must be acknowledged. I first inspected the census registers while on a fellowship provided by the American Research Center in Egypt (ARCE) in the summer of 1994. I did most of my archival research supported by a Fulbright Research Fellowship during 1998–99, supplemented by shorter research trips funded by the Research Board of the University of Illinois in the summers of 2000, 2002, and 2010. I conducted additional research and did most of my writing during sabbaticals in 2006 and 2013 and during leaves from teaching in 2002 and 2011 funded by Humanities Released Time awards from the Research Board of the University of Illinois. The Research Board also provided several semesters of support for research assistants. In addition to the magnificent collection and services of the Library of the University of Illinois, I made use of the collections in the Regenstein Library of the University of Chicago, where Bruce Craig kindly assisted me, and in the Library of the American University in Cairo (AUC), where the staff were friendly and helpful. Akram Khabibulaev, Librarian for Near Eastern, Islamic, and Central Eurasian Studies at Indiana University Bloomington, located some key texts for me. In Cairo I was affiliated with the Department of History of the AUC as a visiting research scholar, and I was always made to feel welcome by my colleagues at the AUC and by the staff of the ARCE, where I could invariably count on the assistance of Madam Amira Khattab. I am grateful to those institutions and persons for their support and assistance.

I wish to thank the staffs of the National Archives of Egypt (Dar al-Watha'iq), the National Library (Dar al-Kutub), and the Public Record Office (Dar al-Mahfuzat). I am grateful for the kind assistance I received and for permission to use their materials. Special thanks are due to Madam Nadia Mustafa and Madam Nagwa Mahmud, the head and deputy head of the National Archives reading room, respectively. My friend and colleague Emad Helal, director of the Documentary Research Unit of the National Archives, was helpful in numerous ways and good company.

My sojourns in Cairo were made more enjoyable by the hospitality and friendship of John Swanson and Sahar Tawfiq. I am also indebted to the late Muhammad Sadiq and Mustafa Sadiq for their friendship and for many of the sources I use in this book.

Will Hanley generously provided me with a copy of the French consular court's decision in the case of Shaykh Ahmad Sulayman Basha and Nafisa Dhuhni, which I discuss in chapter 6. Archana Prakash scanned and gave me a copy of Rifa'a al-Tahtawi's promise of monogamy, which I discuss in chapter 4. That document is in the private archive of the Tahtawi family, and I reproduce it with the kind permission of Ali Rifaah. Samir Ra'fat allowed me to photocopy the special issue of *al-Musawwar* on the marriage of King Faruq and Princess Farida in his possession. I acquired some details of the lives of Ahmad Shafiq and Muhammad Ali Allouba from Hassan Kamel-Kelisli-Morali and his Flickr album. My research assistants, Rosemary Admiral and Aisha Sobh, did valuable work in juridical sources and newspapers.

Michael Reimer originally told me of the existence of the census registers, which he was one of the first scholars to use, and I have profited from discussions of the census with him, Ghislaine Alleaume, Philippe Fargues, Mohamed Saleh, and Terry Walz. Nelly Hanna, Amira El-Azhary Sonbol, and Ron Shaham made useful suggestions, especially with regard to legal sources. Sonbol is the only other scholar that I know of to highlight the importance of the nineteenth-century procedural changes in the operation of the Sharia Courts, including "Hanafization," a term I got from her in a long-ago conversation. Shaham alerted me to the importance of the procedural law of 1897, which authorized the use of police to enforce orders of obedience.

I presented early versions of some chapters at meetings of the Middle East Studies Association and in sessions of the History Workshop of Illinois' Department of History, and I am grateful for the comments and encouragement I received from colleagues. I also presented my findings in conferences and workshops at the University of California–Berkeley (2000), the Institut Français d'Archéologie Orientale du Caire (2002), Harvard University (2003), the University of North Carolina at Chapel Hill (2003), the University of Illinois (2004), the American Historical Association in New York (2009), and Ben-Gurion University (2012), and received valuable feedback. In addition to the persons already named I benefitted over the years from discussing the family in history and family law with Janet Afary, Muhammad Afifi, Iris Agmon, Flavia Agnes, Zehra Arat, James Baldwin, Marilyn Booth, Juan Cole, Manisha Desai, Beshara Doumani, Tarek Elgawhary, Shelly Feldman, Pascale Ghazaleh, the late Muhammad Hakim, Frances Hasso, Emad Helal, Homa Hoodfar, Ahmad Fikri Ibrahim, Baber Johansen, Suad Joseph, Amy Kallander, Liat Kozma, Saba Mahmood, Margaret L. Meriwether, Leslie Peirce, Rudolph Peters, Archana Prakash, Frances Raday, the late Andre Raymond, Zakia Salime, Holly Shissler, Diane Singerman, Judith Tucker, Terry Walz, Anita Weiss, Lynn Welchman, and Kathryn Yount. I am especially indebted to Iris Agmon, Marilyn Booth, Terry Walz, and two anonymous readers for Syracuse University Press for reading and commenting on the penultimate draft of this book.

I published a preliminary version of chapter 1 in *Family History in the Middle East: Household, Property, and Gender*, edited by Beshara Doumani, The State University of New York Press, © 2003, State University of New York. All rights reserved. I am grateful for permission to reprint it here, in an expanded and revised version.

I have taken care in selecting illustrations to avoid the ubiquitous images produced around the turn of the twentieth century for Western tourists and readers by commercial photographers, which merely fed back stereotypes about Muslim women, polygyny, and so on. The illustrations I have chosen were not intended for commercial use nor, with one exception, for public viewing. The first three represent the introduction of family portraiture by professional photographers as well as the diffusion of a conjugal family ideal in the upper and middle classes. The photo of Khedive Tawfiq and Khediva Amina Hanimeffendi and their children in the mid-1880s was originally published in *al-Musawwar*, 1344 (1950), and made available by the Bibliotheca Alexandrina Memory of Modern Egypt Digital Archive. The portraits of Iskandar Abdelmalek and his family and of an unidentified couple posing in wedding attire are published courtesy of the Rare Books and Special Collections Library, The American University in Cairo. My thanks to Ola Seif for her help with those. The photo of the "fallah" family of Sakha, al-Gharbiyya, was originally published in Jean Lozach, *Le Delta du Nil: Etude de Géographie Humaine* (Cairo: Imprimerie E. & R. Schindler, 1935).

Abbreviations

FM The collected fatwas of Muhammad al-Abbasi al-Mahdi, *Al-Fatawa al-Mahdiyya fi al-Waqa'i' al-Misriyya*. 7 vols. Cairo: al-Matba'a al-Azhariyya, 1883–86.

MA Registers of the Sharia Court of Alexandria (Mahkamat al-Iskandariyya), in the National Archives.

MD Registers of the Sharia Court of al-Daqahliyya Province (Mahkamat al-Daqahliyya), in the National Archives.

MM Registers of the Sharia Court of al-Mansura (Mahkamat al-Mansura), in the National Archives.

NAE National Archives of Egypt (Dar al-Watha'iq).

Modernizing Marriage

Introduction

In January 2014 Egyptian voters approved a new constitution for the second time in little more than a year, following the removal of President Muhammad Mursi from power and the installation of an interim government. Many Egyptians considered the constitution written during Mursi's presidency and approved in December 2012 unacceptably Islamist, necessitating a redraft. The new constitution omitted the most objectionable articles, but there were relatively few changes in the articles bearing on the family and the role of women.[1]

Like its predecessors of 1956, 1971, and 2012, the 2014 constitution declared the family to be "the basis of society" and to be "founded on religion, morality, and patriotism." A commitment to preserving the "authentic character" of the Egyptian family was added to the 1971 draft, and in 2012 that commitment was extended to include preservation of its "cohesion and stability" and the upholding of its "moral values," language that was retained in 2014 (Article 10).[2] These declarations express a family ideology constructed by modernist intellectuals beginning in the late nineteenth century. Domesticity, a component of Egyptian family ideology, coexists uneasily with the ideal of women's emancipation, and successive republican constitutions have reflected that tension in addressing the status of women. The 2014 draft committed the state to achieving the equality of women with men "in all civil, political, economic, social, and cultural rights," omitting a phrase included in 1971 and 2012 that made women's equality subject to the principles of the Islamic Sharia. Left unstated was the perpetuation of inequality in the personal status law, which is derived from religious law and governs the domestic sphere.[3] The new constitution also retained the state's commitment to enabling women to "balance

1

between family obligations and the demands of work," and to protecting motherhood and childhood; the latter had first appeared in 1956, along with a more recent commitment to care for and protect "women with dependents, elderly women, and extremely needy women" (Article 11). No article addresses the status of men. Thus although the present constitution supports women's rights less equivocally than before and endorses women's participation in the paid workforce, it also acknowledges their domestic obligations and evinces a special concern for women who lack adequate means of their own or support from a husband or other male relative.

The persistence of these tropes is striking. Successive constitutions written and revised from the early republic through the eras of Arab socialism and structural readjustment, and under secular-nationalist and Islamist regimes, evinced a high degree of consensus on the social importance of the family, childrearing, and motherhood. This book argues that these hegemonic ideas developed in the past two centuries and have only a limited connection with Islamic concepts of an earlier time.

Successive constitutions referred to the family as *al-usra*, a term that in the twentieth century signified the conjugal family,[4] thereby valorizing that particular family form and identifying its cohesion and stability as a social good. Historically, however, Muslim jurisprudence privileged the extended patrilineal family over the conjugal family in such areas as the marital property regime and inheritance, and it permitted polygyny and easy divorce, which were sources of conjugal family instability, as Mounira Charrad has noted.[5] The idea of the conjugal family as the basis of society comes from Enlightenment thought, as does the notion that the purpose of marriage is the formation of a family and childrearing.[6] Precolonial Muslim writings, on the other hand, deemed marriage necessary for licit sexual relations and procreation, but they did not especially emphasize parent-child relations, as Kecia Ali observed.[7] The constitutional reference to women's family responsibilities expresses a domestic ideology, but historical Muslim jurisprudence did not require married women to perform housework or childcare duties.[8]

The concern for (single) women with dependents, those who are elderly, and the extremely needy implies the existence of two classes of adult women, the married and the postmarital, with some of the latter lacking a male provider. Until recently, marriage was nearly universal for Egyptian women, but their treatment as dependents in the constitutional text reflects what Nadia Sonneveld has called "the maintenance-obedience relationship" in marriage, which is the idea that the duty of the husband is to support his wife and children in return for the obedience and submission of the wife.[9] Sonneveld studied marriage and divorce in the 2000s, but the roots of this idea are in precolonial Muslim thought, which, combined with the exaltation of the conjugal family, motherhood, and domesticity in nineteenth-century European thought, produced a modern hybrid that is Egyptian family ideology.[10]

The ideal maintenance-obedience relationship often bears little resemblance to present-day reality, since most married women work out of necessity to contribute to the household income. But the same was true of the late nineteenth century, when the family ideology was formed, as well as of earlier times. Qasim Amin (1863–1908) devoted much of his book *Tahrir al-Mar'a* (The Emancipation of Women, 1899) to the family question, although it is better known for its criticism of the custom of veiling. In it he championed the education of women and wrote of their potential to contribute to society through work, though his point of departure was the maintenance-obedience relationship, which he took as normative. He argued that women should be educated to prepare them for roles as mothers and companions, but that an education would also enable widows and divorcées to support themselves and their children.

This book is a history of marriage and marital relations in Egypt in the nineteenth and early twentieth centuries. During that time the contemporary Egyptian marriage system developed, a family ideology was constructed, and religious norms became the basis of family law, developments reflected in the constitutions of 1956 through 2014. Due to the vastness of family as a topic I have limited my study to marriage and marital relations from the mid-nineteenth century to 1920 or, in other words, before the codification of family law began.

Why study the family in history? Alan Duben and Cem Behar, Lisa Pollard, and Hanan Kholoussy have observed that debates about the family in the late Ottoman Empire and Egypt were often really about society and the nation.[11] This has been true ever since nineteenth-century modernists identified the conjugal family as the elemental unit in society, with the function of raising children. From that time the fate of the family became the fate of the nation, and of course not only in the Middle East. Stephanie Coontz has shown how the family, often misremembered, figures in American social and political discourse.[12] The politicization of the family raises the stakes in the study of family history. One of the tasks of the historian is to clarify the past—as opposed to what some imagine to have happened—in the hope of informing present-day debates.

The study of the family in history necessarily intersects with the history of women and gender.[13] Historians in these proximate fields have had an uneasy relationship, often pursuing different questions, using different methods, and speaking past one another. Women's history, in Louise Tilly's words, was born as "movement history," animated by a desire to uncover the sources of women's oppression, one of the principal sites of which was identified as the family. "Most feminist scholarship ... wishe[d] to go beyond family to individual women and, especially, women who are autonomous actors or struggling to expand their horizons. The questions and problems of women's history in its feminist form focus on oppression and subordination on one hand, and agency and autonomy on the other."[14] Megan Doolittle noted that family historians often use demographic and economic analysis to uncover comparative patterns and changing trends of behavior at the aggregate level. A consequence of that is a tendency to "[treat] families/households as individual social actors," rather than to see them "as networks of relationships, processes, rituals, [and] practices, all of which not only include and reveal gender differences, but have also been fundamentally important in shaping gender relations."[15] Indeed, the story this book narrates of changes in the marriage system, the construction of a family ideology, and the development of family law is also a story of the rearticulation of gender roles and ideology. Scholars of Egypt and other formerly colonized societies have discussed the links between modernist and nationalist projects and domestic ideology, which persist in latter-day secular-nationalist and Islamist discourse,[16] but the family itself has received relatively little attention. In examining marriage as practiced, imagined, and legislated, this book is also a history of how gender shaped and was shaped in those processes.

The study of the family in history also engages questions of modernity and modernization.[17] An earlier generation of scholars who were committed to the theory of modernization held that as societies developed materially and socially they would follow the same route, passing through similar stages. The champion of that view in the area of family studies was the American sociologist William Goode, who argued in *World Revolution and Family Patterns* (1963) that the forces of industrialization and urbanization were promoting similar changes in family life globally. The trend was toward a "conjugal family pattern," which he defined as one in which there were "fewer kinship ties with distant relatives and a greater emphasis on the 'nuclear' family unit of couple and children."[18] That, of course, was the predominant family pattern in mid-twentieth-century Northwestern Europe and its cultural extensions, including North America, which were the assumed models of modernity. Goode's argument was, in essence, that modernizing societies would converge in a common conjugal family pattern resembling that of Northwestern Europe and North America. However, two subsequent developments cast doubt on the theory of convergence. First, there was the discovery by demographic historians that a conjugal family pattern existed in Northwestern Europe centuries before industrialization and urbanization, and thus it cannot have resulted from those processes.[19] The second development, apparent by the end of the last century, was that the conjugal family pattern had not become predominant in every industrializing and urbanizing society, and it was even losing its preeminence in Europe and North America.[20] This posed the question of whether any particular family pattern could be associated with urban, industrial society.

The theory associating the conjugal family pattern with industrialization and urbanization was formulated in the mid-nineteenth century by Frédéric Le Play (1806–82), who proposed a developmental scheme in which family forms became progressively simpler as societies progressed from nomadic pastoralism to peasant agriculture and to industrialism. But a developmental paradigm, as the demographer Arland Thornton calls it, informed theorizing about the family from the beginning of European expansion, and the idea that societies progressed toward civilization through identifiable stages with particular family forms and practices was especially influential in Enlightenment thought.[21] Enlightenment thinkers argued, also, that the status of women was higher at an advanced stage of civilization (the current term is "development"), though some practices they believed to be degrading to women, such as the performance of heavy labor, reflected an ethnocentric and middle-class bias.[22] Nineteenth-century French social theorists argued that women were suited by nature for the domestic roles of motherhood and household management, and that they should not work outside the home.[23] For Egyptian modernist thinkers, nearly all of whom encountered European culture through the French language, that feature of European family ideology was easily reconcilable with the maintenance-obedience relationship, in which the wife was not supposed to go out of the marital home without the permission of the husband.

The "modernizing" of marriage in my title is not an endorsement of the tradition-modernity dichotomy, the theory of convergence, or the idea that modernity happened first in Europe.[24] But I think it conveys the sense of what nineteenth-century civil servants and intellectuals believed they were doing by restructuring state institutions following European models and engaging with European forms of knowledge. They conceived of their project as producing "civilization," a term that was replaced in the twentieth century by "modernization" and "development." Semicolonized[25] and then colonized, they carried out "reforms" that did not replicate European modernity, as Talal Asad noted. Rather, Egyptian modernity was an "[expression] of different experiences rooted in part in traditions other than those to which the European-inspired reforms belonged, and in part in contradictory European representations of European modernity."[26] Modernist intellectuals understood the family to be a key component of civilization but, as Asad observed, they had a different starting point (experiences) than their European contemporaries, and in any event European modernity was not uniform. Moreover it was constantly changing.

The contemporary Egyptian marriage system began to develop in the late nineteenth century, concurrent with but not entirely a result of the construction of a new family ideology. Upper-class polygyny became less common during the last quarter of the century due to the end of the slave trade and the example of monogamy set by the khedival family. In time, polygyny also faced growing social disapproval. After World War I, also, the urban upper and middle classes abandoned large, multiple-family dwellings in favor of apartments that were better suited to conjugal families. Ideological trends may have contributed the most to the decline of polygyny in the long run, but the transition to conjugal family households seems to have been caused by multiple factors, including the development of modern education, a rising age of marriage for both sexes, and the adoption of European architectural styles. Similar changes occurred in Turkey at about the same time.[27] The comparative study of political, social, and demographic factors that influenced the marriage system shows that religion alone did not determine family life and that Western influence was not the only force for change. As Duben and Behar suggested, it raises the question of the usefulness of "Islam" or the Middle East as a unit of analysis in the study of social history.[28]

This period also witnessed important changes in the legal arena. Egyptian officials revised the procedures of the Sharia Courts, which applied the law governing marriage and marital life for Muslims with important consequences, well before the codification of Muslim family law began in the 1920s. These developments were the immediate background to codification and influenced it, and for that reason alone they deserve the attention of historians. The officials who reorganized the legal system were participants in a global circulation of ideas about legal reform that was strongly influenced by colonial knowledge of Muslim family law. New understandings of the Sharia were more textual and rigid than before. However, in Egypt, a postcolonial narrative of national awakening and recovery of the true bases of Islam legitimated twentieth-century Muslim family law as both modern and authentic, obscuring the way it was shaped in the colonial era.[29]

Historiography

While the study of the family in history can contribute to the history of women, gender, and nationalism, social and demographic history, and legal history, it deserves to be studied in its own right for what it can tell us about society and culture in the past. Although the family has long been recognized as a key social institution in the Middle East, its history only began to be written in the 1990s.[30] In the historiography of modern Egypt the family has been discussed mainly as a subsidiary topic in women's and gender history.[31] Households and family practices are also discussed in studies of the early modern (pre-1798) period devoted mainly to political, social, and women's history,[32] and aspects of family history have also been addressed in the study of Islamic law.[33] The relative neglect of family history has left important questions unanswered and even unasked. There is little agreement, for example, on the nature and causes of change in family life during the nineteenth and early twentieth centuries, or whether there even was change. Some scholars believe that no significant changes occurred in the family before World War I,[34] while a larger group argue that the family was subjected to transforming influences.[35]

An obvious weakness of the thesis of no change is the difficulty of reconciling that with other well-known changes in the nineteenth century, such as the expansion and commercialization of agriculture, population growth, internal migration, the decline of certain industries and trades, and the development of new trades and professions. Political-economic and demographic changes influenced family structures in other societies in the past, and there is no reason to see Egyptian society as an exception. Forms of employment and modes of inheritance, both of which changed in the nineteenth century, affected household formation elsewhere, though not in easily predictable ways.[36] It seems to me that the proper question historians should ask is not whether there were changes in the family and the status of women in the nineteenth century but what those changes were.

Most historians assert that transformative influences were at work in the nineteenth century but disagree in their assessment of them. Judith Tucker, in her pioneering work on Egyptian women in the nineteenth century, argued that most families and the women in them were adversely affected by the economic and political transformations of the era,[37] and in his study of the army of Muhammad Ali Pasha (r. 1805–48) Khaled Fahmy asserted that conscription caused the breakup of families.[38] More optimistic was Beth Baron, in her studies of the women's press and gendered nationalism, and Margot Badran, in her work on gender and the feminist movement, who argued in effect that nineteenth-century transformations created the conditions for women's emancipation.[39] Pollard argued that those transformations prompted Egyptians to associate the conjugal family with political maturity,[40] and Kholoussy identified trends in marriage as a source of anxiety.[41]

The pessimistic view of Tucker and Fahmy was consistent, respectively, with Marxist and feminist studies of the development of capitalism and the impact of colonialism[42] and postcolonial skepticism toward the modern national narrative.[43] They were concerned in particular with how new regimes of power affected peasants and the working class, unlike the latter authors, whose subjects came from the literate urban middle and upper classes in the late nineteenth and early twentieth centuries. Baron highlighted two arguably positive effects of colonialism and capitalism, the end of slave trafficking and the rise of the periodical press, which promoted an ideal of companionate marriage (albeit along with domesticity). Badran identified women's education, reformist Islam, and the influence of European culture as additional factors promoting change. Pollard, who, like Fahmy, was influenced by postcolonial studies, emphasized the role of colonial knowledge—European notions of civilization and European criticisms of Muslim family life—in stimulating reformist impulses.[44] In sum, the nature and extent of nineteenth-century changes affecting the family are matters of disagreement, mainly because those changes have not been examined closely by scholars whose main focus was elsewhere. As a result we have an incomplete and somewhat contradictory picture of what happened to the family (or families) during the late nineteenth and early twentieth centuries.

Historians of premodern Egypt have also been influenced by the turn to women and gender. Scholars of this period have examined the elite household system as well as the social and legal aspects of the marriage system. Their studies emphasize the important role played by women in elite household politics, their agency in controlling and managing property, their involvement in business affairs, and their ability to insert favorable conditions in their marriage contracts. The contrast between this image of seventeenth- and eighteenth-century elite women and their counterparts a century later, who were in need of "emancipation," is attributable in part to the different frameworks, questions, and methods brought to bear on the two periods. There is also a stark divergence in the sources used. The premodern historians as well as Tucker and Fahmy relied primarily on manuscripts and archival sources, especially legal documents, which pose certain questions of representativeness and reflectivity.[45] Historians of the late nineteenth and early twentieth centuries have relied mainly on periodicals and printed books, but those sources make it difficult to distinguish actual social behavior from discursive constructions of it.[46] Historians of women and the family in the premodern period should pay more attention to the discursive construction of social norms and conventions by reading premodern literary, medical, and legal treatises; the way has already been shown in two histories of sexuality by Dror Ze'evi and Khaled El-Rouayheb.[47] And more historians working in the era of print should follow the lead of Duben and Behar and Kholoussy in juxtaposing discursive sources with demographic and legal sources. I have attempted to do that in this book.

I have already stated my objection to the notion that there was no change in family structure and the status of women before 1914, but I would not use the term "transformation" to describe changes in the marriage system and marital life before 1920. Despite what the periodicals and books of this era suggest, change was incremental and confined to portions of the upper and middle classes, although they were trendsetters who prepared the way for further developments in the long run.[48] My first two chapters examine the political, social, and demographic factors that contributed to these changes. Chapter 1 discusses the obsolescence of the harem system and the decline of polygyny in Ottoman Egyptian ruling-class culture. Polygyny and harem slavery did "political work" in the system of household government established by Muhammad Ali, founder of the khedival dynasty.[49] Like the Ottoman sultans and similar to other rulers in precolonial Asia and Africa, the khedives bound subordinate men to their household through marriage—in this case, marriage to women from their harem. But khedival autocracy required the ruler's unfettered control of state finances, and it collapsed as a result of foreign intervention brought on by Egypt's bankruptcy in 1876. Foreign financial control provoked the Urabi Revolution (1881–82), which provoked a

British invasion and occupation. During the last quarter of the century the khedives reigned but no longer ruled, and the familial and political realms were separated. Harem slavery was doomed by the demise of household government and the antislavery convention of 1877.

A few years before the bankruptcy the khedival family changed its marriage strategy, abandoning slave concubinage and polygyny in favor of royal endogamy, which entailed monogamy. Monogamy was not an end in itself, but the khedives encouraged Europeans to see it as evidence of their commitment to civilization. The demise of household government, the end of the slave trade, and the adoption of monogamy by the khedival family are examples of how contingent political developments affected elite family culture, which was emulated in other social classes. The publicly monogamous style of the khedives abetted the spread of a new family ideology in which polygyny was disapproved. Egyptian historiography since the 1952 Revolution has been neglectful of the late-nineteenth-century khedives, but to ignore the trendsetting role of the Palace in upper-class culture would be like ignoring the influence of the British monarchy on Victorian culture.

Chapter 2 examines evidence of change in the marriage system in the wider society, beginning with the experiences of several middle- and upper-class men and one woman who were married between 1880 and 1923, and who wrote about it decades later. Their memoirs portray a strongly patriarchal family system in which marriages were normally arranged by fathers or other guardians with little or no consultation of daughters or sons. But men who delayed marriage until they had independent means or their fathers were deceased were able to arrange their own marriages, and the pursuit of higher education and a professional career caused a growing number of men to do that. The delay of marriage by men eroded the custom of forming joint households, which seems to have ceased entirely in the urban upper class after World War I. The establishment of neolocal conjugal family households by young couples was a sign of diminishing family patriarchy.

By the early twentieth century, also, upper- and middle-class families were beginning to permit their daughters to meet prospective husbands. The custom of marrying someone sight unseen was denounced by modernist essayists, and some of our memoirists retrospectively opined that a prenuptial meeting increased the likelihood of marital compatibility. Yet they raised no objection to the involvement of family in selecting a spouse and negotiating the terms of a marriage. Some early-twentieth-century novels extolled love marriage, but none of our memoirists advocated autonomy in spousal choice and certainly not love matches. They thought love should develop after marriage.

Although these memoirs represent the experiences of an elite and mostly male group, legal records and census data enable us to look further down the social scale for social and demographic trends. Polygyny, including slave concubinage, was practiced by all social classes and probably was more widespread than conventional estimates, and it most likely peaked with the surge in slave trafficking of the 1860s. "Slave wives," as they were called, were an alternative to contractual wives as long as the trade was legal.

A sampling of mid-nineteenth-century census registers from Cairo and four villages in the Delta suggests important differences in the age of marriage and in joint household formation between city and village. Mid-nineteenth-century Cairo had a lower age of first marriage than the four villages, and a higher proportion of joint family households. A century later, early marriage and the joint family were associated nearly exclusively with the rural society.

These chapters show how the decline of polygyny and joint household formation in the upper and middle classes resulted from contingent political and demographic changes, the development of education, and the rise of new professions. But these changes were also influenced by a new family ideology promoted by modernist intellectuals and in the periodical press during the last third of the nineteenth century, which is the topic of chapter 3. Egyptian modernists like Rifaʻa al-Tahtawi (1801–73) and their counterparts in the other Ottoman provinces participated in a global circulation of ideas about the family, education, and progress that was influenced by nineteenth-century European social thought, but they were also in dialogue with precolonial Muslim writings on marriage and marital relations, producing the hybrid family ideology mentioned earlier. According to this ideology, the conjugal family was the elemental unit in society and the site where one's character was formed in early childhood. The domestic ideology promoted in late-nineteenth- and early-twentieth-century periodicals was consistent with the new family ideology, which accorded women the important vocation of motherhood and household management. Family stability and harmony were deemed necessary for childrearing, and so the modernists advocated companionate marriage, opposed polygyny, and discouraged divorce. They also advocated the education of women to prepare them for their role as mothers and as companions for their husbands. Their project was civilizational, not feminist, though it had important implications for women. Qasim Amin and certain early feminist women writers embraced that project.

An earlier generation of scholars was concerned with measuring the extent to which Middle Eastern intellectuals adopted modern (that is, European) ideas, the assumption being that "modernization" required the abandonment of "traditional" ideas and institutions. That approach was criticized rightly for portraying Middle Eastern culture as passively receiving Western influence, and also for equating progress with Westernization; thus, postmodernist scholars have questioned what Timothy Mitchell aptly called "the European-centered cartography of modernity."[50] In order to illustrate the process of hybridization that characterized the production of family ideology, I begin chapter 3 with a discussion of precolonial writings on marriage that circulated in Egypt from the eighteenth through the early twentieth centuries, some of the tropes of which survive to the present. My longitudinal study of modernist discourse on the family led me to conclude that it was not a response to negative colonial and missionary views, as some have argued. Modernist intellectuals developed the main theses of a family ideology in the generation before the British occupation and the sharpening of Western criticism of Muslim family life. They drew on a stock of ideas about family, society, and civilization that originated in European social thought, but they sought to use those ideas for social improvement, unlike colonial officials who invoked them to assert Egyptian inferiority.

The new family ideology was transformational in its long-term impact,[51] but before World War I it had only begun to influence social behavior. On the other hand, changes in the legal system had early and important consequences for family life, and these are discussed in the final three chapters. Chapter 4 describes the reorganization of the Sharia Courts and their procedures, along with the impact it had on the application of Muslim family law. There were two major consequences of that reorganization. First, the law became less flexible and less favorable to married women; and second, the requirement that family affairs be recorded in notarized documents enhanced the social role of the Sharia Courts and hence the impact of the first change. Until the mid-nineteenth century the Sharia Courts applied the doctrines of all four schools of Sunni Islamic law, permitting individuals to forum shop to take advantage of the most advantageous rules in each. Individually the schools of law were rigid in what they permitted and did not, but forum shopping gave the legal system flexibility.⁵² From no later than the mid-nineteenth century Sharia Court judges were instructed to apply the doctrines of the Hanafi school exclusively. Hanafization disadvantaged married women by making it more difficult for them to claim arrears of maintenance from their husbands and also by making it impossible for them to seek a divorce for nonsupport, desertion, or abuse. These and other undesirable consequences of the judicial reorganization were not corrected until after World War I. The reform of Muslim family law to protect and strengthen the conjugal family was advocated by modernists such as Qasim Amin and the reforming Grand Mufti Muhammad Abduh (1849–1905), but it was not until the 1920s that the first family law codes restored to women the options their great-grandmothers had exercised by making it easier for them to recover arrears of maintenance and enabling them to seek a divorce for nonsupport, desertion, or abuse.

Chapter 5 returns to the theme of hybridity in discussing the role of the unofficial code of Muslim family law composed by Muhammad Qadri Pasha (1821–88) in the invention of personal status law. Published in 1875 for use as a reference manual in the Mixed Courts, Qadri's code acquired great authority and influence in the absence of a formal codification of family law. It was a step in the transformation of Muslim family law from a jurists' law into positive law. The former was open-ended and accommodated debate and dissension, whereas the latter was explicit and authoritative. Qadri's code introduced Egyptians to the concept of Muslim family law as a law of "personal status," following the terminology in use in colonial Algeria. Subsequently the state restricted the jurisdiction of the Sharia Courts mainly to family and religious matters, and Hussein Ali Agrama has argued that it thereby "sought to regulate Islamic practice by defining the essence of the sharia as comprised of 'family' matters."⁵³ Prior to that, however, Qadri's code habituated Egyptians to thinking about the family and the domestic sphere as the domain of religion. Qadri's code and a subsequent explication of it also influenced family ideology by emphasizing the maintenance-obedience relationship, in which the wife's duty of obedience included remaining at home. Whereas in practice her duty of obedience was contingent on receiving maintenance, the code stated it as an unqualified rule.

Chapter 6 takes up the history of an infamous legal regime, "house of obedience" (*bayt al-ta'a*), that was another consequence of legal modernization. In precolonial Muslim family law a married woman who left her husband's house without his permission was deemed disobedient and undeserving of maintenance. A Sharia Court judge might issue an order of obedience, requiring her to return to her husband's home, but if she refused to return there was little the court or the husband could do. The procedural law of 1897 authorized the police to enforce orders of obedience, returning runaway wives by force if necessary. Twentieth-century advocates of women's rights denounced the enforcement of house of obedience as an un-Islamic custom, but it originated in France, whence it migrated to Algeria and became associated with Muslim culture, and from there it migrated to Egypt.

According to the standard narrative, Muslim family law was unaffected by modernizing change until after World War I and the Sharia Courts were a backwater, but nothing could be further from the truth. Toward the end of the nineteenth century the required use of documents induced women and men to rely on the courts to adjudicate and notarize their family affairs more than ever before, stimulating the discussions that led to codification. Hanafization, Qadri's code, and the enforcement of house of obedience complicate the question of whether nineteenth-century changes benefitted women, and they place subsequent family law reforms favorable to women in a new light. Moreover, Qadri's code and house of obedience are illustrative of the process of hybridization that produced modern Muslim family law. Like contemporary family ideology, Muslim family law was produced as an Islamic personal status law in conditions of colonial modernity.

Sources, Methods, and Terms

I use diverse sources, the technical aspects of which may not always be clear to nonspecialists. Chapter 2 compares demographic data from Cairo published by Ghislaine Alleaume and Philippe Fargues, who sampled the registers of the 1848 census, and similar data from four villages in 1848 and 1868 that I compiled. Alleaume and Fargues gathered a representative sample for Cairo, but the four villages I researched are not statistically representative of the entire rural population. They are, however, suggestive of conditions and trends that may have been similar elsewhere in the countryside.[54]

A census need not be absolutely accurate to be meaningful, and even the best ones have a degree of error.[55] Aggregate Egyptian population counts in the 1840s are considered reliable, unlike some wildly inaccurate estimates by foreigners.[56] The registers of the four villages appear to be reliable due to their plausible sex ratios and age structures. The number of males and females recorded in each register was nearly equal, indicating no significant undercounting of females. In 1848 females were 51 percent of the aggregate population of the four villages, and in 1868 their proportion was reduced to 49 percent due to the presence of a large number of male slaves. Most people did not know their age and reported it as a multiple of five or ten, similar to what occurred in modern censuses in Egypt and India.[57] One can correct for this by grouping individuals in decennial age groups: 0–9, 10–19, and so on.[58] There was a tendency to exaggerate the age of older persons and a deficit in the age cohorts 10–19 and 20–29 in both census years. Similarly, in the Egyptian censuses of 1917 and 1927 people older than 55 exaggerated their ages, and there were deficits of males reported to be 20–24 and of females reported to be 15–20 years old.[59] In sum, the village registers inspected appear to be as reliable as the censuses of 1917 and 1927.

Historians, demographers, and sociologists use a variety of terms to refer to family and household forms, there being no single system. I use the term "conjugal family" to refer to what others call the "nuclear" or "simple" family; that is, a domestic group consisting of one conjugal couple, with or without children. In my discussion I am mainly concerned with the relative proportions of conjugal family households and joint family households. The latter, also known as multiple-family households and extended family households, contain two or more related conjugal couples. I am less concerned with the distinction between conjugal family households and those in which an unmarried sibling lives with the couple and their children, which was and is quite common in Egypt.[60] The crucial distinction is between households with only one couple and those with two or more.

Marriage and its dissolution in Muslim family law differ from Western practices in some respects. Marriage is a contractual relationship, not a sacrament. The groom gives his bride a dower (*mahr* or *sadaq*), or more often a portion of it, the remainder due upon dissolution of the marriage. The dower and a trousseau provided the bride by her parents remain her property, since the norm in marriage is a regime of separate property. This is similar to *séparation de biens* in France or a prenuptial agreement in Britain or the United States providing for any assets brought into the marriage and acquired thereafter to remain the property of the individual spouses. Men may divorce their wives unilaterally and at will by pronouncing a triple repudiation (*talaq*). The first and second repudiations result in a revocable divorce, which is similar to a legal separation in Western law. The husband may recall his wife during a ninety-day period, otherwise the divorce becomes final. Women may initiate divorce but to do so they must convince a judge that there is sufficient cause. I call judicial divorce (*tatliq*) annulment to differentiate it from repudiation. In divorce by repudiation and annulment the husband must pay the delayed portion of the dower to his ex-wife, and he must provide her with temporary maintenance (*nafaqa*) during a waiting period (*idda*), intended to reveal whether she is pregnant. A divorcée is free to remarry after the waiting period. In addition to annulment, women have also had the option of bargaining with their husband for a repudiation in exchange for giving up some or all of their financial rights. This "repudiation for money" (*talaq ala al-mal*), in the form of *khul'* and *mubara'a*, could involve sacrificing the delayed dower, temporary maintenance, and even arrears of maintenance that the wife was owed, as the price of her freedom. In Egypt in 2000 the law was revised to permit women to obtain a *khul'* by judicial decree if they declared they could no longer remain in the marriage and were willing to sacrifice the delayed dower and temporary maintenance.

In my discussion of legal history I refer to Muslim family law rather than "Islamic law" or "the Sharia" to avoid essentialism and to emphasize the contingency and historical specificity of the law applied. Muslim family law in application varied to some extent in the precolonial world due to a diversity of local customs, the sometimes limited reach of the Sharia Courts' authority, the local preeminence of different schools of law, and the development of different judicial procedures. For that reason my account of the application of Muslim family law in nineteenth-century Egypt is drawn from contemporary sources: handbooks, the fatwas of the Grand Mufti Muhammad al-Abbasi al-Mahdi, the authoritative sources upon which he relied, and a sample of the Sharia court records.

Muftis in various times and places have issued authoritative opinions or fatwas that were theoretical, and in general the opinions of muftis have been influential but not binding. The situation in nineteenth-century Egypt was exceptional, however. Muhammad Ali created the position of Grand Mufti (*Mufti al-Diyar al-Misriyya*) in the 1830s as part of his drive to centralize authority. Thus the long-serving (1847–97) al-Abbasi exercised more authority than ordinary muftis. Nearly all of the published cases he heard were forwarded to him from the Sharia Courts, and he evidently saw his role as ensuring that the "correct" or predominant opinions of the Hanafi school of law were applied. He was a conservative, not a reformer.[61] Fatwa collections like his contained exemplary cases intended to present the preferred interpretations, and so the number of cases of a certain type are not an indication of their frequency. As sources for sociolegal history, they are useful, like the court records, in showing the variety of questions that came before the courts and how they were decided. Fatwas usually do not contain the rich detail offered by court records, but they often reference scholarly authorities, which enables us to reconstruct the pedigree of an opinion.

1

Marriage in Politics

*The Obsolescence of Household Government
and the Shift to Monogamy in the Khedival Family*

On Thursday, January 16, 1873, a contract of marriage was agreed to between Tawfiq, the crown prince of Egypt, and Amina Ilhami, granddaughter of the late viceroy Abbas Hilmi I (r. 1849–54). In celebration of the event the reigning khedive, Ismail (r. 1863–79), held a reception at al-Hilmiyya Palace attended by Tawfiq, several ministers of state, and the leading religious dignitaries. Cannon were fired, sweet drinks were had, and the khedive received the congratulations of his guests in order of their rank. Poetry was composed and recited for the occasion by al-Sayyid Ali Abu al-Nasr and Muhammad Qadri Bey. These events initiated a week of receptions, banquets and entertainment, illuminations, and a public procession in which the bride was delivered to the palace of her husband. The next three weeks witnessed similar scenes as the weddings of Tawfiq's younger siblings Fatima, Husayn, and Hasan were celebrated.[1] Like their Ottoman suzerains, the Egyptian khedival (viceregal)[2] family staged public celebrations of births, circumcisions, weddings, funerals, religious holidays, and dynastic anniversaries as a way of cultivating popular legitimacy. The month of celebrations accompanying the four princely weddings was one such calculated display.[3]

In retrospect, these weddings were also significant as the moment when the khedival family abandoned slave concubinage and polygyny in favor of monogamous marriage. Monogamy was subsequently the norm within the khedival family. Tawfiq, as khedive (r. 1879–92), was Egypt's first monogamous ruler. Amina took on a more prominent public role than women in the khedival family had done previously, partly as a consequence of being his sole consort. She was respectfully referred to in the Arabic press as "the wife of the khedive" (*haram al-khidiwi*), and in French and English as the *vice-reine*, *khédiveh*, or "khediva." After Tawfiq's death she retained a prominent role as the *walida pasha*, or mother of the khedive, though English writers often used the French term *khédiveh mère*. Monogamy within the khedival family thus had implications for the role of women at a time in which "the woman question," already much discussed in contemporary Europe, was beginning to be raised in Egypt.[4]

The adoption of monogamy by the khedival family offers a useful vantage point from which we can survey the relationship between family and politics in nineteenth-century Egypt. As Lisa Pollard has noted, Euro-American observers criticized family practices in the Muslim East—or at least, what they understood of those family practices—while upholding an idealized conjugal family as the standard of modern civilization.[5] Westerners understood polygyny, slavery, and the concealment[6] of women to constitute a "harem system" that was incompatible with a healthy family life. The ease and frequency with which Muslim men divorced their wives, disrupting the conjugal family, was an additional target of criticism. This criticism arose in the middle decades of the century, reflecting relatively recent developments in European culture, from idealization of the conjugal family and companionate marriage to the strengthening of antislavery sentiment, and it intensified along with the advance of colonialism toward the end of the century.[7]

Beginning in the 1870s some Westerners noticed that polygyny was on the decline in the Ottoman and Egyptian upper classes. Lord Cromer, the British consul-general in Cairo and de facto ruler of Egypt during his tenure (1883–1907), believed that monogamy was gaining "amongst the more enlightened Egyptians." As examples he mentioned Khedive Tawfiq, his son Khedive Abbas II (r. 1892–1914), and the prime ministers Riyad Pasha and Sharif Pasha.[8] Cromer and others attributed this to the progress of enlightenment under European influence, but cautioned that thorough change would take a long time. The backwardness of the Egyptian family system, which degraded women and deformed men's character, was one of several objections raised by British officials and journalists to the suggestion that Egyptians might reform themselves without foreign tutelage, or that they were ready for self-government. Pollard has described well how Egyptian domestic habits—specifically, those of Khedive Ismail—were invoked to explain the financial and political turmoil that led to the British invasion and occupation of 1882. Similar discourses buttressed other imperial ventures in Asia and Africa as civilizing missions.[9]

Well before the British occupation Egypt's rulers had cultivated European opinion by presenting themselves as enlightened and modern in various ways, including in their family practices. At the time of the four princely weddings, the Palace let Europeans understand that the adoption of monogamous marriage by the khedival family resulted from a desire to emulate European civilization. In reality, however, the shift to monogamy was not an end in itself but a consequence of contingent developments, the most important of which had to do with dynastic politics. Seven years before the four princely weddings, Khedive Ismail had secured an imperial edict changing the system of succession within the khedivate from priority of the eldest male to primogeniture. This meant that the future khedives would all be descendants of Ismail. His son Tawfiq became the crown prince, excluding the princes who had been next in line under the old system. To compensate for the estrangement of the latter, Ismail shored up support among the other lines within the extended khedival family by marrying his children to their cousins.

Family endogamy was common in Egyptian culture but it was alien to the Ottoman sultans, who practiced slave concubinage and polygyny until their deposition in 1924.[10] The ruling class, including Ismail and his predecessors, emulated the imperial style of conjugality. But Ismail's strategy of marrying his sons to their cousins imposed monogamy upon them. Marriage to an Ottoman princess ruled out additional wives or concubines due to her standing,[11] and the same rule applied when the bride was a princess from the khedival family. Subsequently endogamy and monogamy became embedded in the culture of the khedival house and, equally importantly, it became part of the public style of the khedival family.

Some contingent factors abetted this process. It owed something to the weakening of the position of the khedives, with Egypt's bankruptcy and the imposition of European financial control in 1876–78, which precipitated a constitutional revolution known as the Urabi Revolution during 1881–82; this, in turn, was thwarted by British intervention and an open-ended occupation. Thus as time went on the khedives had even more incentive to use marriage to shore up support and ward off rivalry within their extended family. The cultivation of European opinion was no less important, and in this effort the khedives sought to present their monogamy as a sign of enlightenment. It also became more difficult and expensive to acquire concubines after the slave trade was outlawed in 1877, and the fiscal discipline imposed on the Palace after the bankruptcy made it impossible to maintain the large harems of earlier times.

In any event, large harems, which for centuries were integral to the Ottoman political system, became obsolete in Egypt during the last quarter of the nineteenth century. Previously, in addition to maintaining substantial harems, elite Ottoman households trained male *kul/mamluk* slaves who served in the military-administrative apparatus of the state. Upon "graduation" from a household these men typically were married by their masters/guardians to a woman from the harem of another household, thereby forging or maintaining a political alliance and/or tie of dependency with a subordinate house. Succinctly put, the Ottoman household-and-harem system did "political work" comparable to the systems of kinship politics in early modern South and Southeast Asia.[12] But the reorganization of the military and civil service in the Ottoman Empire and Egypt along European lines, known as the *tanzimat,* was well underway by the reign of Khedive Ismail, whose officers and civil servants were now recruited from the free population and trained in government schools. Male slaves were no longer a feature of ruling-class households after mid-century, except for eunuchs, who assisted ruling- and upper-class women in performing their public duties. Ismail maintained the practice of marrying women from his harem to rising state servants in order to attach them to his household, but after the bankruptcy he lost personal control of state finances, and the khedival autocracy collapsed. Although the British rescued the khedivate, they deprived the khedives of power. Closeness to the khedival palace was no longer the sole measure of a man's political standing. A marriage tie to the Palace was still desirable, but it was no longer the only useful alliance that a politically ambitious man might seek.

During the last quarter of the century, also, Egyptian public opinion was moving in favor of monogamy. Modernist intellectuals promoted a new family ideology that posited the conjugal family as the elemental unit of society, and the new family ideology was also promoted in the burgeoning periodical press of the era. Monogamy and companionate marriage were key features of the new family ideology, and the example set by the khedival family undoubtedly promoted it among the ruling and upper classes. The extent and rate of change in public opinion at the turn of the century cannot be measured with any exactness, but it is telling that when Tawfiq's son, Khedive Abbas II, contracted a polygynous marriage in 1910, the Palace was careful not to publicize it, even though polygyny was still legal. The Palace was sensitive to the image of the khedive among an Egyptian public that increasingly associated monogamy with enlightenment and civilization.

Constructing the Harem System

Any serious discussion of the Ottoman household-and-harem system requires an unpacking of Euro-American perceptions of it, which continue to influence latter-day views. Nineteenth-century Westerners understood family life in the Muslim East through the frame of "the harem system," by which they referred to a cluster of practices, the most salient and objectionable of which were slavery, polygyny, and the concealment and covering of women. Before the abolition of the slave trade, slavery was usually said to be the linchpin of the system. Without a ready supply of slave concubines and domestics, it was believed, polygyny would become impossible, and Ottoman domestic culture would be transformed.[13] After that thesis turned out to be mistaken, Europeans persisted in regarding polygyny and the concealment of women as constituting a "harem system" that was, in the words of one writer, "fatal to the idea of the family, which forms the basis of all true civilization."[14] The term "harem system" was not used in contemporary Ottoman Turkish or Arabic.

Notwithstanding their disapproval of the "harem system," the more perceptive European observers sought to explain it rather than condemn it outright. Although the harem was (and still is) imagined by some to be a site of sexual debauchery, few women writers (who unlike men were able to enter harems) failed to note how far from reality those fantasies were. To be sure, during the first three-quarters of the nineteenth century the Ottoman imperial and Egyptian khedival households contained anywhere from several hundred to over a thousand female slaves. But relatively few of these women became consorts of the household head. The majority performed household work while others were trained for a role as upper-class consorts, and either gifted or married into other households. They remained celibate and subject to a strict rule of discipline under the master's mother and wives. Harem discipline was compared by some observers to that of a convent; to suggest that harems were like "brothels" was "outrageous."[15]

Hardly any Western account of harem culture failed to point out that slavery in the Muslim East bore little resemblance to the harsh system known in the Americas. Harem women could look forward to manumission and marriage with a trousseau after a period of service. Legally, a slave concubine who bore her master's child, known as an *umm walad* or *mustawlada*, could not be sold. Her child was free and, as an heir, had the same rights as the children of contractual wives. It was not unusual for such concubine-mothers to be freed and married by their masters.[16] Women travel writers tended to write against the notion that harem slaves were exploited or sexually degraded, emphasizing that they had certain legal rights, their condition of enslavement was transitory, and that "they became integrated in the extended Muslim family and the Ottoman political system."[17] As Billie Melman has pointed out, the Victorian women who penned these accounts were doing more than pushing back against the outlandish sexual fantasies of some of their male contemporaries. At times they used a representation of the Muslim East as a foil to their own society and its shortcomings. Their emphasis on the autonomy and legal rights enjoyed by married Muslim women was intended to be read against the debates over married women's autonomy and control of property in Britain.[18] Typically, also, the accounts of harem life by European women were based on access to elite households.[19] They wrote, in addition, in great detail about the interior décor of the harem, the clothing and jewelry worn by the women, and the elaborate protocol, details that were deemed of interest to their readers.

Slavery in the Ottoman domains and especially in Egypt became a focus of European criticism following its abolition in the British and French empires in 1838 and 1848, respectively.[20] Slave ownership was never outlawed in Egypt but it atrophied quickly as a consequence of the Anglo-Egyptian Convention for the Abolition of Slavery in 1877. The convention outlawed the importation of African slaves immediately, and seven years later the ban was extended to the importation of white slaves, who by then were mainly Circassian women, and to the selling of previously acquired slaves between households. The convention also enabled slaves to apply for manumission either at one of four bureaus established in different parts of the country or at the British consulate. Thousands per month did so in the following years.[21] By the end of the century slavery was no longer commonplace and it had ceased to be a target of Western criticism.

As for polygyny, foreign observers believed it to be limited in extent and characteristic of urban upper-class society, if for no other reason than because of the cost of maintaining multiple wives and the slaves or servants necessary to serve them.[22] Moreover, in the major cities, including Istanbul and Cairo, by the 1870s it was reported to be "the now prevailing fashion among the upper class of having only one wife."[23] That impression was shared by Lord Cromer, as we have seen, in the years leading up to World War I.

The Politics of Marriage and Reproduction

During most of its history the reproduction of the Ottoman ruling class took place within its elite households. The imperial household in Istanbul was not only the home of the sultan, where he reproduced his dynasty, but also a place where thousands of male and female slaves were trained, the men being prepared for service in the military-administrative elite and the women, in most cases, to become the wives of these state servants. The military-administrative elite assembled smaller versions of the sultan's household, commensurate in size with their rank and revenues.[24] In much the same way, the founder of Egypt's khedival dynasty, Muhammad Ali Pasha, ruled through a "household elite" consisting of blood relations, in-laws, freed slaves, and others "who had entered his service by private agreements or were clients by virtue of their household affiliation."[25]

As in the imperial household, in Muhammad Ali's household male and female slaves were prepared for entry into the political elite. The Pasha employed male "graduates" of his household (freedmen or *mamluks*) as military commanders, ministers of state, and provincial governors, as is demonstrated by Emad Helal in his study of slavery in nineteenth-century Egypt.[26] Slave women trained in the viceregal harem were married to men in the Pasha's service as a way of binding them to him. P. N. Hamont, a French veterinarian in Muhammad Ali's service, wrote, "Among Turkish princes it is a very ancient usage, and one that Muhammad Ali has continued in the government of his *pashalik*, to give female slaves from the harem to the officers of his nation. . . . Each of the functionaries who receives a female slave is given money and a furnished house."[27] Writing a few years later, Sophia Lane Poole observed similarly that the elite often arranged the marriages of their harem women to men with whom they had a relationship of patronage: "the man chosen . . . is almost always something of a dependent."[28]

In the late 1830s, as Muhammad Ali faced fiscal difficulties and a growing Anglo-Ottoman political challenge, he adopted policies of economic and political retrenchment, including making grants of land to family members, officers, and officials. The grants had the dual purpose of converting peasant tax arrears into the responsibility of the Ottoman Egyptian elite, and binding those men, who were from various provinces, more closely to Egypt.[29] Now, also, the Pasha married off the majority of his harem slaves to state servants, strengthening their ties of loyalty to his palace. As evidence of this, nearly every female "graduate" of the Pasha's harem in Helal's list was married to an official or officer.[30] These were prudent moves in a time of fiscal straits and political uncertainty, and they illustrate the operation of the household-and-harem system that was central to the rule of Muhammad Ali. But that system seems to have been too alien for contemporary Westerners to grasp, so they resorted to the stereotype of the harem as a site of unrestrained sexual activity. Hamont reported that the Pasha was advised by friends to reduce the size of his harem "on account of his age and to conserve his energy," and in a later account the aged pasha was said to have done so on the advice of physicians.[31] In reality, a minority of the women in the Pasha's harem became his sexual partners. Most were trained for marriage to subordinate men of the elite.

The large slave households maintained by the ruling class were thus an integral part of the political system. Westerners found this incomprehensible, but the Ottoman system of household-and-harem politics would have been legible to someone from precolonial South or Southeast Asia, where family and household were also integral to the political system. In Siam (modern Thailand), for example, polygyny served to establish networks and ties of dependency between the king and provincial notables, who gifted their daughters to him. The kings' many wives and children symbolized their sexual prowess in a culture in which political power was associated with masculinity, and their numerous sons provided them with a cadre of loyal officials.[32] In India, the early Mughals pursued a comparable strategy of alliance by marriage with subordinate ruling families, which led to the assembling of huge harems. These grand harems guaranteed the Mughal emperor an heir, made a display of his grandeur and virility, and symbolically embodied his claim to be the protector of the world.[33]

While the married-in daughters of subordinate families comprised the royal Siamese and Mughal harems, the Ottoman imperial and Egyptian khedival harems trained women of slave origin to be married-out to subordinates. According to Leslie Peirce, the sultans "claim[ed] a preeminence that dictated a disdain for alliances with lesser powers,"[34] hence other Muslim rulers and members of the Ottoman elite were not expected to gift daughters to the imperial harem. After the mid-fifteenth century the sultans reproduced exclusively through slave concubines, very few of whom were elevated to the status of legal wife after the late sixteenth century.[35] Although the sultans had multiple consorts the great majority of their harem women were married off to men in the military-administrative apparatus. In the fifteenth and sixteenth centuries these men were themselves often former slaves trained in the imperial palace. From the seventeenth century to the mid-nineteenth century, former slaves trained in other elite households as well as freeborn men entered military-administrative careers, and if they rose high enough they might be married to a woman from the imperial harem and thereby bound to the imperial household.

Muhammad Ali and his successors built the khedival autocracy upon a foundation of "household government" that employed these methods. The ruler's household, including his harem, was an instrument through which a dependent elite was created and reproduced. However, the khedival and princely households were superseded in this role toward the end of the Pasha's reign by new government schools inspired by the French *grandes écoles*, which trained men to serve in the officer corps and civil service. A growing proportion of the graduates were native Egyptians, and their advance into the middle and upper ranks of the military and administration is celebrated in the semi-official national historical narrative as a step toward self-rule. The acquisition and training of male slaves except for eunuchs ceased, though the khedival harem continued to do political work. Harem women were married to rising officers and civil servants, establishing a personal tie between them and the ruler, through the reign of Khedive Ismail. He, along with other princes and princesses, gave freed slaves in marriage along with houses and grants of land of anywhere from 50 to 1,000 feddans (1 feddan = approx. 1 acre).[36] Three prominent actors in the Urabi Revolution were connected to the khedival palace by marriage. The most prominent of these men was Mahmud Sami al-Barudi, an Egyptian-born scion of an old Circassian family and a prominent neoclassical Arabic poet, who served the khedives in several military and civilian roles, rising to the rank of brigadier and becoming Minister of Religious Endowments. He sided with the Urabists, who insisted on his appointment as war minister in 1881 and prime minister in 1882. Prior to those events he had married the daughter of Khedive Ismail's nurse and, later, Adila, the sister of Mansur Pasha Yakan, a cousin of Ismail who was also married to his oldest daughter Tawhida.[37] The officers Ali Fahmi and Muhammad Ubayd were also married to women from Ismail's harem. The February 1881 petition of Ali Fahmi and his fellow officers, Ahmad Urabi and Abd al-Al Hilmi, for the dismissal of the war minister was the opening event in the revolution. For that act of insubordination they were stripped of their rank and imprisoned, but then rescued by soldiers of the khedival guard led by Muhammad Ubayd. Marital ties to the Palace failed to ensure the loyalty of these men once the khedive had ceased to wield independent power and was unable to resist a European takeover. However, under the old system, wives from the khedival harem were highly desired, since they had "influence . . . in pushing husbands to the front."[38]

Despite their slave origin, these women had high status due to their affiliation with the khedival household. They were socially equal or superior to their husbands, even when the latter were freeborn. When Muhammad Ali decided to marry off his harem the number of women was so great that the grooms selected were said to include relatively minor government employees. Hamont attributed the following words to an official "burdened" with one of these wives:

> With one of the Pasha's slaves . . . our position is extremely unfavorable. It is a master that the viceroy gives us, and a master that it is extremely difficult to satisfy. At every moment of the day, this woman recalls her origin, she has visits that require expenses, and our monthly salaries are insufficient for the demands of one day. As soon as they leave the [viceroy's] palace, all of these slaves want to command, and henceforth it is we who respectfully kiss the hand of a lady. A woman from the great harem . . . evinces no deference, no respect for her husband, and when he goes to her, the former slave remains sitting, and hardly looks at him! If we show bad humor, if our attitude is not respectful to her taste, the new wife returns to the palace of the viceroy and complains against the man that the master has given her![39]

Sophia Poole made a similar observation. A man chosen by a grandee to receive one of his harem women in marriage "is almost always somewhat of a dependent; and the lady generally treats him as if he were somewhat of a dependent with respect to herself."[40] Men such as these, who married "up" to women from the khedival and princely harems, were constrained from taking additional wives or concubines.

Men who married free but high-born women were similarly often limited to one wife out of deference to their wives' families. This was the situation of al-Barudi, who married the sister of Mansur Yakan, as well as of Sharif Pasha and Riyad Pasha, whom Cromer singled out for praise on account of their monogamy. Sharif married Nazli, the daughter of Sulayman Pasha al-Faransawi (the French convert *né* Sève), one of Muhammad Ali's top commanders. Riyad married the daughter of Husayn Pasha Tapuzada, a Balkan Turk from Kavala who had come to Egypt with Muhammad Ali.[41] Outside the boundaries of the ruling class, a woman of sufficient social standing could insist as a condition of her marriage that her husband promise not to marry an additional wife or take a concubine, thereby imposing monogamy on him.[42]

Plural marriage was out of the question when one married an imperial or khedival princess. Previously wed wives had to be divorced, and previously acquired concubines were let go. The imperial household arranged endogamous marriages for Ottoman princesses to cousins and, more often, to prominent men of imperial slave background, including grand vezirs and commanders.[43] Muhammad Ali's daughters were wed to top commanders and officials, and later generations of khedival princesses were married to prominent state servants.[44] Like the weddings of imperial princesses, the weddings of khedival princesses were celebrated publicly, but the nuptials of Crown Prince Tawfiq and Amina in 1873 was the first occasion in which the khedival dynasty celebrated the wedding of a prince, since the acquisition of a concubine or the elevation of a concubine to the status of legal wife did not occasion any public celebration.

In sum, then, elite men who married their social equals or superiors were often constrained from taking another wife or a concubine, even if they could easily afford to do so. The sultans and the military-administrative elite who emulated them, including the first five khedives of Egypt, reached "down" by acquiring slave women as consorts. To be sure, these women were refined and well trained in the accomplishments deemed suitable for ruling-class consorts, and at least some of them were literate. But as slaves they were in no position to object to being part of a polygynous household. Westerners' impressions of a trend toward monogamy in the Ottoman and Egyptian upper classes began to be recorded in the last third of the nineteenth century, on the eve of the antislavery convention and for decades after that. Thus the end of the slave trade and the elimination of concubinage was undoubtedly an important factor in the decline of polygyny in upper-class households, but not the only one. The evidence consistently points to the status of the bride as the main factor limiting ruling- and upper-class men to a single consort before World War I.

Egypt's bankruptcy not only destroyed khedival autocracy but hastened the obsolescence of the system of marrying harem women to servants of the khedivate. The next several years witnessed the Urabi Revolution and the onset of the British occupation. Shorn of control of state finances and deprived of real power, the khedives no longer had exclusive control of government appointments nor of political patronage. Following Ismail's abrupt deposition and exile in 1879, his son and successor Tawfiq was responsible for marrying off the many women left behind in his father's harem.[45] Tawfiq and later khedives maintained more modest households, being subject to the financial discipline of a civil list. Now, also, slaves were more costly and difficult to procure since the trade in slaves was prohibited. The palace of Ismail reportedly had no fewer than seven hundred slaves, while those in Tawfiq's palace numbered only sixty.[46]

In addition to maintaining large harems, the khedives, from Muhammad Ali through Ismail, emulated the imperial practice of reproducing through slave concubines and limiting their consorts to a single son. The one exception was Muhammad Ali's first wife, Amina Hanim (d. 1824), whom he married long before becoming the viceroy of Egypt and rising to the rank of pasha. Her father was a pasha and the governor of Kavala, in what is now Greece.[47] She gave birth to four sons who survived to adulthood, Ibrahim, Ahmad Tusun, Ismail Kamil, and Abd al-Halim, and two daughters, Tawhida and Nazli.[48]

Amina did not accompany Muhammad Ali to Egypt, and after his appointment as viceroy in 1805 she and her daughters resided for a period of some two years in Istanbul, where they would have become thoroughly acquainted with imperial palace culture. There is a story told that upon her arrival and installation in the harem of the Citadel Palace in Cairo, in 1808, Amina became estranged from Muhammad Ali due to the many slave concubines he had acquired, reportedly telling him, "I have been your wife until today, henceforth we are strangers."[49] Although the story appeals to our modern sensibilities, it is likely that Amina's "estrangement" was a consequence of Muhammad Ali's elevation into the upper rank of the Ottoman ruling class. That rank required that he assemble a household and that it emulate the imperial household, including the sexual behavior of the ruler and his consorts. It was a long-standing Ottoman practice to limit an imperial consort to only one son, and Amina had already given birth to four sons who were potential heirs. Within Ottoman ruling-class culture she would have arrived at what Leslie Peirce has called "postsexuality," which consisted of "the cessation of childbearing, either through postmenopausal incapacity or forced sexual abstinence, and motherhood." But for imperial consorts postsexuality meant an enhanced role, not a diminished one, as evidenced by "their public display of political power and wealth (symbolized by their assumption of the privilege of public building)."[50] I have been unable to find any information on public building projects by Amina Hanim, though in 1814 her high standing was on display when she made the pilgrimage, processing from Jidda to Mecca with a train of 500 camels carrying her servants, entourage, and goods. She was met by Muhammad Ali at Mina, a stage in the pilgrimage, in a public acknowledgment of her status as first consort. Due to the grandeur of her train and guard, and the sumptuousness of her tent, the local inhabitants are said to have called her "the Queen of the Nile."[51]

Each of the other consorts of the first five khedives was of slave origin. The names of twenty consorts of Muhammad Ali, including Amina, have been preserved. Except for Amina, none had more than one son, evidence that in his new rank the Pasha followed the Ottoman policy of "one-mother-one-son." In addition to the known children of these women Muhammad Ali had another five sons, the names of whose mothers are unknown. Assuming that the "one-mother-one-son" principle was applied consistently, the Pasha would have had well more than twenty-five consorts, since not all the names of the mothers of his daughters are known, and there were others who bore no children at all.[52] The population of his harem would have been much greater still, since it included numerous celibate slave women being trained for out-marriage as well as domestic slaves.

In some other respects the behavior of the khedival family departed from the imperial model. Since the seventeenth century Ottoman princes had been confined in the imperial palace compound. They were kept in a state of sexual and political immaturity, not allowed to father children or establish their own households, in addition to being denied a public role.[53] But khedival princes married and had their own households, and were employed in political offices and commands. The viceroys also married some of their consorts, in another departure from the example set by the sultans. Muhammad Ali reportedly married Mahduran (d. 1880) some years after the death of Amina.[54] His son and successor as regent, Ibrahim, had seven consorts, two of whom became legal wives, though none bore more than one son. One of the five consorts of Abbas I bore the title *hanim*, indicating she was a legal wife, while the others were *qadin*s or recognized concubines. None had more than one son.[55] The famous consort of Said Pasha (r. 1854–63), Inji Hanim (d. 1890), also appears to have been a legal wife. Some otherwise perceptive foreign residents, like Sophia Lane Poole, sister of the orientalist Edward Lane, and the American consul Edwin de Leon and his wife Ellie, believed that Inji Hanim was the sole consort of Said Pasha, which is a measure of the obscurity of Melekber Hanim (d. 1886), the mother of Said's two sons, in a departure from the Ottoman model. Perhaps her obscurity was deliberate. Like the other khedives, Said was attuned to international opinion and "courted publicity." He may have put Inji Hanim forward as his "diplomatic" wife, or in other words the consort designated to receive the wives of foreign diplomats and various lady visitors while the others were kept behind the scenes. Inji Hanim became a favorite of foreign women, who admired her beauty and intelligence.[56]

Khedive Ismail, the son of Ibrahim Pasha, assembled the largest household of any ruler since his grandfather. He had fourteen recognized consorts, each of slave origin, four of whom were legal wives. He married the "First" and "Second" Princesses, Shahinat Faza Hanim (d. 1895) and Jananyer Hanim (d. 1912), before his accession, and the "Third Princess," Cheshm-i Afet Hanim (d. 1907), sometime afterward. He married Shafiq Nur Hanim (d. 1884), often referred to in the sources as *Walida* or "Mother," in 1866, elevating her to the position of "Fourth Princess" about fourteen years after she gave birth to his oldest son, Tawfiq.[57]

Contemporary Europeans, and especially the British, had an interest in portraying Ismail as incapable of controlling his impulses, whether sexual or financial, in justifying the occupation, the ostensible aim of which was to restore financial and political order. Lisa Pollard has shown how fantastic rumors about the sexual lives of the khedival family were taken seriously by British officials and journalists.[58] The relationship between Ismail and Shafiq Nur was the object of lascivious speculation. She was supposedly a lowly domestic slave to whom the khedive had once taken a liking, but whom he did not see fit to wed. The same stories attributed the supposedly weak character of Tawfiq to the low origin of his mother. These tropes flourished in the Western imaginary, so that by the 1930s, in one source, the number of Ismail's consorts had grown to more than seventy, and the mother of Tawfiq had become a peasant woman.[59]

The verifiable elements of the story of Shafiq Nur Hanim are less titillating when read in the context of elite Ottoman culture. To begin with, the production of an heir out of an encounter with a chambermaid was a scenario more typical of French novels and lawsuits than the khedival household. Indeed, contemporary French discourse on adultery and out-of-wedlock births may partly explain the assumptions made by Europeans.[60] However, the conjugal lives of princes and their consorts were carefully controlled in Ottoman ruling-class culture, as Peirce has shown, and the khedival family was part of that culture. The future Khedive Ismail began sexual activity at about the age of twenty under the watchful eye of his mother Hoshiyar Qadin, who sent Shafiq Nur to him from her own harem.[61] With her he fathered his second child and first surviving son, Tawfiq, in 1852. No stigma attached to the child of a concubine, who had equal standing with the children of legal wives as an heir and successor. Said and Ismail were the sons of never-married concubines. It can only be speculated why Ismail married the first three princesses ahead of Shafiq Nur, but she undoubtedly had high standing in his household both as the mother of his oldest son and as a former member of his mother's harem.

It was the sultan, upon decreeing primogeniture as the law of succession in Egypt, who required Ismail to marry the mother of the heir apparent. Not long afterward, she and her son established a separate residence in al-Qubba Palace.[62] Tawfiq would have been no more than fifteen at the time, and still being schooled. But as the crown prince he quickly took up a public role, touring the country, performing the ceremony of turning over the reins of the sacred litter (*mahmal*) to the Commander of the Pilgrimage, and acting as regent during Ismail's trip abroad in 1867.[63]

Ismail's Strategy of Endogamous Marriage

The rule of succession of the eldest prince became established in the Ottoman sultanate in the early seventeenth century. As one consequence, father-to-son succession became extremely rare, occurring only three times in twenty-two generations.[64] The same system of succession of the eldest was prescribed in the imperial decree of 1841 that created an autonomous Egyptian province under the rule of Muhammad Ali's descendants. Thus after the brief regency of the Pasha's son Ibrahim, the viceroyalty went to the latter's nephew, Abbas Hilmi I. Abbas was succeeded by his uncle, Muhammad Said, and Said was succeeded by his nephew, Ismail.

Ottoman princes were denied a public role, and confined even during adulthood in an apartment (*kafes*, literally "cage") within the imperial palace, so that they would not pose a threat to the reigning sultan. With some exceptions, the *kafes* system was eased only in the later nineteenth century.[65] But the khedives in Cairo never followed that practice, routinely employing princes in military commands and high offices. Rivalries and factions developed among the khedival princes, the sharpest cleavage occurring between Muhammad Ali's son Ibrahim and his grandson Abbas. Ibrahim forced Abbas into exile in the Hijaz and tried to deny him the succession. As viceroy, Abbas purged many of the Egyptian and French officials who were associated with Muhammad Ali and Ibrahim, and became embroiled in a dispute with the other senior princes over the division of Muhammad Ali's estate. After his death, Abbas's loyalists attempted unsuccessfully to raise his son, Ibrahim Ilhami, to the throne. These divisions and rivalries within the extended khedival family tempted each of Muhammad Ali's successors to consider changing the law of succession to primogeniture.[66]

Khedive Ismail also had to contend with family divisions. He became the heir apparent when his older half-brother, Ahmad Rif'at, was killed in a railroad accident, and there were persistent rumors that Ismail was somehow behind this tragedy.[67] When in 1866 Ismail obtained the change in the rule of succession to primogeniture, it caused a rupture with the princes previously next in line, his half-brother Mustafa Fadil and his uncle Muhammad Abd al-Halim, who were obliged to live in exile. Mustafa Fadil began financing Young Ottoman exiles in Paris, reportedly to pressure the sultan to restore his right of succession. During the next several years, relations between Cairo and Istanbul worsened to the point of crisis, due in part to the khedive's behavior as an almost independent sovereign. Things were eventually patched up, and a new imperial decree in June 1873 confirmed primogeniture as the law of succession along with other privileges, such as official use of the title "khedive," that the sultan had granted earlier.[68] But in the intervening years Ismail was concerned lest the sultan change his mind and revise the law of succession once again.

It was in those circumstances that Ismail decided upon a strategy of endogamous marriage within the extended khedival family. Having restricted the succession to his own progeny, he intended to conciliate the collateral lines and enlist their support for his heirs. Consequently nine of the khedive's twelve children married endogamously (Table 1). Three spouses were children of Ahmad Rif'at, and a fourth was his granddaughter, indicating a concern to conciliate that line. Two other spouses were daughters of Ilhami, the son of Abbas I, evidently chosen for the same reason. None were the children of Mustafa Fadil or Abd al-Halim. The breach with them was irrevocable, and Ismail bought up their properties in Egypt to discourage them from returning.[69] Even after his deposition and exile in 1879, most of Ismail's remaining children married endogamously, which may indicate that the ex-khedive hoped to return to the throne.

In the context of Ottoman Egyptian politics and culture, then, the really significant change heralded by the four princely weddings of 1873 was the shift to royal endogamy. Although Ismail imposed monogamy on Tawfiq and his other sons as a necessary consequence, monogamy was not his principal goal. Ismail seemed to have had no qualms about his own polygyny, and an incident that occurred a few years before the four weddings suggests that he was not at all convinced of the virtues of monogamy. The famous playwright and journalist, Ya'qub Sanu', was asked to present three of his comedic plays in a command performance at the

Table 1
The First Marriages of the Children of Khedive Ismail

Prince or Princess	M. Year	Spouse
Tawhida (1850–88)	1868	Mansur Pasha, son of Ahmad Pasha Yakan[a]
Muhammad Tawfiq (1852–92)	1873	Amina, daughter of Ilhami, son of Abbas I
Fatima (1853–1920)	1873	Muhammad Tusun, son of Said
Husayn Kamil (1853–1917)	1873	Ayn al-Hayat, daughter of Ahmad Rif'at, son of Ibrahim
Hasan (1854–88)	1873	Khadija, daughter of Muhammad Ali the Younger, son of Muhammad Ali
Zaynab (1859–75)	1874	Ibrahim Fahmi, son of Ahmad Rif'at
Ibrahim Hilmi (1860–1927)	?	Qamar, Circassian
Mahmud Hamdi (1863–1921)	1878	Zaynab, daughter of Ilhami, son of Abbas I
Ahmad Fu'ad (1868–1936)	1895	Shivakyar, daughter of Ibrahim, son of Ahmad Rif'at
Jamila Fadila (1869–96)	1879	Ahmad, son of Ahmad Rif'at
Amina Aziza (1874–1931)	1896	Mustafa Shakib Bey
Ni'mat Allah (1876–1945)	1890	Ibrahim Fahmi, son of Ahmad Rif'at[b]

Sources: *al-Waqa'i' al-Misriyya*; Khanki, "Zawjat Hukkam Misr"; Tugay, *Three Centuries*; Hilal, *Al-Raqiq*; *Burke's Royal Families of the World*, 1980; http://www.royalark.net/Egypt/egypt9.htm.
Note: Ismail had at least 18 children (10 sons and 8 daughters). Only those who lived long enough to marry are shown above, and only their first spouses.
[a]Nephew of Muhammad Ali.
[b]Widower of the late Zaynab (above); marriage contracted but not consummated.

khedival palace. Each was a farce satirizing contemporary mores. According to Sanu' the khedive enjoyed the first two, titled "A Fashionable Young Woman" and "An Egyptian Dandy," telling Sanu', "You are our Molière and your name will be immortal." But the third play was "The Two Cowives," an exposé of the evils of plural marriage. This time the khedive was not pleased, saying, "Master Molière of Egypt, if you aren't man enough to please more than one woman don't [try to] make others do as you."[70]

Nevertheless, the new marriage strategy inaugurated with the four princely weddings was presented opportunistically to Europeans as a decision to adopt monogamous marriage. Ellen Chennells, the governess of one of Ismail's younger daughters, recalled:

> We were told that four royal marriages were to take place during the winter, and rather a new state of things was to be inaugurated with them. Mohammed Ali had had the same kind of harem as the Sultan, consisting exclusively of slaves, and this custom had been continued by his successors down to the Khédive. But the latter in mature age wished to adopt the European law of one wife, and direct succession from father to son, instead of the old Mussulman custom of inheritance through the eldest male of the family. The second he succeeded in establishing, by fixing the succession in the person of his eldest son, Mohammed Tewfik Pasha, and the first, by restricting each of his sons to one wife of equal rank with himself.[71]

The way in which these weddings were represented to Westerners as the beginning of "a new state of things" is striking. The khedive was said to desire to adopt monogamy and primogeniture, in that order of priority. The four princely weddings were represented to Egyptians through the official gazette, *al-Waqa'i' al-Misriyya*, which never mentioned monogamy, though elsewhere the gazette celebrated the change in the rule of succession. Primogeniture was justified as giving the khedivate greater stability, and as something favored by (civilized) European states.[72] The restriction of Ismail's sons to a single wife as a consequence of marrying princesses was a familiar aspect of Ottoman Egyptian culture that occasioned no comment. In the marriage system of the time monogamy and polygyny were not thought of as alternatives, since a man might transition between monogamous and plural marriage at different points in his life.

The contrasting manner in which the four princely weddings were represented to Westerners and to Egyptians bespeaks a sophisticated Palace strategy aiming to present the khedival government in the best light, and to flatter Europeans at the same time, by foregrounding the adoption of monogamous marriage. Chennells's account even hints at what was behind the supposed shift to monogamy by linking it with the change to primogeniture and the princes' marriage to women of "equal rank," namely, princesses from the extended khedival family.

The Reigns of Tawfiq and Abbas II and the Conjugal Family Ideal

In the first half of the twentieth century the "emancipation of women" was written into the modernist-nationalist narrative of Egyptian history at the same time that the conjugal family ideal and its corollary, companionate marriage, became accepted among the educated as integral to a modern way of life. Reflecting that trend and the rhetoric of the ruling dynasty, which portrayed itself as a force for progress, certain historians in the 1930s credited Khedive Ismail and his descendants with contributing to the advancement of women and the improvement of family life,[73] and the publicity surrounding the wedding of King Faruq and Princess Farida in 1938 presented them as a modern domestic couple.[74]

An early example of that rhetoric is the following statement attributed to Tawfiq, the first monogamous khedive, in 1881:

> The great thing . . . is to educate women. They will then not only become true companions to their husbands, but will take an interest in the primary education of the children, which at present is so neglected, and adds so much to our difficulties when they first come to school. Family life is the greatest blessing, and it is impossible unless both men and women are educated. It is the aim of my life to achieve that result; and in time, I trust, we may be able to do away with slaves in the harem. I hate the very idea of slavery, and am doing all I can to put it down: moreover, a harem is only wanted for many wives; with one wife there won't be any necessity for seclusion. It is wrong to imagine that our religion requires us to have more than one wife, or to make the wife our slave instead of our equal. The Hanefite rite [school of law] defines clearly the position of women, and assigns to them almost a leading place; but how can women lead if they are ignorant and uneducated?[75]

This quotation appeared in a sympathetic portrait of Tawfiq published at the beginning of the Urabi Revolution, and seems to have been intended to shore up European support for him. He was, according to the author, "an excellent husband and father."[76]

Tawfiq's views were consistent with Egyptian and Ottoman modernist writing on the family, which emphasized the need to educate girls to prepare them for a domestic role and to be "companions to their husbands." Tawfiq's concern over "the divorce question in the lower classes" reflected another concern of the reformers.[77] Such views were attributed to Tawfiq only in European sources, but by all accounts he was genuinely monogamous and often professed opposition to slavery. None of the slave women in his household were concubines.[78]

Figure 1. Khedive Tawfiq and Khediva Amina Hanimeffendi and their children, mid-1880s. From left to right: the khediva, Prince Abbas Hilmi (1874–1944); Princess Nimatallah (1881–1966); the khedive, Prince Muhammad Ali Tawfiq (1875–1955); and Princess Khadija (1879–1951). Professional photographers introduced the family portrait in Egypt in the last quarter of the nineteenth century. Source: Bibliotheca Alexandrina Memory of Modern Egypt Digital Archive.

Tawfiq's ability to articulate an agenda of family reform and women's advancement on the eve of the British occupation is evidence of the state of development of these ideas in Egypt and their circulation at the highest levels.[79] But to the extent that he was committed to these ideas, Tawfiq's freedom of action was constrained at first by informal European control and after 1882 by the British occupation: he reigned but did not rule. His first priority was to restore the legitimacy of his khedivate, which had been rescued by the British from a broadly based revolution. The Palace cultivated his popularity by scheduling regular public appearances and activities, and by facilitating press coverage of them, as well as of ceremonial events. The Khediva Amina's presence at official events was also mentioned regularly, and notices of her and the khedive's movements—attending the opera, traveling from one palace to another—were published.[80] Pollard has drawn a connection between the publicly reported activities of Tawfiq and Amina and a growing trend in the contemporary press to link the reform of family life to national regeneration, but, as she noted, the reported views and activities of Tawfiq preceded the explosion of didactic writing on household management, childrearing, and other domestic topics in the late 1880s and 1890s.[81] Had Tawfiq not died suddenly in 1892, his and Amina's public activities might have enabled them to become, symbolically, the nation's leading bourgeois couple, and to associate the khedival dynasty closely with the conjugal family ideal. But by the measure of that ideal his successor was less than a perfect family man.

If Tawfiq sincerely opposed slavery and polygyny, the same cannot be said for his son and successor Abbas II, or even his widow Amina, who now occupied the influential position of mother of the khedive. At his accession Abbas II was only seventeen years old and unmarried, and Amina took charge of the search for an appropriate princess for him to wed. She passed over his first cousin, setting her sights instead on an Ottoman princess with whom she nearly succeeded in arranging a union. In the meantime, Abbas began to have sexual relations with Iqbal (1876–1923), one of three Circassian slave women that Amina had assigned to his personal service. On February 12, 1895, Iqbal gave birth to a girl, named Amina in honor of her grandmother. A contract of marriage between her and the khedive was written seven days later. At the public celebration the mother of the khedive hosted the women's reception.⁸² Iqbal Hanim eventually bore all of Abbas's six children.

Amina's gift of Iqbal and two other slave women to Abbas recalls the gift of Shafiq Nur to the future Khedive Ismail by his mother, and suggests that this was a way of controlling a young prince's sexual activity. Fathering a child with a slave concubine was still unexceptional in ruling- and upper-class culture, but public expectations had changed during the forty years between the birth of the late Khedive Tawfiq and his granddaughter Amina with regard to the domestic lives of the khedives. Abbas immediately freed Iqbal and raised her to the status of legal wife. *Al-Waqa'i' al-Misriyya* announced the birth and the subsequent wedding, and published some poetry written in honor of the khedival daughter,⁸³ evidence that no sense of scandal attached to these events. The public announcements did not allude to Iqbal's previous slave status, but the circumstances were obvious to anyone familiar with upper-class culture.

Amina may have acquired Iqbal, and almost certainly acquired other slaves, after the importation of white slaves into Egypt became illegal in 1884. She and Abbas II seem not to have found slavery objectionable in principle, since they kept slaves in their households until World War I.⁸⁴ In spite of breaking with some aspects of traditional harem culture (such as permitting her unveiled portrait to be published in 1923 and later), she continued to conduct herself in accordance with the culture of harem slavery for the rest of her life. She established an extensive endowment, one of the purposes of which was to pay pensions to sixty former slaves, including ten eunuchs.⁸⁵ Most of the others were women, a slight majority of whom were married or widows, indicating that they had left Amina's service at some earlier date. Others, like her chief servant (*bash qalfa*) Lady Qamar, apparently remained in Amina's service until her death in 1931. As for Abbas's attitude toward slavery, in Istanbul in 1894 he gave his personal physician Comanos Pasha the task of purchasing additional white female slaves "for his harem." The khedive complained that he had but two or three slaves, just enough to serve him personally. He could not procure slaves in Egypt, where the trade was forbidden, so it was necessary to acquire them, discreetly, in Istanbul. Comanos bought six, to serve as domestics and not as concubines.⁸⁶

Abbas II also departed from his father's example by practicing polygyny. His second wife was Javidan (Djavidan) Hanim (1877–1968), the former Countess May Torok von Szendro, of Hungarian noble lineage, whom he met during a holiday in Europe. They were married secretly some time after 1900, and she used to accompany him on trips in disguise. She converted to Islam and she and the khedive were remarried, officially, at the end of February 1910, probably to avoid a scandal. The marriage was dissolved three years later. In her memoirs Javidan mused, "It is curious to think that my husband has two wives."[87] Unlike Abbas's marriage to Iqbal, his marriage to Javidan was not announced publicly, even though it was presided over by the Grand Mufti. No notice of the event appeared in *al-Waqa'i' al-Misriyya* or in private newspapers like *al-Ahram*, even though the activities of the khedive routinely received press attention. Knowledge of the khedive's polygyny may not have become public until the 1930s.[88]

Khedive Ismail had multiple wives and concubines, public knowledge of which displayed his grandeur and masculinity. Abbas's clandestine polygyny resembled less his grandfather's style than the behavior of an adulterer in a legally monogamous society, or, as is the case in Egypt today, in a society in which polygyny is legally permissible but socially disapproved.

The transition to monogamy in the khedival house epitomized a number of complex and ambiguous changes in nineteenth-century ruling- and upper-class domesticity. In a culture that permitted plural marriage, monogamy and polygyny were not thought of as opposites, and so the adoption of a monogamous style of marriage by Khedive Ismail's sons was a cause for comment only among Westerners. After securing the decree of primogeniture Ismail adopted a strategy of endogamous marriage to conciliate other branches of the khedival family, and royal endogamy was incompatible with polygyny. European observers saw the adoption of monogamy as a significant change, but there is no evidence that it was intended or understood within Ottoman Egyptian culture as a departure of major proportions. Nevertheless, the upper class emulated the khedival family in such things as architecture, clothing, and the employment of European governesses to educate their daughters, and the public example set by the khedives seems to have contributed to a decline in upper-class polygyny.

The cultivation of European opinion was a perennial concern of the Muhammad Ali dynasty, and the khedives and their publicists made much of the transition to monogamy. Despite the difficulties Abbas II had with Egypt's British occupiers, until he married Javidan Hanim British writers generally portrayed his domestic life as irreproachable. Edward Dicey praised Abbas's monogamy, as did Cromer in his book *Modern Egypt* (1908), though in *Abbas II* (1915) he refrained from comment.[89] Western observers insisted that polygyny was incompatible with a sound family life, and that Muslims had to adopt monogamy to advance toward modern civilization. Thus the Palace sought to preserve the "irreproachable" image of the khedive's family life in Britain and other "civilized" countries.

The Palace was also concerned to cultivate Egyptian public opinion. Juan Cole has described how the rapid development of transport, schools, and publishing in the last third of the nineteenth century contributed to the formation of a "public" who consumed the print media and were interested and active in public affairs.[90] While desiring an end to the British occupation, many leading Egyptian public figures were unenthusiastic about the prospect of returning to strong khedival rule. They favored a constitutional regime that would restrict the power of the monarch and permit them to run things by means of a representative parliament. The new family ideology was most influential among the literate public whom Abbas needed to cultivate, and the conjugal family and companionate marriage were important features of that ideology.[91] In marrying polygynously the khedive was exercising what even today is the legal right of Muslim men in Egypt. The Palace strategy of covering up his polygyny indicates the extent to which public sentiment had changed between the four princely weddings, when the transition to monogamy in the khedival house went unremarked by Egyptians, and the eve of World War I.

2

Marriage in Practice

The Changing System of Marriage and Household Formation

Khedive Tawfiq, who succeeded Ismail upon the latter's deposition and exile in 1879, was responsible for marrying off the many harem women his father left behind. The young Ahmad Shafiq (1860–1940) was a palace official involved in the task of selecting husbands for the women, providing them with trousseaus, and paying their wedding costs. One day his superior astonished him with the news that he, too, would be married to a Circassian woman whom the khedive had chosen for him. His father advised him to accede to the wishes of the khedive, who was his benefactor.[1]

Shafiq's memoirs are a useful source for reconstructing marriage practices in ruling- and upper-class families in the late nineteenth century, starting with his own experiences. His first marriage illustrates the persistence of elements of the culture associated with household government in the generation following the end of the slave trade and the demise of khedival autocracy. He was the son of a government official and a protégé of Tawfiq, who paid for his advanced education. Slaves acquired the status of the households to which they belonged, and so a well-born official like Shafiq was considered a fitting match for a woman from the harem of the former khedive.[2] His marriage strengthened the tie between him and the khedival household, just as earlier generations of civil servants and officers had been attached to the khedival household through marriage to women from its harem. His account also illustrates how the system of family patriarchy limited the autonomy of both men and women when it came to selecting a spouse, although in this case it was the khedive, as his patron, who was making the decision and not his father. As a young, subordinate man, Shafiq had as little say as his bride did in choosing when and whom to marry.

This and other aspects of the marriage system began to change in the next generation, at least among the literate middle and upper classes. This chapter discusses those changes, starting with an examination of the memoirs of eight Egyptians who married between 1880 and 1923.[3] The central feature of the marriage system as depicted in these autobiographical accounts was the process of arranging marriage, which included selecting a spouse and negotiating the terms of the marriage contract. The younger the bride or groom was, the less they participated in the selection of their spouse. Upper-class conventions discouraged prospective brides and grooms from meeting before the day of their wedding. Most of our memoirists, who were men, objected to that practice, but not to arranged marriages in principle. However, none of them were married as minors. The sole woman among these authors, the feminist leader Huda al-Sha'rawi (1879–1947), was married at the age of thirteen to a much older cousin, which was a wrenching experience. Later in life she championed the cause of setting a minimum age for marriage.[4] Thus the age at marriage is another issue posed in these memoirs, and not only as a political question, since older grooms and brides exercised more autonomy in spousal choice and were more likely to form conjugal family households separate from their parents. Secondary education and especially an advanced education tended to push the age of marriage for men upward, and that seems to have been a factor in the disappearance of large, joint family households among the urban elite after World War I.

A third issue raised in these memoirs was polygyny. Women intensely disliked it, and al-Sha'rawi was no exception. She separated from her husband for seven years due to his polygyny. However, our memoirists appear to confirm the impression of foreigners that polygyny was waning in the upper classes. Polygyny had no place in the new family ideology, in which the ideal of companionate marriage was an important component. Although our male memoirists did not express opposition to polygyny directly, those who desired prenuptial meetings with their prospective brides justified it in terms of both their religion and their desire for a companionate relationship with their wives. Even though they were describing their sentiments decades later, their accounts reinforce the impression that the clandestine polygyny of Khedive Abbas II was an indicator of changing ideals of marriage and family life at the time.

Our memoirists were successful lawyers, politicians, and writers. They were from elite families or rose into the elite. There are no working-class or peasant autobiographies from this period that I know of. Yet in spite of their limited representativeness, these memoirs are valuable for their description of the methods of spousal selection and marriage negotiation; their depiction of the involvement of family, friends, and others in the process; and the authors' portrayal of their own attitudes and sentiments at the time. While the memoirs privilege elite experience, we can apprehend some aspects of marriage and marital life among the majority of Egyptians from other sources, including the registers of the Sharia Courts and the fatwas or legal decisions of the long-serving Grand Mufti of Egypt, Muhammad al-Abbasi al-Mahdi. If the memoirs represent an elite perspective, until the end of the nineteenth century the court records mainly represent the middle strata. Census registers are yet another source that offer evidence of the lives of the more marginal members of society who rarely appeared before the courts, such as laborers, Bedouin, and slaves. Literally a snapshot of numerous urban and rural households in the middle decades of the nineteenth century, these census registers contain quantifiable data that permits us to test, and sometimes revise, long-standing notions of Egyptian social history that are based on little more than the impressions of foreign travelers.

Remembering Marriage in the Late Nineteenth and Early Twentieth Centuries

Informed of his Circassian bride-to-be, Shafiq would have known better than to ask to meet her in advance of the wedding. Upper- and ruling-class households practiced the strictest seclusion of women, ostensibly to guard their modesty, but also making ostentatious displays of wealth and respectability. It was not acceptable for families of standing, and certainly not the khedival household, to permit their young women to be seen by or even described to men other than their closest relations. The norm was for brides and grooms to meet one another for the first time at their weddings, although women had some ways of obtaining a view of a prospective groom, as shall be seen.

Shafiq and some of our other memoirists were unhappy with that custom, desiring to meet their prospective brides or at least to be informed about them by a third party. As men with a modern education, they were conversant with contemporary discourse on the importance of a couple meeting before their wedding in order to establish the beginning of a relationship.[5] The recollection of their sentiments is a sign of the inroads made by the new family ideology, in which marriage was idealized as a lasting, companionate relationship. The more conservative families resisted prenuptial meetings between their daughters and fiancés well into the twentieth century, which is why some of our authors, even when writing decades later, emphasized the point that Islam permits such meetings. Mid-twentieth century religious authorities made the same point for the same reason.[6]

Sometime before his marriage, Shafiq had been identified as a suitable match for another woman whose family called the affair off when his mother asked to see her.[7] The same thing happened on a later occasion, after he was widowed. By then Shafiq was in his thirties. He had spent some time in Europe and nearly married a French woman, whom he identified as one Isabelle Contal. Shafiq wanted to get to know his prospective bride as he had done with Isabelle.[8] His mother cautioned him that it would not be acceptable to a noble family, though he might be allowed to see her picture. However, the family of the prospective bride were upset by his mother's request to see her, and refused to continue the negotiations.[9] Shafiq eventually remarried in 1894. Although he omitted the name of his wife from his memoir, she was Aziza Rashed Rakem Hanim, the daughter of a general in the army of Khedive Ismail.[10] At the time she and her mother were in the entourage of the ex-khedive, then living in exile in Istanbul. Khedive Abbas II personally intervened to overcome the reluctance of the mother to allow her daughter's photograph to be sent to Shafiq in Cairo. Still, Shafiq and his bride met for the first time on their wedding day.[11]

Shafiq was, of course, not a typical Egyptian but a well-born palace official, whose brides should come from the most elite families. Only the wealthiest households could afford to maintain a regime of strict concealment, with separate housing quarters and large staffs of slaves and servants. Public space expanded in the second half of the nineteenth century with the development of public transportation, public architecture, and city planning on the European model, making concealment more difficult and thereby more expensive and exclusive. Upper-class women did venture into public space, but to do so they needed eunuchs as escorts, curtained carriages, and the like. There were screened boxes for ladies in Cairo's Opera House, which opened in 1869, but no separate women's section in the general seating.

The burgeoning popular press of the late nineteenth century fanned anxiety over the presence of women in public space, with contributions and letters describing local acts of crime and public immorality that often involved women. Together with prescriptive writings for women, the press framed a dichotomy between respectable and disreputable women. The former guarded their chastity by covering and not mingling with men, while the latter behaved licentiously by not covering fully, mingling, and even flirting.[12] Popular as well as official concern for the policing of women's behavior in public was not new, as Liat Kozma has shown.[13] But it grew with the advance of urbanization, the expansion of public space, and the emergence of a popular press that echoed and intensified such concerns. The desire of the elite to maintain respectability through the covering and concealment of their women was thus an effect of modernization as much as it was a legacy of the past.

A convention related to women covering themselves was the custom of not revealing their names in public. Shafiq did not mention the name of his Circassian wife, who died three years after their marriage, nor that of his second wife, Aziza Hanim, although he published his memoirs at a time in which the emancipation of women was being written into the modern national narrative.[14] All but two of our male authors omitted the names of their wives from their accounts, and Salama Musa (1887–1958) recalled that as a child his older sister slapped him for calling out her name in public.[15]

The working-class and peasant majority also divided themselves into homosocial spaces, though they lacked the means to observe the degree of gender separation practiced by the elite. In those strata men and women often married within their extended family or urban or village quarter, and some families were known to intermarry across generations. In the villages, according to the feminist writer Malak Hifni Nasif, who wrote under the pen name Bahithat al-Badiya (1886–1918), brides and grooms normally met each other before marrying,[16] though it is likely that the more prominent rural families emulated the restrictive customs of the urban middle and upper classes.

One of Shafiq's contemporaries was the lawyer and politician Ibrahim al-Hilbawi (1858–1940). Al-Hilbawi's father was a Nile boatman who later worked as a farmer and merchant, learning to read late in life. Al-Hilbawi married for the first time in 1880 in his native village of Kafr al-Dawar, located in the Lower Egyptian province of al-Buhayra. When he began practicing law in the city of Tanta, in the adjacent province of al-Gharbiyya, his wife refused to accompany him out of a dislike for urban life, and went to live with her family. Unlike married women in Western Europe, she was under no legal obligation to accompany him to a distant locale.[17] The implication is that they divorced. His second wife was a Circassian ex-slave from the harem of Princess Jamila (1869–96), one of the daughters of the former Khedive Ismail. The wife of a colleague, acting as an intermediary, assisted in selecting her.[18] This match bespeaks al-Hilbawi's ambition and his ability to achieve it, as a result of entering the nascent legal profession and acquiring the proper connections. Al-Hilbawi's readers would have understood that a prenuptial meeting with his bride was out of the question since he was forging a marriage link with the aristocracy. The marriage took place in 1888, but his wife died the following year.

Al-Hilbawi's third attempt at marriage demonstrated the limits of his social-climbing ability. This time he asked the wife of a different colleague to select a Circassian woman for him from the entourage of the late Princess Parlanta (d. 1892),[19] the mother of Khediva Amina, who was supervising the marrying off of her mother's former harem women. Al-Hilbawi was ordered to present himself at the door of the harem of Abdin Palace, the khedival residence, where he stood for a while to allow himself to be inspected. Later he was informed that he did not impress the intended bride (or perhaps the khediva herself) as a man of stature.[20] Following this rejection he turned again to the Palace of Princess Jamila; she married him to the daughter of a grandee who had been raised in her Palace. This was an unhappy marriage, and he divorced this wife not long after moving his law practice to Cairo.[21] He married a final time in 1897, this time happily, to another Circassian ex-slave from the harem of one of the wives of the late Khedive Ismail.[22] Al-Hilbawi's several marriages illustrate the continued desirability of ties of marriage to the ruling family for ambitious men of his generation. But by the end of the century it was probably easier for rising men with talent but an undistinguished background, like al-Hilbawi, to marry harem women, since the harem system had by then become obsolescent. The last cohort of harem women had to be married off, and rising professional men like al-Hilbawi were suitable grooms.

The memoirs of Huda al-Sha'rawi offer a rare female perspective on the marriage system in this era. She was the daughter of Muhammad Sultan Pasha (1825–84), known as the "king" of Upper Egypt due to his landed wealth and political influence.[23] In 1892 she was married at the age of thirteen to her cousin and guardian, Ali al-Sha'rawi, who was in his forties. Their marriage ensured that the land she had inherited from her father would remain in the family.[24] Huda was not informed of the marriage at first, and lacking older sisters she did not recognize the early wedding preparations for what they were. Then she was pressured to accept her cousin's offer of marriage for the sake of the family.[25]

In the upper class it was not unusual for the guardian of the bride to negotiate an agreement committing the groom to monogamy by making divorce automatic if he violated his promise, or by giving her the power to pronounce a divorce if he did so. The former device was known as a conditional divorce (*ta'liq al-talaq*) and the latter as a delegated divorce (*tafwid al-talaq*). In either, the divorcée would receive all that she was due financially. Both were accepted in Hanafi jurisprudence, which was in effect in the court system at the time.[26] Huda's mother Iqbal insisted, as conditions of the marriage, that Ali promise to leave his concubine, who had borne him a number of children, and not take an additional wife. But she was doubly disadvantaged in these negotiations by her illiteracy and because she was not Huda's legal guardian. Huda's guardian, who should have represented her interests, was Ali. On the morning of the wedding Ali gave Huda a notarized declaration of a conditional divorce in a sealed envelope, which she put aside unread.

Less than fifteen months later Huda discovered that Ali had either not ceased relations with the mother of his children—his *mustawlada*—or had resumed relations, and also that she was again pregnant. At first she and Iqbal believed that she was divorced under the terms of the conditional divorce, but it turned out that Ali had worded it to say that if he "took back" his *mustawlada*, then the *mustawlada* would be "divorced," not Huda. Huda's description of the document and of these events is brief and not very detailed. Her account suggests that Ali freed his *mustawlada* and then surreptitiously married her, which is the only way their continued sexual relationship could be licit; hence the promise to "divorce" her.[27] Huda's readers would have sympathized with her assumption that the conditional divorce applied to her, since that was the commonplace formula. Though not divorced, Huda responded to the situation by separating from Ali for seven years.[28]

Her response is an indication of how strongly women disliked polygyny. That dislike was shared by her mother, a Circassian who had come to Egypt as a refugee. Though not enslaved, Iqbal was raised in an upper-class harem and groomed for elite marriage, eventually becoming a younger wife of Sultan Pasha. Huda grew up in the family home in the Ismailiyya quarter of Cairo—the fashionable district inspired by Haussmann's Paris that was built in the late 1860s—where she and her brother lived with their mother and her senior co-wife, Hasiba, and Hasiba's son. Huda and her brother addressed Hasiba as *Umm Kabira* or "Elder Mother." Sultan Pasha maintained a second residence in the Upper Egyptian province of al-Minya, where he presumably kept other consorts. Although Iqbal had a tranquil relationship with Hasiba, she was angered by Ali's initial resistance to an agreement guaranteeing his monogamy. Then when Huda separated from Ali, Iqbal negotiated on her behalf, but did not pressure Huda to reconcile with him. That pressure came later from men, including her brother.[29]

Huda's contemporary, Muhammad Ali Allouba (1875/1878–1956) made a career as a lawyer, politician, and diplomat. He was the son of a civil servant and notable in the town of Asyut in Upper Egypt. He married in 1904, a year after being accepted as a lawyer in the appeals court. Following the convention of that time, his family undertook the search for a suitable bride for him in Asyut, and then in Cairo, where his father rented a house for six months as a base of operations. Eventually a match was suggested by a relative and family friend. Reciprocal visits by family members ensued, and the engagement was agreed upon by the two fathers. It was the custom in the bride's hometown of Cairo to view her prospective husband from behind a *mashrabiyya* lattice. But Allouba, a man with modern ideas, objected on the ground that while she could see him, he was not permitted to see her. The issue was resolved when his prospective bride consented to her father traveling to Asyut to see him. On the wedding day, in Asyut, the marriage contract was drawn up by the two fathers, and Allouba and his bride met for the first time. Although he did not name her in his narrative, she was Nefisa Amin Hanafi.[30] Looking back at these events from the mid-twentieth century, Allouba wrote that the custom of not meeting before marriage persisted to that day, especially in Upper Egypt, but he thought it was better for couples to meet and get to know one another beforehand. Even so, popular opinion held that a daughter should accept a marriage decision made for her by her parents, who were the most capable of assessing a prospective groom and his family without being swayed by emotion. He added that love can cloud one's judgment; it should come after marriage, but not before.[31]

The famous writer and scholar Ahmad Amin (1886–1954) grew up in a middle-class family in Cairo. His father taught at al-Azhar and ran a stern, patriarchal household, though he saw to the education of the author's older sister at the al-Siyufiyya School, which was the government's only girls' secondary school at the time.[32] But the changing attitude in favor of women's education had no counterpart when it came to arranging a marriage. Having started his career as a teacher in the School for Qadis and after some hesitation, Amin decided at the age of twenty-nine to marry. Finding a bride was difficult, in part because some young women and their families assumed from the turban he wore—indicating his religious education—that he was humorless and unsophisticated. Eventually a fellow teacher identified a family that he found acceptable and who also accepted him. He dispatched his mother, his sister, and a colleague's wife to meet the young woman. They approved of her but their descriptions gave him little idea of what she was like. In the end, he wrote, "I trusted the matter to God," and they met for the first time when they married in 1916. Nearly four decades later he compared the process to opening a fortune cookie or buying a lottery ticket.[33] His account makes it clear that he endorsed the idea of couples meeting before marriage.

Amin's contemporary, the writer and journalist Muhammad Lutfi Jum'a (1886–1953), grew up in a middle-class family in Alexandria. After living several years as a bachelor by choice, he decided to marry at the age of thirty-two. His wife, whom he identified as Nafisa Muhammad al-Ibrashi, was recommended to him by a close female relative, and after meeting they wrote the contract together in 1918. Two decades later he was still satisfied with the marriage, while expressing skepticism toward the idea of a marriage based on romantic love. Romantic love lasts a short time but a marriage will last if there is sincerity, truthfulness, and esteem, he wrote. In this context Jum'a noted that Nafisa did not demand as a condition of the marriage that he not marry an additional wife, and she turned down his offer to delegate the right of divorce to her.[34]

The lawyer and nationalist Abd al-Rahman al-Rafi'i (1889–1966) also vacillated between bachelorhood and marriage, eventually deciding to marry because "[marriage] is the natural, normal state of humanity in society." Due to his love for his deceased mother he decided to look among his maternal relations for a bride. While visiting them he noticed Aisha, the daughter of one of his maternal uncles. This was at the beginning of the 1919 Revolution, the nationwide uprising against British colonial rule. Aisha was a "revolutionary" who participated in the now-iconic demonstration of March 16—the first women's demonstration, which marked the beginning of the public participation of women in Egyptian politics (Huda al-Sha'rawi was one of the organizers of the demonstration).[35] Al-Rafi'i admired Aisha for her activism and her strong convictions, qualities that he could only have noticed as a result of conversing with her. Yet, he wrote, he could not broach the subject of marriage to Aisha directly, since that was not done in those days, especially in conservative families. Al-Rafi'i's readers would have understood that he approached her father, or perhaps he asked another relative to act as an intermediary. The contract was agreed to one year after the beginning of the revolution, in March 1920. Al-Rafi'i went on to speak of his love for Aisha and his indebtedness to her, calling her "the partner of my life" who assured him "a happy domestic life, and . . . family tranquility that helped me in work."[36]

The socialist writer Salama Musa married at the age of thirty-six, in 1923. From a Coptic family, he was the son of an official in the Lower

Figure 2. Iskandar Abdelmalek and Liza Henein, their daughter Margueritte (standing), and their son Amin by a photographer called Phoebus, sometime before 1919. Family portraiture grew in popularity from the late nineteenth century, along with diffusion of the conjugal family ideal in the upper and middle classes. Regardless of whether they lived in a joint or conjugal family household, couples who posed for intimate photos such as these presented themselves as bourgeois conjugal families. Courtesy of the Rare Books and Special Collections Library, The American University in Cairo.

Egyptian province of al-Sharqiyya, and grew up in the town of Zaqaziq. His father died when he was only two, but he left his wife and several children a pension and a substantial landholding. Musa was able to pursue an advanced education, including four years in England. Like Jum'a and al-Rafi'i, he described himself as giving little thought to marriage in early adulthood, in spite of his mother's urging. He met his future wife, whom he did not name, while visiting her family along with a friend. He was able to speak with her, and on the second visit they spent two hours together. The couple spent even more time together after their engagement. Although she had attended a French school, Musa discovered that his wife had little interest in the world of books and ideas to which he belonged, so he undertook her advanced education by involving her in his work, thereby raising her intellectual level. "A fine harmony" developed between them, he wrote, and "[s]he became my friend as much as my wife." But for that to be possible the wife and husband must be nearly equal in education and intellect.[37]

Arranging Marriage

These autobiographies illustrate the variety of ways in which middle- and upper-class marriages were arranged in the late nineteenth and early twentieth centuries, from being selected or selecting someone through matchmakers who were professionals, patrons, or friends, to contacts and negotiations conducted by family patriarchs and matriarchs, to following up on the suggestion of a relative, friend, or colleague. The idea of young, never-married women and men meeting before their wedding was only beginning to be accepted by World War I. In an 1881 article Muhammad Abduh, the reformer and future Grand Mufti, was much more critical of marriage customs in the countryside than Malak Hifni Nasif would be almost thirty years later. Abduh claimed that the main concern of a young man's parents in choosing a bride for him was not her character but the wealth and status of her family.[38] Abduh was likely reflecting on the habits of the prosperous landholding element whence he came. Nasif, an upper-class Cairene, encountered peasant women in al-Fayum, where she lived in the home of her husband, but she wrote at a time in which nationalist writers were constructing the peasantry as authentic Egyptians and their ways were often used as a foil to urban upper-class norms that required women to veil, restricted them from working away from the home, and discouraged prenuptial meetings with their fiancés.[39]

According to Shafiq, in the urban middle and upper classes there were times when a family knew hardly anything about the woman to whom their son was engaged except what they were told by a matchmaker.[40] Amin described a more or less similar system among the Cairene middle class in the early twentieth century:

> Marriage was mostly subject to the old traditions: a young man would hear from a friend or a relative of his that so-and-so had a marriageable daughter, or he might learn this from a professional woman called *khatiba* (matchmaker) who visited homes, gathered information from them, saw there the young women of marriageable ages or the young men desiring to marry, and acted as a go-between for the families of the future husband and wife by introducing the ones to the others; a relative of the young man would then approach the young woman's father or guardian and propose to him the young man's desire; if he accepted, the latter would send his mother and some of his womenfolk to see the girl; if they described her to him in a manner to convince him, he would proceed to the marriage without having seen her or known her appearance, her disposition, and her character; he would know all that only after concluding the contract and after the wedding.[41]

Of our memoirists only Jum'a, al-Rafi'i, and Musa, who married between 1918 and 1923, met their prospective brides before becoming engaged to them. That and the willingness of Jum'a and al-Rafi'i to mention the names of their wives gives their narratives a modern tone compared to those of the earlier memoirists.[42]

Marriages were normally "arranged," not only in the process of choosing a spouse but in the sense that negotiations preceded the writing of the marriage contract. These negotiations were almost a necessity because there were so few requirements for a legally valid marriage. The "pillars" of marriage, as they were called in the legal texts, were a properly worded contract between the bride and groom or their guardians; a groom and a bride legally free to marry; qualified marriage guardians; an agreed-upon dower; and qualified notary-witnesses.[43] But in addition to the dower and the portion of it to be paid promptly, the bride and groom or their guardians could negotiate a number of other issues, including the trousseau (*jihaz*) provided the bride by her parents. The bride's side might seek a commitment to monogamy by the groom, or other guarantees concerning her freedom to visit relatives and friends, the place of the marital residence, and so on.[44] The higher the status of the bride's family, the more likely they were to seek such stipulations. Thus it was unexceptional for the mother of Huda al-Sha'rawi to try to secure a commitment to monogamy from her prospective husband. Evidently Ali al-Sha'rawi also agreed that Huda would continue to reside in her mother's house in Cairo, where a suite of rooms was prepared for her new life as a married woman.[45]

Marriage at a relatively young age meant dependence on one's father or another guardian to pay the costs. Although men as well as women of the age of discretion were entitled legally to arrange and contract marriages on their own,[46] without recourse to a guardian, the cost of marriage, which included the dower, the trousseau, and various ceremonial costs, were important reasons for the involvement of elder family members in marriage decisions, especially for those marrying for the first time.

Although it was not legally required, the parents of a bride normally provided her with a trousseau. In urban society this usually consisted of household goods—linens, utensils, and even furniture. In the villages a woman might be given a head of livestock as a part of her trousseau, "according to the custom of the peasants" as was noted in one court case.[47] Weddings included a public procession (*zifaf*) of the bride to the home of the groom, during which the trousseau was displayed, and along with hired musicians and dancers it was an occasion for her family to show off.[48] The groom or his family paid the prompt portion of the dower (usually two-thirds of it), provided additional gifts to the bride, and either family might pay the cost of food and entertainment.[49] In 1856 al-Abbasi considered the sad case of a man who desired to marry and who claimed that his father was obliged to marry him off, pay the costs, and give him some of the land and buildings he owned. But his father was not legally obliged to do so. Since the man lived and worked in his father's household and had no independent income, he lacked the means to pay for a dower and a feast on his own.⁵⁰ Muhammad Lutfi Jumʻa, Abd al-Rahman al-Rafiʻi, and Salama Musa arranged their own marriages in part because their fathers were deceased, and moreover they were well established in their professions and able to pay their own marriage costs. Thus a man's ability to arrange and contract his own marriage depended on his means. Younger men and women were less likely to opt to marry themselves off due to a lack of means and fear of alienating their family.⁵¹

In large families the ceremonial costs of marriage were sometimes mitigated by staging more than one wedding at a time. Shafiq's parents saved money by marrying off his brother and sister on the same day, and al-Hilbawi, who took responsibility for his siblings, married off his brother, sister, and half-sister on the same day while staging a single celebration in the family home.⁵² Ceremonial costs were greatest in the middle and upper classes, of course, and lower-income families made do with less pomp and ceremony. Widows and divorcées usually remarried without staging a wedding procession.⁵³

Marriages necessarily had to be arranged for slaves, who could only marry with the permission of their masters. Many Circassian slaves in upper-class households were trained to become the consorts of high-placed men, but the majority of slaves were trans-Saharan African women who worked as domestics in urban upper- and middle-class households.⁵⁴ Ghislaine Alleaume and Philippe Fargues' analysis of the 1848 census of Cairo revealed that wealthy as well as middle-class households contained slaves along with free resident servants.⁵⁵ The ratio of female to male slaves in the towns was about three to one, and so most slave women who entered conjugal relationships did so with free men. Men who were temporary residents or unable to afford the cost of marriage could acquire a slave woman in lieu of a contractual wife for housekeeping and sexual companionship. The 1848 census of Cairo describes some of these women, particularly Abyssinians, as "slave wives" (*zawjat jariya*). The term is contradictory, because legally, a man was required to emancipate a woman he owned in order to marry her. But the imprecise terminology undoubtedly reflected popular usage. "Slave wives" were sometimes substitutes for contractual wives.⁵⁶ Edward Lane, who sojourned in Egypt during the

1820s and 1830s, noted that "some [men] prefer the possession of an Abyssinian slave to the more expensive maintenance of a wife."[57] He also discovered that single men were distrusted and not welcome to live outside the European quarter of Cairo, but that could be rectified by acquiring a slave woman, or marrying a widow with the understanding that he would divorce her in one to two years when he left Egypt.[58] A decade later Gérard de Nerval was advised that to live in an Egyptian neighborhood he should acquire a slave woman, because "slaves are much cheaper [than wives]." Some European men developed long-term relationships with slave wives, but others abandoned them when convenient, even when pregnant.[59]

There were very few slaves in the four villages of Damas, Sandub, Zafar, and Ikhtab, all in al-Daqahliyya province, according to their census registers in 1848, though twenty years later African slaves accounted for between 3 and 6 percent of the population in each. Three-quarters of them were male, reversing the ratio of enslaved men to women in the towns. Most of the male slaves were in landholding households, presumably employed in agriculture.[60] Due to the greater proportion of male slaves, in the four villages in 1868 twenty-five of the forty married slave men had free Egyptian wives. These marriages potentially violated the rule of status suitability (*kifa'a*) since enslavement made a man an unsuitable match for a free woman. But a misalliance could be declared invalid only as a result of a suit brought by the bride or someone entitled to act as her guardian.[61]

Age of Marriage and Household Formation

Nowadays large, multigenerational households are associated with the rural society,[62] but they were ubiquitous in nineteenth-century Cairo. Demographers refer to households such as these as "extended," "multiple," and "joint" family households. The distinctive feature of a joint family household is that it contains two or more related conjugal couples.[63] Most of the time a joint family household is formed when a son marries and brings his bride to live with him in his father's household. Hence, joint households usually evolve out of conjugal family households (also known as "simple" or "nuclear" family households). But two conditions are necessary for that to be likely: sons need to marry relatively early, and patrilocal marriage needs to be the norm. A joint household comprising a father and two or more married sons might continue after the father's death if the brothers stay together, but as with all family forms the joint household cycle involves a constant process of forming, developing, and breaking up.[64]

Systems of household formation in past time are of interest because of their role in political and economic life.[65] Scholars have also identified the joint household as a site of strong domestic patriarchy, or as David Ludden defined it, "patriarchal power that is located historically inside institutions of kinship." Deniz Kandiyoti famously described the area stretching from North Africa through South and East Asia as a region of "classical patriarchy," and argued that "[t]he key to the reproduction of classic patriarchy lies in the operations of the patrilocally extended household,"[66] or in other words the joint household, in which the women and younger men are subordinated to a senior head of household. Kandiyoti later modified her thesis of how women in these household systems coped by "bargaining with patriarchy," but continued to associate joint households with patriarchal forms of control.[67] Other scholars have zeroed in on patrilocal and early marriage (for women) as essential factors in the reproduction of domestic patriarchy, arguing that, historically, the absence (or decline) of these practices favored companionate marriage and greater equality between the spouses.[68]

In Cairo, middle- and upper-class families largely abandoned the joint family household in favor of conjugal households by about the second quarter of the twentieth century, more or less at the same time that Istanbulites did.[69] That development was evident about a generation after observers first noted a decline in the practice of polygyny in those classes. It also correlated with a rising age of marriage for both sexes.

Joint family households accounted for 29 percent of all Cairene households in 1848, according to Alleaume and Fargues' sample of the census, while the aggregate proportion of joint households in the four villages was only 17 percent (Table 2).[70] Joint households were favored by the elite of Cairo. The men most likely to preside over them were engineers (84.5 percent), copyists (64.5 percent), teacher-scholars (63.7 percent), and large merchants (60.6 percent). The scholars, large merchants, and copyists

Table 2
Proportion of Household Types in the Four Villages and Cairo, 1847–48

	The Four Villages	The Cairo Sample
Solitaries and No-Family Households	17.2%	16.4%
Households with One Conjugal Couple	65.1%	54.6%
Joint Family Households	16.9%	29.0%
Incompletely Classifiable	0.8%	

Sources: NAE, Census registers of Damas, Sandub, Zafar, and Ikhtab, 1847–48; Allaume and Fargues, "Naissance d'une Stastique."

were also the most likely to have slaves and live-in servants in their households,[71] a sure sign of wealth. In the villages, similarly, it was mainly the village headman or *umda*s, the lesser shaykhs of village sections, and other landholding villagers who headed joint households. Land was the principal economic resource in the countryside, and there was a strong correlation between household complexity and landholding.[72]

The large merchants who engaged in wholesale and international trade (*tujjar*) were part of Cairo's historic elite, as were the high ulama, or teacher-scholars, who held positions in the major mosque-colleges such as al-Azhar. Before the nineteenth century some ulama became wealthy as the administrators of religious endowments, through official patronage, and by engaging in private commercial ventures. There were close ties between the large merchants and high ulama, who were often from the same families and/or intermarried. Some ulama also worked as copyists and in related trades such as bookselling, which may explain the presence of copyists in the upper class.[73] After about 1820 the position of the large merchants and high ulama began to be eroded by the policies of Muhammad Ali, who relied more on men recruited from abroad than local notables in governing, who assumed administrative control of the religious endowments, and who attempted to control most production and trade for the benefit of the treasury.[74] Nevertheless, these old elite elements still held an upper-class position at mid-century, maintaining large joint households with numerous slaves and servants in emulation of the ruling class. The engineers were a new element, created by the Pasha's regime as part of its drive to modernize the army and administration, but they too conformed to elite culture by forming joint households and acquiring more than a few slaves and servants of their own.[75]

In the countryside, the rural notables maintained joint households as a way of keeping the family landholding undivided and to maximize their command of labor and local political influence.[76] In the village of Ikhtab in 1848, the headman or *umda* Ahmad Atarbi headed a household of fifty-seven comprising three generations: Ahmad and his wives, his several sons, one of whom was married, plus the widows of two deceased sons, and the wife of an absent grandson. Another household headed by Muhammad Khatir, the shaykh of a section of the village, contained forty-eight individuals in three generations: Muhammad and his wives, a married brother and his wives, and his sons and their wives and children.[77] Ahmad Atarbi was the largest landholder in the village, with 460 feddans, and Muhammad Khatir had the second largest holding with nearly 300 feddans.[78] Both households supplemented their own labor with nonrelations. The Atarbi household included eighteen slaves (fifteen males) and four servants. There were no slaves in the Khatir household, though the inmates included two servants and two young field workers.

Twenty years later, al-Hajj Muhammad Atarbi had succeeded his late father as the *umda* of Ikhtab and as the head of a household now numbering forty-one, but still comprising three generations: Muhammad and his wives, his sons and their wives, and the children of the latter. Three of his adult brothers had separated to form their own joint households (Table 3). The household of the aging Muhammad Khatir still numbered forty, though it now included several slaves.[79] These were still the leading landholding households, with 484 feddans and 229 feddans, respectively.[80] By then,

Table 3
Proportion of Household Types in the Four Villages, 1868

Solitaries and No-Family Households	10.54%
Households with One Conjugal Couple	64.95%
Joint Family Households	24.51%

Sources: NAE, Census registers of Damas, Sandub, Zafar, and Ikhtab, 1868.

families like these were establishing urban branches, and toward the end of the century their scions became part of the modern political and cultural elite.[81] In the cities they maintained the joint-household formation cycle.

Joint family households were not exclusive to the upper class. One-third or more of Cairene men in professions in which a son could assist or be trained in apprenticeship, such as textile weaving, leather work, metal work, and various retail trades, headed joint households.[82] In one riverine village, Badaway, joint households were headed by retail merchants, boatmen, and fishermen, in addition to landholders. In these occupations, also, the need for labor favored joint household formation.[83]

The reproduction of joint households required men to marry relatively early, while their fathers were living. Moreover, joint households made early marriage relatively easy, since a young man did not require the means to support a family on his own if he were to remain a dependent in his father's household. The Egyptian scholar Ahmad al-Dayrabi (fl. 1690–1711) wrote disapprovingly of child marriage in the countryside on the ground that boys were married even though they lacked the means to pay for a dower.[84] Of course, the dower was paid by their fathers.[85]

Late marriage reduced the likelihood of joint household formation due to a greater probability that the groom's father would be deceased. In

Table 4
Married Men by Age in Cairo and the Four Villages, 1847–48

Age Group	The Cairo Sample	The Four Villages
<15	0.7%	0.9%
15–19	51.0%	3.2%
20–24	79.7%	48.0%
25–29	92.4%	
30–34	96.6%	72.4%
35–39	98.6%	
40–44	99.4%	85.7%
45–49	99.6%	
50+	99.5%	81.7%

Sources: NAE, Census registers of Damas, Sandub, Zafar, and Ikhtab, 1847–48; Fargues, "Stages of the Family Life Cycle."

the early twentieth century a man who fathered a son at the age of twenty could expect on average to live to the age of fifty-three,[86] and if his son married in his teens or twenties they were likely to form a joint household. In Fargues' analysis of the 1848 Cairo census most men married in their late teens, and four-fifths of them were married before the age of twenty-five.[87] This was consistent with a high proportion of joint family households. Men married much later in the four villages: only about 3 percent were married in their teens, and a little less than half were married before the age of thirty (Table 4),[88] a difference that was consistent with the lower proportion of joint households in the villages.

There was a similar disparity in the age at which women married (Table 5). Using Fustat or Old Cairo as a proxy for Cairo proper, where women's ages were not recorded, Fargues found that nearly half of all women were married before the age of fifteen, the age of legal majority in Islamic jurisprudence, and nearly 90 percent of women were married before the age of twenty.[89] But in the four villages less than a fifth of the women were married before the age of fifteen, and a little more than half of them married before the age of twenty. By 1868 the age of marriage in the four villages

Table 5
Married Women by Age in Old Cairo and the Four Villages, 1847–48

Age Group	Old Cairo	The Four Villages
<5	0.5%	0.0%
5–9	4.4%	0.4%
10–14	49.1%	17.5%
15–19	89.0%	56.8%
20–24	99.0%	83.8%
25–29	96.7%	
30–34	100.0%	88.4%
35–39	98.4%	
40–44	96.0%	82.6%
45–49	100.0%	
50+	100.0%	43.7%

Sources: NAE, Census registers of Damas, Sandub, Zafar, and Ikhtab, 1847–48; Fargues, "Stages of the Family Life Cycle."

had risen for both sexes (Table 6). Men still married early enough and in sufficient numbers to enable joint households to continue, but relatively few minors were married: less than 2 percent of boys younger than fifteen and less than 5 percent of the girls.

The marriage of nearly half of all girls in mid-nineteenth-century Cairo between the ages of ten and fourteen corroborates the statement of Lane that many girls were married at the age of twelve or thirteen, and few were unmarried at sixteen.[90] But the lower proportion of minor marriages in the four villages, which was even lower by 1868, would still have been sufficient to provoke al-Dayrabi's comment, especially since the marriage of minor girls and, less often, boys correlated with wealth and status, making them noticeable events. Thirty percent of married women ten to fifteen years old were in landholding households in 1848 and more than two-thirds of them in 1868. The correlation with household complexity is even stronger: more than half of married women ten to fifteen years old were in joint households in 1848 and nearly three-quarters of them in 1868. Many of these households were headed by village shaykhs and *umda*s. Thus although child marriage was relatively rare in the nineteenth-century countryside, it occurred most often in families of wealth and standing. We have no comparable data from Cairo, though two famous women of the urban upper class, Aisha al-Taymur (1840–1902) and Huda al-Sha'rawi,

Table 6
Married Men and Women by Age in the Four Villages, 1868

Age Group	Married Men	Married Women
<5	0.0%	0.0%
5–9	0.0%	0.0%
10–14	1.7%	4.6%
15–19	8.4%	28.8%
20–29	34.2%	82.4%
30–39	73.6%	89.3%
40–49	87.2%	81.2%
50–59	90.2%	68.3%
60+	82.2%	28.3%

Sources: NAE, Census registers of Damas, Sandub, Zafar, and Ikhtab, 1868.

were married off as minors at the ages of fourteen and thirteen. A minimum marriage age was enacted in 1923, but by then child marriage was construed as a practice of the rural and uneducated,[91] reflecting the change in attitude and the disappearance of child marriage among the urban elite.

The "ruralization" of the joint household in our imaginary is a measure of how completely it disappeared from urban society during the twentieth century. Beginning in the last quarter of the nineteenth century ambitious young men began to postpone marriage until after they had finished an advanced education and begun their careers, as Allouba did, to marry in his mid- to late twenties.[92] Amin, Jum'a, al-Rafi'i, and Musa married even later, between the ages of twenty-nine and thirty-six. Thus one of the effects of the development of modern education was to delay marriage among educated men. Although the age of marriage rose for both sexes throughout the country after 1900,[93] the trend was especially noticeable among the *effendiyya*, the middle- and upper-class graduates of the new government schools. Men like the last four, who remained bachelors as young adults, contributed to popular anxiety about the fate of the Egyptian family and hence the nation, fueling discussion of a "marriage crisis" in the 1920s and 1930s, as Hanan Kholoussy has shown.[94]

The urban upper-class joint household system, in which families maintained households of up to sixty inmates, including servants, persisted until around the time of World War I.[95] According to Shafiq, "A son would reside in the family house even though he was married or a civil servant without paying anything of the expenses; that was the responsibility of the head of the family. As for the salary of the son, it was left to him to spend on his personal needs and, similarly, the cost of supporting his wife. Each son had his own wing of the house in which to reside with his wife, amid the [larger] family."[96] Allouba, who married in 1904, described a similar relationship with his father. Although he was a lawyer in the appellate court his father negotiated his marriage contract, paid his dower, and added a wing to the family home in Asyut for him and his bride.[97]

Among our memoirists, the third generation, who married between 1916 and 1923, departed from that pattern by forming separate conjugal-family households with their brides. Amin chose to live apart from his parents, albeit nearby them, to avoid problems between his mother and his wife.[98] At the age of twenty-nine his career was well established, and he had the means to set up an independent household. Jum'a and al-Rafi'i delayed marrying into their early thirties and after their fathers were deceased. They too had established careers and independent means, as did Musa, whose father died when was young.

The rising age of marriage among the *effendiyya* occurred at a time of changing marital ideals. Already by the time the latter four men married, the periodical press was promoting the new family ideology, with its emphasis on a companionate relationship between husband and wife.[99] This conjugal family ideal encouraged young couples to establish separate (neolocal) households to enable them to develop their relationship and to nurture their children, while avoiding the problems to which Ahmad Amin alluded. In Muslim family law a married woman was entitled to lodging separate from her in-laws, but this criterion could be met by a set of rooms within a larger structure or compound containing a joint household.[100] The wings added to the family home by Shafiq's and Allouba's fathers are examples of that. However, that was not compatible with the new family ideology, in which "the family" was defined as the conjugal couple and their children rather than the extended lineage.

The transition to conjugal family households diminished the power of family patriarchs who had exercised authority over the younger men as well as the women in the joint household system. By virtue of having an independent income and control of a separate household budget, young men in the middle and upper classes enjoyed more autonomy, as did their wives. However, it is commonplace nowadays for urban extended families to reside in adjacent or nearby apartments, often within the same building, which they may own, like the Pamuk family building in Istanbul described by the novelist Orhan Pamuk.[101] In the census data these next-door related families appear as separate conjugal family households. Familial and other social relations extend beyond the formal boundaries of households in all societies, but the preference for close proximity of related conjugal families illustrates how an originally Northwestern European ideal, the neolocal conjugal family household, was adapted and indigenized in the Middle East. This phenomenon has not been studied in Egypt, but Duben and Behar described a comparable situation in Turkey

Figure 3. An unidentified couple posing in wedding attire, photographed by the B. Edelstein studio in Cairo, 1920s. Photos of married couples, not necessarily taken on the day of the wedding, also became popular around the turn of the twentieth century. Like the family tableau in Figure 2, they express a couple-centered notion of family. Upper-class women took a keen interest in European fashion from the middle of the nineteenth century, and in the new century brides began to wear the white wedding dress, originally popularized by Queen Victoria. Courtesy of the Rare Books and Special Collections Library, The American University in Cairo.

where "functional connections" between households were common in all social strata in the late nineteenth and early twentieth centuries, and such connections "are not uncommon even today in Istanbul or other major Turkish cities, where intergenerational, interhousehold, extended family ties are particularly strong, even in a situation where nuclear family households overwhelmingly predominate as the statistical norm. These vital ties still provide, and appear to have then provided, services, often for childcare, that the demographically modest circumstances of most households could not otherwise afford."[102] My impression from years spent in Cairo is similar. This arrangement affords a young couple some autonomy while enabling them to rely on the extended family for assistance, especially in childcare, and to look after aged parents.

Polygyny

The recollections of our memoirists lend weight to the impression that upper-class polygyny was waning in the late nineteenth century. None of our male writers were polygynous, but in the preceding generation Huda al-Sha'rawi's father Sultan Pasha had multiple consorts, and her older cousin and husband Ali either maintained or renewed a relationship with his *mustawlada* after marrying Huda in 1892. The father of Ibrahim al-Hilbawi married a second wife in 1876, and while not divorcing al-Hilbawi's mother he became estranged from her. Al-Hilbawi conveyed the anguish of his mother, writing that he and his brothers made an effort to ease her feelings. As an adult he supported his mother and younger siblings financially while his father devoted his earnings to his second wife and their children.[103] An exception to the waning of upper-class polygyny was the marriage in 1907 of Malak Hifni Nasif to a Bedouin shaykh who already had a wife and a daughter.[104] Nasif became a strong public opponent of polygyny.

Until recently the extent of polygyny in the nineteenth century was a matter of informed guesswork on the part of foreign observers like Lane, who ventured that no more than 5 percent of married men in Cairo had multiple wives. Fargues found a lower rate in his sample of the Cairo census of 1848, putting it at 2.7 percent of married men.[105] In each of the four

Table 7
Polygynous Married Muslim Men in the Four Villages

	1847–48	1868
Damas	6.27%	7.8%
Sandub	6.34%	6.22%
Zafar	17.19%	7.96%
Ikhtab	12.29%	13.19%
Total	9.03%	8.52%

Sources: NAE, Census registers of Damas, Sandub, Zafar, and Ikhtab, 1847–48 and 1868.

villages, however, the rate of polygyny was several times higher: an aggregate of 9 percent of married men in 1848 and 8.5 percent in 1868.

Despite the common association of polygyny with urban upper-class households,[106] polygyny was widely practiced among village notable families and it was not unusual in middle- and lower-income households (Table 7). In Sandub, for example, there were twenty-four polygynous men in twenty households. Five were village shaykhs or brothers of a village shaykh living with him in a joint household, and a sixth was also listed as a landholder. The remaining upper-crust polygynous men were a government employee, a silk merchant, and a tobacco merchant. In the middle to lower strata there was a Sufi shaykh, a blind man "in the mosque," a disabled soldier, and six men employed in a factory (*fawriqa*). The status and occupation of the remaining six could not be determined. Sandub is adjacent to al-Mansura, and some of its residents were employed in the manufactories established in that town under Muhammad Ali. The blind man "in the mosque" most likely was a Qur'an reciter. The only man with more than two wives was one Shaykh al-Awni, a *murabit* (*marabout*) or Sufi holy man, who had four.[107] The pattern was similar in the other three villages, except that without a nearby town they had no resident factory workers or retailers. Landholders were the overwhelming majority of polygynous men, with a village judge here and a mosque imam there. Nearly all had had but two wives.

The practice of polygyny is easy enough to explain for the village notables and others in the upper tier. For the notables, who as shaykhs exercised authority over sections of their villages, polygyny made a statement about their wealth and sexual prowess, facilitated alliances with other notable families, and ensured that they would have sons to succeed them. In Sandub the polygyny of Muhammad Agha, the government employee, mimicked the style of the ruling class, and the plural marriages of the merchants are comparable to marital patterns among the merchants of al-Mansura.[108] As for the wives of the Qur'an reciter, the holy man, the soldier, and especially the factory workers, it is likely that their labor contributed to the income or subsistence of their households. Women spun most of the yarn consumed by Egypt's weavers,[109] hence they were recruited to work in Muhammad Ali's spinning factories. The wives of the factory workers may have been among those employed in the *fawriqa*, but the census enumerators did not record occupations for women since only men were taxed and subject to conscription. Lane noted that the plural wives of poor men paid for their own maintenance, or nearly so, "by some art or occupation."[110] That made polygyny affordable to low-income men. It was a financial burden in the middle and upper classes, since the norms of covering and concealing constrained women from working outside the home.

In addition to polygyny being practiced in all social classes, more families were affected by it than the census data indicate directly. Polygyny was underrepresented in the census in at least two ways. First there was what might be called transitional or temporary polygyny. That is, men would (and still do) marry polygynously and divorce the first wife after a short interval. This is evident from a comparison of modern census returns with marriage data. In the 1937 census, for example, only 3.4 percent of married men were reported to be polygynous, but in the same year 9.6 percent of all marriages were polygynous.[111] It was and still is not uncommon for a man to conceal a polygynous marriage from his first wife, and for its revelation to lead quickly to a divorce or informal separation, as occurred with Huda and Ali al-Sha'rawi as well as with Ibrahim al-Hilbawi's parents. The situation is so common that, since 1979, the personal status law has enabled married women to seek an annulment within twelve months of learning that their husband made a second, polygynous marriage. Contrary to the Qur'anic injunction to treat multiple wives equitably and not to leave one

Figure 4. "Fallah Family of Sakha," in al-Gharbiyya province, late 1920s. The relationship of the individuals to one another in this household is unknown, though presumably the man in the center was the household head. His tarbush suggests some education and that he may not have been a "fallah" in the sense of a cultivator. The stiff poses and the girls looking off-camera contrast with the conscious self-representation of the urbanites in the previous photos. Source: Jean Lozach, *Le Delta du Nil: Etude de Géographie Humaine* (Cairo: Imprimerie E. & R. Schindler, 1935), planche 1.

of them "suspended" (Q 4:3, 4:129), men who married polygynously were apt to neglect the first wife, as al-Hilbawi's father did. Lane noted that this often provoked the first wife to take refuge with her parents or a brother and refuse to return, resulting in a judgment of disobedience that relieved her husband of the obligation to support her.[112] This abuse still occurs.[113]

The second way in which the census registers underrepresented polygyny was by not accounting for concubinage consistently. The enumerators recorded each married woman as the wife of so-and-so, making it easy enough to identify men with plural wives. However, some men combined concubinage with contractual marriage or substituted a concubine for a contractual wife. In the census registers of Cairo the male partners of "slave wives" were recorded.[114] But in the village registers inspected, female slaves who might have been concubines or *mustawlada*s were not identified as such. For example, in the census register of Ikhtab in 1848 the headman Ahmad Atarbi, who was forty-five, had three wives: Raqiyya, seventy (*sic*), Siriyya, forty-five, and Fatuma, twenty-five. Fatima, a twenty-five-year-old slave woman, was also a member of his household. Ahmad died some thirteen years later. His probate inventory, recorded at the provincial Sharia Court, shows that in the interval he had married a fourth wife, Fatir al-Badawiyya. Another heir listed was his daughter Nafisa, the daughter of his now-deceased *mustawlada* Fatima. Nafisa had appeared in the 1848 census as the one-year-old daughter of Ahmad Atarbi, but with no indication that Fatima was her mother. It is only because her daughter survived to become an heir of her father that there is a record of Fatima's role as a *mustawlada*.[115] The growth of the slave population during the third quarter of the nineteenth century almost certainly resulted in an increase in concubinage and polygyny. In the four villages in 1868 there were seventy-six slave women in their teens, twenties, and thirties, only sixteen of whom were contractually married. One can only speculate about how many of the sixty remaining women were concubines.

A sample of probate inventories recorded between 1860 and 1885 in the Sharia Court of first instance of al-Mansura and the provincial court of al-Daqahliyya suggest certain patterns of concubinage. Urban as well as rural notables enjoyed concubines. Twelve notables of al-Mansura were survived either by a wife whom they had manumitted before marrying, or by children born to them by a *mustawlada*.¹¹⁶ The urban notables were either men with ties to the political regime who tended to have Circassian or Abyssinian concubines, or large merchants who tended to have "black" trans-Saharan Africans (*Sudaniyya, Zanjiyya, sawda'*). The eleven rural notables who had concubines were in most cases *umda*s or shaykhs, or from families of *umda*s and shaykhs, and most of the women were trans-Saharan Africans or Abyssinians. The concubines who appeared in the probate inventories represent an uncertain proportion of all concubines, and possibly a minority, since only those who were married by their masters and survived them would be listed among their heirs, and only those *mustawlada*s whose children survived their fathers would possibly be mentioned as the mother of an heir.

Companionate Marriage

Until around the time of World War I the middle- and upper-class marriage system discouraged prospective brides and grooms from meeting before their wedding day, effectively foreclosing the possibility of mutual attraction and compatibility playing a role in spousal selection. Attraction was a factor in the marriage choices of only al-Rafi'i, who developed an admiration for Aisha before making a marriage offer, and Musa, who spent considerable time with his future bride before becoming engaged. Yet by the early twentieth century the question of whether mutual attraction and even love ought to be a factor in choosing a spouse had become a subject of discussion, and it was addressed by Nasif in essays published circa 1908–9. She opposed what she aptly called "blind" marriages in which the spouses met for the first time at their wedding, arguing that prenuptial meetings were necessary to permit a man to arrive at an estimate of the learning and character of his fiancée and her family. But she opposed "the European practice of allowing the engaged pair to get together for a period of time so that they can come to know each other." That might indeed result in love, which was undesirable, because it could blind one to the other's faults.¹¹⁷ The idea of love preceding marriage was more widespread by the middle of the twentieth century, at least in novels and in films if not always in practice, which is why both Allouba and Jum'a addressed the issue with the same perspective as Nasif. Thus while enlightened opinion in the early twentieth century held prenuptial meetings to be desirable, there was too much at stake in marriage to allow young men and women to follow their hearts and freely choose their spouses.

From Ahmad Shafiq to Salama Musa, the desire for prenuptial meetings was justified on the logic that they would enable a couple to establish some knowledge of one another, as a sound beginning to a companionate relationship. Or, alternatively (it was implied), a prenuptial meeting would enable the couple to discover a lack of mutual attraction or compatibility. But none of our memoirists mentioned a desire to act autonomously in choosing a spouse. None objected to the involvement of family or others in the selection process or the premarital negotiations. Literate Egyptians at the time were familiar with the ideal of marriage for love, since it was a trope in novels, including the many translated from European languages,[118] and, increasingly, in journalism. But when looking back at their early lives, our memoirists recalled no desire for complete autonomy in selecting a mate, and nearly half a century later two of them wrote expressly against that idea.

The spread of the new family ideology did not lead to the abandonment of arranged and negotiated marriages, though the system of spousal selection and prenuptial negotiation has changed considerably since the early twentieth century. Unlike then, young men and women today have the opportunity to meet and get to know potential spouses at school and in university, and they are much more involved in prenuptial negotiations. But in the late twentieth century, arranged marriages remained the norm.[119]

3

Marriage Reformed

Modernist Intellectuals and the New Family Ideology

While changing political, social, and demographic factors influenced patterns of marriage and family formation in the ruling class and the emergent *effendiyya*, the nineteenth century witnessed important developments in the realm of ideas. Beginning in the late 1880s, through the burgeoning periodical press, a new family ideology began to be disseminated and debated among literate Egyptians, and by the 1920s its main tenets had gained widespread acceptance in the middle and upper classes. The foundational idea in the new family ideology was that in any society the conjugal family was the elemental unit, and that the strength and welfare of the society depended upon a sound family life. The main function of the family was to raise children, who were the future of the nation. For the nation to advance, children must be raised so as to instill in them desirable character traits in addition to their formal instruction, and that process needed to begin in early childhood within the home.

The new family ideology comprised a number of corollary ideas. Due to the importance of the home environment for childrearing, the stability and harmony of the family became a social good. The conjugal couple and their children were idealized as "the family" and companionate marriage was valorized. Domesticity (domestic ideology) accorded women the principal role in household management and childrearing—as wives and mothers. These ideas had implications for women beyond constraining them to the private sphere. Proponents of the new family ideology held that women should be educated so as to be able to fulfill their domestic roles properly, and their education had the additional merit of making them better companions for their husbands. Together with prenuptial meetings to allow prospective spouses to get to know each other, an educated bride increased the likelihood of marital compatibility and, hence, the harmony and stability of the family. In the interest of family harmony and stability, polygyny and easy divorce were also discouraged. The new family ideology was not oriented primarily toward expanding the rights of women, but it was an important precursor to feminism. It valorized companionate and hence monogamous marriage. It also valorized women's education and domestic vocation, constituting them as participants in the project of modernization. As such it was a discursive foundation upon which the early feminists could build a case for women's participation in public life.

Prior to the advent of the new family ideology, diverse aspects of family life were addressed in a variety of genres, including prose and poetry, works on proper comportment (*adab*), and juridical compendia and commentaries. In precolonial juridical literature, chapters on marriage, divorce, inheritance, and guardianship were interspersed with chapters on taxation, business partnerships, lawsuits, and sales. There were shorter handbooks on the legal technicalities of marriage and the proper conduct of marital relations, but the modern concept of the conjugal family (the monogamous couple and their children) as the elemental unit in society is an artifact of the last third of the nineteenth century. It was in the last third of the nineteenth century as well that the family became a subject of public discourse and government policy, including the invention of family law as a distinct category of law known as "personal status law." In this respect precolonial Egyptians were like premodern Europeans. In Western Europe, the term "family" acquired its modern connotation in the early nineteenth century, referring to a domestic group comprising a couple and their children. In earlier times a family was either an extended kinship group that did not live together or a single household, including inmates such as slaves and servants who were unrelated by blood or marriage.[1] In Europe, also, family law was "invented" as a distinct category of law in the nineteenth century.[2]

Egyptian family ideology had a number of features in common with Euro-American family ideology since both drew upon Enlightenment thought. The modernist intellectuals who produced it were participants in the transnational circulation of a cluster of ideas about civilization, education, childrearing, women, and the family, which they hybridized with precolonial Muslim ideas.[3] The modernists desired to emulate the civilization that Europe had achieved but they did not regard themselves as westernizers. They understood civilization to be the highest stage of human advancement, something that Muslim society was capable of achieving. Omnia El Shakry has described how twentieth-century Egyptian social scientists adopted "much of the language and many categories" of colonial social science, including "notions of backwardness, improvement, [and] progress," though they employed them in the service of social improvement.[4] The nineteenth-century modernists anticipated the social scientists in adopting European theories about marriage and family formation, the status and role of women, childrearing, and education for the improvement of Egyptian society, even while Europeans deployed the same theories in asserting Egyptian difference and inferiority.[5] To uphold European civilization as a model was not necessarily to adopt a colonial perspective. The modernists observed superior European wealth and power, and it was rational to ask what the cause of that superiority was.[6]

The modernists, moreover, were able to locate the sources of modern civilization within their own cultural heritage—that is, within Islam. Reform of the marriage system, opposition to polygyny and easy divorce, and the education of women—all were supported by certain readings of Qur'anic verses and hadiths, and some were anticipated in the precolonial juridical and conduct literature. That these reforms would produce an advanced civilization like Europe's made them desirable, but the religious texts made them permissible if not incumbent upon believers. Still other ideas having no scriptural basis—like domestic ideology, which posited women's place as the home—became sacralized. If women were suited to domestic pursuits by nature, so the argument went, then surely that was ordained by God.

The new family ideology was constructed in dialogue with precolonial writings on marriage and marital relations in a process of hybridization. European notions were sometimes modified, such as on the question of plural marriage, which is explicitly permitted in a Qur'anic text. The modernists disapproved of polygyny but advocated restricting it instead of banning it. Certain ideas in the precolonial writings were carried over into the new family ideology, the most important of which was the maintenance-obedience relationship.[7] In that relationship women were due maintenance (*nafaqa*, or financial support) from their husbands, and their husbands were due obedience from them. The precolonial norm of obedience obligated a married woman to remain at home but exempted her from any obligation to cook, do housework, or care for children. In the new family ideology, however, the maintenance-obedience relationship lent authority to an ideal of domesticity in which women's vocation of household management and childrearing was emphasized while the exemption of women from household duties was elided.

This chapter begins with a discussion of precolonial Muslim writings on marriage, and then it follows the articulation of the new family ideology in the work of modernist intellectuals during the last third of the nineteenth century and the first decade of the twentieth century. Perhaps the closest thing to a literature on family in the precolonial writings was a genre of handbooks or manuals on marriage and marital relations used for teaching and reference, several of which circulated in Egypt before and after the advent of printing. They were of two types. One was concerned primarily with the legal aspects of marriage, and since the Sharia Courts of Egypt applied the doctrines of all four Sunni schools of law until the mid-nineteenth century, some of these books were studies in comparative marital law. Two that I have relied upon are Hasan al-Idwi al-Hamzawi's *Ahkam Uqud al-Nikah* (The Legal Rules of Marriage Contracts, 1859), and Ahmad b. Umar al-Dayrabi, *Kitab Gayat al-Maqsud li-Man Yata'ati al-Uqud* (The Intended Aim for Whoever Is Concerned with Marriage Contracts, 1880). Al-Idwi (1806–86) was a Maliki shaykh who taught at al-Azhar.[8] Al-Dayrabi, a Shafi'i scholar who also taught at al-Azhar, wrote his book between 1694–95 and 1711,[9] and it was printed more than a century and a half later.

The other type of manual offered instruction in the proper conduct of marital relations. Two examples of the latter genre are Abd al-Majid Ali al-Hanafi's *Matla' al-Badrayn fima Yata'allaq bi-l-Zawjayn* (The Rising Moons on Matters of Married Couples, 1862) and Muhammad b. Umar al-Nawawi, *Sharh Uqud al-Lujayn fi Bayan Huquq al-Zawjayn* (An Explication of the Silver Necklace on an Explanation of What the Two Spouses Are Due, 1878). Abd al-Majid Ali identified himself as a Hanafi scholar and a servant of the shrine of al-Sayyida Zaynab in Cairo. He probably lived in the eighteenth century, since the latest authority he cited was al-Haskafi (d. 1677).[10] His treatise, like al-Dayrabi's, seems to have circulated in manuscript until it was printed a century or more later. Al-Nawawi was a Shafi'i and a native of Java, in today's Indonesia, who resided in Mecca after making the pilgrimage. His *sharh*, or explication, of *Uqud al-Lujayn* was printed in Cairo,[11] where it contributed to Egyptian discourse. *Uqud al-Lujayn* itself was attributed to "a group of scholars," and a reference to the Egyptian scholar Ibn Hajar al-Haythami (d. 1567) suggests that it was composed in Egypt in the late sixteenth or seventeenth century. These two books framed marital relations in terms of what each spouse was entitled to from the other and what each owed the other, or in other words, "what the spouses are due" (*huquq al-zawjayn*), the phrase that appeared in the title of al-Nawawi's book.

These handbooks tell us how proper marital relations were construed by religious scholars in Ottoman Egypt. They continued to be popular in the late nineteenth and early twentieth centuries, at a time in which modernist intellectuals were promoting an alternate vision of family relations in books and the periodical press. The modernists were in dialogue with the precolonial writings even while they were profoundly influenced by European thought, and in particular French thought, due to the preeminence of the French language among officials and intellectuals and the emulation of French models in the new government schools and legal system. The intellectuals whose works are discussed below are Rifa'a Rafi'i al-Tahtawi (1801–73), Ali Mubarak (1823–93), Muhammad Abduh (1849–1905), Qasim Amin (1863–1908), Aisha al-Taymur (1840–1902), Zaynab Fawwaz (ca. 1850–1914), and Malak Hifni Nasif (1886–1918), who wrote under the pen name Bahithat al-Badiya ("Searcher in the Wilderness/Desert"). Al-Taymur and Fawwaz were the only members of this group who were not literate in French. The women are better known as feminists than modernists, but to a large extent they shared the modernist orientation of their male counterparts. They were no less feminist for that, as they wrote of women's perceptions and experiences from an intimate knowledge and they believed women's education and the protection of women's rights to be not only necessary for social improvement but also goods in themselves.

The modernist texts examined in this chapter are fairly well known but until now they have not been examined together as a body of literature on the question of the family. Some latter-day authors detected feminist sentiments in the writings of al-Tahtawi,[12] the famous reformer whose career was devoted to developing educational institutions on the European model and who advocated for the education of women. Al-Tahtawi's promise to remain monogamous to his cousin and wife, Karima bt. Muhammad al-Farghali, has been cited as further evidence of his feminism; but his promise was in the form of a conditional divorce, which was a device commonly used by women to deter their husbands from taking additional wives or concubines, as we have seen.[13] Al-Tahtawi's main concern was with education as the basis of civilization, and with the important role of the conjugal family in the raising of children. The anachronistic search for his feminism has distracted attention from his foundational contribution to a modern family ideology that identified the conjugal family as the basic unit in society, and his encouragement of stable and harmonious families as a social good. Al-Tahtawi set forth his views on education and the family in his book *Al-Murshid al-Amin li-l-Banat wa al-Banin* (The Trustworthy Guide for Girls and Boys, 1872).[14] The *Murshid* was commissioned by Khedive Ismail when plans were afoot to expand elementary education. It is a statement of the bases upon which a modern educational system should be developed.[15]

Al-Tahtawi studied the religious sciences at al-Azhar and read philosophy with his mentor, Shaykh Hasan al-Attar (1766–1835), an early supporter of Muhammad Ali's educational project. He encountered French culture while serving as the imam of the first student "mission" to Paris (1826–31). There he read widely, interacted with intellectuals, and began translating books. His well-known account of France and the French, *Takhlis al-Ibriz fi Talkhis Bariz* (The Extraction of Pure Gold in the Abridgment of Paris), was published in 1834. The following year he was appointed director of the newly organized School of Languages, which also functioned as a translation institute.[16]

Al-Tahtawi's younger colleague, Ali Mubarak, belonged to the first generation of Egyptians educated in the new government schools. He participated in a student mission to France (1844–49), and returned to Paris later for a few months as a government official in 1867–68. Under Khedive Ismail he directed the departments of public works and education more than once, and was a principal contributor to the plan to restructure the educational system that led to the commissioning of al-Tahtawi's *Murshid*. His best-known work is the multivolume *al-Khitat al-Tawfiqiyya*, a social and historical geography of Egypt,[17] but his ideas on family life were expressed in two lesser-known works. *Tariq al-Hija* (The Path to Understanding, 1868) was a primary school textbook that included essays for students to practice reading, and which were intended to "embellish the[ir] minds . . . with items of refined and exact knowledge."[18] The other was a novel-like prose work, *Alam al-Din* (1882), the plot of which featured the eponymous Shaykh Alam al-Din, an Azhari who encountered a British Orientalist in Cairo, and who, along with his son, accompanied the Orientalist to France. *Alam al-Din* was probably written a decade before its publication.[19] It and *Tariq al-Hija* were didactic in purpose, and addressed a variety of topics that included but were not limited to education, family life, and the position of women. Mubarak's experience of marriage, widowhood, and divorce[20] is not reflected in them.

Toward the end of the century the Muslim reformer and Grand Mufti of Egypt Muhammad Abduh and the lawyer Qasim Amin promoted the conjugal family ideal out of the conviction that a sound family life was necessary for social improvement. Abduh was a graduate of al-Azhar and also studied with the Iranian scholar al-Sayyid Jamal al-Din, known as al-Afghani (1838–97), who introduced him to the rational sciences.[21] Amin attended government schools, including the School of Law, capping his education with a law degree from the University of Montpellier. Unlike al-Tahtawi and Mubarak, who were educators and civil servants, Abduh and Amin served as judges in the National Courts and were exposed to many of the practical problems faced by married women. Thus, in addition to valorizing women's education and the conjugal family, they advocated reforming Muslim family law so as to strengthen family life. Abduh contributed to the development of family ideology in several articles in *al-Waqa'i' al-Misriyya*, which he edited during 1880–82. Later as a judge and mufti he addressed the family question in a report on the reform of the Sharia Courts (1900), an uncompleted Qur'an exegesis serialized in the journal *al-Manar*, known as *Tafsir al-Manar* (1900–), and in reports and fatwas recommending specific reforms to the Ministry of Justice. Abduh grew up in a polygynous household and was married at the age of sixteen, while still a student, to a woman from his village. She died years later while he was in exile in Beirut, and he was said to have been unable to teach for several days out of grief. He soon remarried.[22]

Qasim Amin took up the question of the family initially in *Les Égyptiens: Réponse a M. le Duc d'Harcourt* (1894), which took issue with Harcourt's thesis that Egyptian backwardness was attributable to Islam and offered a defense of women's covering and concealment.[23] That year he married Zaynab Amin Tawfiq, who had been tutored by an English governess in the harem. Like many women of her generation she would not uncover her face in public until long after her husband changed his view and became an advocate of uncovering.[24] In *Tahrir al-Mar'a* (The Emancipation of Women, 1899) Amin argued that Islam permitted women to reveal their faces and to enter public space in the presence of men, and moreover that this was necessary for their education and social progress. He was not the first to make these points, but his distinguished position as a judge and his frontal attack on conventional gender norms stirred a major controversy. Admirers called him "the Luther of the East" and a founder of Egyptian feminism.[25] The indelible association of Amin with the cause of women's emancipation has left his ideas on the family in relative obscurity, even though they account for the major part of *Tahrir al-Mar'a*.

In recent decades historians have tended to emphasize writings by women that antedate *Tahrir al-Mar'a* so as to properly credit women as the founders of Egyptian feminism.[26] Women writers took up the family question as well as the woman question in the late 1880s, and subsequently it was a frequent topic for female as well as male writers in periodicals and books. Like the male modernists, they expressed support for women's education, companionate marriage, and monogamy, and they embraced the new domestic ideology in which women were understood to have a vocation in household management and childrearing, although they did so with some different emphases.

The three writers discussed here had diverse backgrounds. Aisha Ismat al-Taymur came from a distinguished Ottoman Egyptian family that was close to the khedival family. Through tutors she received a classical education in Persian, Arabic, and Ottoman Turkish, but her studies were interrupted when she was married off at the age of fourteen to an Ottoman official. After her husband's death she returned to her studies and writing, but her publishing career was delayed further by grief over the premature death of her daughter. She published in three languages, poetry, essays, an allegorical tale entitled *Nata'ij al-Ahwal fi al-Aqwal wa al-Af'al* (The Results of Circumstances in Statements and Deeds, 1886), and a treatise on family and domestic affairs, *Mir'at al-Ta'ammul fi al-Umur* (The Mirror of Contemplation on Matters, 1893).[27]

Zaynab Fawwaz grew up in southern Lebanon. As a youth she acquired literacy as a member of the household of an educated mistress. The sources disagree on her marriages and divorces and the circumstances of her migration to Alexandria. She divorced her first husband before beginning her publishing career. She married again later, but initiated a divorce after discovering that her husband, whom she had known only through correspondence before her marriage, already had three wives. Fawwaz published a biographical dictionary of famous women, two novels, and a play, and in the 1890s she began publishing essays in *al-Nil* and other newspapers, several dozen of which were preserved in a volume entitled *al-Rasa'il al-Zaynabiyya* (The Zaynab Epistles, 1905 or 1906), in which she anticipated some of the ideas of Qasim Amin on women's education and work.[28]

Women of al-Taymur's and Fawwaz's generation could get an advanced education only through tutoring in the home. The younger Malak Hifni Nasif, daughter of a distinguished judge, educator, and poet, was able to attend government primary and secondary schools for girls, which had opened by then in Cairo. After finishing her education she taught in the girls' section of the Abbas Primary School, which she had attended as a student. At the age of twenty-two she was persuaded to marry a Bedouin shaykh and to reside with him in the desert near al-Fayum. She had to give up teaching, but in arranging the marriage her father had insisted on her right to publish and give lectures. Neither she nor her father were aware that the shaykh already had a wife and a daughter. Nasif was especially outspoken against polygyny in the essays she published in the newspaper *al-Jarida*. Two dozen of them, along with speeches and poetry, were collected in *al-Nisa'iyyat* (Feminist Pieces, 1910).[29]

What the Wife and Husband Are Due from (and Owe to) Each Other

The theologian al-Ghazali (1058–1111) noted that in his time there was disagreement on the virtues of marriage. The benefits included children, a legitimate outlet for sexual desires, companionship, and someone to manage the household and to see to domestic chores. One also earned merit in the eyes of God by caring for dependents. The drawbacks included the burden of earning a lawful income to support one's dependents; treating a wife (or wives) properly, including putting up with one who may be difficult; and being distracted from spiritual concerns by worldly matters.[30] Al-Ghazali wrote from a male perspective and addressed a male readership, which was not unusual. The precolonial writings on marriage expressed an exclusively male sensibility. Later scholars were less reserved in recommending marriage for men who had the means to support a family and/ or who feared sinning out of lust. The Damascene mufti Ibn Abdin (1783–1836), whose works were considered authoritative in nineteenth-century Egypt, noted that in Hanafi books of jurisprudence the chapter on marriage came just after those on the obligatory acts of worship, having priority over *jihad*, or striving, including warfare, in the service of God. Like *jihad*, marriage ensured the perpetuation of the Muslims, and to devote oneself to it was preferable to other supererogatory acts of devotion.[31]

The contract of marriage was described in this literature as establishing an asymmetrical relationship in which the husband's authority was explicit. It was not unusual to compare marriage with slavery. Ibn Abdin explained the juridical rule that prohibited a woman but not a man from marrying someone of inferior status by saying, "Marriage is slavery (*riqq*) for the woman while the husband is an owner." The man would suffer no loss of status because the husband wielded an authority over the wife comparable to that of the master over a slave. Al-Ghazali also described marriage as "a kind of slavery" due to the obedience a wife owed her husband. Their comparison of marriage with slavery made reference to a hadith attributed to one or two of the daughters of Abu Bakr, the first caliph, the original point of which was that the guardian should have the welfare of his daughter in mind in arranging her marriage.[32] The fourteenth-century jurist Ibn Qayyim al-Jawziyya idealized a husband's maintenance of his wife by comparing their relationship with the master-slave relationship.[33] According to Kecia Ali, comparisons between marriage and slavery were present in early juridical interpretation and "[t]he terminology of *milk* saturate[d] the jurists' writings." Normally *milk* meant ownership, but in the context of marriage it meant the husband's "control or authority" over his wife or else his "prerogative" or legal ability in the marital relationship.[34] In the Hanafi school of law the marriage contract accorded the husband *milk al-muta'*, the ability to enjoy his wife, and *milk al-hubs*, the ability to confine her in his home.[35]

Ottoman-era writings compared the wife less often to a slave than to a prisoner or a captive, in a comparison that came from the Prophet's farewell sermon: "Treat women well, for they are prisoners with you."[36] But these authors also understood the quality of marital life to be important. To get off on the right foot some jurists recommended that a man be permitted to see his fiancée with her face and hands uncovered before the wedding, as that would call forth congeniality and affection (*al-ulfa*), and fathers were encouraged not to marry their young daughters off to elderly men for the same reason.[37]

The normative ideal in marital relations was expressed in terms of reciprocal obligations and entitlements, or *huquq*, as has been noted. To read the plural *huquq* (sing. *haqq*) as "rights" in the modern sense strikes me as anachronistic, though admittedly the concept is similar, and it is usually translated that way. In premodern usage one's *haqq* was what one was due or entitled to, or conversely what was obligatory upon someone. Both Abd al-Majid Ali and al-Nawawi included chapters in their books on "what the wife is due from the husband" (*huquq al-zawja ala al-zawj*), and "what the husband is due from the wife" (*huquq al-zawj ala al-zawja*).[38] These formulae echoed two well-known passages in the scriptural sources.

One is Qur'anic verse 2:228: "And they [women] are due in like manner to what is due from them [to men] according to what is just, but men are due a degree more." The other is from the Prophet's farewell sermon: "You are due certain things from your wives and your wives are due certain things from you."[39]

These entitlements and obligations were not symmetrical, as the Qur'anic verse states, and together they comprised the maintenance-obedience relationship. The wife was entitled to a dower, financial maintenance, clothing, proper housing, and good treatment from her husband. If she had co-wives she was entitled to equitable treatment with them in those matters as well as in companionship. Her husband was obligated further to instruct her, if needed, in what she ought to know about the obligatory acts of worship, about menstruation (which affected ritual purity), and about her duty to obey him. Since an obedient wife restricted herself to the home she was like a prisoner or a captive, and this was another reason for treating her with consideration. If disobedient, her husband was to correct her by depriving her of his companionship and of sexual relations, and as a last resort by striking her with a blow that was not harsh.[40] Al-Nawawi stressed the virtue of a husband's forbearance, citing the story of a man who sought out the Caliph Umar to complain that his wife spoke to him overbearingly. Waiting outside Umar's door the man heard the Caliph's wife speaking to him overbearingly while he remained silent. When Umar came out, he explained that he put up with that on account of what his wife was due from him (her *huquq*), since she cooked his food, baked his bread, washed his clothes, and nursed his child even though she was not obliged to do those things, and because with her his heart was free from desiring what was forbidden. He then advised the man to take the same attitude toward his own wife.[41]

In addition to enjoining men to be patient and forbearing with their wives—and here again, it is only men who were being addressed—this anecdote highlighted the point that, legally, married women were not obliged to do housework or childcare. Abd al-Majid Ali stated it directly: a woman was not to be compelled to bake, cook, or clean if she declared herself unwilling to do so.[42] To be sure, most women performed housework and cared for children, tasks that were so strongly gendered that Lane and de Nerval were expected either to marry or acquire a slave woman to keep house and for licit sexual relations. But in the middle and upper classes housework was performed by slaves and free domestics, and wet nurses were employed often to suckle infants. The mistress of an upper-class household supervised these activities but did not perform them herself.

Another reason mentioned by both al-Nawawi and Abd al-Majid Ali for treating women with patience and forbearance was their deficiency in intellect and faith. This canard came from a well-known hadith,[43] though two of the three men who related it, Abd Allah b. Umar and Abu Hurayra, were identified by Fatima Mernissi as transmitters of dubious misogynist hadiths.[44] Other scholars have contrasted the gender-egalitarian content of most Qur'anic verses with post-prophetic interpretations based on hadiths that enshrined male superiority in general, and which are still invoked today to justify gender inequalities as God-given.[45]

Toward the end of al-Nawawi's chapter on what the wife was due from the husband his discussion turned to the authority the husband exercised. It closed with a hadith reported by Ibn Umar in which the Prophet is said to have articulated a relationship between political sovereignty and the authority of family patriarchs. Every man, he said, is a shepherd (*ra'i*). The man who tends to the interests of his flocks (*ra'iyya*)—that is, his dependents—will be rewarded with good fortune, and if he does not do so, each of them will demand their due (their *haqq*) from him in the next world. Extending the metaphor, the Imam or head of state is a shepherd, as he is responsible for his flocks/subjects, tending to what they are due (their *huquq*); a man is a shepherd of his family, his wife and others, as he is responsible for his flocks/dependents, fulfilling what they are due (their *huquq*) in the way of clothing, maintenance, and so on; and a woman is a shepherdess in the house of her husband, in its good management, in advising him, in her compassion, and in safeguarding herself, his wealth, and his children, as she is responsible for its flocks/inmates.[46] The use of this hadith in the late Ottoman era illustrates how social and family relations were hierarchically constructed in relation to the political order. It also suggests the compatibility of precolonial Muslim thought with the Enlightenment idea of the family as the elemental unit in the social and political order.

Al-Nawawi and Abd al-Majid Ali composed their chapters on what the husband was due from the wife differently but made similar points. Al-Nawawi began with the Qur'anic verse, "Men are in charge of women in that God has favored one over the other and in that they spend of their wealth" (4:34).[47] Notwithstanding other verses that imply women's equality within and responsibility to the Muslim community, this well-known verse, according to Barbara Stowasser, "stipulates that the godly Muslim family order rests on the husband's authority over his wife as occasioned by his responsibility for her economic support and on the wife's obedience to her husband's authority; that is, his *qiwama* (being in charge)."[48] This verse was, in other words, the basis of the maintenance-obedience relationship. Al-Nawawi explained it by saying that men have authority over women because of what they provide them in the form of a dower and maintenance. Further, he noted, the exegetes said that men were also favored over women in having greater measures of intelligence and knowledge, patience in difficult endeavors, strength, literacy, and chivalry. He then listed the occupations of men that were denied to women, such as religious and political offices (i.e., positions in which authority was exercised over men). In the family men acted as the guardians of women, they received larger shares of an inheritance, and descent was figured patrilineally.[49] Thus the marital authority of the husband was justified by his responsibilities, consistent with innate differences between the sexes, and reflected in social conventions.

Abd al-Majid Ali began his discussion by saying that a husband could forbid his wife from doing certain things because she had the ability to injure him in word and deed. She should not belittle him or injure him in any way, but be submissive and show him deference. Abu Hurayra reported that the Prophet said, "If I were to order anyone to prostrate to anyone, then I would order the wife to prostrate to her husband."[50] Of course Muslims only prostrate themselves before God, in prayer. Al-Nawawi also mentioned that a man's wife should show him respect: she should rise when he enters, maintain silence while he speaks, and so on.[51]

The main thing a husband was due from his wife was obedience. That included staying in the marital home and not leaving without his permission, submitting to him sexually, guarding his home and possessions in his absence, and guarding her chastity. The first two duties occasioned more commentary than the others, which indicates where marital conflicts arose most often. Al-Nawawi and Abd al-Majid Ali both cited a hadith reported by Abu Hurayra, namely that if a wife spent the night away from her husband's bed the angels would curse her until the morning.[52] The angels would also curse a wife who went out of the house without her husband's permission until she returned. Even if she went out with his permission she was to avoid drawing attention to herself by wearing old clothing, seeking uncrowded places, and staying away from the major streets and markets, taking care not to let a strange man hear her voice or learn who she is, and so on.[53] Abd al-Majid Ali added that a man could forbid his wife from visiting strangers (that is, nonrelations), going to their celebrations, to feasts, or to the public bath, and from following funeral cortèges.[54]

These restrictions on women were normative ideals that were not realized in most families. Only the upper class was able to apply those standards with any strictness, in emulation of the rulers and to make a show of their wealth and respectability. The chronicler al-Jabarti drew an admiring portrait of the al-Shara'ibi merchant family of eighteenth-century Cairo, saying "a woman would not go out of their house except to the cemetery." Their house, in the wealthy district of al-Azbakiyya, was a large structure or compound containing a joint household with twelve married couples in separate residences. Since the family practiced endogamy to keep their capital intact, the al-Shara'ibi women did not process on their wedding day in public to the residence of their husband. Rather, they were able to do so without leaving the family compound, and they did it at night, while the men were at prayers.[55] Al-Jabarti may have exaggerated for effect, but his description illustrates how upper-class social norms conformed closely to the ideals upheld by writers such as al-Nawawi and Abd al-Majid Ali. That these norms were acted upon in the upper class is also evident from the conditions routinely negotiated by women at the time of their marriage to guarantee their mobility—that is, their ability to visit socially, to receive visitors, to go to the public bath, and so on.[56] Most upper-class women did venture out of the home, properly covered, though some highly secluded women (*mukhaddarat*) would not permit themselves to be seen by anyone outside their immediate household.[57]

Working-class and peasant women—the vast majority—could not come close to observing these norms. Village women performed various tasks in the fields, tended poultry and livestock, spun and sold yarn to weavers, and regularly went to market as vendors and buyers. Urban working-class women also spun, sewed, and worked in the markets as vendors, and there were certain trades that women necessarily performed, such as bathhouse attendants, midwives, corpse washers, matchmakers, and the *dallalat* or saleswomen who plied their wares to harem women.[58] However, working women were looked down upon as having bad morals because their work brought them into regular contact with unrelated men.[59] Thus women of middling social status, such as the wives of artisans and small merchants, would emulate their social superiors by observing the restrictive norms as best they could. Their respectability and the maintenance they were due from their husbands was at stake: "the presumption in the obligation of maintenance," Ibn Abdin wrote, "is confinement (*al-ihtibas*)."[60] Many middle- and upper-class women earned an income by performing needlework at home and thus remained "obedient" and deserving of maintenance.[61] Thus while a relatively small part of the population were able to observe the ideals of obedience strictly, those ideals set a standard of propriety that had a real influence on social attitudes and behavior.

To sum up at this point, the precolonial writings on marriage were produced by men to be read by men. They defined the purpose of marriage as the perpetuation of the Muslims and a licit outlet for sexual desire. Marital relations were framed in terms of mutual entitlements and obligations, or what the spouses were due from each other, though in return for receiving maintenance the wife owed her husband obedience. Qur'anic verses, hadiths, supposed innate differences between the sexes, and social conventions were invoked to justify the authority of husbands over their wives. But within the context of family patriarchy the quality of marital relations received a certain emphasis. In the interest of spousal compatibility prenuptial meetings were recommended and the marriage of young women to older men was discouraged. Married men were encouraged to treat their wives with consideration and patience. At present we cannot venture an opinion as to how common affection in marriage was, but it existed in at least some marriages. Abduh grieved at the passing of his wife, and the poet al-Barudi composed a touching elegy for his deceased wife Adila.[62] A century earlier the scholar Murtada al-Zabidi (1732–91) expressed his grief in an elegy for his deceased wife Zubayda bt. Dhu al-Fiqar al-Dumyati that bespoke their loving relationship: "She has gone, and with her there has gone from me all pleasure. My eyes which rejoiced in her have been cut off altogether."[63]

Rifaʻa al-Tahtawi and Ali Mubarak on Education, Childrearing, and Marital Life

Though of different generations and educational backgrounds, Rifaʻa al-Tahtawi and Ali Mubarak had similar careers as civil servants and educators, and they wrote about education, childrearing, and marital life during the same span of years, from the mid-1860s to the mid-1870s. While in France or shortly after returning, al-Tahtawi may have followed the discussion leading to the Guizot law (1833) that mandated a national elementary school system for boys. The *Murshid* appeared more than twenty years after the Falloux law (1850), which called for a system of girls' elementary schools, and it shows that al-Tahtawi was well informed about developments in European education. By training an engineer, Mubarak shared al-Tahtawi's belief in the importance of education, and he too was strongly influenced by European educational models.[64]

In the views of both men education was essential to the attainment of civilization, a conviction they acquired from their own experiences, their observations in France, and the social sciences they encountered in French. Al-Tahtawi translated two works that according to Pollard became "staple" texts in the Egyptian schools in the nineteenth century. In his *Geographie Universelle* Conrad Malte-Brun distinguished between civilized, barbarian, and savage nations on the basis of learning. Barbarian nations were half-civilized, possessing written laws and organized religions, but they lacked advanced sciences and arts, while civilized nations possessed advanced sciences, fine arts, refined literature, and the rule of law. G.-B. Depping, in his *Aperçu Historique sur les Moeurs et Coutumes des Nations*, held that family systems and the status of women were indicators of a nation's barbarity or civilization: "The higher the regard for women in a nation, the more advanced is that nation in civilization." Among other things he condemned early marriage and polygyny, and the ease with which "Turks" divorced their wives, for depriving women of "the authority and influence they hold among civilized peoples." Malte-Brun also opposed polygyny and divorce as inimical to population growth. Al-Tahtawi completed the translation of Depping while in Paris, and it was published in 1833; he finished translating the first volume of Malte-Brun in 1835. In 1848 Mubarak was presented with a copy of Malte-Brun's *Geographie Universelle* by Muhammad Ali's son and regent, Ibrahim Pasha, as a prize for excelling in his studies in Paris.[65]

The imprint of the ideas of authors like Malte-Brun and Depping on education, progress, the family, and women is evident in al-Tahtawi's *Murshid*. Education, according to al-Tahtawi, was the basis of civilization. Greek civilization was based on learning, and advanced countries like Prussia, Switzerland, Belgium, the Netherlands, and the United States had public education systems. Countries that lagged behind in educational attainment were backward.[66] Al-Tahtawi insisted that elementary education be made available to all children, poor as well as wealthy, and girls as well as boys. Girls and boys should attend school together and have the same curriculum, consisting of reading, writing, grammar, and calculation, in addition to instruction in the Qur'an. In this discussion he qualified the words for children, *awlad* and *abna'*, which are masculine plurals that could be read as "boys" and "sons," by adding afterward "males and females" or "boys and girls" so as to leave no ambiguity in his meaning. However, he made it clear that only the brighter *male* students should continue to secondary and higher education.[67] Women, he wrote, were not suited for men's work, such as heavy labor, higher learning, and politics, but rather to the domestic roles of housekeeping and raising children for which an elementary education is adequate.[68] This was consistent with contemporary French social and educational thought, according to which women needed only to be educated for a domestic role.[69]

Drawing on precolonial Muslim writings and echoing the likes of al-Nawawi and Abd al-Majid Ali, al-Tahtawi added that women who engaged in men's activities risked immodesty (*al-tabarruj*), and that women should not appear at public gatherings nor walk in the streets and markets. The custom, he wrote approvingly, was for women to not leave the home without a male escort, nor to travel unaccompanied by their husband or a closely related man (*mahram*).[70] Here he invoked the maintenance-obedience relationship to indigenize European domestic ideology, with its strongly gendered notion of separate public and private spheres. Domestic ideology was alien to the precolonial writings, which prescribed work for married women that could be done in the home, like spinning, sewing, and embroidery, so that they could preserve their modesty, while exempting them from housework and childcare. Although French social thought prescribed housework and childcare for women it did not object to women appearing in public space in the presence of unrelated men. Indeed, heterosociality was one of Depping's indices of civilization.[71]

A common objection to educating women was their supposedly deceitful nature, and the fear that literacy would enable them to engage in illicit correspondences. Al-Tahtawi addressed that concern, first, by asserting the benefits of women's education for family life. Educating girls and boys together would promote good marital relations in the future. (His readers understood that the sexes need not be separated before puberty.) Education was an antidote to the naiveté and frivolity of ignorant women. Improving their refinement and intellect would suit them to share in conversation with their husbands and become more endearing to them. Education would also enable them to work productively (i.e., within the home), thereby keeping them from idleness and pointless chatter.[72] The idea of education as a corrective to women's idleness, frivolity, and empty chatter was a trope in European writings[73] that seems to have been taken up by al-Tahtawi and other modernists of his era, such as the Lebanese Butrus al-Bustani (1819–83) and the Ottoman Namık Kemal (1840–88).[74] Al-Tahtawi added that the Prophet married literate women such as Hafsa bt. Amru and Aisha bt. Abi Bakr, and argued that there are no historical accounts of educated women misbehaving. Rather, education would enlighten their intellects and have a positive effect on their childrearing abilities. Many countries experienced the benefits of women's education, and the books of hadith have many accounts of pious, educated women. There were literate women in the Prophet's day, some of whom taught reading and writing to other women, and the Prophet approved of that.[75]

Mubarak too believed in the necessity of elementary education for girls to prepare them for a domestic role. In an essay in *Tariq al-Hija* he argued that the proper treatment of women included giving them a general education in addition to the necessary obligatory training in the principles of childrearing, sewing, embroidery, and household management. Like al-Tahtawi, he fused European domestic ideology with the maintenance-obedience relationship, eliding the precolonial exemption of women from housework. Education, he continued, would increase the beauty, purity, and perfection of women, making them better mates for their husbands. The idea that women should not be taught to read was an ancient delusion and a faulty understanding that was neither revealed by God nor supported by any proof.[76] In *Alam al-Din* Mubarak expressed the same ideas through fiction. Some time after arranging to marry the sister of a friend, the eponymous Shaykh discovered that his wife, Taqiyya, had an inclination toward learning, so he began teaching her the elements of religion and writing. She practiced writing and memorized the Qur'an. Then she asked him to teach her all he knew, and so he taught her works of comportment (*adab*), jurisprudence, hadith, Qur'anic exegesis, and more, so that eventually she equaled him in learning. Yet even while reading these books with him "she fulfilled all the marital obligations (*huquq al-zawjiyya*) that were incumbent upon her," catering to him when he entered the home and turning to her work or to reading when he went out. In time they had four children, and she busied herself with them.[77] These passages asserted the aptitude of women for learning on a par with men, going beyond the endorsement of a limited education for women in *Tariq al-Hija*. Taqiyya's ability to fulfill her marital obligations while engaged in rigorous study suggested that the education of women posed no threat to the domestic order.

The influence of European domestic ideology on al-Tahtawi and Mubarak is especially evident in their elision of the exemption of women from housework, cooking, and childcare found in precolonial Muslim writings. In late-eighteenth and early-nineteenth-century France, a turn against the employment of household servants and nannies was closely related to the Enlightenment notion of the conjugal family as the appropriate site for the raising of children. According to Patricia Mainardi, "the social reformers of the Enlightenment . . . mounted a major campaign in the cause of marriage, motherhood, and the nuclear family—indeed *invented* childhood as a separate and special period of life.... [G]reat care was taken to set forth a program of child-rearing and education that would make them into happy, healthy, and productive citizens.... [W]omen ... were now called upon to nurse their children at home, to educate them, and to set a good example as both wife and mother."[78] In the *Murshid*, similarly, al-Tahtawi upheld a version of domestic ideology out of a concern for childrearing, which was closely connected with education.

The word he used most often for education was *tarbiya*, literally "raising" or "rearing." Timothy Mitchell found that al-Tahtawi may have been the first to use this word with the meaning of education, and argued that as a neologism it referred to the new organization of formal education in which al-Tahtawi was involved.[79] According to al-Tahtawi the *tarbiya* of children began in the home before they were old enough for formal instruction. The term connotes both upbringing and moral formation; instruction (*ta'lim*) is but a part of *tarbiya*. It was women, as mothers, who were best suited to oversee this initial stage of their children's formation. Women must be educated to fulfill this role properly, and education will also ensure their compatibility with educated husbands.

Mubarak also highlighted the importance of the early years of childhood and the role of the home environment in childrearing. An essay in *Tariq al-Hija* emphasized the virtue of loving and nurturing one's children, citing hadiths that identified the continuance of the species and the propagation of Islam as among the purposes of marriage. But the essay went on to mention the view of some scientists that a child's character begins to form even in the womb, and that children have the potential to contribute as adults to the benefit of their religion and homeland (*watan*).[80]

Al-Tahtawi's and Mubarak's belief in the importance of childrearing at home led them to emphasize the necessity to society of stable and harmonious families. The marriage contract, al-Tahtawi wrote, connects the spouses in a union the purpose of which is virtuousness (licit sexual activity) and procreation. Since affection is an important part of the relationship a guardian should not marry off a girl before she reaches maturity/young adulthood (*bulugh*), and not until after the prospective groom has seen her (i.e., uncovered), as that is more likely to result in affection between them. It is also recommended that a man marry a woman of equivalent age.[81] Although these recommendations were to be found in the precolonial writings, al-Tahtawi may have been responsible for popularizing the idea of a prenuptial meeting between the bride and groom in the last quarter of the nineteenth century. Perhaps he was aware of the turn in French literary culture against arranged "marriages of convenience" in favor of consensual marriages based on attraction,[82] but if so he did not challenge the role of the marriage guardian nor advocate autonomy for the young in spousal choice. However, in recommending against the marriage of minor girls he was in effect advocating consensual marriage, since the Hanafi doctrine applied in the Sharia Courts required the consent of adult women in marriage and even permitted them to arrange and contract marriages on their own.[83]

It was also in the interest of good marital relations that al-Tahtawi recommended men limit themselves to one wife unless there was a clear need for plural marriage.[84] Polygyny was permissible only on condition of the equitable treatment of wives ("If you fear you will not be just, then one" [Q 4:3]), and men who failed to treat their wives equitably would be punished on the Day of Judgment. Moreover, polygyny was a source of family discord, a point al-Tahtawi illustrated with some lines penned by the thirteenth-century Sufi, Shaykh Abd al-Aziz al-Dirini:

> I married two women in my hyper-ignorance
> > But a husband of two has a calamity
> I said, I will live between them as a sheep
> > Living a blessed life between the noblest two ewes
> But the situation was always the opposite
> > A perpetual agony with two trials
> The contentment of this one activated that one's wrath
> > So I was never free from one resentment
> For this one a night and that one another
> > And an ongoing quarrel on both nights
> If you want to live happily
> > With your hands full of good fortune
> Then live as a bachelor, and if you can't
> > Then marry just one, or else it's a battle![85]

Al-Dirini used a sly double entendre in calling himself a male sheep (*kharuf*), for in colloquial Egyptian Arabic a *kharuf* is a man who has lost control of his family.[86] His comical depiction of himself alternating nights between two jealous wives refers to one of the norms men were supposed to observe in fulfilling the requirement of equitable treatment. Beyond the rueful humor the poem suggests that while men regarded polygyny as a lawful way of increasing their sexual pleasure, for women it was a cause of hurt feelings and jealousy, disrupting the harmony that ought to reign within the marital home.

Despite his disapproval of polygyny al-Tahtawi was circumspect on the subject of slave concubinage, mainly quoting other works, including advice on the selection of slaves, whether brown or white women were preferable, virgins or non-virgins, and the plump or lean.[87] That discussion seems out of place in a book that otherwise upheld an ideal of companionate (and monogamous) marriage, but it may have been prudent to avoid any suggestion of disapproval of the domestic life of Khedive Ismail, who had fourteen recognized consorts, all of slave origin, and who, a few years earlier, had expressed his displeasure at a play lampooning polygyny.[88]

Returning to the subject of marriage, al-Tahtawi stressed the need for husbands and wives to respect and love one another.[89] Love, affection, and trustworthiness (or fidelity) were important marital obligations (*huquq al-zawjiyya*), the fulfillment of which was a duty that the spouses owed each other in equal measure.[90] His words recalled the formulae "what the wife is due from the husband" and vice versa, though affection and trustworthiness were not a part of the maintenance-obedience relationship in the precolonial writings. He did not neglect the established norms in that relationship, however, noting that a husband must maintain his wife and not abuse her, and so on, and that she must surrender to him, obey him, protect his property, and observe the rules of modesty by remaining in the house.[91] Earlier, also, he made it clear that he saw no inconsistency between good marital relations and women's subordination within marriage. God created woman for man so that they could assist one another; she is his helpmate and for his enjoyment. She looks after his affairs and attends to his children and other dependents.[92] But she should not dispute with him, he wrote, paraphrasing Qur'anic verse 4:34, since "men are in charge of them [women] and not the opposite."⁹³ Yet he repeatedly emphasized the importance of a harmonious marital relationship.⁹⁴

A chapter in Mubarak's *Alam al-Din* suggests that he too believed in the importance of a companionate marital relationship. It took the form of a conversation between the Shaykh and Taqiyya about what could be done to alleviate their poverty. The two spoke to one another as intellectual equals. Her education had refined her intellect, enhancing her role as a helpmate, and enabling her to be a sounding board for his ideas. Taqiyya stressed the importance of education and the responsibility of the educated to engage with the world and use their talents toward its improvement.⁹⁵ Yet despite her intellectual ability it did not occur to her or the Shaykh that she should do anything other than attend to her domestic duties.⁹⁶ Like al-Tahtawi, Mubarak did not believe that the education of women had any purpose other than to improve their performance of domestic duties and to enhance their marital relationships. In a later chapter the Shaykh encountered European women in Alexandria who were good conversationalists—another testament to women's education—but he rejected uncovering and the mixing of the sexes in Egyptian society for moral and religious reasons.⁹⁷

Like al-Tahtawi, Mubarak disapproved of polygyny, though his perspective changed from strong disapproval in *Tariq al-Hija* to a less than wholehearted defense of it in *Alam al-Din*.⁹⁸ In *Tariq al-Hija* he discouraged polygyny, first, on the ground that the equitable treatment of wives stipulated in the Qur'an (4:3) is unachievable, an idea that is widely accepted nowadays. He anticipated al-Tahtawi's argument in the *Murshid* by saying that polygyny disrupted the good order of a household, and he expounded on the virtue of sexual self-restraint, likening polygyny to the behavior of animals, and asserting that one woman, if agreeable and not harsh, was more than sufficient for a man.⁹⁹

In *Alam al-Din* the Shaykh and the Orientalist discussed polygyny and agreed that only the ruling class had large harems guarded by eunuchs, since it was they who kept multiple wives and concubines. The practice, according to them, originated with the Byzantines, and the concealment of women it necessitated was imposed by the Turks. Love and intimacy are impossible between a master and multiple concubines. Since the common people emulate their rulers, if the rulers behave virtuously the country's condition will improve.[100] This criticism of the domestic style of the Ottoman Egyptian ruling class was likely one of the reasons why *Alam al-Din* was not published until after the deposition of the polygynous Khedive Ismail and the succession of his monogamous son Tawfiq.

Elsewhere Mubarak's characters offered a defense of polygyny. During the voyage to Marseilles the Shaykh pointed out to the Orientalist that polygyny was not unique to Muslim societies. It was nearly universal outside Christendom, and even Christians practiced it in earlier times. He speculated that divine wisdom permitted polygyny due to men's stronger physique, their ability to have children later in life than women, and because women are not always available for sexual relations (due to menstruation and childbirth). He added that such scandalous things as infanticide and abortion were unknown in his country.[101] The press in Second Empire France was filled with articles on infanticide, abortion, and the suicides of young women, whose extramarital lovers were shielded by the law if they refused to acknowledge paternity when children resulted.[102] Mubarak was saying in effect that adultery and illegitimate births did not occur in polygynous Egypt.

Polygyny came up in another conversation involving the Shaykh's son, Burhan al-Din, a French dinner hostess, and her daughter. The women asked whether polygyny was not contrary to a sound family life, making relations between a man and his wives difficult and engendering conflict among the children—nearly the same criticism that appeared in *Tariq al-Hija* and al-Tahtawi's *Murshid*. Burhan al-Din replied that most Muslim men were not polygynous, although it was permitted by the Sharia. The daughter persisted: Is it possible for a man to divide his affections among more than one wife? Burhan al-Din deflected the question by saying that one's affections are changeable, that the Sharia gave a man who disliked his wife the option of divorcing her, and that she could buy her freedom or ask him to divorce her to end their misery, while the French had no such options. The hostess admitted that Burhan al-Din had carried his point.[103] Here again Mubarak put Egyptian family practices in a more favorable light than French practices. Before the legalization of divorce in 1884 the indissolubility of marriage in France was said to be a cause of spousal abuse and women's suicide. But in Egypt men could divorce their wives easily by repudiation, and women could induce their husbands to divorce them by offering to cede their financial rights, hence "buying" their freedom.[104] Earlier, in *Tariq al-Hija*, Mubarak had been more critical of divorce, citing the well-known hadith that "the most hateful of permissible things to God is divorce," and saying that it should only be resorted to out of necessity.[105] The fictional discussions of polygyny and divorce in *Alam al-Din* show that Mubarak was reading contemporary French accounts of spousal abuse, married and unmarried women's suicide, infanticide, and abortion. But European criticism of Muslim family life was also growing sharper. In addition to voicing modernist ideas, Mubarak wrote in defense of his culture, perhaps replicating conversations he had while in Paris in 1867–68.

The writings of al-Tahtawi and Mubarak were foundational in the construction of an Egyptian family ideology. They and a number of other Middle Eastern contemporaries participated in the transnational flow of a set of ideas about civilization, education, childrearing, and family that originated in the Enlightenment, selectively combining those ideas with precolonial Muslim normative ideals to produce a hybridized ideal of the family. Both men adopted the Enlightenment notion of the conjugal family as the elemental unit in society, the main purpose of which was to nurture children. They introduced the novel idea that women were naturally suited for the roles of childrearing and household management and not for work outside the home, while advocating the education of women to prepare them for their domestic vocation. In their formulation domesticity was congruent with the maintenance-obedience relationship, although that required elision of the exemption of married women from the duties of housework and childcare. Concern for the stability and harmony of the conjugal family was another new feature of the family ideology promoted by the two men. Both men believed that the compatibility of husbands and wives would be enhanced by the education of women, and both understood polygyny to be a source of family discord. Al-Tahtawi stressed the importance of marital harmony based on love and respect, and he put new emphasis on precolonial prescriptions for marital compatibility such as marriage between women and men of comparable age and prenuptial meetings. Although neither al-Tahtawi nor Mubarak was a feminist, the family ideology they formulated had favorable implications for women. In promoting family stability and harmony they necessarily had to oppose polygyny; in supporting the education of women they discarded the idea that women were conniving and deficient in intellect and faith; and in ascribing a domestic vocation to women they distanced themselves from the idea that married women were mere "captives" in the home.

Muhammad Abduh and Qasim Amin on Family, Education, Marriage, and Divorce

Like al-Tahtawi and Mubarak, Muhammad Abduh and Qasim Amin belonged to different generations and had different educational formations, but their ideas on the family question tended to converge, which is explainable in part by their close association. In the 1890s Amin was part of the circle around Abduh known as "the Imam's party," and he read portions of *Tahrir al-Mar'a* to Abduh before its publication.[106] The book undoubtedly reflects the influence of Abduh's ideas but there is little reason to believe that Abduh wrote it, or parts of it, as was alleged at the time of its publication and later. The most prominent proponent of the co-authorship theory is Muhammad Imara, editor of the complete works of both men, who based his conclusion on their educational backgrounds and not on an analysis of the style of *Tahrir al-Mar'a* or its arguments. According to him Abduh, the Azhari, must have written the passages requiring knowledge of Islamic jurisprudence, and the secular-educated Amin must have written the parts displaying sociological and philosophical knowledge.[107] The problem with this supposed division of labor is that, on one hand, Abduh was well read in Western philosophy and social science,[108] and surely would have been able to write the passages Imara attributed to Amin. On the other hand, the jurisprudential content of *Tahrir al-Mar'a* is minimal, and not written in anything like the abstruse style typical of juridical writings. Amin was introduced to Muslim family law in the School of Law, and those passages were not beyond his ability.[109] Finally, the suggestion that Abduh concealed his authorship to avoid controversy is belied by his willingness to take controversial positions in his public lectures and publications.

Albert Hourani noted that al-Afghani and Abduh were influenced by François Guizot's *History of Civilization in Europe*, published in translation in 1877, which presented civilization as a process of social development together with the development of individuals.[110] Guizot's developmentalist historical scheme included the separation of conjugal families out of larger, more communal family forms like tribes and clans, and social differentiation based on property. The supposedly high status of women in Europe had its origins in the emergence of the conjugal family, where "the importance of women, the value of the wife and mother, at last made itself known."[111] This historical interpretation projected the conjugal family ideal of early-nineteenth-century France, with its placement of women in the domestic sphere as wives and mothers, into the feudal past as a foundational element of modern civilization. It was consistent with the theses of Malte-Brun and especially Depping, who associated the status of women with the advance of civilization.[112]

Abduh's early contributions to Egyptian family ideology, in several articles in *al-Waqa'i' al-Misriyya*, showed the imprint of these ideas. In an essay on the necessity of marriage he used a developmental scheme, starting with the assertion that women by their nature were unable to provide all the necessities of life for themselves and their children, hence they needed to form an exclusive relationship with a man who would protect them and provide what they are due (*huquqaha*). But men would not do that without the assurance of kinship that marriage provides. Thus the various holy laws established rules for marriage, so that a couple was able to maintain a good home life (*husn al-mu'ashara*) and preserve the system of domestic society (*nizam al-ijtima' al-manzili*). The needs of individual members of the family (*al-a'ila*) would be fulfilled through the family, and they would have no interest apart from promoting its happiness and wellbeing.[113] In his report on the reform of the Sharia Courts nearly twenty years later he articulated more clearly the concept of the family as the elemental unit of society, writing, "it is clear that the populace (*al-sha'b*) is composed of houses (or households, *buyut*) that are called families (*a'ilat*), and the basis of every nation (*umma*) is necessarily its families because the whole consists of its parts."[114] Thus the ills that afflicted Egyptian family life threatened the greater social order.

Abduh believed that these ills in general resulted from the poor character of the people, which could be rectified with education. He was keenly interested in improving and extending the system of education, a topic he addressed in numerous writings and speeches, and in the necessity of education for both sexes.[115] His mentor al-Afghani had argued that if Muslim societies were to advance, women as well as men must be educated:

> [I]t is impossible for us to emerge from stupidity, from the prison of humiliation and distress, and from the depths of weakness and ignominy as long as women are deprived of rights and ignorant of their duties, for they are the mothers from whom will come elementary education and primary morality. . . . If the mothers are educated, know human rights, and what the precepts of honor and civilization require, there is no doubt that their children will adopt their characters and will acquire from them these virtues. I think that when women's education is neglected, then even if all the males of a nation are learned and high-minded, still the nation is able to survive in its acquired stage only for that generation. When they disappear, their children, who have the character and educational deficiencies of their mothers, betray them, and their nation returns to the state of ignorance and distress.[116]

That al-Afghani lived in Iran, Afghanistan, India, and Istanbul before coming to Egypt is suggestive of the ubiquity of these ideas on civilization, education, women, and the family in educated circles in the Muslim world in the late nineteenth century.

Qasim Amin wrote in *Les Égyptiens* that women should have "un instruction relative" to attain a scientific understanding of their world and to enable them to impart morality and virtue to their children. Egypt would benefit as more women became educated. However, education should prepare them for a domestic role and not for intellectual pursuits.[117] He elaborated at length on the need for women's education in *Tahrir al-Mar'a*, saying like al-Tahtawi that girls should receive an education at least equal to what boys received at the elementary level, so as to enable them to raise children, manage a household, and be companions to their husbands. Like other modernists he had in mind formal instruction on the European model for the acquisition of literacy, as well as some knowledge of history, geography, and the sciences, and instruction in religion and proper comportment. With such an education women would be able "to accept sound opinions and to reject the superstitions and the idle prattle that now destroy the intellects of women." The trope of the uneducated woman as ignorant, idle, and susceptible to superstition was embedded in the family ideology along with the ideal of women's improvement through education, as we have seen. Amin and other modernists of that era equated ignorance with a lack of formal education, referring to "ignorant" women when he meant uneducated women, though he softened this by faulting men for depriving women of educational opportunities.[118]

The most important reason for the education of women was their role in childrearing and household management. From birth to the age of discretion children were raised in a female environment, he wrote. A boy lived in the company of his mother, sisters, and aunts, and their servants and friends, seeing his father only occasionally. An ignorant mother could not instill good traits in him because she did not understand what those traits were. Ignorant of the rules of hygiene, she would let him roam the street and play in dirt, and would allow him to become lazy and inattentive. She would expose him to superstitions with tales of *jinn* and other spirits and by taking him to visit the tombs of saints. This "disease," the ignorance of women, afflicted families of all classes.[119]

Of course, the reference to servants signaled that Amin had in mind mainly middle- and upper-class homes. He was clearer about the class context when he came to the topic of household management, which, he said, in the cities had become an art requiring a woman to possess a diversity of knowledge for such things as managing the family budget, supervising the servants, and making the home a pleasant and relaxing place for her husband. Above all it was her duty to raise children soundly "in body, intellect, and character." In the countryside peasant women were able to keep house and assist in the fields without an education because rural life was relatively simple. But household management in the towns had become as challenging as the management of a large government bureau.[120] Amin put more emphasis on household management (*tadbir al-manzil*) than his predecessors had done, which reflected the growing popularity of that topic in the periodical press from the 1880s onward.[121]

Like al-Tahtawi and Mubarak, Amin emphasized that the education of women was necessary for good marital relations. Men and women were naturally attracted to one another, he wrote, but the passion in a marriage will wane with time, while an educated man will continue to enjoy the intellectual and spiritual aspect of marriage to an educated woman. "Complete love" consisted of both the physical and intellectual/spiritual aspects. But for it to exist there necessarily had to be proportionality between the spouses in their education.[122] The likelihood of compatibility between husband and wife would also be increased if there were prenuptial meetings between prospective brides and grooms, and if guardians consulted with brides to give them a say in the selection of their husbands.[123]

While the importance of women's education for their roles as mothers, wives, and housekeepers had become unexceptional in modernist circles, Amin went beyond the domestic ideology of his time in suggesting that the education of women should enable them to manage their affairs and even to work to support themselves. Were it not for the neglect of their education, he wrote, women would be capable of working in the sciences, letters, fine arts, trade, and manufacturing, and of producing in the measure that they consumed rather than being dependent upon others. Fewer families would be impoverished if their female members became productive, and society in general would be enriched by women's productive and intellectual activity.[124] Here and elsewhere Amin made it clear that he did not intend women to limit their productive work to tasks that were performed in the home, like spinning and needlework, though he did not attempt to reconcile the idea of women entering the workforce and the primacy of their domestic roles, which he upheld elsewhere in the text. Another practical reason to educate women was to enable them to handle legal and financial matters. Uneducated women sometimes handed over their affairs to unscrupulous guardians or were persuaded to affix their seal to legal documents without knowing their content.[125] Presumably Amin had seen such cases as a judge.

Muslim family law obliged men to maintain their wives and children, and that was enforceable in the courts, as shall be seen. But not all women were able to rely upon male relatives for support. Amin gave as examples the unmarried girl without relatives, the divorcée, the widow, and the mother without sons or with minor sons. A proper education would enable such women to support themselves and their children. The alternative, impoverishment, caused some women "to sacrifice themselves in the dark of night to the first one who asks—and how great an abasement this is for a woman!"[126]

Amin's argument for modifying the system of covering and concealment followed from his argument in favor of women's education. The veil of that era covered a woman's face and was commonly called *hijab*, a term that had the generic meaning of "cover" as well as "concealment." Amin used *hijab* in both senses, referring to covering with the veil as well as concealment by seclusion.[127] Echoing the fictional Shaykh Alam al-Din, he noted that the practices of covering and concealment were neither unique to Muslim societies nor immutable, and that in Egypt they had changed in the past generation. These were customs "like other harmful customs that became established among the people in the name of religion, while religion is innocent of them."[128] Nevertheless, for the sake of morality he did not advocate that women uncover completely or immediately, but rather that they cover in conformity with what the faith actually required—what he called the "religiously ordained covering" (*al-hijab al-shar'i*).[129] Muslim jurisprudence did not require women to cover their hands and faces. The imams of the four schools of law were in accord that a woman's face and hands could be seen by her prospective husband and that the face and hands could be revealed in business dealings as well. The principle was that the faces and hands of women were not *awra*, that is, they were not like private parts that must be covered at all times, and could be revealed in situations in which they would not cause temptation (*fitna*).[130] Covering and concealment put women at a disadvantage in conducting business and in testifying in court, Amin continued. The Sharia granted women the same legal rights as men, including the right to control and manage their own wealth, but women needed to be seen to conduct business: How can one make a contract with a woman without seeing her and verifying her identity? Nor can covered women work in a craft, trade, or service, and so on. Out of necessity the veil was not worn by female servants, workers, or villagers.[131]

Furthermore, concealment, which amounted to the "confinement" of women in their homes, deprived even literate women of the necessary experience to be truly educated. Girls were concealed/confined starting at the age of twelve to fourteen, which was the beginning of their transition to adulthood and a formative age. These restrictions deprived them of the opportunity to inform themselves about the world and to investigate life and what it requires—in other words, they were deprived of the opportunity of learning about life by experience, which required social interaction, or "mixing with people, becoming informed about them, and learning about their character." In being cut off from the wider world they lost even what they had learned in elementary education.[132]

Even though Amin qualified his arguments by saying that the covering and concealment of women ought to be gradually lessened and that he did not want Egyptian women to go to the extremes of European women in uncovering, it is easy to see why conservatives found these arguments so provocative and others found them so praiseworthy. By the turn of the century the education of women was becoming accepted as desirable even in conservative circles, as was the domestic component of the new family ideology. But Amin went farther, linking the backwardness of women and hence of society not only to their lack of education but also to the norms of covering and concealment, and he declared those norms to be un-Islamic to boot. He also legitimized women's work outside the home without resolving the apparent contradiction between that and the new family ideology, which incorporated the maintenance-obedience relationship and the expectation that middle- and upper-class women would remain at home. To be sure, the norms of covering and concealment were becoming more permissive,[133] as he noted, and rural and working-class women had always worked outside the home. But *Tahrir al-Mar'a* offered a coherent argument—and in its time a radical one—not only for the education of women but for ending their "confinement" in the home and behind the veil. This evidently was the "emancipation" to which the title referred.

Abduh and Amin were in accord on the need to address three other issues that affected the welfare of the conjugal family, namely polygyny, maintenance, and divorce. The previous generation of modernist intellectuals had identified polygyny as incompatible with companionate marriage and a harmonious family life. In Abduh's and Amin's time a number of new concerns were raised in the press and in official circles over abuses that were believed to threaten both the stability of the family and public morality. These were, first, the failure of married men to maintain their wives and children financially; second, divorces pronounced irresponsibly by men; and third, the inability of women to escape marriages in which they suffered from nonsupport, desertion, or abuse. It appeared to both men that these issues could be addressed through legal reforms, and the solutions they proposed, while not identical, were broadly similar.

Abduh and Amin eventually went farther than al-Tahtawi and Mubarak in arguing that polygyny should be restricted if not prohibited. Abduh opposed polygyny in his early writings on grounds similar to al-Tahtawi and Mubarak, namely that men rarely treated plural wives equitably as stipulated in the Qur'an, and that the jealousy between co-wives and enmity between their children disrupted family life. Men often divorced one wife to placate another, breaking up the family. The divorcées and their children suffered poverty and degradation when the ex-husband neglected their maintenance, and it was difficult for women to use the courts for redress. Upper-class men were no better than others in this regard, neglecting older wives and their children to appease their younger wives, depriving the former of companionship for years.[134] The conventional exegesis of that era explained the Qur'anic verse 4:3 ("If you fear that you will not act justly then one") as requiring equity in maintenance and companionship, including equal numbers of nights spent with each wife. Thus, according to Abduh, equitable treatment (*al-adl*) was a marital obligation (*min huquq al-zawjiyya*) that polygynous men incurred. But since so few men could live up to that standard it was better for them to limit themselves to a single wife.[135] The standard interpretation of a later verse, 4:129 ("You will not be able to be equitable between your wives, be you ever so eager; yet do not be altogether partial so that you leave her as it were suspended"), was that men were not expected to have equal affection or passion for their wives, nor to treat them equally in sexual intercourse.[136]

Nearly twenty years later, in *Tafsir al-Manar*, Abduh advanced a radically different reading of verses 4:3 and 4:129, arguing that they implied the abolition of polygyny. Now he understood that verse 4:129 "may refer to equal treatment (*al-adl*) in the inclination of the heart." Moreover, he understood the phrase ("yet do not be altogether partial so that you leave her as it were suspended") to refer to men who left one wife without companionship and/or support in favor of another, something that happened all too often, as we have seen.[137] Since polygyny harmed individuals, it was harmful to families and society as a whole, and so Abduh concluded that it could be forbidden in the public interest (*maslaha*).[138] In a posthumously published fatwa Abduh addressed those who defended polygyny as a part of Egyptian culture, reiterating the points that it was not specific to the East, and was a tendency among rulers and the rich in lands where women were more numerous than men. Rather than legitimizing polygyny, he argued, Islam restricted it and prohibited it to men who could not treat their wives equitably. Moreover, since polygyny was associated with the mistreatment of wives and their deprivation of what they were due (*huquq-ihinna*), it could be prohibited. The only allowable exception would be the barrenness of a first wife, and that should be established before a judge.[139]

Amin's discussion of polygyny in *Tahrir al-Mar'a* made nearly the same points. He too noted that polygyny was not a specifically Muslim practice, and that it became less common as the status of women rose in a society—indeed, it had waned over the previous twenty to thirty years in some sectors of Egyptian society due to the abolition of slavery and advances in the education and understanding of men.[140] Polygyny was a source of conflict between wives, between them and their husbands, and between their children. Hence it was contrary to the conjugal family ideal of "a united family in which children live in the embrace of their parents, a sincere love holding them together."[141] He too juxtaposed the Qur'anic verses 4:3 and 4:129 in arguing that they contained both "a permission and an interdiction" of polygyny, making it justifiable only if the wife had an illness that prevented her from fulfilling her marital duties or if she were barren.[142]

Abduh's and Amin's hardened attitude toward polygyny reflected the progressive strengthening of family ideology, at the center of which stood the conjugal family ideal, and their concern with the issues of maintenance and divorce was informed by what they observed in numerous cases as judges.[143] But it also seems to have reflected anxiety over the moral peril supposedly posed by women who were left unsupported and/or unsupervised by men. At the time and later, popular anxiety over the presence of women in public space resounded in the periodical press. What was often described as indecent and immoral behavior included nearly any activity that brought women into public space and/or contact with unrelated men.[144] The breakdown of the maintenance-obedience relationship was implicitly at fault.

In July 1900 Abduh sent the Ministry of Justice an eleven-point list of reforms in response to a request for a fatwa concerning men who failed to maintain their wives, divorced wives, and children. This, he wrote, was one of four comparable situations that arose frequently, in which women and children were left destitute, resulting in "corruption," "the destruction of morals," and "evil doings" that affected the entire nation. There was, first, the question of men condemned to prison, whose wives were left without maintenance. Second, there was the issue of men who would not or could not support their wives, "as occurs with the majority of individuals of the lower class and many individuals of the middle and upper class." Third, there were husbands who went missing without a trace, or who were absent for lengthy periods without providing for the maintenance of their wives. Fourth, some men treated their wives so harshly that they could not continue to live together. In these situations a judge should be able to divorce the women from their husbands and to declare long-missing husbands deceased, but that was not permissible in the Hanafi doctrine that was applied in the Sharia Courts at the time. Therefore Abduh proposed that the normative rules of the Maliki school be applied in these cases. Maliki jurists permitted women to petition a judge for an annulment on grounds of nonsupport, desertion, and "harm," including harsh treatment, and they allowed a judge to declare a man deceased after going missing for four years.[145] Abduh justified his proposal on the principle of necessity (*darura*), which, like the public interest, could be invoked to permit a change in policy, in this case the adherence of the Sharia Courts to Hanafi doctrine. Abduh closed with an appeal to the khedive to implement this reform, and although it was not acted upon at the time it was eventually adopted in Law No. 25 of 1920.¹⁴⁶

Amin also thought it necessary to expand women's access to divorce in these cases, and in *Tahrir al-Mar'a* he proposed doing so by one of two methods. One would be to resort to the Maliki school of law, as Abduh suggested. The other would be to make more use of the delegated divorce and the conditional divorce, both of which were accepted in the Hanafi school. He preferred the former, which he thought was more likely to preserve family stability, since the decision would be in the hands of a judge.¹⁴⁷

Amin's concern with family stability was expressed clearly in his opposition to the abuse of men's privilege of unilateral divorce. Although divorce was socially necessary it was, in the words of the hadith cited earlier by Mubarak, "the most hateful of permissible things to God," and so Muslims should only resort to it for a necessary cause.¹⁴⁸ But the behavior of men fell short of that standard. Some broke up their families by repudiating their wives carelessly and unintentionally, since the Hanafi school accepted a repudiation as valid and binding even if it was declared under duress, out of negligence, in jest, in anger, or while intoxicated. Men also abused the conditional divorce by swearing that their wives would be divorced if such-and-such a thing happened or did not happen. To remedy that Amin proposed a mandatory period in which arbiters representing the spouses would attempt to reconcile them. No repudiation should be effective unless declared before a judge or another authorized official, in the presence of witnesses, and recorded in an official document.¹⁴⁹ A version of the latter proposal had recently been implemented in the Sharia Court system, which all but required the civil registration of marriages and divorces, and provided for a cadre of marriage registrars (*ma'dhun*s) to record them.¹⁵⁰ Some of Amin's other points were taken up in Law No. 25 of 1929, which rendered all conditional divorces ineffective along with divorces pronounced unintentionally or while intoxicated.

Due to the beginning of civil registration of marriages and divorces Amin was able to present data on both, which he cited as "evidence of the decline of the state of our families and the ease with which their structure is being destroyed."¹⁵¹ His handling of the data was naïve, but using it we can calculate a crude divorce rate of about 3.3 per thousand population in 1898, while data reported by Cromer in 1903 suggests a rate as high as 5 per thousand. These rates are plausible in light of divorce rates (including revocable divorces) of anywhere from 3.2 to 4.7 per thousand during the 1930s and 1940s.[152] By way of comparison the crude divorce rate in the United States peaked at 5 per thousand around 1980 in conditions of greater longevity; at the time roughly half of all marriages ended in divorce. Thus at the turn of the twentieth century the unfettered ability of Egyptian men to repudiate their wives meant that divorce was relatively frequent. Zaynab Fawwaz wrote that frequent divorce made married women feel insecure,[153] and Abduh and Amin emphasized that it broke up families and caused women's poverty and degradation.

Abduh and Amin wrote at a time in which the periodical press was beginning to popularize certain aspects of the new family ideology, in particular domesticity. The two men reprised the themes of the previous generation of modernists, identifying the conjugal family as the basic unit in society, the site where children are nurtured, and advocating women's education and domesticity as well as companionate monogamous marriage. They went a step farther than their predecessors in advocating legal reforms to promote family stability and to alleviate some of the problems faced by women in Muslim family law. Their participation in the judicial system had made them aware of these legal issues, and by the 1890s the state had begun to take a more active role in managing family affairs, as will be seen in the next chapter. The advocacy of Abduh and Amin influenced the first wave of codification of Muslim family law in the 1920s, which improved the situation of married women. However, their ideas and the consequent reform legislation were premised on the maintenance-obedience relationship, upholding a norm in which the husband provided maintenance in return for the obedience of the wife, including her not working without his permission. Even Amin, who recognized that not all women had male guardians on whom they could rely for support, and who held that women if properly educated could contribute in all fields of work, accepted the maintenance-obedience relationship as the norm.

Amin's views have come under criticism in recent years from a postcolonial perspective. Timothy Mitchell argued that freeing women from the harem and producing an educated "generation of mothers" to reform

Egypt was a goal of Cromer and his colonial secretary Harry Boyle that was "taken up" by Amin. Leila Ahmad asserted that the ideas of Cromer and missionary critics of Islam were the basis of *Tahrir al-Mar'a*, and Lila Abu-Lughod too detected striking resemblances between his views and the views of missionaries and colonial officials.[154] There is a similarity between the discourse of the nineteenth-century modernists, including Amin, and colonial and missionary discourse, since both drew on a stock of ideas about family, society, and civilization that were articulated in the Enlightenment and developed in nineteenth-century European social thought. But if missionaries and colonial officials deployed those ideas to assert Egyptian and Muslim inferiority, Amin and other modernists sought to use them for social improvement, as El Shakry and Hibba Abugideiri have argued in similar contexts. Moreover, Amin's arguments that polygyny disrupted family life and that women's lack of education left them ill-prepared to raise children were not new, but drew upon modernist ideas developed before the British occupation. Cromer made his views public in a postretirement book that appeared in the year Amin died and nearly a decade after *Tahrir al-Mar'a*. Boyle's thoughts were published even later.[155] Cromer's criticisms of Egyptian family life were similar to what modernists had been saying for decades. His claims that the concealment of women stunted their intellectual development and that polygyny was evidence that Muslim men despised women were remarkably similar to assertions made earlier by Amin.[156] Amin and Abduh are best understood as participating in an evolving modernist discourse on the family and women, the main theses of which were developed before the intensification of colonial and missionary critiques of Muslim family life that accompanied the expansion of empire near the end of the nineteenth century.

Aisha al-Taymur, Zaynab Fawwaz, and Malak Hifni Nasif on Marriage, the Family, Women's Education, and Work

Women began publishing in the 1880s in spite of far fewer opportunities and less encouragement to acquire literacy than men.[157] The three authors discussed here are better known as feminists than modernists, but a reading of their works with those of the male modernists makes it clear that they embraced the new family ideology and its corollaries, the conjugal family ideal and domesticity. Nevertheless, their viewpoints and emphases differed in some telling respects.

The women's acceptance of domestic ideology was linked with the goal of educating women. In an 1889 essay Aisha al-Taymur endorsed the education of girls, saying it would enhance their ability to manage a household and to rear children. Zaynab Fawwaz also supported girls' education, seeming to echo al-Tahtawi and al-Afghani in an 1896 essay in which she declared that "women are the basis of civilization, as the first school for every one of the human race," and that individuals acquired their good or bad characters from their mothers as children. She also agreed that educated women made better helpmates for their husbands and were more able to share in family life with them. During 1908–9 Malak Hifni Nasif, the professional educator, wrote often about girls' education. She disparaged the things they were taught by foreign governesses and in foreign schools, like the piano and French history, and argued that Egyptian government schools were the best when it came to preparing girls for the roles of household management and childrearing.[158] The support of the three women for girl's education and domesticity was consistent with the message in a growing number of publications by men and women on the art of household management in the 1890s and later.

The modernism of the women was also evident in their recognition of European civilization as more advanced than their own. Al-Taymur and Fawwaz anticipated Qasim Amin in holding up Europe as an example of how the education of women correlated with civilization, or what is called "development" today. Nasif opposed the aping of all things European and was critical of the *alafranka* style (in emulation of Europeans or "Franks") of youth in her day, but she still found much to admire and worthy of emulation in European "knowledge, vigor, perseverance, and love of work," and in their teaching methods.[159]

Nasif wrote some years after the publication of *Tahrir al-Mar'a*, but the points made by al-Taymur and Fawwaz on women's education and work anticipated some of the arguments of Qasim Amin. All three rejected any suggestion that women, as mothers, were to blame for the backwardness of society, saying as Amin did that their deprivation of an education by men was the real problem.[160] Fawwaz and Nasif argued that women should be free to pursue an education beyond the elementary level and to engage in work activity outside the home. That was not forbidden by religion, they noted, and family life would not suffer as a result.[161] For them and other women writers, as Marilyn Booth noted, there was a difference between valorizing the domestic vocation of women and limiting all women to the domestic sphere.[162] Fawwaz insisted that neither religion nor nature required women to be confined to the home and domestic duties. In Europe, with its advanced civilization, women worked. Egyptian women also worked in trades, crafts, and construction; "the markets are full of women vying with men in business transactions," and of course peasant women worked. Only women in the urban middle and upper classes stayed at home and that was a matter of custom.[163] Nasif argued that women were underrepresented in productive work because the introduction of labor-saving machinery like the sewing machine deprived them of opportunities; the implication was that men monopolized technology. But there were many women who needed to work—those who were unmarried, barren, widowed, divorced, or whose husbands needed assistance in supporting a household. Nor should they be expected to take lowly jobs; they should have the opportunity to become teachers or doctors. The unstated point was that women as teachers and doctors could work in a homosocial environment, unlike working-class women, whom Nasif described as having bad morals because of their contact with unrelated men in the workplace.[164] Amin, alone among the male modernists, addressed the need of some women to support themselves by working and the potential of women to contribute in all fields of endeavor, and he was not opposed to women and men mingling chastely and for some purpose. Abduh and other modernists who feared the breakdown of the maintenance-obedience relationship seem to have imagined it would result in women leaving the home to work and immorality.

The women writers valorized companionate marriage. In *Nata'ij al-Ahwal*, in the reading of Mervat Hatem, al-Taymur portrayed the ideal wife (in this case the wife of a ruler) as having "mature opinions, intelligence, good management skills, beauty, and grace," and as counseling her husband and being a positive influence on him.¹⁶⁵ In *Mir'at al-Ta'ammul* al-Taymur approached the ideal of marriage from the perspective of the spouses' mutual obligations in a way that made clear her familiarity with the precolonial writings. Her starting point was an explication of the phrase "what men are due from women and women from men" (*huquq al-rijal ala al-nisa' wa al-nisa' ala al-rijal*):

> [God] said, "Men are in charge of women in that God has favored one over the other and in that they spend of their wealth" [Q 4:34], for the man is concerned with the wife, striving to protect and shelter her, and to provide everything she needs. Moreover the [male] entitlement is not satisfied legally unless the cause, in His words "in that God has favored," is evident, meaning in matters having an abundance of intelligence and faith. Thus He invested them with authority and political leadership, and appointed caliphs and imams among them. And He gave them an advantage as notaries within the community, for He stated in another verse, "if there are not two men then a man and two women from the witnesses of whom you approve, so that if one of them errs then the other will remind her" [Q 2:282]. That is but a confirmation of their "favor" and the firmness of their justice. And in the words of the Almighty and Exalted, "and in that they spend of their wealth," that is, in the dower, food, drink, lodging, and clothing according to the financial condition of husbands and wives, as He pointed out in another verse in which the Exalted said, "The father shall bear the cost of her maintenance and clothing according to what is just, and no soul shall be burdened with more than it can bear" [Q 2:233], namely [a burden] on mothers.¹⁶⁶

The last verse referred to the mother of a newborn. Al-Taymur's comment that God "favored" men "in matters having an abundance of intelligence and faith" was a sly reference to the hadith in which women were said to be deficient in these qualities.

In this and subsequent passages al-Taymur used a strategy of linking the family responsibilities imposed on men in the maintenance-obedience relationship to the "favor" granted them in revelation. And the problem, she wrote, was that young men often shirked those responsibilities, thereby forfeiting their position of leadership within the family, which she constructed as a conjugal family. Al-Taymur illustrated this point with a parable about a lion that was too lazy to hunt, forcing his mate to do so, which resulted in a role-reversal. When the lion objected to eating after the lioness had eaten, she informed him of the new situation, saying that now "I am due from you what was due you from me."[167] Discussing the verse "They [women] are due in like manner to what is due from them [to men] according to what is just" (Q 2:228), al-Taymur explained that women are due certain things from their husbands which their husbands are required to provide as part of a proper marital relationship. The marital obligation (*haqq al-zawjiyya*) is not fulfilled unless each spouse respects what is due to them and due from them. The husband must provide all that she is due, just as she must obey him and be bound by his command. But if the situation is reversed and she has authority over him, then her obligation of obedience is in doubt. "Why not loose the band of the drapes [of the women's quarters] and discard the cloth of modesty?"[168]

Hatem pointed out that in these passages al-Taymur went "beyond the conventional religious views of the time" in making male privilege contingent on the fulfilling of male responsibility.[169] Indeed, in the Sharia Courts the maintenance-obedience relationship was applied with a double standard. A married woman was not entitled to maintenance if disobedient, and her husband could be excused from that obligation. For women, on the other hand, collecting arrears of maintenance was an arduous legal process. If they were forced to work outside their home to support themselves and their children they risked forfeiting their right to maintenance and a loss of reputation and status.[170]

It is difficult to tell from texts like *Mir'at al-Ta'ammul* whether in actuality men were behaving more irresponsibly than in the past, though that seems to have been a commonplace perception. Al-Taymur asserted that many young men married for money and were lazy and dissolute, putting an undue burden on their wives.[171] Fawwaz wrote that a man often would leave his wife and children in want when taking up with another wife, illustrating her point with a popular saying, "The father runs off and the mother makes do."[172] Nasif denounced the behavior of young men toward women in public, saying she was not asking men "to prostrate themselves" to women but merely to make way for them in the streets, not to stare at them, and not to make rude comments and gestures.[173] Her choice of words inverted the hadith mentioned earlier about women prostrating to their husbands in a show of respect. She also objected to young, dissolute dandies who preferred having girlfriends instead of marrying, and families who allowed material values and superficiality to influence their decisions in choosing spouses for their children.[174] Abduh and Amin were also concerned over the failure of men to maintain their wives. Regardless of whether the behavior of men was worsening in reality, it often fell short of a standard upheld by these writers. That standard was influenced by the new family ideology, which incorporated the maintenance-obedience relationship as part of the conjugal family ideal. In articulating a behavioral standard for men, these and other modernist writers defined masculinity in terms of shouldering family responsibilities as providers, rather than male privilege or an innate superiority, as Hatem noted.[175]

A commitment to the conjugal family ideal and companionate marriage was most evident in the hostility expressed by Fawwaz and Nasif toward polygyny. Fawwaz described it as "a curse" on all members of the family that condemned women to jealousy and extreme hardships, men to a lifetime of misfortune, and children to enmity toward their half-siblings. Nasif called it "the fiercest enemy of women, their unique devil." It broke women's hearts and led men to dissemble and be subjected to spiteful accusations.[176] Both Fawwaz and Nasif had experienced plural marriages, and Nasif in particular invoked her own experience and those of the women with whom she spoke. While the women writers did not go beyond the male modernist argument that polygyny was destructive of family life, they conveyed the special anguish it caused women. Abduh was the only male modernist to oppose it with similar emotion, perhaps due to his mother's experience.

The embrace of the new family ideology, including its component of domesticity, by modernist-feminists like al-Taymur, Fawwaz, and Nasif has posed a problem for historians of women and the feminist movement. They have explained domesticity as an expression of conservative religious values or, alternatively, of developing bourgeois values; and they have suggested that it was a response to "socioeconomic and technological changes" or, alternately, to social "upheaval" and a desire for stability.[177]

However, the core ideas of domesticity were articulated decades earlier by the likes of al-Tahtawi and Mubarak in Egypt, and Namık Kemal and Butrus al-Bustani elsewhere in the Ottoman domains. Rather than restrict women to the domestic sphere, their concern was to create a domestic sphere, which they understood to be necessary for social improvement. They believed that the key to social and national advancement was the proper education of children, including the formation of their character, which began in early childhood or even in the womb, as Mubarak wrote. Thus it was necessary to create the proper domestic environment, that is, in a conjugal family household. The education of women and their domestic vocation were means to that end. Subsequent generations of modernists advocated enforcement of the maintenance-obedience relationship and reforming Muslim family law to promote stable families. The late-nineteenth- and early-twentieth-century periodical literature that promoted domesticity on social and scientific grounds drew upon this family ideology.

Although domestic ideology constrained women's access to higher education and their participation in the professions after World War I, a generation earlier it was not reactive but a force for change, pushing against the ideas expounded in the precolonial writings, which were still influential. Al-Nawawi's *Sharh Uqud al-Lujayn* had four printings between 1878 and 1919, which is a rough measure of its popularity and of the continued vitality of a popular vision of marital relations in which women were deficient in intellect and faith, and once married were the equivalent of prisoners or captives of their husband. The new family ideology ascribed to women the ability to acquire an education equivalent to what most men received and to shoulder the responsibility of managing households and rearing children, responsibilities upon which the improvement of the nation depended. Metaphorical references to the home as a married woman's "empire" or "kingdom," and a description of her as the "mistress of the house," may have been more empowering than constraining in that era.[178] Afsaneh Najmabadi argued this point in the context of Iranian history, in which the issues were similar: "For women of the early twentieth century, [the domestic ideology] provided the very grounds from which the male domain of modern education could be opened up to women. To claim the position of the learned . . . manager and head of the household, far from frustrating the dynamics of women's move into public life, provided the empowering grounds for their national recognition."[179] El Shakry and Abugideiri have argued in a similar vein that Egyptian domestic ideology in the early twentieth century was part of a nationalist agenda of social improvement.[180]

According to Najmabadi the new family ideology in Iran offered women a vision of a "new husband-wife-centered family," that is, the conjugal family. Companionate marriage was an essential component of that vision, and to achieve it "men had to reform, and women had to acquire education." Men were expected to commit to monogamy and women to become "worthy companions." It was later, in both Egypt and Iran, as she noted, that domestic ideology was invoked to frustrate women's ambitions for full citizenship and participation in public life.[181]

4

Marriage in Law

Transformations in the Law Applied

Egyptian Muslim family law was transformed over the course of the nineteenth century and in the first few decades of the twentieth century through two processes. Beginning in the mid-nineteenth century the Sharia court system was reorganized, and new procedural rules were introduced that both changed the application of the law and enlarged the role of the Sharia Courts in people's lives. A few decades later, and in concert with those changes, Egyptian officials began to discuss the codification of Muslim family law, although codification was delayed until after World War I. This chapter discusses the new judicial organization and procedures and their effects, and the next chapter deals with the issue of codification.

The organizational and procedural transformation began with the creation of the position of Mufti al-Diyar al-Misriyya—Mufti of the Egyptian Domains or "Grand Mufti" as rendered here—by Muhammad Ali in 1835, and gained momentum with laws issued in 1856, 1880, and 1897. For the sake of brevity I shall refer to these laws as "procedural laws," even though they dealt with the organization and administration of the Sharia court system as well as with court procedures.[1] A few years after the elevation of a Hanafi scholar to the new supreme muftiship, the right of giving fatwas on matters of public policy was restricted to officially appointed muftis, all of whom were Hanafis.[2] Subsequently the procedural laws required that Hanafi law be applied exclusively in the courts. The new procedures were a departure from a centuries-old system in which the normative rules of all four Sunni schools of law were applied in the courts. The older, pluralistic system allowed litigants and the makers of contracts to engage in a kind of "forum shopping" or "venue shopping" by having recourse to the school of law that best suited their purpose. Each of the schools of law tended to be rigid in what it permitted and did not, but the pluralist nature of the system allowed a degree of flexibility.³ The "Hanafization" of the Sharia Courts eliminated that flexibility.

Before the mid-nineteenth century family affairs, including disputes, were often conducted apart from the Sharia Courts, with witnesses to establish a record. But the Hanafization of the courts had a significant impact as a result of the second major aspect of the procedural laws, namely the encouragement and, eventually, requirement of the use of documentary evidence in legal proceedings, including in family matters. By the turn of the twentieth century civil registration of marriages and divorces was all but required, as the courts would not hear any claims regarding marriage or divorce that were not supported by official documents.⁴ The Sharia Courts, along with a cadre of marriage registrars or *ma'dhun*s, were the venue for producing and notarizing family-related documents. Women and men had to use them to establish an unassailable record of their marital status and rights, and consequently the courts were busier than ever.

Hanafi legal norms were imposed on the population as a consequence of the new emphasis on documentation in legal affairs. Hanafi norms made it more difficult for women or their guardians to negotiate stipulations when arranging a marriage or for married women to collect arrears of maintenance, and they also made it impossible for women to escape marriage to a husband who failed to support them or abused them. Thus the first stage of legal modernization put married women at a greater disadvantage than their mothers and grandmothers had been. However, they were able to take advantage of the requirement of documentation by using the courts to establish a record of the maintenance they and their children were due. The problems caused by Hanafization, and the failure of men to support their dependents, vexed officials and intellectuals who were concerned not only for the welfare of women and children but also for the moral consequences of women being left unsupported and unsupervised. Eventually some of the problems caused by Hanafization were addressed in the laws of 1920 and 1929 governing marriage and divorce.

The important consequences of the reorganization of the Sharia Court system have largely escaped the notice of historians. The standard narrative of legal modernization focuses mainly on the creation of a "secular" legal system inspired by the French example, and in particular on the creation of the Mixed Courts and National (*Ahli*, or "Native") Courts in 1876 and 1883, respectively.[5] In doing so it elides two earlier legal-modernizing processes. One was the creation, beginning in 1842, of a system of judicial councils headed by a Supreme Judicial Council (*Majlis al-Ahkam*) that, along with newly established police forces, dealt with criminal, administrative, and eventually civil cases; this system operated until the opening of the National Courts in 1883.[6] The other process was the transformation of the Sharia Courts, which is discussed in this chapter. The common purpose in creating the judicial councils and reorganizing the Sharia Courts was to make the application of the law more predictable and uniform, a hallmark of modern legal systems. In the standard narrative the Mixed and National Courts were "modern" due to their French structure and procedures and their reliance on formal codes of law. The Sharia Courts met neither of those criteria. Even though Hanafization resulted in more uniformity and predictability in the law applied, the Sharia was still a jurists' law[7] embodied in numerous compendia, commentaries, and fatwa collections, and it lacked the simplicity and easy access characteristic of a code. Because Muslim family law was not codified until the 1920s it is a commonplace—though a mistaken one—that no significant changes in family law occurred until then.[8] Historians have neglected the Sharia Courts out of a belief that they were declining in importance, but in the late nineteenth century they became more central to family life and their workload grew correspondingly.

Pluralism and Custom in the Premodern Legal System

Although the Hanafi school of law was the official school of the Ottoman Empire, the acceptance of the doctrines of the three other Sunni schools of law and local custom gave the Sharia court system a certain amount of flexibility in applying the law before the mid-nineteenth century. The judges appointed from Istanbul to the major provincial towns were Hanafis and graduates of the imperial *madrasas* in the central part of the empire. But in the many districts where the population included adherents of the other schools of law, deputy judges representing those schools were also appointed to preside in the courts. The latter came from local scholarly families and were designated as deputy judges (*na'ibs*) in recognition of the superior position of the Hanafi judge. But the decisions of the deputies were accepted as valid and, if necessary, enforced by the authorities. Thus, in addition to Hanafi judges, Shafi'i deputies were appointed in some Anatolian provinces and in all of the provinces of Greater Syria and Iraq, and Maliki deputies were appointed in the North African provinces.[9] All four schools of law were represented in the courts of Ottoman Cairo, a legacy of the appointment of co-equal judges from the four schools during the Mamluk Sultanate (1250–1517).[10] The court in the Lower Egyptian town of al-Mansura had deputies representing the Hanafi, Shafi'i, and Maliki schools but not the minority Hanbali school.

The four schools of law differed in their methods of deriving normative legal rules from the foundational texts of the faith, the Qur'an and Sunna, doing so in part by relying to different extents on the other two bases of the law, analogy (*qiyas*) and consensus (*ijma'*). The consequent differences in the rules they derived were sometimes significant, and pluralism made it possible for the sultan's subjects to forum shop when conducting their business and family affairs in order to take advantage of the most favorable legal doctrine. A judge affiliated with a particular school was not permitted to apply the doctrine of another. But as Yossef Rapoport has shown, judges in the Mamluk Sultanate referred cases to colleagues representing other schools to achieve the desired result, and religious scholars "accepted—indeed, supported—the plurality of *madhhabs* as a remedy for the[ir] limitations."[11] This continued in the Ottoman period. The Hanafi chief judge of Cairo permitted petitioners to rent endowed (*waqf*) property according to the Maliki and Hanbali schools, which allowed a more flexible contract,[12] and forum shopping was not unusual when it came to family issues. The Palestinian mufti Khayr al-Din al-Ramli (d. 1671) was asked about a woman whose husband deserted her without support, and who had gone to a Shafi'i judge to have her marriage annulled. The Shafi'i school allowed a marriage to be annulled for the husband's nonsupport, desertion, or disappearance, but not the Hanafi school, to which al-Ramli adhered. Nevertheless, the Hanafi judge executed the decision of his Shafi'i colleague, as was the practice. Now the woman had finished her waiting period, and the question was whether she could remarry on her own according to the Hanafi rule. Only the Hanafi school permitted an adult woman to contract her own marriage, while the other schools required a woman to be married off by a guardian without exception. Was she free to do that, or must she remarry according to the Shafi'i rule? Al-Ramli responded that she could marry according to either school, since the earlier decision by a Shafi'i had been enforced by a Hanafi judge. In this example of forum shopping the woman took advantage of the Shafi'i rules to obtain an annulment of her marriage due to her husband's desertion and nonsupport, and then she made use of the Hanafi rules in order to marry herself without recourse to a guardian.[13]

According to Judith Tucker, Syrian women obtained annulments in similar circumstances from Shafi'i and Hanbali judges, and in Cairo, James Baldwin found that women went to Maliki and Hanbali judges for annulments.[14] Nor was forum shopping unique to the Ottoman Empire and that era. In his answer al-Ramli cited as a precedent a case decided by the Central Asian jurist al-Marghinani (d. 1197). In India under the Mughals as well as the British, Muslim women forum shopped between the minority Shafi'i and the majority Hanafi schools to obtain annulments and to self-marry, and forum shopping was also a well-known practice in the nineteenth- and twentieth-century East Indies, Malaya, Yemen, East Africa, and West Africa.[15]

The Ottomans in seventeenth-century Cairo sought to limit forum shopping for annulments and other practices not permitted in the Hanafi rules, and toward the end of the century they even attempted to prohibit non-Hanafi judges from granting annulments. But Baldwin was doubtful about the effectiveness of the Ottoman order,[16] and indeed, non-Hanafi judges were still granting annulments to abandoned women a century and a half later. In 1849, for example, the Grand Mufti Muhammad al-Abbasi al-Mahdi considered the case of a woman whose husband had left her four years earlier, and who remarried after receiving an annulment from the judge in her village. Al-Abbasi responded that, legally, she was still married to her first husband, saying that a judge was not permitted "to divorce a missing man for non-payment of maintenance under any circumstances, even if the judge sees that as proper according to his school of law, because of the ruler's prohibition of that."[17] This and similar cases from the mid-nineteenth century show that by then the higher authorities were enforcing the application of Hanafi law in the Sharia Courts, but that non-Hanafi judges had been accustomed until recently to apply the rules of their own schools of law, including the annulment of marriages for desertion and nonsupport.

In addition to pluralism and forum shopping, the recognition of local custom also gave the Sharia court system flexibility in adjudicating family matters and other affairs. Colonial-era and Islamic-modernist discourse has tended to draw a line between customary practice and the Sharia, presenting them as separate and often contradictory.[18] More recent scholarship has, on the contrary, emphasized the important role custom played in the legal system in the past. Ottoman Sharia Court judges were expected to take account of local custom as well as of the administrative laws decreed by the sultans (the *qanun*s) in applying the Sharia.[19] Moreover, the legal system as a whole, understood as the system of social regulation and conflict resolution in its entirety, comprised extrajudicial venues of a customary nature. Public behavior was supervised, norms were enforced, agreements were recorded and validated, and disputes mediated within numerous autonomous social units: urban guilds and residential quarters; villages and village quarters; and extended families, clans, and tribes.[20] Judges validated contracts, marriages, and divorces made outside the courts so long as they conformed to the basic requirements of the law and were attested to by qualified witnesses.

 Muslim jurists recognized custom as a source of law. The Egyptian Hanafi scholar Ibrahim Ibn Nujaym (d. 1561 or 1563) expressed this as the principle that "what is generally accepted in custom is like what is stipulated in the holy law."[21] He cited the example of the trousseau (*jihaz*) commonly provided by fathers to their daughters upon marriage, which was not a legal requirement but was (and still is) an accepted custom. Disputes over whether the trousseau was a loan or a gift arose often enough that the issue merited a discussion in Ibn Nujaym's book on general legal principles. It was recommended to take custom into account, he wrote, when a father claimed without proof that the trousseau was a loan. If customarily the trousseau was given to the bride, then the father's word was not accepted. But if the custom was either to give or lend it, then his word was accepted. Citing other scholars, Ibn Nujaym said that all of them recommended taking account of custom, and that the custom of a locale should be examined in rendering a legal opinion.[22]

Marriage before the Mid-Nineteenth Century: Minors and Adults, Men and Women

When it came to marriage and divorce, each of the schools of law offered advantages and disadvantages to men and women, as we have already seen in the example of the woman who divorced according to the Shafi'i rules and married according to the Hanafi rules. The basic elements or "pillars" of marriage were at a minimum a properly worded offer and acceptance, a contract, and a bridal gift or dower (*mahr* or *sadaq*) that was given to the bride.[23] The groom assumed full marital authority upon payment of the dower, including entitlement to his wife's obedience (*ta'a*) and sexual relations with her. A contractually married woman was not required to join her husband, or to obey him, or to submit to him sexually until the dower was paid. A young girl in any event was not required to join her husband until she was physically capable of sexual intercourse, and so payment of the dower was often delayed until that time.

The Hanafi and Hanbali schools accepted the groom's payment of a portion of the dower as sufficient to permit a couple to begin marital life. The remainder could be delayed until the marriage ended in death or divorce. This was the common practice in Egypt.[24] The prompt portion of the dower (*muqaddam* or *mu'ajjal*) was often one-third. Payment of the "delayed" portion (*mu'akhkhar* or *mu'ajjal*) was due upon divorce or, if the husband died, it was treated as a debt and deducted from his estate before its division. The delayed dower may have deterred some men in the middle and upper classes from exercising their right of unilateral divorce, but if they did so the delayed dower and temporary maintenance provided some security to their ex-wives. Every school of law imposed a dower at the going rate (*mahr al-mithl*), commensurate with the economic standing of the bride and groom, when the amount was not specified in the marriage contract or when the dower was subject to an invalid stipulation.²⁵

The four schools differed on the role and authority of guardians in arranging and contracting marriages, and also on the extent to which brides and grooms had a say in the process of choosing a spouse. The preferred marriage guardian (*wali*) for both the bride and the groom was the father, followed by the paternal grandfather, and after him the male agnates in the order of priority they would have in inheritance.²⁶ The extent to which brides and grooms had a say in the choice of their spouse depended upon their age and sex. Legal majority consisted of attaining young adulthood (*bulugh*) as well as discretion (*rushd*). Girls reached adulthood between the ages of nine and fifteen and boys between twelve and fifteen. It was discernible in outward bodily signs of puberty, by ejaculation or menstruation, or by impregnation or insemination. If none of those signs were present then adulthood was considered to be reached at the age of fifteen.²⁷ Discretion was manifested through sound conduct after young adulthood was reached, and was nearly synonymous with it.²⁸

Minors lacked full legal capacity, and every school of law required the marriage of a minor, whether a girl or a boy, to be contracted by a guardian. In his role as a marriage guardian, the father or paternal grandfather of a minor virgin was a *jabbar*; that is, he could marry the girl or boy off by compulsion (*jabr*). The right of a father to marry off his minor child was so ironclad that cases contesting that right rarely appeared in the fatwa collections. However, an illustrative case was heard by al-Abbasi in 1849 involving a man who desired to marry off his nine-year-old daughter without her authorization and against the wishes of her mother, whom he had divorced earlier. After ascertaining that he had paid child support, that the groom was suitable, and that the dower was at the going rate, the mufti replied, "The aforesaid father may compel his minor daughter to marry and [that] does not depend on the authorization of anyone [else]."²⁹ The minor children of divorced couples were usually left in the custody of their mother, and it may have been the opposition of the mother that made this case unusual enough to be included in al-Abbasi's collection.

The decision of a marriage guardian other than the father or paternal grandfather required their ward's assent, though both the Hanafis and Shafi'is accepted the silence of a minor girl as assent.³⁰ Hanafi jurists permitted a minor to reject a marriage arranged by someone other than her father or paternal grandfather, but to preserve her option of choice upon reaching legal majority (*khiyar al-bulugh*) she had to object at the time she was informed of her betrothal, otherwise her silence was taken as assent. Although some did so,³¹ it was probably rare, since it meant defying their male relations and going before a judge to invalidate the marriage. Women were married off at a younger age than men, and minor girls more often than minor boys, to judge from the legal records and census data available. Most urban women were married at the age of fifteen or older, while in the four villages in al-Daqahliyya women and men married later, as we have seen. In the villages the most likely to be married off at a young age were the children of notables and others whose families had land and status and a strong interest in preserving both through strategically arranged unions.³² The early marriages of Aisha al-Taymur and Huda al-Sha'rawi suggest there was a similar pattern in the urban upper class.

The rules for arranging marriage were different for adults and nonvirgins. Three of the schools of law still required the involvement of a marriage guardian for women, but adults and nonvirgins had to give their expressed assent in order for the marriage to be valid. Silence would not do.³³ The Hanafi school was unique in allowing women of the age of discretion, including virgins, to dispense with a guardian and to arrange and contract a marriage on their own. In the premodern era it is likely that most of the women who took advantage of this rule either lacked close male kin nearby or were widows and divorcées of independent means. Because it was the custom for parents to transfer property to their daughter at the time of marriage, and afterward for her to rely on them and her brothers for support if marital difficulties arose, it is not likely that many never-married women from intact families defied their male relations to choose a husband on their own. According to the marriage handbooks, even some Hanafi jurists objected to self-arranged marriages by women, and others said it was a last resort if a guardian was lacking.³⁴

Stipulations

A Muslim marriage is a contract, and a common practice was to stipulate the amount of the dower even though that was not required. Hanafi jurists accepted those stipulations as valid but would not enforce them: if the groom failed to pay the agreed-upon amount the marriage would still be valid if he paid the going rate (*mahr al-mithl*). The Shafi'is held that stipulating any amount other than the going rate was invalid. But the Hanbalis accepted a stipulated dower as binding and would annul the marriage if the groom failed to pay what was agreed.[35]

The Hanbali school was unique in permitting a woman to annul her marriage on the ground of nonpayment of the stipulated dower and nonfulfillment of any other stipulations in the contract. Nelly Hanna sampled marriage contracts inscribed in the Sharia Courts of seventeenth-century Cairo and found that a third of them contained stipulations of one sort or another. The consistent goal of stipulations was to mitigate the asymmetrical maintenance-obedience relationship in its standard form, and thus "to keep the wife from being under the complete control of her husband, either by imposing direct limitations on him or by power sharing between the husband and his father-in-law."[36] According to al-Dayrabi, the more commonplace stipulations that women (or their guardians) inserted in the marriage contract were: that a husband would not marry an additional wife or acquire a concubine; that if already married he would divorce his first wife, or if in possession of a slavewoman he would sell her; that he would not remove his bride from her hometown or village; that he would not move her far from her parents; that he would allow her to continue nursing a small child by a previous marriage; and that he would not remove her far from her children by a previous marriage. The last stipulation referred to the rule whereby divorcées received the custody of their minor children, but could lose custody if they married a man unrelated to those children. The contract could also stipulate that a husband would not remove his bride from her father's home, and/or that he would reside with her there instead of removing her to his own house.[37] The latter two stipulations would accomplish the goal of "power sharing," or the balancing of marital and paternal authority.

Other stipulations found by Hanna guaranteed women the right to work or to carry on a social life. A working-class woman, for example, stipulated that her husband would not prevent her from pursuing her trade as a vendor.[38] A woman from a prominent family not only stipulated that her husband would have no other wives or concubines but also that he would not prevent her from "going to the public bath; visiting her lady friends whenever she wished; receiving the visits of her children, companions, relatives, and friends, whenever they wanted and for as long as they wished." She would also be permitted to make the pilgrimage to Mecca and to return.[39] This evidence shows, again, that the premodern Muslim writings on a wife's obligation of obedience were more than theoretical. They not only expressed but informed social attitudes and practices. A man could withhold maintenance from his wife if, without his permission, she went out to work or to visit, or if she received visitors. The legal records show how women in the premodern era were able to negotiate exemptions from those sanctions.

Women's dislike of polygyny made it a popular target for stipulations.[40] Historically, the jurists read the Qur'an as permitting men to have up to four wives and unlimited concubines, and so the strategy was to deter them from exercising that privilege by stipulating that a woman could annul her marriage if her husband violated his promise of monogamy. Only the Hanbalis permitted stipulations of that sort to be inserted in the marriage contract itself, but within the other schools of law there were different ways of achieving the same results.

Maliki doctrine held it was illicit to insert stipulations into the marriage contract, but that principle was sidestepped in Moroccan Maliki judicial practice (*amal*). Maliki jurists elsewhere in North Africa enabled women to restrict their husbands' right to plural marriage in agreements subsequent to the marriage contract. The latter were enforceable, they held, because in popular custom they were considered to be part of the marriage agreement. A man might agree, for example, not to marry an additional wife or acquire a concubine, stipulating that if he did so his first wife would have the option of declaring herself divorced. Agreements of this sort were so common in Tunisia that they were known as "the custom of al-Qayrawan." Those agreements deterred polygyny either by automatically divorcing a wife, giving her the option of declaring herself divorced, or giving her the ability to divorce her husband from a second wife and to free a concubine he had acquired.[41] The third option is a reminder that men would practice polygyny and concubinage clandestinely.

Hanafi and Shafi'i jurists accepted two legal devices discussed previously, namely the delegated divorce and the conditional divorce. In the former a man would give the right of unilateral divorce (*talaq*) to his wife in a separate agreement before the marriage contract, at the time of it, or afterward. According to the jurists a delegated divorce might be granted for only a moment, say if a man uttered the proper words in the heat of an argument with his wife. One man told his wife, "I give you the ability (*mallaktuki*) to divorce yourself by yourself," and she replied, "what should I say?" He said, "Say 'I divorce myself from you,'" and so she used those words in the presence of witnesses, and al-Abbasi accepted it as a single, revocable divorce.[42] However, for a delegated divorce to serve as a deterrent to polygyny or some other objectionable act by the husband, it was granted as an option that the wife could exercise when she wished, as in the case of Sharifa Umm Isa of Damietta, who divorced herself irrevocably from her husband in 1911.[43] In either a momentary or open-ended delegation of divorce, the husband gave his wife (*tamlik*) the ability to divorce herself. Normally a married woman was said to be in the custody of her husband (*fi ismatihi*), but a woman who was the recipient of a delegated divorce was described as being in custody of herself or in charge of her own custody (*ismatuha fi yadiha*) or else as being in charge of herself/her own affair (*amruha bi-yadiha*).[44] This device was well known in nineteenth-century Egypt: Ahmad Shafiq offered to delegate the right of divorce to Isabelle Contal as a guarantee of his monogamy in an unsuccessful attempt to persuade her mother to sanction their marriage; Muhammad Lutfi Jum'a offered a delegated divorce to his wife at the time of their marriage; and Qasim Amin raised the possibility of incorporating either the delegated divorce or the conditional divorce into marriage arrangements to guarantee that women could escape marriages in which their husbands failed to support them, deserted them, or abused them.[45] Delegated divorce was also commonplace in South Asia.[46]

If delegated divorce gave a woman the option of repudiating her husband, a conditional divorce was automatic upon the fulfillment of the specified condition. Judith Tucker distinguished three ways in which men used and abused conditional divorce.⁴⁷ Men often swore oaths of divorce to emphasize their seriousness in an argument, or in social or business affairs. For example, one man swore a triple divorce of his wife during an argument with their son, and al-Abbasi ruled it valid.⁴⁸ Men also used the threat of divorce to control their wife, swearing that if she did something they forbade, like leaving the house or going to the home of a relative, they were divorced. Of course, for some women this was an opportunity to free themselves of an unwanted husband.⁴⁹ In addition to those abuses a man could swear a conditional divorce in support of a promise of good behavior: his wife would be repudiated (with all the financial consequences) if he failed to fulfill his promise to remain monogamous, to maintain her, not to remove her from her family home, not to leave for an extended period, and so on.⁵⁰ A man could also declare a conditional delegated divorce, as when one man agreed that if he took his young wife from her father's house against her will "she would be in charge of her own affair" (*yakuna amruha bi-yadiha*). When he removed her she divorced him.⁵¹

Rifaʻa al-Tahtawi's famous commitment to monogamy was in the form of a conditional divorce (see Fig. 5). In 1839 he signed a document declaring to his cousin and wife, Karima bt. Muhammad al-Farghali, "that he shall abide with her by herself in marriage without any other wife or slave woman for its duration, and he made her custody [*isma*] conditional upon the taking of any other women or the enjoyment of another [sic] slave woman. And so if he marries a wife at any time the daughter of his maternal uncle by a document and the [marriage] contract is freed thrice, and likewise if he enjoys a slave woman as [his] property."⁵² Decades later Ali Shaʻrawi swore a conditional divorce at the time of his wedding to Huda Shaʻrawi to guarantee that he would break off relations with his *mustawlada*, a promise he failed to keep. Qasim Amin also raised the possibility of using the conditional divorce to enable women to escape a marriage in which they were not supported or abused. In the end, concern over the whimsical abuse of conditional divorce outweighed its utility, and so it was invalidated in 1929.⁵³ However, it was incorporated in the Ottoman Law of Family Rights (OLFR,

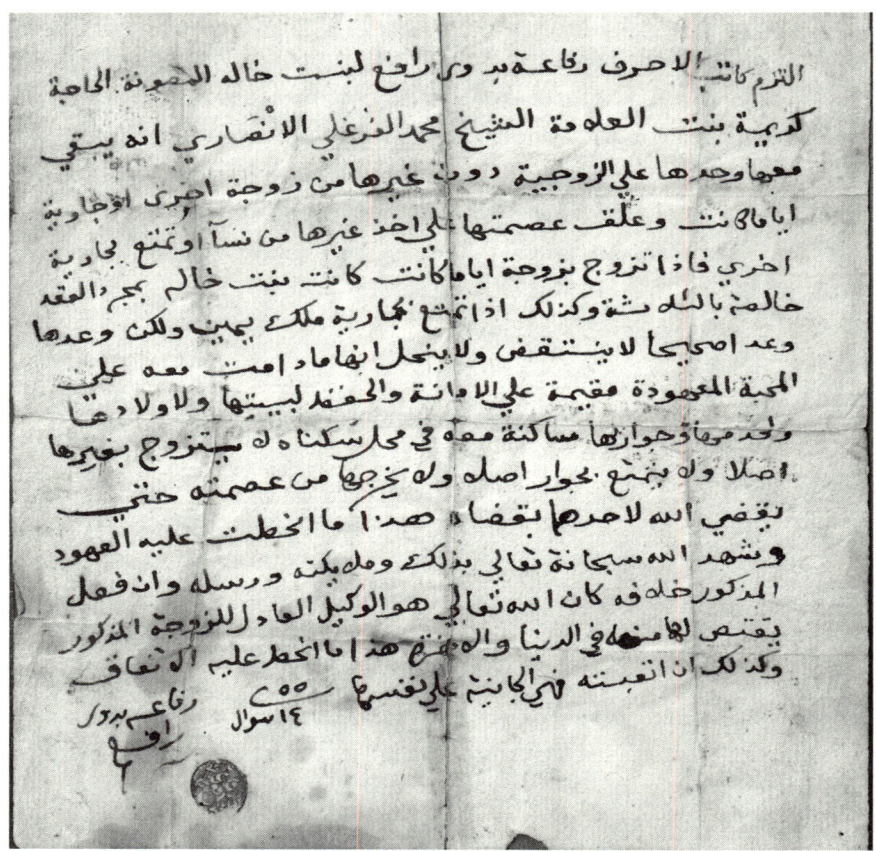

Figure 5. Al-Tahtawi's promise of monogamy: an example of a conditional divorce. Source: al-Tahtawi family archives. Courtesy of Ali Rifaah.

1917),[54] which did not apply in Egypt, as a way of controlling the behavior of the husband. It was widely used in Southeast Asia for that purpose, but it was rare in South Asia, where the delegated divorce was preferred.[55]

After the Mid-Nineteenth Century: Hanafization and Documentation

Nineteenth-century procedural laws ended the era of Islamic legal pluralism in Egypt and required the use of documents as evidence in the courts.

By the middle of the century the Grand Mufti was enforcing Hanafization by invalidating Sharia Court decisions based on non-Hanafi rules, as we have seen.

Adherence to Hanafi law was inscribed in the subsequent procedural laws. The law of 1856 stated that Sharia Court decisions should be made according to the "sound opinions" (*al-aqwal al-sahiha*) of the Hanafi school.[56] That particular wording meant that only the mainstream opinion or predominant view within the school should be applied, not any dissenting or minority views. At the same time and later, efforts were stepped up to promote the Hanafi school with newly endowed professorships at al-Azhar.[57] Khedive Ismail promoted the Hanafi school aggressively, restricting the appointment of religious officials to Hanafis and appointing the first Hanafi Shaykh al-Azhar. The Shaykh al-Azhar, the head of al-Azhar seminary, was the most prestigious religious official in the country, and the position had been occupied by Maliki and Shafi'i scholars in previous generations. Although most Egyptians adhered to the Shafi'i or Maliki school, the khedive's pro-Hanafi policy induced many religious students to switch to the Hanafi school.[58]

The procedural law of 1880 reiterated the instruction to judges to apply the predominant opinion (*arjah al-aqwal*) of the Hanafi school in their decisions.[59] By 1897 Hanafism was so well established that the law of that year referred to rendering judgments "in accord with the established doctrine of the school (*al-madhhab*)," it being obvious that "the school" was the Hanafi school of law.[60] Although these laws did not explicitly require it, evidently Ismail and his successors reserved Sharia Court judgeships to Hanafis. In his report on the reform of the Sharia Courts in 1900, Muhammad Abduh claimed that this policy resulted in the appointment of some poorly qualified judges and urged that adherents of the other schools be considered for judgeships since they understood Hanafi law and were capable of applying it.[61]

The Hanafization of the Sharia court system had important consequences because it coincided with an enhancement of the role of the courts in family affairs. Until the mid-nineteenth century the preferred way of establishing the validity of a document or the truth of testimony was through the use of witnesses. But as the managerial role of the state expanded, more reliance was placed upon documentation. Regulations issued in the 1840s required transactions in land to be recorded on officially stamped paper and notarized in a Sharia Court, and the authorities also accepted inscription in the cadaster or the tax rolls as proof of landholding rights.[62] The procedural law of 1856 expanded the role of documentation in all legal affairs. It established guidelines for inscribing decisions in the court registers and for provision of an official copy of each decision to the party in whose favor the judge had ruled. If the losing party sought to raise the case again it would not be heard so long as the court record and the winning party's document matched.[63] Similarly, the courts were instructed to record sales, gifts, and other property transactions and to issue official documents to the parties involved. So long as the privately held documents and the court records matched, no suits denying the terms of those transactions would be heard. Further, the law declared that the following would be admissible as evidence in the courts without the need of verification by witnesses: a document in someone's hand, stamped with their signet; and account books kept by merchants, tax collectors, and brokers.[64]

The law of 1856 also provided for the Sharia Courts, which were located in the major towns, to deputize "learned men" in each village or two for the purpose of overseeing and recording marriage contracts, divorces, and related legal affairs. Previously an individual had been authorized in some of the larger villages to notarize contracts and transactions and was known as either a judge (*qadi*), a jurist (*faqih*), or a court deputy (*na'ib al-shar'*).[65] The 1856 law established guidelines for these village officials in recording and reporting marriages and divorces, and it set a schedule of fees for each notary action.[66]

This law and the subsequent procedural laws enhanced the role of the Sharia Courts by making them the venue for producing, notarizing, and verifying legal documents. This expanded role is evident in the Sharia Court registers of al-Mansura, which are preserved in the National Archives. Before 1856, all kinds of cases—contracts, torts, and litigation—were inscribed in a single register series in each court. The law of that year instructed the courts to keep separate register series for different types of legal actions: inheritance and related cases; property transactions;

lawsuits; marriages, divorces, and marital reconciliations; and legal depositions. The keeping of discrete register series was a rationalizing measure, made all the more necessary by the increased volume of court business. The new rules did not explicitly require documentation, but by guaranteeing that proper documents would be accepted in the courts it encouraged contractual parties to ensure the protection of their interests by having documents notarized in the courts. The fees charged do not seem to have been a serious deterrent.

The procedural law of 1880 restated the rule that court decisions would be written up in a notarized document at the request of a litigant, and that no such documents would fail to be accepted as valid in a court.[67] Chapter 8 of this law detailed the selection and duties of an official now called the marriage registrar or *ma'dhun*, the successor to the "learned man" specified in the 1856 law. Registrars knowledgeable in the rules of marriage were to be appointed in every district of Cairo and Alexandria and in the other towns and villages. Their duties included ascertaining the eligibility of women to marry—that they were unmarried and free of a waiting period—in addition to recording marriages. They were instructed to write down in triplicate the names and patronymics of the spouses, their guardians, and the witnesses; the amount of the dower paid; and the delayed portion due. The copies were to be stamped with a signet or signed by the registrar and the bride and groom. The bride and groom each received a copy, and the *ma'dhun* inscribed the third copy in his register. If a couple married in front of him later divorced, the law instructed him to make a notation in the marriage register. He also was to keep a separate register for divorces. At the end of each month he was to provide the court with accounts of the marriages and divorces he had recorded and the fees he collected.[68] Marriage and divorce registers compiled by the *ma'dhun*s of Damietta, Rosetta, and Alexandria from the 1880s through the early 1900s are preserved in the National Archives. Though couples were still not required to have their nuptials recorded by a registrar, a notarized document attesting to their marriage or divorce guaranteed that their rights would be acknowledged in the courts. To judge from the sheer number of registers preserved in the archives, that practice motivated many to use the services of a *ma'dhun*. Thus the 1880s witnessed the beginning of systematic civil registration of marriages and divorces, which resulted in the data used by Qasim Amin nearly two decades later.

The law of 1897 stated that no claim of marriage or divorce would be heard by a court after the death of one of the spouses unless it was supported by documents that were free of suspicion.[69] The previous laws had offered positive inducements for the documentation of family affairs, but now the 1897 law offered a punitive inducement, saying in effect that the courts would not hear postmortem claims regarding marriages or divorces that were not supported by properly notarized documents. This all but required civil registration of marriages and divorces—that is, notarization in the courts or by the *ma'dhun*s—in order to protect one's rights in the event of future disputes over financial maintenance, child support, the prompt or delayed dower, and inheritance, to mention the most common sources of litigation. The new emphasis on documentation in legal affairs gave rise to a neologism, namely the "customary contract" (*aqd urfi*), which referred to contracts, including marriages, that were done in the old way in front of witnesses and apart from the court or the *ma'dhun*. Customary contracts could be formalized in a Sharia Court, which would draw up the proper documents.[70]

In the early twentieth century there were reports of the persistence of informal marriages—that is, unregistered marriages or marriages that went unregistered for a period of years, especially for the purpose of evasion of the minimum marriage age enacted in 1923.[71] Typically that was attributed to the peasants, though informality was undoubtedly characteristic of the poorer and more marginal elements in urban as well as rural society. Marriage, even for families of modest standing and wealth, was an important event in which careful consideration was given to the prospective spouse and his or her family, and it involved a significant transfer of wealth between generations. Civil registration protected the interests of the families involved, and so there would have been an inverse relationship between informality and wealth.

Hanafization and the new emphasis on documentation had a number of effects on family life and family ideology in the second half of the nineteenth century. Hanafization confronted married women with difficulties that their mothers and grandmothers had not faced. No longer could they avail themselves of the Hanbali rule that allowed them to insert stipulations directly into a marriage contract. The Hanafi rules still permitted conditional and delegated divorces, but it is not clear how often those devices were used. Beyond the anecdotal evidence already mentioned, al-Abbasi's fatwas contain only a handful of references to delegated divorces and conditional divorces designed to control the behavior of men. Hanafization clearly disadvantaged married women whose husbands failed to maintain them, were absent, or went missing, though to some extent that handicap was balanced by the ability of women to use the Sharia Courts to guarantee the maintenance to which they were entitled. The Hanafi rules also permitted adult women to make their own decisions in marriage. Nevertheless, the difficulties encountered by married women became a matter of public concern during the last quarter of the century. The failure of men to fulfill their responsibilities in the maintenance-obedience relationship was a theme taken up in the press, by intellectuals, and by members of the General Assembly, which advised the Council of Ministers.

The Problem of Nonmaintenance

The schools of law were in accord on the responsibility of husbands for the maintenance of their wives and children. In the maintenance-obedience relationship it was the fulfillment of his obligation to provide his wife with a dower, and financial maintenance, clothing, and housing (collectively referred to as "maintenance," or *nafaqa*), that entitled a man to her submission and obedience. Maintenance was commensurate with the economic status of the couple, and the wife was entitled to it regardless of her personal wealth.[72] But the schools of law differed on the consequences of a man's failure to provide maintenance. In the Shafi'i, Maliki, and Hanbali schools, unpaid maintenance was a collectable debt that accumulated from the time a man ceased to provide it. A judge could determine a "going rate" according to the economic standing of the couple. In the Hanafi school unpaid maintenance did not become a collectible debt unless and until the rate was set formally, either by mutual agreement or a judicial order.[73] Women deprived of maintenance who delayed going to court lost any claim to what was unpaid in the interval.[74]

Men who traveled were still obligated to support their wives and children, and the most common ways of doing so were to leave money and/or provisions with their wife or to appoint a legal agent to see that their wife received what she was due. However, some men left without making any such arrangements, and others stayed away longer than anticipated. In the 1840s one man planned on being away for a year and left his wife adequate provisions for that time, but he was actually absent for three years. His wife was unable to claim the unpaid maintenance because the amount due had not been formally set.[75] Since upper-class women usually had sufficient means of their own and working women were often able to support themselves, nonmaintenance seems to have posed the greatest difficulty for women of the middle stratum. The obligation of obedience required them to remain in the home even if their husbands were away. Women who went out to work without their husband's permission became disobedient (*nashiza*) and undeserving of maintenance,[76] and they would suffer a loss of reputation if they came into regular contact with unrelated men. Deserted women who moved in with their parents or other relatives also became disobedient and forfeited their entitlement to maintenance.[77] The legal system did not accept the logic of Aisha al-Taymur's argument that the marital authority of men should be contingent on them meeting all of their obligations, but it did make women's entitlement to maintenance contingent on their obedience.

Some women found ways of supporting themselves and their children while remaining at home and preserving their status as obedient wives. One woman supported herself and her children for over a month out of her own resources while her husband was away, but in the absence of a prior judgment or agreement setting the amount of their maintenance she was not entitled to compensation. Another woman left unsupported for a year and a half resorted to borrowing to support herself. She too was unable to collect any arrears of maintenance after her husband returned due to the absence of a prior judgment or agreement. Nor was her husband legally responsible for the debts she incurred. One woman whose husband left her without support for two years was permitted by a judge to collect some debts he was owed, and another was able to sell some goods her husband had left with her. However, when Muhammad Afandi went to

Istanbul and left his wife and children destitute, she was not permitted to liquidate his real property.⁷⁸

Women whose husbands left them without support could still petition a court to set the daily amount they were due, so that it would begin to accumulate as a debt.⁷⁹ Many women did so, but these rulings only enabled them to sue their husbands if and when they returned. Ignorance of the law, fear of scandal, and despair over the return of an absent husband may have discouraged some women from going to the court promptly, but by delaying a month or longer they lost the right to claim the arrears for those days.⁸⁰ The length of time some women waited before going to court suggests that it was a last resort, after they had exhausted their own resources or the support of their natal families. Three and a half years after a man fled and went missing, leaving his wife and sister without support, the women secured a decision setting the maintenance they were due, but they had no claim to the unpaid amount up to that time. Another woman waited seven years before obtaining a ruling setting her maintenance.⁸¹

Although Hanafization made it more difficult for women to collect unpaid maintenance, many adapted to the situation by using the courts to establish the amounts they were due as a hedge against their husband's future desertion or failure to support them. Al-Abbasi's fatwas are not statistically representative of all the cases he heard, but in the chapter on maintenance, suits by women seeking to fix the maintenance they and their children were due while their husband was present and their marriage intact were more numerous than post-desertion suits. The fatwas offer few details, but some of them state that the woman went to court to establish her maintenance after a quarrel with her husband.⁸² The laws of 1880 and 1897 encouraged that strategy by requiring documentary evidence for claims regarding marriage and divorce. Marriages and dowers were inscribed in the *ma'dhun*'s register by then, but not maintenance.

In the register of legal proceedings (*murafa'at*) of the Sharia Court of al-Daqahliyya for 1899, these preemptive lawsuits were by far the most common, accounting for a little under a third of all the entries.⁸³ These proceedings offer greater detail than the fatwas and give us a better sense of women's strategies. In January Sadiqa, the daughter of Muhammad al-Bahri, sued Ali Muhammad Siraj al-Katib ("the Scribe"), of al-Mansura, testifying that they were married and had a one-year-old son. She demanded that he provide her with a legal domicile and maintenance for herself and her son. Ali acknowledged her testimony to be true and agreed to provide the domicile and maintenance.[84] In June Muhammad Muhammad Kashif, the shaykh of his own agricultural settlement (*izba*), part of the village of Shubra Hur, and his wife Hanifa, the daughter of Ibrahim, sought to establish a formal record of the maintenance he owed her and their three daughters. Monthly, that came to 6 *kayla*s of grain, half in wheat and half in maize, plus 50 piasters, one-third of all of that for her and the remaining two-thirds for their children. For clothing he owed them eight piasters per year, and he also owed Hanifa a legal domicile. Finally, she stated that the delayed portion of her dower came to 600 piasters. Muhammad affirmed all of that, and Hanifa requested the court to record it. However, the judge refused the request as legally unsound, since there was no dispute and nothing irregular about the details in the testimony.[85] The response of the judge indicates that it was necessary for a woman to sue her husband in order to secure a ruling setting the maintenance that she and her children were due. Hanifa's mistake was her failure to use that strategy.

A month after that Sayyida, the daughter of Ahmad al-Sandubi, was represented by her brother Muhammad Afandi in suing her husband Ibrahim Layla al-Attar ("the Pharmacist"). She demanded that her husband provide her and her children a legal domicile, maintenance, and clothing, and that these be legally recorded. The children, she testified, were five-year-old Bakhiyya, Muhammad, about three years old, and Hafida, an infant. Ibrahim acknowledged his wife and children and said he was able to provide the domicile. But he claimed to be poor and unable to pay more than one and a half piasters per day in maintenance. The judged delayed his decision while deputizing two notables of the town to look into his affairs and determine whether he was wealthy, of middling status, or poor. They concluded that he belonged to the middle stratum and should pay a daily maintenance of four piasters, half of that for the children, and for clothing 75 piasters every six months, one-third of that for the children. The judge ordered him to do so.[86] This is a good example of how the court determined the "going rate" for maintenance.

The women who brought these suits acquired a legal guarantee that even a single day of unpaid maintenance would be counted as a debt against their husband, and the experience of going through the legal process, which was public, may have deterred some husbands from shirking their responsibilities. Moreover, women who brought these suits often had children, and they were able to secure their husband's acknowledgment of them and their inclusion in the maintenance order.

Most of the couples in these cases represented the middle stratum of urban society. Their daily maintenance was in the range of one to two piasters, comparable to the amount assigned Sayyida, and most of the men were artisans and tradesmen, along with a handful of waged workers and professionals. The preponderance of families of the middle stratum in these cases seems to suggest, again, that nonmaintenance was not as great a problem for upper-class women. Women in the middle stratum were concerned with preserving their status as obedient wives and their respectability through displays of modest behavior. They may have engaged in needlework, but they would not have worked outside the home, and it is noteworthy that Sayyida, the wife of a pharmacist, engaged her brother to represent her in court rather than venturing there herself. Working-class and poorer women necessarily went out to work to contribute to the income of their households, though women such as these who appeared in public and interacted with unrelated men were disparaged by Aisha al-Taymur and Malak Hifni Nasif as immoral.

Absent and Missing Husbands

Within the logic of the maintenance-obedience relationship the absent (*gha'ib*) or missing (*mafqud*) husband posed a problem similar to nonmaintenance and desertion, for these too were situations in which married women and other dependents were deprived of support that they were due. Absent and missing husbands were a standard topic in precolonial jurisprudence, and al-Abbasi's fatwas testify that it was a continuing issue in the nineteenth century. In the juridical texts the given examples were traveling merchants and tradesmen, migrant workers, and pilgrims who left their homes and wives without being heard from for lengthy periods or who disappeared without a trace. In nineteenth-century Egypt, in addition, soldiers and civil servants were posted away from home, and military action abroad increased the number of men who went missing.

During the regime of legal pluralism, women with absent or missing husbands could seek an annulment before a Shafi'i or Maliki judge, and a Maliki judge would declare a man deceased if he had gone missing without a trace for four years. But the rules of the Hanafi school of law offered no such relief. They did not allow annulments for nonmaintenance or desertion, and they would not permit a missing man to be declared deceased until he would be in his nineties. By the middle of the nineteenth century, to judge from al-Abbasi's fatwas, the Egyptian authorities had succeeded nearly completely in suppressing the practice of granting annulments to the wives of absent or missing men. Only a few of the mufti's decisions referred to such annulments, each of which he invalidated.[87] Ironically, Hanafism was adhered to more strictly in Egypt than in the rest of the Ottoman Empire, where the imperial government permitted decisions to be made in accord with the school of the parties in cases of desertion and nonsupport, and the OLFR of 1917 drew on non-Hanafi sources to enable judges to annul the marriage of a woman whose husband was absent and from whom no maintenance could be collected, and likewise a woman whose husband had gone missing for four years.[88]

No such compromises were made in the Muslim family law of Egypt. However, in Hanafi judicial practice (*amal*) it was possible for the wife of an absent or missing man to report "hearing by word of mouth" either that he had divorced her or that he was deceased, and on the basis of such a report a judge could permit her to remarry after completing her waiting period. This was an unusual departure from premodern Sharia Court procedure, in which the testimony of two witnesses was required to establish a fact. Nevertheless, it was accepted by judges in seventeenth-century Kayseri, eighteenth-century Ankara, and eighteenth-century Syria-Palestine.[89] News of a divorce or the death of a husband was acceptable in court if it came from trustworthy people and the woman "believe[ed] it in her heart."[90] This was also the judicial practice in nineteenth-century Egypt, though the evidence we have of it comes from situations that went wrong. Al-Abbasi's collection contains a number of cases concerning women who were allowed to remarry after hearing that their absent husbands had divorced them or that they had died, and who later were taken to court when their original husbands returned.[91] Of course, no fatwa would result when the divorce or death of the absent husband actually occurred and the legal procedure worked properly. But the cases at hand raise the possibility that some women were so desperate that they made fraudulent claims. In four of six fatwas issued during 1849–53 the husbands were absent for periods of two to seven years.

The engagement of Egyptian troops in foreign wars left an untold number of women with missing husbands, and some light on that is cast by two remarkably similar cases heard in the Sharia Court of al-Mansura in 1857. The gist of the story was the same in both. A village woman was married to a reservist who was called to duty at the beginning of the Crimean War (1853–56). The Egyptian force sailed from Alexandria in July 1853. Roughly two years later in one case, and a year and a half later in the other, the women claimed to have heard that their husbands had perished, and remarried. When their original husbands returned and discovered what had happened, they brought the matters to court. In both cases the original marriages were ruled to be still valid and the second marriages invalid, but the women were not subject to any penalty since the judges found that they had acted sincerely on the basis of erroneous information.[92] However, in one of the cases the woman gave a rather detailed description of how word of her husband's supposed death reached her, saying that a man in a nearby village received a letter from two soldiers who came from her and her husband's village. Her husband asked the court to summon the two men, who denied all knowledge of the letter. The case was referred to the mufti of al-Mansura, Shaykh Muhammad al-Tahiri, who was unwilling to pursue the possibility that the story of the letter was fabricated and who accepted the woman's testimony that she acted "based upon news that registered in the heart [as] truth."[93] We cannot tell how often the wives of absent and missing men made use of this Hanafi legal practice to free themselves from marriages to absent or missing men, nor how often they invented a story for that purpose. But it is clear that married women with long-absent or missing husbands were in difficult straits. It was better to be a widow with the possibility of remarriage.

The Role of the Marriage Guardian and Self-Marriage by Women

The application of Hanafi law in the Sharia court system meant that the near-absolute authority of fathers and paternal grandfathers to arrange the marriage of minor children was upheld,[94] but that was relatively uncontroversial since the other schools of law had similar rules. A minor could reject a marriage arranged by someone other than her father or paternal grandfather, but she had to object at the time she was informed of her betrothal. Huda al-Sha'rawi's experience is illustrative of the kind of pressure to which minor girls in the upper class were subjected to persuade them accede to a match made by a non-*jabbar* guardian. The jurists of all four schools agreed that men became capable of contracting their own marriages at the age of discretion, though in the strongly patriarchal family culture of the nineteenth and early twentieth centuries they did not always do so. A case in point was the marriage of Muhammad Ali Allouba in 1904. His father of took charge of finding him a bride and then co-wrote the marriage contract with her father.

The Hanafi school treated an adult woman almost like a man in permitting her to negotiate and contract her marriage on her own without recourse to a guardian or even securing his permission. This legal rule conflicted with the patriarchal culture of the era in which fathers assumed the prerogative to arrange the marriage of adult sons, not to mention daughters, and so the self-marriage of daughters was a very contentious issue. Many of the fatwas in al-Abbasi's chapter on marriage were occasioned by fathers attempting to compel their adult daughter to accept a marriage that they had arranged, which was something the father could not do legally.[95] Fatwas upholding the right of an adult woman to marry herself off against the wishes of her father or another agnate are roughly as numerous.[96] Here the number of fatwas is a sign of the contentiousness of the issue and not the frequency with which it arose. The reasons why a woman would arrange and contract her own marriage are speculative. There was nothing to deter poor women and/or women lacking kin from arranging their own marriages, which may explain the marriage of free women to slaves in the four villages. Widows and divorcées with some means might also act independently when remarrying, and in defiance of the wishes of agnates seeking to control their choice and the disposition of their wealth. Women of the middle and upper strata marrying for the first time were the least likely to exercise that prerogative since they had the most to lose by doing so. They had little opportunity to meet a potential husband, and it was the norm for a young woman to be married off by her father. In the mid-twentieth century, according to Allouba, popular opinion still held that a daughter should accept a marriage decision made for her by her parents, who were considered to be the most capable of assessing the prospective groom and his family. A lack of independent means and fear of estrangement from her family would have deterred most young women from independently choosing a groom.

Although the legal system upheld the right of adult women to marry themselves off, self-arranged matches were subject to the same conditions that applied to marriages arranged by guardians, namely that the dower be at the going rate for someone of their standing and that the groom be suitable in status. The man otherwise qualified to act as her guardian could object to the self-marriage of a woman on those bases. Since the amount of a dower could be adjusted easily but not the status of the groom, the mufti more often heard cases involving misalliances, or marriages contracted by women with unsuitable men.[97]

The rule of status suitability restricted the choice of a husband to someone of equal or higher standing than the bride. A freed slave could marry her former master, but a woman from the respectable middle class could be prevented from marrying a man who practiced a vile or unclean trade, and a woman of noble lineage—one of the Prophet's descendants, say—might be prevented from marrying a commoner.[98] This issue did not concern the authorities, who never dreamt of creating a system to investigate the status suitability of grooms. When the marriage registrar system was created in 1880 the *ma'dhun*s were instructed to ascertain only that the bride was unmarried and free of a waiting period. It was up to the father of a self-marrying woman or another agnate, as her guardian, to raise an objection to her choice of a groom. If they failed to do so or gave their permission for the marriage, then the marriage was considered valid. But if they could prove the unsuitability of the groom, the marriage would be invalidated.

These legal issues were involved in the celebrated case of the marriage of Safiya al-Sadat and Ali Yusuf in 1904. Safiya was the daughter of Shaykh Abd al-Khaliq al-Sadat, head of the Wafa'i Sufi order, and Ali was the editor of the popular newspaper *al-Mu'ayyad*. Shaykh al-Sadat traced his lineage to the Prophet, while Ali Yusuf had humble origins. The former objected to the marriage on the ground of the groom's unsuitability and won his case in court, although later he reconciled with Ali Yusuf and allowed him and Safiya to remarry. His actions suggest that he was motivated more by a desire to assert his paternal authority than by concern over the groom's suitability. In any event this dramatic incident has been misunderstood variously as evidence of the advent of romantic marriage; of a new trend of women challenging patriarchal authority by asserting the right to choose their husbands; and of Safiya's modern subjectivity.[99] The first two interpretations presume that Safiya's self-marriage was unprecedented, but it and her father's lawsuit closely resembled those of the preceding century. Samira Haj argued that Safiya's assertion that she was "adult, sane, and in full possession of myself (*baligha rashida malika li-amr nafsi*)" expressed a modern "rhetoric of rights and individualized subjectivity." However, in Maliki jurisprudence an adult woman who had reached the age of discretion (*baligha, rashida*), and as a result had full legal capacity, was described as in charge of herself or of her affair (*malika li-amr nafsiha*, as I prefer to translate it).[100] In the Hanafi school similar terms were used to describe a woman to whom the right of divorce was delegated, as we have seen. Thus Safiya used familiar legal language to assert her rights in the Sharia, not to express a new sensibility. Nevertheless, as Haj and others have noted, this incident fueled a public debate in the popular press over choice in marriage that expressed tensions generated by social change.

The "Family Crisis" and the Irresponsibility of Men

Once the conjugal family was identified as the elemental unit in society and the fate of the nation was tied to it, discussion of the family was no longer just about the family. The crisis of the family was a trope in late-eighteenth-century French painting and novels, and Lynn Hunt saw a connection between the attack on prerevolutionary royal absolutism and opposition to tyrannical paternal authority. Family crisis was a theme in late Ottoman literature, and Duben and Behar drew the similar conclusion that criticism of the family was a safe way to express discontent with political and social conditions in the Hamidian era. Deniz Kandiyoti went a step farther in proposing that Ottoman and early Republican critiques of the Turkish family were a way of "articulat[ing] a new morality and a new discourse on the regulation of sexuality," and Afsaneh Najmabadi, in a tip of the hat to Hunt, detected a "family romance of nationhood" in turn-of-the-century Iranian family discourse.[101]

In Egypt in the late nineteenth and early twentieth centuries, Marilyn Booth saw multiple connections between family discourse and nationalist discourse, Lisa Pollard argued that the family was a "framework" for discussing national issues, and Mervat Hatem understood Aisha al-Taymur's *Nata'ij al-Ahwal* as linking marital relations and political relations.[102] But Egyptians did not criticize the family as a proxy for the political regime because, unlike in Iran or in the Ottoman center, the regime they opposed was colonial. Here the modernist family discourse aimed at social improvement, and the theme of family crisis was tied to the failure of men to fulfill their responsibilities in the maintenance-obedience relationship. Al-Taymur's *Mir'at al-Ta'ammul* posited a crisis of the family caused by irresponsible men unwilling to support their wives, and the capricious abandonment of wives and children by polygynous men was denounced by Zaynab Fawwaz and Malak Hifni Nasif. Muhammad Abduh often wrote of the irresponsibility of men who married polygynously and divorced on a whim. The wreckage they made of family life was detrimental to the nation.[103] Proponents of the reform of Muslim family law also posited a family crisis or at least the threat of one that could only be averted by certain legal changes.

This crisis was often constructed by male writers as fundamentally a moral one. A key component of the maintenance-obedience relationship was the notion that women could not support themselves; that was the responsibility of men. Men who shirked that responsibility left their wives, children, and other dependents to fend for themselves. Families were broken up and women and children reduced to poverty. Moreover, women who were left unsupported and unsupervised threatened the moral order.

As Abduh put it, the failure of men to support their wives and children resulted in "corruption," "the destruction of morals," and "evil doings" that affected the entire nation.¹⁰⁴

The failure of men to maintain their wives was not a new phenomenon. In Muhammad Ali's time peasant women reportedly complained routinely to Ottoman-Egyptian officials of nonmaintenance by their husbands and ex-husbands, and the officials responded with threats to induce payment.¹⁰⁵ Fear of unsupported and unsupervised women underlay some criticisms of military conscription, as evidenced in the assertion of James Augustus St. John that the taking of the conscripts "condemned" their wives and children "to poverty and want, or [drove them] to support a wretched existence with the wages of humiliation and vice." The wives and daughters of the soldiers would be "irremediably lost: many families are thus entirely broken up."¹⁰⁶ Elsewhere he elaborated:

> [T]heir wives, if abandoned for a short time to their own guidance, easily slide into prostitution; and it is the opinion of many persons in the country, that when Ibrahim Pasha's soldiers shall return from Syria they will all find their moieties among the almé [dancing girls, associated with prostitution]. Though assertions so sweeping are necessarily exaggerated, it is nevertheless certain that the Egyptian women are naturally lascivious. All their looks and movements indicate this. Even their walk is lewd and immodest, and they turn upon the stranger so sensual an eye that it would be difficult not to discover the character of their thoughts.¹⁰⁷

"[T]he opinion of many persons in the country" was that of the Ottoman-Egyptians, urban upper-class Egyptians, and possibly foreigners, who were St. John's informants. St. John was a popular writer with no knowledge of Turkish or Arabic.¹⁰⁸ There is no evidence in his text that he spoke to any conscripts or village women, though his eyesight was keen enough to detect their lasciviousness.¹⁰⁹ Conscription undoubtedly left some women in poverty, but St. John's informants imagined its effect on peasant families within the blinkered frame of the maintenance-obedience relationship, in which women were defined solely as dependents. They failed to acknowledge that village women worked; that absent husbands, including conscripts, were obligated legally to support their dependents; and that at the time women were able to annul their marriage and remarry if their husband failed to support them or went missing.

The concern of St. John and his informants over the destitution of women owed much to the specter of immorality they believed it raised, and the twin bases of that anxiety were women's supposedly powerful sexuality and their presumed inability to support themselves with licit employment. The same perception of moral peril was a trope in most proposals to reform Muslim family law in the later nineteenth century. For example, the difficulties caused by missing husbands were addressed in an unsigned essay in the newspaper *al-Adab* in 1889.[110] The essay referred specifically to the problem of the wives of soldiers who had gone missing in the Crimean War and the subsequent wars in Ethiopia and Sudan. It identified the crux of the problem as the rules of the Hanafi school, "the one in force in our country today by a decision of the government," and it pleaded with the ruler to allow Shafi'i and Maliki judges to apply the doctrines of their schools in cases of missing husbands. Otherwise, the wives of missing husbands would be reduced to poverty with possibly dire moral consequences. Women, who were deficient in intellect and faith, might be driven by necessity to dispose of "the cloak of honor and chastity."[111]

Far more concern and commentary was generated by the failure of men to live up to their responsibilities in the maintenance-obedience relationship by supporting their dependents. Once a judge had fixed the amounts of maintenance due and ordered payment, unpaid maintenance accumulated like any other debt, and a man could be imprisoned for nonpayment unless he could prove he was impoverished and unable to pay. That juridical rule was incorporated into the 1856 procedural law.[112] As an alternative to imprisonment a woman whose husband or ex-husband failed to provide her maintenance could ask that his wages or property be garnished, but the failure of the civil authorities to execute Sharia Court orders was a perennial issue. In 1884 the Ministry of Justice noted the failure of provincial officials and police to act on Sharia Court decisions,[113] and in his report on the reform of the Sharia Courts sixteen years later Abduh identified the haphazard enforcement of Sharia Court decisions, including orders to pay maintenance, as a serious flaw in the judicial system. The administrative authorities, he wrote, were neither trained properly nor prepared to execute Sharia Court rulings, and as a result no more than one percent of them were enforced. To address this shortcoming he proposed giving the Sharia Courts the ability to enforce their orders directly through bailiffs.[114]

Concern over the enforcement of Sharia Court orders continued to be voiced in the new century. In April 1903 the journal *al-Ahkam al-Shar'iyya* editorialized on the "neglect" of Sharia Court decisions by the civil authorities, reprinting relevant passages from Abduh's report.[115] In 1909 four members of the advisory General Assembly submitted memoranda to the Council of Ministers raising the issue of creating a bureau in each provincial court to enforce the payment of maintenance and related issues. Shaykh Abd al-Rahim al-Damurdash[116] also took the occasion to point out the constraints of Hanafi law:

> In this country of ours there are issues the likes of which may not be found elsewhere, and that is that men do not respect the entrustment of women [to them] by God, for they leave them without maintenance nor anything to maintain them, and so wives are left in a condition which may compel them—God forbid!—to that which does not please Him. The Hanafi masters have ordered them [the abandoned wives] to make debts against their husbands, but it is not easily done nowadays for a number of well-known reasons, while in the Shafi'i and Maliki schools there is help for the likes of them, and so it is incumbent that their affairs be conducted according to one of these two schools because they are among the schools of Islam that the majority of people in this land follow.... Verily it is something made requisite by the era.[117]

Here also, al-Damurdash raised the specter of women acting immorally due to the failure of men to maintain them. Like Abduh, he suggested that the problem of nonmaintenance could be addressed by recourse to the rules of the Shafi'i and Maliki schools of law, both of which accounted arrears of maintenance from the time nonpayment began and permitted annulments for nonsupport. In another of the memoranda Muhammad al-Shinnawi Bey opined that the nonenforcement of court orders to pay maintenance especially affected poor women, and thereby could result in "transgressing of the bounds of the faith, the committing of sin, and the corruption of morals."[118]

The following year another member of the Assembly, Ibrahim Afandi al-Jarim, submitted a similar memorandum to the Council of Ministers proposing that the Sharia Courts be enabled to enforce their own decisions. In it he described the steps a woman had to take to collect arrears of maintenance or, failing that, to garnish her husband's wages or property. She would begin by securing a Sharia Court judgment ordering her husband to pay what she was due. The court would notify her husband of the order up to three times, and if he failed to respond at all the court order would then be transmitted to the administrative authorities for action. This alone could take up to four weeks. In order to proceed with garnishment the woman had to provide the authorities with information about her husband's property.[119] Ten years earlier Abduh had noted that fees were due at each step in that process, and most women needed the services of an advocate or an agent, which discouraged poor women from recourse to the courts.[120] The men whose wives were able to pursue the issue resorted to various tricks to avoid garnishment of their wages and property. Workers connived with their employers in claiming they had abandoned their work and had nothing that could be garnished. The head of a joint household would claim he had expelled a wayward husband, who in any event possessed nothing to garnish, while hiding him in the household. Perhaps later his father would arrange his marriage to another woman, using resources denied to his first wife. A man engaged in trade would place his wealth in his partner's name so there was nothing in his own name to garnish, even though everyone knew he was the partner of so-and-so. A typical civil servant made a meager salary but had many children, so if the maximum permitted portion of his salary was garnished the remainder would not suffice for him and his children to live on.[121] Abduh mixed hyperbole and class bias in this passage. Men's neglect of maintenance left women and children to die of hunger or beg in the street. Civil servants, workers, and day laborers were the worst offenders, and in addition to that they married multiple wives and had too many children.[122]

Yet not all men were able to evade their responsibilities. During the decade bracketed by Abduh's report and al-Jarim's memorandum, the official gazette carried regular announcements of public auctions of property that had been seized by the government to pay arrears of maintenance as well as the delayed dower due divorcées. A typical notice in January 1901 mentioned the upcoming auction of 25 *qirat*s of farm land belonging to Muhammad Nasr Hasuna of the village of al-Barajil in Giza province in order to pay the 6 pounds and 40.5 piasters of maintenance and clothing allowance he owed his wife Shu'ur, the daughter of al-Samad Khalil, through mid-October 1900.[123]

The failure of irresponsible men to maintain their wives was a preoccupation of the elite in the late nineteenth and early twentieth centuries, as evidenced by Abduh's report on the reform of the Sharia Courts, essays in periodicals, and the discussion in the General Assembly. This discussion occurred entirely among men, and their construction of nonmaintenance as a significant social problem was infused with gendered notions of women's inferior abilities and character. Their calls for more effective enforcement of orders of maintenance were accompanied by the express fear that women left unsupported and unsupervised would resort to immoral activity.

Legal modernization in the nineteenth-century Sharia Court system transformed Muslim family law in application, and by the end of the century the requirement of civil registration meant that these changes affected the lives of most Egyptians. Even upper-class families began to bring their affairs before the courts after the First World War.[124] The transition from Islamic legal pluralism to Hanafism put married women at a disadvantage, especially when it came to collecting arrears of maintenance, but women used the courts to establish a legal record of what they and their children were due in the event of non-payment. Pursuing arrears or the garnishment of a wayward husband's property or wages was an arduous process, though some women succeeded in doing so. Women whose husbands deserted them or went missing were unable to have their marriage annulled, though some were able to convince a judge that they had received word of their absent husband's death or pronouncement of divorce. The legal difficulties women faced in marriage led to several proposals to reform family law during the decade and a half before the First

World War, all of which seem to have been inspired by the proposals suggested by Abduh in 1900. These were, first, to utilize the rules in Maliki and Shafi'i jurisprudence to make it easier for women to collect arrears of maintenance and to enable them to annul their marriage if their husband deserted them, was absent without supporting them, or went missing. Second, Abduh and his followers suggested giving the Sharia Courts the means to enforce their decisions directly.

The discourse of family crisis that accompanied these reform proposals, all of them by men, consistently raised the specter of unsupported and unsupervised women resorting to immoral activity. The law could be amended to alleviate the problem of non-maintenance, but the cause of the problem was men who failed to fulfill their responsibilities in the maintenance-obedience relationship. This discourse assumed a socially normative world made up of households consisting of obedient and dependent women and the men who supported them, and it either elided the reality of working women or regarded them as a threat to morality. This perspective was not very different from the view of early twentieth-century female upholders of domesticity.[125]

5

Marriage Codified

The Invention of Egyptian Personal Status Law

According to Ali Pasha Rifaʿa, the son of Rifaʿa al-Tahtawi, Khedive Ismail approached the scholars of al-Azhar with a request "to compose a book on laws and penalties suitable to the conditions of the era, easy in its phrasing, and organized topically in a way similar to the organization of the books of European laws." Rebuffed, the khedive turned to al-Tahtawi, himself a graduate of al-Azhar, in the hope that al-Tahtawi could persuade the Azharis of the merits of such a project. But al-Tahtawi excused himself, saying he did not wish to be denounced as an infidel. Decades later, Muhammad Rashid Rida used this anecdote to portray the religious establishment of the nineteenth century as narrow-minded, blaming their obstinacy for the adoption of French law in the National Courts instead of a code based on the Sharia.[1]

Rida's polemic aside, the story of the khedive proposing a compilation of Muslim "laws and penalties" in a kind of code rings true. Majlis al-Ahkam and the judicial councils were said to lack a proper civil law and their decisions were all too often a matter of opinion. Ismail undoubtedly was aware of the Ottoman project, begun in 1868 and completed in 1876, to compose a civil code based on Hanafi jurisprudence, known as the *Mecelle*. But Egypt's viceroys were jealous of Egypt's autonomy and preferred to issue laws that were appropriate to local conditions.[2] The khedive's other efforts to promote legal modernization included the revival of the study of French law in the School of Administration and Languages, established in 1868, out of which a separate School of Law was created in 1873. The study of French law had begun in al-Tahtawi's School of

Languages, but that school had been reduced to a translation bureau in 1841 and was closed ten years later. Now under the khedive's patronage, al-Tahtawi and his students published translations of several French codes during 1866–68.³

In addition to those steps Ismail authorized his prime minister, Nubar Pasha, to negotiate the establishment of the Mixed Courts between 1867 and 1875.⁴ The Mixed Courts were a response to the growing presence of resident foreign nationals, who dominated commerce and finance, and the unequal treaties (Capitulations) imposed on the Ottoman Empire, including Egypt, that privileged foreigners with extraterritorial status. Extraterritoriality was justified on the ground that non-European law did not meet an international (that is, European) standard of civilization.⁵ Mixed Law was therefore based on French law, and applied to commercial and civil cases involving persons of different nationalities, taking the place of multiple consular jurisdictions.⁶ Following the establishment of the Mixed Courts Egyptian officials began to design a system of National (*Ahli*) Courts to replace the judicial councils. This work was interrupted by the Urabi Revolution and the British invasion and occupation. Initially the officials intended to draft a civil law based upon the Sharia, but when work was resumed at the end of 1882 that idea was abandoned in favor of adapting the Mixed Law codes for use in the National Courts. The Council of Ministers hoped (in vain as it turned out) that this would persuade the Europeans to permit the abolition of the Mixed Courts. The Council of Ministers was also concerned to establish clear jurisdictional boundaries between the National Courts and the Sharia Courts. The National Courts would deal with civil, commercial, and criminal law, while the Sharia Courts would be limited to personal status and religious law.⁷ Thus between 1875 and 1883 the judicial system was transformed. Majlis al-Ahkam and the judicial councils were abolished, and now three major court systems operated in parallel: the Mixed Courts and the National Courts, which were modeled on the French system and applied mainly French law; and the Sharia Courts, reorganized in accord with the procedural laws of 1856 and 1880, which applied a still uncodified Muslim family law.⁸

Nowadays the association of religion with the domestic realm and the derivation of family law from religious law is taken for granted, but that is a consequence of the reorganization of the judicial system, which was influenced by colonial-era knowledge of Islamic law. The Ottomans composed a viable civil code based on Hanafi jurisprudence (elements of which are still in use in some Ottoman successor states), and a similar project was mooted more than once in Egypt. The decision to use French law in Egypt had more to do with the contingent political situation than the relative merits of French and Muslim law. This was consistent with transnational trends in which legal systems in colonies and semicolonial states were either created or reorganized in conformity with the "civilized" norms of European law and practice. As Tamara Loos wrote, describing the process in Siam, the men involved "engaged in an international circulation of ideas about colonial-era jurisprudence and customary law." They and local rulers participated "in a global circulation of legal reform . . . link[ing] Siam to a network of ideas that went beyond national boundaries."[9] The new and reorganized legal systems applied versions of English Common Law or French Civil Law, which were deemed to have universal applicability in such areas as criminal law, commercial law, and property law. On the other hand, as Brinkley Messick noted, colonial-era scholars identified family law as the "core" or "heart" of the Sharia, and the same was true of indigenous "customary" and religious law elsewhere. In European thought the family was the elemental social unit, and hence the site in which the indigenous culture was reproduced. It was thought that the culture could be safeguarded by leaving the regulation of domestic relations to local customary or religious law. This logic appealed to nationalists as well.[10] The upshot is that in most postindependence Muslim countries it was unthinkable that family law would not be derived from religious law.

This chapter discusses the invention of Egyptian personal status law in the last quarter of the nineteenth century, not only as a consequence of the contingent reduction of the jurisdiction of the Sharia Courts but also in the context of the circulation of an influential body of colonial knowledge about Muslim family law. French legal scholarship influenced the process in Egypt due to the preeminence of the French language and the adoption of French law. Earlier, in Algeria, French colonial administrators created a Civil Law system in which the Sharia Courts administered Muslim family law separately, as personal status law. That model migrated to Egypt with the publication of a code of personal status by Muhammad Qadri Pasha (1821–88), which acquired great authority and influence in the application of Muslim family law in Egypt and elsewhere. Historians have neglected Qadri's code, and so this chapter examines how it and the process of codification influenced the modern understanding of Muslim family law.

Delaying Codification

Nineteenth-century European scholars regarded the Sharia as ill-suited for use in a modern legal system. In their explication of Algerian Muslim family law published in 1873, Édouard Sautayra and Eugène Cherbonneau asserted that the most authoritative Maliki juridical text, the *Mukhtasar* of Khalil b. Ishaq (d. 1365), was not a proper law book at all. It contained "extraneous" material of a moral character, it was repetitive, and it lacked order.[11] The authors presented a selective translation of it, and rearranged it in conformity with the order of topics in the French code to make it intelligible to their intended readers, who were trained in French law. To this they added the jurisprudence of the other three Sunni schools of law when it differed from the *Mukhtasar* of Khalil, making use of other colonial-era translations of juridical texts, and they also included recent Algerian jurisprudence.[12]

Sautayra and Cherbonneau's book served colonial officials as a guide to Muslim family law in the absence of a codification, which, when proposed a decade earlier, had encountered vigorous opposition. The Algerian ulama may have suspected that codification would undermine their authority as the sole qualified interpreters of the holy law, and in any event they mistrusted the motives of the French, who regarded it as an opportunity "to systematize and rationalize Islamic law, and surreptitiously introduce reforms."[13] The Tunisian ulama also resisted codification,[14] and so the Azharis were not alone in refusing the khedive's request that they draw up a code. In Istanbul, the imperial center, the ulama were less capable of defying the rulers, and key officials saw the utility of the codification of Sharia for its application in a reorganized legal system. The explanatory memorandum that accompanied the *Mecelle* emphasized the diversity of opinion within the Hanafi school of law from which it was derived and consequently the difficulty faced by judges in arriving at an appropriate opinion. This justified the composition of the *Mecelle* as a code drawn from "the most authoritative works" in the Hanafi school. On issues in which the opinions of those works diverged, the *Mecelle* adopted those that were "more suitable for the needs of our times."¹⁵

Not long after Khedive Ismail failed to initiate a similar project of civil law codification in Egypt, Qadri's code of personal status law according to the Hanafi school was published for use as a reference manual in the new Mixed Courts. *Al-Ahkam al-Shar'iyya fi al-Ahwal al-Shakhsiyya* appeared in 1875 in Arabic, French, and Italian, the languages used in the Mixed Courts. An English translation appeared later.¹⁶ Qadri had trained in the School of Languages and attended lessons at al-Azhar, fashioning himself into an expert on comparative French and Islamic law. He participated in the translation of the French codes, and served twice in Khedive Tawfiq's cabinet as Minister of Justice and Minister of Education. He is best known for composing codes of Hanafi law. In addition to the code of personal status, he published unofficial codes of civil law and of the law of charitable endowments (*waqfs*).¹⁷

Qadri's personal status code has not received the attention it deserves from legal historians or historians of women and the family because of its unofficial status,¹⁸ but its importance to the modern understanding of Muslim family law cannot be overstated. Its use spread well beyond the Mixed Courts, and twentieth-century legislatures and courtrooms in various Muslim countries treated it as an authoritative source of law. Multiple printings over the past fifty years in Cairo, Damascus, Beirut, Amman, and Riyadh attest to its continued importance.¹⁹

Qadri's personal status code acquired a position of influence in the first place because it was easy to use and uncontroversial. It was concise and accompanied by a detailed table of contents, and it presented the mainstream juridical opinions of the time. Second, and as intended, it was relied upon by judges and practitioners, including Egyptians, in the Mixed Courts and, later, the National Courts, as an authoritative statement of Hanafi family law. Third, it acquired authority by virtue of its use for the teaching of Muslim family law in the School of Law. The School of Law prepared men to serve in the Mixed Courts, the National Courts, and the civil service, and accordingly the curriculum emphasized French law, but courses in Muslim family law were also required.[20] Many of the leading men in politics and letters in the late nineteenth and early twentieth centuries were graduates of the School of Law, where Qadri's personal status code was their introduction to Muslim family law, and likely one of the few books they read on Islamic law.[21] Finally, Qadri's code gained influence due to the delayed codification of family law. Codification was a contentious issue due to the advent of the new family ideology and the interference of British colonial officials in Egyptian legal affairs. Consequently, although the codification of Muslim family law was discussed in official circles as early as the 1890s, it did not begin until the 1920s, and for decades it was a gradual and piecemeal process. Successive family laws, including Law No. 1 of 2000, currently in force, contained an article stating that, in any matter not directly addressed, the predominant view (*arjah al-aqwal*) of the Hanafi school should be applied. There are fewer unaddressed questions now than in the early twentieth century, but they still require knowledge of Hanafi law, and Qadri's code is still a commonly used source.[22]

In the 1890s the Ministry of Justice proposed that Qadri's code be the basis of a draft family law. A revised version of it was prepared and approved by the Grand Mufti, Shaykh Hasuna al-Nawawi (served 1895–99), though no further action was taken.[23] In his report on the reform of the Sharia Courts published in 1900, Muhammad Abduh, who succeeded al-Nawawi as Grand Mufti, proposed convening a committee of scholars to compose a book of legal rules derived from Muslim jurisprudence and that judges be required to follow it. Rather than revising Qadri's code, he proposed the inclusion of non-Hanafi rules when that was justified by the public interest.[24] The method of selecting rules from various schools of law, or *takhayyur*, was controversial due to its innovativeness. For some sixty years only Hanafi law had been applied in the Sharia Courts, and the norm in interpretation was to stay within the bounds of the school. The Ministry raised the issue of codifying family law again in 1904, asking the Grand Mufti Abduh and the Shaykh al-Azhar to consider, among other reforms, convening a group of Hanafi shaykhs to agree on a method of compiling the rules of the Sharia (*al-ahkam al-shar'iyya*) in a reference manual to aid the work of judges. Qadri's code was recommended again as the starting point.²⁵

The codification of Muslim family law was thus one of a number of reforms in the Sharia court system supported by the khedival government, especially from the 1890s onward. Abduh and his allies advocated recourse to Maliki jurisprudence to ameliorate the situation of married women whose husbands failed to support them, abused them, or went missing.²⁶ Other proposed reforms included better training of court personnel and increasing their salaries, the reform of the procedural law to improve the courts' operations, and, as we have already seen, a better mechanism for enforcing the decisions of the courts.²⁷ However, proposals for Sharia Court reform, including the codification of Muslim family law, stood little chance due to the controversies of that time. Abduh was involved in a struggle over the reorganization of al-Azhar in the mid-1890s, and the reformist views he expressed as Grand Mufti made him an object of attack.²⁸ In 1899 British interference in the appointment of judges to the Supreme Sharia Court outraged public opinion, and then in 1903 Cromer sealed the fate of Sharia Court reform by endorsing it in his annual report. Cromer's reports were public and immediately translated, and the nationalist press denounced his intervention.²⁹

If the codification of Muslim family law was not a politically neutral process, neither was it a simple matter of compiling a set of legal rules, for within the Hanafi school alone there were multiple, contingent interpretations to choose from on key issues, as the explanatory memorandum of the Ottoman *Mecelle* had noted. Moreover, Abduh and his followers saw codification as an opportunity to introduce certain reforms in the marriage system, such as limiting the right of men to plural marriage and unilateral divorce. Today these reforms are remembered in Egypt as good and necessary, but at the time they added to the contentiousness of the issue of codification.

Inventing Personal Status Law

Family law in the Middle East and North Africa is referred to nowadays as the law of "personal status" (in Arabic, *al-ahwal al-shakhsiyya*, and in French, *statut personnel*), a term that was unknown in Muslim jurisprudence before the late nineteenth century. In European law, where it originated, personal status referred to the legal status and capacity of individuals, which in different systems was determined either by one's domicile or nationality.[30] It acquired a new use in colonial Algeria, where the French applied "the principle of *personnalité*, that is, different justice for different categories of person,"[31] on the basis of religion. In the early years of French rule the Muslim Algerians were allowed a degree of legal autonomy, but that was progressively reduced until by 1873 the jurisdiction of Algeria's Sharia Courts was restricted to matters of personal status (*statut personnel*), which was defined as family law, or the law concerning marriage, divorce, children, and inheritance.[32] The application of French law to landed property facilitated its acquisition by European settlers,[33] while the refusal of most Muslim Algerians to renounce the Sharia and to embrace the French civil code meant they were denied full French citizenship.[34] This difference also signified Algerian backwardness in the eyes of Europeans, but adherence to Muslim family law expressed Algerian communal identity, and, eventually, their national identity.[35]

Here we are concerned with another aspect of that legal history, namely the invention of Muslim personal status law. Justified by the French as an expression of their respect for the indigenous culture and their desire to preserve it, Muslim Algerian law (*droit Musulman Algérien*) was developed as a distinct and hybridized version of Islamic law.[36] The French also reorganized the Sharia court system, centralizing it, staffing it with judges trained in official *médersas* (religious schools, or *madrasa*s), and subordinating it to French appeals courts.[37] The approved *médersa* curriculum and the translations relied upon by the magistrates in the appeals courts emphasized the law as embodied in selected canonical texts, like the *Mukhtasar* of Khalil, at the expense of custom and judicial practice. Councils of ulama were convened to address aspects of the religious law that the French found objectionable or irrational, such as child marriage and the "sleeping baby."[38]

The Algerian model for incorporating Sharia jurisprudence and courts within a modern—that is, a European—legal system acquired the form described above during the mid-1860s. Subsequently the reorganization of the Egyptian legal system resulted in a situation similar to the one in Algeria. That is, a Civil Law system became dominant in Egypt with the establishment of the Mixed and National Courts, which applied codes derived mainly from French law, and it became necessary to define a relationship between the new Civil Law system, on one hand, and the preexisting Sharia Courts on the other. The dominant position of French legal studies in Egypt and the growing cadre of officials trained in French law ensured that French colonial legal studies would be a point of reference when Egyptian officials undertook the reorganization of their legal system, even if they did not follow the Algerian model in every respect.

As in Algeria, in Egypt the family was preserved as the principal domain of the religious law through a separation of the law of personal status (*statut personnel*) from the law of real status (*statut reél*).[39] The migration of the term "personal status" to Egypt coincided with the establishment of the Mixed Courts, which heard cases involving real property but were instructed to leave questions of family law—that is, personal status law—to the Sharia Courts. The term was introduced to Arabic-reading Egyptians in the Mixed Law codes[40] as well as in the title of Qadri's personal status code, and in subsequent years it became indigenized. It appeared in the procedural laws of 1880 and 1897, and early in the next century it was used in journalism without any gloss of its meaning.[41] The adoption of this term in legal and journalistic writing was a sign of the naturalization of the new system of legal pluralism associated with it, including the notion that Muslim family law and other religious family laws should be applied separately from the universally applicable laws administered by the state.

From Jurists' Law to Positive Law

If in legal scholarship Qadri's code was valued as a clear and concise statement of family law according to the Hanafi school, that was also its principal contribution to the modern understanding of Muslim family law: its (re)construction of Hanafi jurisprudence in the form of positive law, as a code. Rudolph Peters described Islamic law as a "jurists' law" in the sense that it was defined by a corps of legal scholars, or jurists, working independently of the state. They did so "in a scholarly, academic debate, in which conflicting and often contradictory views were opposed and discussed. . . . Because of differences in understanding the texts and in the use of the hermeneutical tools, the shari'a as laid down by the jurists is not uniform."[42] In his code Qadri eliminated that lack of uniformity so as to make Muslim family law legible to foreigners and Egyptians who were trained in French law.

Messick observed that in Yemen, the modern state's extension of regulatory control over legal proceedings coincided with a change in the composition of documents from spiral-shaped writing to straight-ruled writing. This, he argued, reflected "changes in the basic epistemological structure of the document, with the principles underpinning the document's construction and its authority." Contents determined form in the older style of document, including its length, while the composition of modern documents tends to conform to preestablished criteria (including actual fill-in forms). Thus in modern documents "form is separate from, prior to, and more determinate of the shape of the textual contents."[43] A comparable difference in form exists between the earlier juridical literature and Qadri's code, which may be illustrated by comparing pages from both (compare Figs. 6 and 7). Figure 6 is a page from Ibn Abdin's *Radd al-Muhtar ala al-Durr al-Mukhtar*, which was an authoritative statement of Hanafi law in nineteenth-century Egypt. *Radd al-Muhtar* is a commentary on an earlier work by Ala al-Din al-Haskafi (1616–77) explicating a compendium of Hanafi legal rules by Shams al-Din al-Timurtashi (d. 1595). The design of the printed page, which mimicked the format of earlier manuscript versions, facilitates a parallel reading of all three texts. Ibn Abdin's commentary occupies the main part of the page, and al-Haskafi's explication is in the margin. Ibn Abdin's commentary refers to passages in the text of al-Haskafi within parentheses, beginning each time with the word *qawluh* ("his statement") in boldface type, followed by a word or part of a phrase. Similarly, al-Haskafi's explication quotes the text of al-Timurtashi within parentheses.

The purpose of Ibn Abdin's commentary and similar works was to arrive at a statement of the preferred legal opinions in the school of law, and hence of the rules for judges to apply. The mode of presentation preserved the preceding juridical discussion, including disagreements and

Figure 6: Chapter on the Marriage Guardian in a juridical text. Source: Ibn Abdin's *Radd al-Muhtar* (Bulaq: al-Matba'a al-Amiriyya, 1905–8).

dissenting views, which led to the formulation of the preferred opinions.[44] By preserving a record of the discussion and debate behind a given opinion, the text made it clear that the opinion was an artifact arrived at by human endeavor in specific circumstances. In signaling the contingent construction of an opinion, the text implied that under the right circumstances a different opinion might be preferred, although that happened rarely. Only the most eminent jurists could issue opinions on unprecedented questions or attempt to revise the prevailing view. The Grand Mufti Muhammad al-Abbasi al-Mahdi, who often cited Ibn Abdin, frequently mentioned in his rulings that he was following the preferred rule (*al-mukhtar*), the recommended opinion (*al-mufti bi-hi*), or the juridical practice (*al-ma'mul bi-hi*) of the Hanafi school in his time.

The radically different form of Qadri's personal status code was due to its mimicking of the form of the French code. It was arranged in topical chapters and sections comprising 647 numbered articles (Fig. 7). In contrast to the five thick tomes filled by *Radd al-Muhtar*, Qadri's code was a slim volume of 138 pages. Qadri was not a reformer in the mold of Abduh and Amin. On the contrary, he consulted the Hanafi authorities in use in his time to arrive at the rules stated in his code, and as a result they were uncontroversial. However, each article in his code stated a rule or a set of rules without any acknowledgment of the historical scholarship that led to its formulation. There was no hint that these rules resulted from generations of discussion and debate or that they might be subject to disagreement and revision in certain circumstances. With regard to that difference, Peters observed that juridical works "are discursive and include various, often conflicting opinions on the issue. They are open texts in the sense that they do not offer final solutions. Provisions of a law code, on the other hand, must be authoritative, clear and unequivocal. In a law code there is no room for contradictory opinions or argumentation and its provisions must be definitive and final. Therefore, choices have to be made when codifying the shari'a."[45] For most of the literate public, who had little knowledge of the methods and multiple contingent views that were characteristic of Islamic jurisprudence, Qadri's code may have made Muslim family law appear to be an unvarying set of rules.

Figure 7: The introduction and beginning of Qadri's personal status code. The headings are (on right): Part I, On the Rules Applying to Humanity; Book 1, On Marriage; Chapter 1, On the Preliminary Steps of Marriage; and the heading of Article 1. The body of Article 1 and the numbered Articles 2, 3, and 4 continue on the next page (on left); then Chapter 2, On the Conditions of Marriage, Its Pillars, and Its Rules, and Articles 5, 6, and 7. Source: Muhammad Qadri's *Al-Ahkam al-Shar'iyya*, 2d ed. (Bulaq: al-Matba'a al-Amiriyya, 1881)

Choices and Elisions

What effect did Qadri's (re)construction of Hanafi jurisprudence as positive law have on the substance of the law? As Peters noted, Qadri selected among multiple opinions within the Hanafi school of law in order to state a single rule on a given question, as was called for in a statutory code. Peters illustrated this point by comparing Qadri's personal status code with a popular juridical text of the Ottoman period on the question of a woman's right to arrange and contract a marriage on her own. This, as we have already seen, was a contentious issue. The juridical text was Damad Afandi's (d. 1667) *Majma' al-Anhur fi Sharh Multaqa al-Abhur*, an explication of a compendium of Hanafi law by Ibrahim al-Halabi (d. 1549),[46] which in style and arrangement was similar to Ibn Abdin's *Radd al-Muhtar*.

Damad Afandi included three contrasting opinions in his discussion of this question. The first opinion was that a legally capable woman had an absolute right to marry on her own except in the case of a misalliance due to the unsuitability of the groom, in which case her guardian could petition a judge for an annulment. The second opinion held all such misalliances to be invalid regardless of whether they were contested. According to the third opinion the validity of any marriage contracted by a woman on her own was contingent on the guardian's approval.[47] A legally capable woman (*mukallafa*, the term used in the Hanafi school) was one who was free and had reached the age of discretion. Her marriage guardian was the most qualified male relation, starting with her father, then her paternal grandfather, and then her agnates in the order of inheritance. A suitable (*kuf'*) groom was someone of equal or higher status than she. The practical difference between the three opinions was that, according to the first one, a misalliance contracted by a woman on her own was legally valid and in effect unless or until annulled by a judge at the request of her guardian. If the guardian raised no objection until she gave birth, then his ability to oppose the marriage was void. Thus if someone in a misalliance died, then in the first opinion the survivor would inherit from the deceased. In the second opinion the survivor would not inherit since any misalliance was invalid. In the third opinion, any self-marriage was invalid without the approval of the guardian, even if the groom were suitable, and so the survivor would not inherit.

Damad Afandi signaled the preferred opinion by weighing each of these views in its historical context. The first opinion was in "the authoritative doctrine" (*zahir al-riwaya*) attributed to the eponymous founder of the Hanafi school, Abu Hanifa (d. 767), and his principal student Abu Yusuf (d. 798). The second opinion was attributed to Abu Hanifa by a later figure who heard it related by Abu Yusuf. It became the preferred opinion by the twelfth century, and prominent scholars still endorsed it in the sixteenth century. It was considered the prudent view, since among other things not all guardians were effective in opposing misalliances and not all judges were just. The evident concern was to protect the interest of the patriline from a rash decision by a woman. The third opinion was expressed by Muhammad al-Shaybani (d. 805), the most prominent student of Abu Yusuf. Damad Afandi made it clear that al-Shaybani's opinion did not come from Abu Hanifa, indicating that it should be treated with circumspection.[48] Thus the second opinion was preferred.

Writing a little over a century later and commenting on a different text, Ibn Abdin took up the same question but presented only the first two of the above opinions,[49] apparently giving too little credit to the third one to include it. Ibn Abdin did not differ from Damad Afandi on the first opinion and in accepting the second opinion as the preferred one. However, he qualified that by saying that a misalliance contracted by a woman on her own was invalid in three of four scenarios: first, when the guardian was informed of the prospective groom and refused to agree to him; second, when the guardian was not consulted; and third, when the guardian agreed to the groom without knowledge of his unsuitability. In the fourth scenario, the marriage was valid when the guardian agreed to the prospective groom in full knowledge of his unsuitability. The agreement of the guardian had to be before the marriage; afterward it would not suffice.[50]

In responding to questions regarding misalliances arranged by women on their own, the Grand Mufti al-Abbasi ruled consistently in accord with the second opinion, identifying it as the recommended one in language similar to that used by Damad Afandi and Ibn Abdin.[51] Considering the case of a high born woman descended from the Prophet who married a "common . . . lowly, and vulgar" man against the wishes of her agnates, he noted that in the authoritative doctrine of the Hanafi school this marriage would be in effect but it would be annulled at the request of her guardian if she had not yet given birth. However, the preferred opinion (*al-mukhtar*) as well as the recommended one (*alayhi al-fatwa*) was the noneffectiveness of the marriage due to the "corruption of the times," which was another way in which the second opinion was justified.[52]

The opinion adopted by Qadri in his code was the same one endorsed by Damad Afandi, Ibn Abdin, and al-Abbasi, though he included the additional point raised by Ibn Abdin. The rule he set down was that a free and sane woman of age, whether a virgin or not, could contract her own marriage without the mediation of a guardian, and that the marriage would be effective if the husband were suitable and the dower at the going rate. But if she married an unsuitable groom without the clear and prior agreement of her agnatic guardian, then the marriage was impermissible from the beginning, and the subsequent agreement of the guardian would not suffice. Her marriage to an unsuitable groom was permissible only if agreed to in advance by her guardian or if she had no agnatic guardian at all.[53] Although he adopted the preferred opinion of his time, Qadri elided discussion of the alternative opinions. The purpose of his code was to make a definitive statement of the legal rules as a guide for legal practitioners.

A question that casts additional light on Qadri's method of choosing among multiple opinions concerned the prerogative of a man to remove his wife to a domicile away from her hometown or village or, as the issue was usually formulated, "to travel with her." In the authoritative doctrine of the school, a man who paid the prompt portion of the dower had an unqualified right to move his wife elsewhere. Later opinions restricted that prerogative, invoking "the corruption of the times." Scholars in the tenth through the twelfth centuries held that a married woman could not be compelled to move or to travel without her consent.[54] Some scholars in the later Middle Ages and the Ottoman period inclined toward permitting a man to move his wife a relatively short distance, described variously as less than from a city to a village, or to a nearby village that one could go to and return before nightfall.[55] The Egyptian mufti al-Shurunbulali (d. 1659) supported the latter view, casting doubt on the opinion that she could be moved farther.[56] The juridical discussion referred to unscrupulous men who exploited women whom they removed far from their families, and suggested the social and psychological difficulties a woman faced when removed from familiar surroundings and placed among strangers.[57]

After an extensive review of the opinions on this question, Ibn Abdin identified the last one as the preponderant opinion. A married woman could be compelled to move only a relatively short distance, less than from a city to a village or else to a village less than a day trip away. Nevertheless, he argued against adhering rigidly to that rule, saying that cases like these ought to be decided by a mufti on their specific merits. A woman might be harmed by being removed from her hometown, he wrote, but it was not necessarily true in every case, and also a man might be harmed by having to move without his wife.[58]

Al-Abbasi usually ruled that a man was permitted to move his wife a distance less than *masafat al-qasr*.[59] *Masafat al-qasr* is the minimum distance someone must intend to travel to permit them to abbreviate their prayers. In the Hanafi school it was a journey of three days at a normal speed, and according to modern scholars the equivalent of 82 kilometers or 51 miles.[60] That was considerably more than the day trip permitted by jurists as recently as the eighteenth century. It is not clear when or how *masafat al-qasr* came to be the distance short of which a man could move his wife without her consent, but courts in nineteenth-century Palestine also applied that standard.[61]

However, in at least one decision on this issue al-Abbasi abandoned what he otherwise regarded as the preferred opinion. The case involved a man who moved with his wife from Cairo to the city of Tanta in the middle of Lower Egypt, after paying the advance portion of the dower and consummating the marriage. Tanta was a distance greater than *masafat al-qasr* from Cairo,[62] but she did not object to the move. After some time he desired to move back to Cairo, but she refused to accompany him. The question was whether she could be compelled to go with him, or in other words whether she could be declared disobedient if she persisted in her refusal, which would relieve him of the obligation of her maintenance. Shaykh al-Abbasi began his answer by noting that there had been differences of opinion on this question. He cited the authoritative doctrine, namely that he could travel with her, and the subsequent opinion that he could do so only with her consent. Then he quoted at length Ibn Abdin's argument that each case should be considered by a mufti on its merits to determine the potential for harm. The quotation concluded with a situation that Ibn Abdin had foreseen if the second opinion was applied literally at all times. A man's wife might consent to accompany him to Mecca for the pilgrimage, and if they stayed there awhile she could refuse to return with him to their hometown. Ibn Abdin concluded that scenario with the rhetorical question, "Would any [jurist] rule that he leave her by herself to do whatever she wanted?" Al-Abbasi added, "His intent is that from [the scenario] the answer to what happened shall be understood, and God the Exalted knows best!"[63] Thus in certain circumstances al-Abbasi was willing to waive the rule that limited the distance a married woman could be compelled to move.

This is how Qadri formulated the issue in his personal status code: "The husband is permitted, if he is trustworthy and he paid the woman the prompt dower, to move her from where he married her, so long as it is less than *masafat al-qasr*, regardless of whether the move is from city to city, or city to village, or the opposite. He may not compel her to move the distance of *masafat al-qasr* nor more than that, even if he has paid her the entire dower."[64] Here again, Qadri adhered to the preferred opinion of his time, eliding other opinions, including Ibn Abdin's argument for judicial discretion in these questions.

On the Husband's Marital Authority

Another important difference between Qadri's personal status code and the Hanafi juridical literature was in the organization of the topics. Just as Sautayra and Cherbonneau had done when translating parts of the *Mukhtasar* of Khalil, Qadri organized his code to conform broadly to the order of topics in the sections of the French Civil Code that dealt with marriage and divorce. Book I of Qadri's code, "On Marriage," corresponded with Title V of the Civil Code, "Of Marriage." Qadri's Book II, "On That Which Is Due Each of the Spouses from the Other," corresponded with chapter 6 of Title V in the Civil Code, "Of the Respective Rights and Duties of Married Persons." Subsequent Books in Qadri's code on divorce, children, and guardianship came in the same order as their equivalent titles in the Civil Code.[65] The content of the articles in Qadri's code on marriage and divorce conformed to the standard Hanafi texts, often including the sequence of topics. However, Qadri's Book II had no equivalent in those texts, in which marital entitlements and obligations were mentioned in separate chapters. For example, in Ibn Abdin's *Radd al-Muhtar*, the exercise of the husband's authority over his wife after payment of the advance portion of the dower was discussed in The Book of Marriage, but his obligation to provide maintenance was discussed in a separate chapter at the end of The Book of Divorce.

In assembling the sixty-seven articles comprising Book II, Qadri may have drawn from the precolonial manuals on marital relations that juxtaposed the entitlements and obligations of husbands and wives. The first chapter in Book II addressed the husband's obligation of good conduct with his wife, which consisted of treating her properly and companionately and providing her with maintenance comprising food, clothing, and lodging. He was obligated to have sexual relations with his wife at least once during the marriage. The rest of the chapter (and the majority of the articles in it) consisted of the regulations for treating plural wives equitably. The next chapter discussed in detail the maintenance the husband was obligated to provide his wife upon the completion of the marriage contract, how to determine the amount of the maintenance, and the circumstances in which the wife forfeited her entitlement to it by an act of "disobedience" (*nushuz*). Consistent with Hanafi jurisprudence, she lost her entitlement to maintenance while disobedient and recovered it when she returned to obedience. This chapter also dealt with the issue of the husband who was absent without leaving adequate money or provisions for the maintenance of his dependents. His possessions and any debts owed him could be taken for maintenance. If he left nothing and his wife was not disobedient, a judge could determine the maintenance he owed, and it would begin to accrue as a debt against him. But if she requested an annulment it was to be denied.[66]

There was no difference between these rules and the decisions of the Grand Mufti al-Abbasi. Decades earlier Ibn Abdin had explicated the rule that a Hanafi judge could implement an annulment decided by a Shafi'i deputy judge in the case of an absent or missing husband, and in the late nineteenth century the Ottomans allowed some of these cases to be decided using Shafi'i jurisprudence.[67] However, the Egyptian procedural laws required strict adherence to Hanafi law.

The third chapter of Book II, entitled "On the Authority of the Husband and His Entitlements," is an interesting example of how Qadri addressed the provisions of the French code while stating the Hanafi law. It began with Article 206:

> The authority (*wilaya*) of the husband over the wife is disciplinary, for he has no authority over her personal wealth and moreover she may dispose of all of it without his permission or agreement, and without him having a cause for opposing her on the basis of his authority. She may collect the earnings of her properties, engage agents other than her husband to manage her interests, and her contracts are legally valid without depending on his permission at all, nor the permission of her father or grandfather or their trustee in the event of his [the husband's] loss, if she is of the age of discretion and capable of managing [her own affairs].[68]

This article addressed directly some of the effects of the marital authority of the husband in French law (*puissance maritale*), which was that upon marriage a woman entered a state of legal tutelage or incapacity, as if she were a minor. The Napoleonic Code gave her husband control of her property and any earnings, and his permission was necessary for her to engage in contracts or to testify in court.[69] The term "authority" (*wilaya*) did not appear often in Hanafi discussions of the marital relationship, and only in reference to his authority to discipline her for disobedience.[70] Thus in order to express the sense of the unfamiliar French legal term *puissance maritale*, Qadri resorted to a word used infrequently and in a narrower context in Hanafi jurisprudence, rendering it in Arabic as *wilayat al-zawj ala al-mar'a* or "the authority of the husband over the wife."[71]

A Muslim married woman did not incur legal disability, as Article 206 made clear, though she was subject to her husband's discipline (*ta'dib*) or "correction," as it was expressed in contemporary French and English.[72] Subsequent articles in this section explained that the husband was allowed to discipline his wife "lightly" for acts of disobedience for which no punishments were specified in the law, but he was not permitted to strike her violently on any account.[73]

The husband's other prerogatives were, like his disciplinary authority, contingent on payment of the advance dower. These included, first, the ability to restrict his wife to the marital domicile, as stated in Article 207: "The husband, after providing the wife with the advance portion of her dower, may forbid her from going out of his house without his permission in circumstances other than those in which she is allowed to go out, such as visiting her parents once each week and her close relatives once each year. He may forbid her from visiting female non-relations and attending their celebrations, and from going out to feasts even at the home of close relatives."[74] Here the husband's ability to forbid his wife from leaving the house was stated as an absolute right without reference to the rules of maintenance, which were stated separately in the preceding chapter of the code. This was the double standard in the maintenance-obedience relationship that Aisha al-Taymur highlighted in *Mir'at al-Ta'ammul* nearly twenty years later. That is, a married woman who was "disobedient," say by going out without the permission of her husband, risked at least a temporary loss of maintenance, while the failure of a man to provide maintenance did not entitle his wife to disobedience. However, in al-Abbasi's fatwas and court records of the era a judge would not issue an order of obedience to a recalcitrant wife unless her husband pledged to provide her maintenance.[75]

Payment of the advance dower also enabled a man to remove his wife from her father's house to his own, if she were mature enough for sexual relations, and provided his house was in a good location and less than a distance of *masafat al-qasr*.[76] These rules differed from contemporary French law, which had a higher minimum age of marriage but obliged the wife to live with her husband wherever he chose.[77]

The fourth and last chapter in Book II was "On the Entitlements and Obligations of the Wife." The obligations of the wife to her husband were discussed in Article 212:

> The obligations of the wife to her husband include her being obedient to him in those marital duties he orders her to perform and which are legally permissible, and to restrict herself to remaining in his house, after his payment to her of the advance dower, and not to go out from it except with his permission, and to be quick to go to his bed if he requests her after that [i.e., after payment of the advance dower] when

she has no legal excuse, and to guard herself, and to protect his property and not to give any of it to anyone that it is not customary to give except with his permission.[78]

As in Article 207, by virtue of receiving the advance portion of the dower the wife incurred the obligation to submit herself to her husband and to obey him. Until she received it she could refuse sexual intercourse and refuse to leave her home to reside with him. If she took up residence with him, she could still go out of the house without his permission until he paid her the advance dower. After receiving the dower she was entitled to visit her family and to receive visits from them, and to tend to an ill parent if the parent had no one else to look after them.[79]

Al-Ibyani's Explication of Qadri's Code

In 1893 the School of Law published a *sharh*, or explication, of Qadri's code by Muhammad Zayd al-Ibyani (1862–1936), a member of the faculty who had been using it for some years to teach personal status law.[80] Between 1893 and 1924 al-Ibyani's *Sharh* had no fewer than six printings in four editions, and a *mukhtasar* or condensation of it had at least five printings in four editions, which indicates that both were widely used in the early twentieth century.

There was a long tradition of composing explications of important juridical texts and, subsequently, condensations of and commentaries on the explications. Explications such as the one by Damad Afandi on al-Halabi, or by al-Haskafi on al-Timurtashi (which was followed by Ibn Abdin's commentary on al-Haskafi), reviewed the history of the discussion of each question, often including contradictory opinions, before arriving at a preferred opinion. That method informed the reader that the preferred opinion was the contingent result of the reasoning of fallible scholars. But al-Ibyani's explication of Qadri's code did not fit that mold. It made no reference to the history of juridical discussion and debate leading up to the formulation of the rules Qadri listed. Rather, al-Ibyani glossed the articles in the code with references to Qur'anic verses, hadiths, and the opinions of Abu Hanifa, Abu Yusuf, and Muhammad al-Shaybani. He utilized subsequent opinions but without attribution to the jurists who developed them, in contrast to the careful method typical of late Ottoman-era religious scholars. Readers lacking solid training in Muslim jurisprudence would not have realized that these were the opinions of later scholars, nor was it apparent that the opinions were the result of a contingent historical process of discussion and debate. Al-Ibyani was aware that most of his readers would be nonspecialists. Qadri's code, he wrote in his introduction, was intended for easy comprehension by those who were unfamiliar with the mode of expression of the jurists, but it was not always free of the sometimes obscure language of the sources on which it was based, which justified the production of a *sharh*.[81] Indeed the majority of literate Egyptians, including many of the political and literary elite, were unfamiliar with the mode of expression of the jurists. They would have been unable to recognize the original context of the opinions that al-Ibyani selected for emphasis.[82] Al-Ibyani's method of explication, I suggest, had the opposite effect of the method employed historically by Muslim jurists. It imbued Qadri's code and his own explication with a sacred authority. If the historical Muslim jurisprudence presented an open-ended discussion, Qadri's code, and especially al-Ibyani's explication, closed off discussion.

An example of this can be found in al-Ibyani's explication of the rule mentioned in Articles 207 and 212 that a husband who had paid his wife the advance dower could forbid her to go out of the house with limited exceptions. One of the most important of those exceptions, mentioned only in Article 207, was her ability to go out on weekly visits to her parents and pay an annual visit to her other close relations. In his explication of Article 207 al-Ibyani added this qualification:

> According to Abu Yusuf her going out is conditional on the inability [of her parents] to come [to visit] her and so if they are capable of that then she should not go out. It is an acceptable opinion (*hasan*), for if their going out might not inconvenience them and her going out will be troublesome for the husband, then she is forbidden, for in frequent outings the door of *fitna* is opened, especially if she is a young woman and the husband is someone of standing, as opposed to the going out of [her

parents], for it is easier. Therefore it should be investigated whether there is no harm in someone's going out, and they shall [be permitted to] go out, and the other shall be forbidden.[83]

The word *fitna* means temptation, discord, and strife, and Egyptians still invoke the specter of *fitna* to warn against the consequences of immodest public behavior by women.

Qadri's Article 207 appears to have been based upon the view of Ibn Nujaym, who held that a married woman was permitted to go out to visit her parents once a week and her close relatives once a year with or without her husband's permission. As usual, though, there were differences over this question. It was an earlier Egyptian jurist, Ibn al-Humam (d. 1456–57), who stated that if her parents were unable to visit her a woman's husband "should give her permission to visit them from time to time in accord with general norms," but to do so every Friday would be excessive, "for in frequent outings the door of *fitna* is opened, especially if she is a young woman and the husband is someone of standing, as opposed to the going out of [her] parents, for it is easier."[84]

Qadri's preference for the opinion of Ibn Nujaym was probably consistent with the view of contemporary Egypt jurists, to judge from his method of selection of opinions in other issues.[85] He likely would have disagreed with al-Ibyani's explication. Be that as it may, al-Ibyani used the words of Ibn al-Human without attribution, leaving the impression that they represented the view of Abu Yusuf, and his use of Ibn al-Human's words shifted their emphasis from instructing the husband to permit his wife to go out to see her parents, if necessary, to discouraging the husband from permitting his wife to go out at all. Thus in al-Ibyani's explication the right of the husband to forbid his wife from going out of the home was more absolute than it was in Qadri's code.

Continuing his explication of Article 207, and after reviewing all of the situations in which a married woman might or might not be permitted to go out of the home, al-Ibyani added: "In every situation in which we permit her to go out, she is permitted on condition of not adorning herself nor altering her appearance in a way that would attract the gaze of men and garner attraction, on account of the words of the Exalted, 'and display not your finery, as did the pagans of old.'"[86] Those words were taken almost verbatim from Ibn al-Humam: "Whereas we permit her to go out, she is permitted on condition of not adorning herself nor altering her appearance in a way that would attract the gaze of men and garner attraction. The Exalted said, 'and display not your finery, as did the pagans of old.'"[87] Ibn al-Humam's words appeared in his chapter on maintenance together with a list of the demands a husband could make of his wife in return for payment of it. The Qur'anic verse was addressed to the wives of the Prophet, who were admonished in the preceding verse that they "are not as other women" (33:32). But in conservative circles this was upheld as exemplary behavior for all women.

It bears repeating that juridical discussions like these did not reflect everyday reality, rather they expressed an ideal that influenced popular attitudes. Malak Hifni Nasif captured a version of that reality when she wrote, "Isn't it odd that we see our young women being disgraced daily in the breadth of the streets, crowding the sales shops, and shamelessly doing everything conceivable, for they speak to the tram conductor and stand leaning and exposing their bosoms immodestly in front of the photographer, but if a prospective enlightened fiancé asks a young woman's father to permit him to see her and speak with her with her father chaperoning them that is considered a horrible thing."[88] Women were getting out but respectable families were still reluctant to agree to prenuptial meetings between their daughters and prospective husbands. Even though she was critical of immodest behavior, Nasif opposed what she called the "extremism" of some families that would not let women out of the house for visits,[89] which indicates that at least some families attempted to live according to the norm that al-Ibyani articulated.

Al-Ibyani broke no new ground in interpretation, though he inclined toward conservatism on the question of the freedom of mobility of married women. His method of referring only to the Qur'an, hadiths, and the founder-scholars of the Hanafi school conferred a sacral authority on Qadri's code and his own explication. The rules in Qadri's code and al-Ibyani's explication of them were derived from centuries of jurisprudence, but to the uninitiated they appeared to come directly from the Qur'an, the Sunna, and the founders of the Hanafi school of law.

Codification and the Legacy of Qadri's Personal Status Code

The codification of Muslim family law in twentieth-century Egypt was a gradual and piecemeal process. Codes governing marriage and divorce were enacted in 1920, 1923, and 1929, and inheritance and bequests in 1943 and 1946. The drafters of these laws adopted the method of *takhayyur* to incorporate non-Hanafi jurisprudence on various points, but Hanafi doctrines remained the basis of family law, and the predominant opinion of the Hanafi school applied to any questions not addressed directly in the codes. Beginning in the 1920s a number of professors in the School of Law (which became the Faculty of Law of Cairo University) published their own texts on Muslim personal status law. The latter studies tended more often to include the references to the juridical literature that al-Ibyani elided. A recent edition of Qadri's code includes al-Ibyani's *Sharh* but also the appropriate juridical discussions in the four schools.[90] Thus recent scholarship has to some extent restored the study of Muslim family law to its historical juridical context. The inclusion of the jurisprudence of the four schools invites readers and, potentially, legislators to practice *takhayyur*, whereby some of the flexibility of the old system of legal pluralism can be recovered. However, latter-day scholars seem to be committed to preserving the predominant view in each school as it was in the nineteenth century. The discussion and debate that was characteristic of historical jurisprudence has ceased.

Although this chapter has examined Qadri's code mainly in an Egyptian context, it was part of a transnational process of selective codification of the Sharia that included colonial translations of key texts, selective and reordered translations like Sautayra and Cherbonneau's code-like rendering of the *Mukhtasar* of Khalil, and, eventually, actual codes incorporating Shariatic principles. Translation and codification contributed to the end of discussion and debate within the schools. As Robert Crews noted in his study of Islam and the Russian Empire, codification promoted a new understanding of Sharia "as a uniform and static 'law' whose meanings were fixed in texts and codes."[91]

Another enduring legacy of the judicial reorganization of the nineteenth century was the close association of the family with religion and religious law. This was a contingent development and neither inevitable nor an expression of "the centrality of the family in Islam,"[92] as is often claimed. "The family," understood to be a related domestic group, is an artifact of the nineteenth century. Colonial scholarship produced the idea that family law is the "heart" of the Sharia. The narrowing of the jurisdiction of the Sharia Courts to family affairs was contingent on local politics, influenced by the example of Algeria, and in conformity with transnational trends. Since the late nineteenth century the association of religion and the domestic realm has obliged those proposing the reform of family law to invoke Qur'anic verses, hadiths, and jurisprudence for support. To be sure, proponents of change have also appealed to the changing times and modern values, but even the most recent reforms in the personal status law have been justified (as well as opposed) on religious grounds. The widespread acceptance of the idea that religion should govern family relationships has contributed to the persistence of the maintenance-obedience relationship in law and social norms.

6

Marriage Modernized?
The Curious History of "House of Obedience"

For many Egyptian women the maintenance-obedience relationship was epitomized in the term "house of obedience" (*bayt al-taʿa*), which refers to the obligation of the wife to obey her husband, and especially to reside with him. Those of a certain age can still recall when that obligation was enforceable by the state authorities. A man whose wife left him could obtain a judicial order of obedience (*hukm al-taʿa*) instructing her to return, and, if she refused, he could request the police to execute the order, returning her by force if necessary. The Ministry of Justice suspended the execution of orders of obedience by the police only in 1967, after decades of campaigning against it by feminists and liberal men.[1]

Among Egyptians it is commonplace that enforcement of house of obedience was a retrograde custom left over from an unenlightened past. In reality it was a modern practice without precedent in custom or Muslim family law. It originated in France, where courts enforced the duty of a married woman to live with her husband wherever he chose by authorizing the police to return runaway wives to their husbands. It migrated into Algerian jurisprudence during the colonial-era reorganization of the Sharia Courts, becoming indigenized as a feature of Muslim Algerian law. French colonial knowledge of Muslim family law was the likely vector of its transmission to Egypt. In Egypt the enforcement of orders of obedience was sanctioned in Article 93 of the procedural law of 1897. It stated that "the execution of a decision [ordering] the obedience of a wife (*al-hukm bi-taʿat al-zawja*), keeping a child in the custody of a close relation (*mahram*), separating two spouses, and the like having to do with personal status, may be by compulsion (*qahran*) even if it leads to the use of force and entry into houses." The article went on to direct the administrative personnel to follow the instructions given by the Sharia Court in such cases.[2]

This chapter situates the enforcement of house of obedience in the context of the "modernization" of marriage. Rather than a comprehensive history, the aim is to locate its origin and to trace its indigenization in Egypt.

House of obedience was a concept in precolonial Muslim jurisprudence, but its enforcement by the state was an expression of several of the social, ideological, and legal processes of change discussed in the preceding chapters. In the late nineteenth century modernist writers, religious officials, and civil servants raised concerns over the fate of the family. The conjugal family, the elemental unit in society, had to be protected for the sake of the nation, and so it was deemed appropriate for the state to enforce the maintenance-obedience relationship. Irresponsible husbands caused more concern than disobedient wives, and so the procedural laws permitted the garnishment of the wages and property of men who failed to maintain their dependents, as well as their imprisonment. The enforcement of orders of wifely obedience was of less concern; the earliest discussion of it that I found was in Abduh's report on the reform of the Sharia Courts, published three years after the procedural law of 1897. Orders of obedience as well as those concerning child custody and the separation of illicit couples[3] were evidently difficult to enforce in the face of resistance by families and due to the sanctity of their homes. Thus the police were authorized to carry out those orders by entering homes and using force.

Enforcement of house of obedience was one outcome of state centralization and the expansion of its managerial role in family affairs, which by the turn of the century included civil registration of marriages and divorces as well as enforcement of other aspects of the maintenance-obedience relationship. That development overlapped with a second factor, namely the articulation of a family ideology that emphasized the importance of the conjugal family and its role in childrearing, and the corollary domestic ideology, which fit with the maintenance-obedience relationship. Although Qasim Amin advocated against the "confinement" of women, and respectable women were reportedly venturing out more often, that was ostensibly with the permission of their male guardians. According to handbooks like al-Nawawi's *Sharh Uqud al-Lujayn*, which was still in circulation, men were entitled to restrain the mobility of their wives.

A third and closely related factor was the changing understanding of Muslim family law among civil officials. Qadri's influential code of personal status, designed in the form of a European code, stated mainstream Hanafi legal norms as positive law and elided the historical discussion that produced them, including the variant opinions. The rules in Qadri's code, including the duty of a married woman to remain at home, consequently appeared to be more absolute than they were in the juridical discussions, and al-Ibyani's explication sacralized those rules. The civil officials who drafted Article 93 of the 1897 law were exposed to Muslim family law mainly through Qadri's code. They very likely also were influenced by French-Algerian writings on personal status law. Thus the transnational circulation of colonial knowledge of Muslim family law was a fourth factor in the composition of Article 93. Ironically, the French courts abandoned the practice of forcibly returning runaway wives to their husbands by the end of the nineteenth century, and afterward it survived as an indigenized practice in North Africa, Egypt, and other parts of the Muslim world. In the next century European scholars regarded it as a Muslim tradition, and conservative Muslims defended it as sanctioned by revelation.

A Marital Dispute in Alexandria

A marital dispute that became a public scandal in Alexandria in the early twentieth century offers us a vantage point on the complicated genealogy of house of obedience in Egyptian law. The dispute involved a conditional divorce allegedly declared by Shaykh Ahmad Sulayman Basha to his wife Nafisa Dhuhni.[4] Nafisa claimed that Shaykh Ahmad declared that if she left his house on Muharram Bey Street she would be "free of his custody" (*khalisa min ismatihi*), an expression meaning that she would be irrevocably divorced. In the event she left and went to stay with her brother, Mustafa Dhuhni Bey, several blocks away in al-Raml, in February 1902. Then she petitioned the Sharia Court to recognize the divorce.[5]

Both husband and wife were from prominent families. Shaykh Ahmad and his brothers were among the senior ulama of Alexandria, and Nafisa's brother and their late father were government employees with the title of *bey*.⁶ Families of this stature were normally loath to air their dirty linen in public, but to gain legal recognition of her divorce Nafisa had to sue in the Sharia Court to establish that the conditional divorce had been declared and that the condition had been fulfilled. Men often tried to control the behavior of their wives by swearing conditional divorces, as we saw previously, and forbidding them to go out of the house or to the house of a relative was one of the more common tactics. Lawsuits of the kind raised by Nafisa were also not unusual, since for some women these oaths of conditional divorce offered an opportunity to be freed from an unpleasant marital situation. Shaykh Ahmad contested the alleged divorce in the Sharia Court, and while doing so he took advantage of his status as a protégé of France to sue Nafisa in the French consular court for abandoning the marital domicile.⁷ Invoking her duty of obedience, he asked the court to order her to return immediately and to authorize the use of force if she refused.⁸ The consular court issued its verdict in early April, ordering Nafisa to return to the house of her husband. Two months later the Sharia Court also ruled against Nafisa due to her inability to produce witnesses to verify that the alleged oath of conditional divorce had been uttered.

The scandal that ensued was not caused by Nafisa's suit but by Shaykh Ahmad's countersuit. Ali Yusuf, editor of the popular newspaper *al-Mu'ayyad*, turned this case into a cause célèbre. From the public reading of the verdict of the consular court in April to the decision of the Sharia Court in June, *al-Mu'ayyad* rallied public opinion against the involvement of the French consular court in a personal status case concerning Muslim Egyptians. The opening salvo was an article titled "French Consulate Seizure of the Judicature of the Islamic Sharia." This and subsequent articles hammered on the theme that the French consulate had arrogated to itself the power to make decisions on intimate matters involving the personal status of Muslim Egyptians, where it had no business. *Al-Mu'ayyad* criticized Shaykh Ahmad for resorting to the consular court, but its main theme was the interference of a foreign, Christian power in matters of "the Islamic Sharia."⁹ The term "personal status" appeared in these articles without any explanation, evidence that the readership was by then familiar with this term.

In addition to the relevant court records, the articles in *al-Mu'ayyad* offer a detailed portrait of the relationship between Nafisa and Shaykh Ahmad, albeit a one-sided one, for Nafisa (or more likely her lawyer) used the columns of *al-Mu'ayyad* to generate public sympathy. She agreed to return to Shaykh Ahmad after the Sharia Court ruled against her, but only after publishing her personal account of the affair.[10] In it she wrote that she was previously married to Shaykh Ibrahim Sulayman Basha, a brother of Shaykh Ahmad who died in 1890. The deceased had named Shaykh Ahmad as the guardian of her daughter Zaynab. She was persuaded to appoint another brother, Shaykh Muhammad, as her legal agent, but after marrying Shaykh Ahmad she named him as her legal agent. Not long after that she learned that Shaykh Muhammad and Shaykh Ahmad had connived to persuade her to release (*takharuj*) her portion of her late husband's estate to his two children, namely Zaynab and Ali,[11] Ibrahim's son by Nafisa's co-wife. Nafisa claimed that in doing so the brothers took advantage of her lack of knowledge of affairs and her state of grief. The release was recorded informally and not registered in the court until after her marriage to Shaykh Ahmad, which is when Nafisa realized she had been deceived. That, she wrote, was when she left Shaykh Ahmad the first time.

Thereafter the couple reconciled, though Nafisa also alleged that Shaykh Ahmad, as her husband and agent, mismanaged the property she inherited from her late father, so that she became virtually penniless. Now, a decade later, Nafisa received another shock when she was informed of a marriage contract betrothing her daughter Zaynab to the son of Shaykh Ahmad by another wife, Zaynab's first cousin Abd al-Latif. The contract had been made between Shaykh Ibrahim, Zaynab's late father, and Shaykh Ahmad. There was a tradition of endogamous marriage in that family, Nafisa wrote, which was their way of preserving the family's wealth. But she said she wanted her daughter to marry someone with whom she would be happy, regardless of whether he was from the family.

Nafisa left Shaykh Ahmad a second time over the issue of Zaynab's marriage in February 1902, presumably taking Zaynab with her. In March, at about the same time that Shaykh Ahmad brought his obedience suit against Nafisa in the consular court, his son Abd al-Latif sued Zaynab in the Sharia Court to oblige her to join him as his wife in his home. Zaynab countered with a suit in the National Court alleging that her late father's signature on the contract of marriage was a forgery. Abd al-Latif and several witnesses who signed the contract were convicted of forgery, but the verdict was reversed upon appeal, and in March 1903 Zaynab had no choice but to accept the legality of her marriage to Abd al-Latif.[12] In Hanafi law the father of a minor had the authority to marry her or him off without their consent, and so neither Zaynab nor her mother could contest the contract once her father's signature and seal were authenticated.

This family drama posed a number of issues regarding marriage and women that had begun to be discussed publicly during the previous decades. Three years earlier Qasim Amin had argued in *Tahrir al-Mar'a* that an education would enable women like Nafisa to handle their own affairs and to avoid being taken advantage of, as she claimed had been done by her second husband and her brother-in-law. Her daughter Zaynab's marriage seemed to epitomize the evils of child marriage and marriages of convenience as opposed to the merits of companionate marriage.[13] Nafisa or her lawyer may have tailored her account of the affair to evoke those issues in a bid for public sympathy, but that would indicate the extent to which those ideas were being aired in the press and the ground they had gained.

However, *al-Mu'ayyad* focused its indignation almost entirely on the issue of foreign intervention in an Egyptian personal status case. For Ali Yusuf, the editor, the overriding issue was national sovereignty and non-interference in Muslim affairs, not the rights of women or the need to reform marriage practices. But the consular court applied Muslim family law in its ruling, not French law, a point that *al-Mu'ayyad* omitted in its coverage of the case. In its decision the consular court asserted its jurisdiction in cases involving French nationals, including Muslims, and it asserted the competence of French consular courts in Muslim personal status cases.[14] Left unstated was the source of that competence: the body of French legal scholarship on Muslim family law and the availability of translations of certain legal texts, on the basis of which French magistrates had heard appeals from the Algerian Sharia Courts for decades. In the case of Shaykh Ahmad and Nafisa the consular court applied Muhammad Qadri's code of personal status, which it described as forbidding a married woman from leaving the marital domicile without permission: "Whereas this law in its article 212 forbids the woman from leaving the conjugal domicile without authorization."[15] That reading reflected an understanding of Qadri's article 212 as positive law. It stated that a married woman was obliged "to restrict herself to remaining in [her husband's] house ... and not to go out from it except with his permission," but it did not mention physical restraint. In ruling that Nafisa must return to the house of Shaykh Ahmad, the consular court drew on knowledge of Muslim family law that had developed in Algerian jurisprudence.[16]

In addition to *al-Mu'ayyad* the Egyptian government objected to the involvement of the consular court in this case, and the Ministry of Interior instructed the Alexandria municipality not to enforce the consular court's ruling that Nafisa must return to Shaykh Ahmad. Neither the government nor *al-Mu'ayyad* raised an objection to the idea of the police using force to return Nafisa to her husband, which was authorized in the 1897 law. However, the legal journal *al-Ahkam al-Shar'iyya* was indignant at the possibility that she might be brought back to the house of her husband, "cowering [and] humiliated, surrounded by police armed to the teeth to prevent her from fleeing."[17]

The Wife's Duty of Obedience in Muslim Family Law

In the applied Muslim family law of the Ottoman era, as represented in legal commentaries and fatwa collections from the sixteenth through nineteenth centuries, a wife's duty of obedience included submitting herself to her husband and not leaving his house without his permission, with certain exceptions, contingent on payment of the prompt dower and the provision of maintenance by her husband. The ideal of a married woman keeping to the home presumed a certain level of household income. Urban working-class and rural women routinely worked in public or semipublic space, and/or they passed through public space on their way to work. The juridical literature recognized the reality and even the necessity of working women, but those women had no legal claim to maintenance if their husbands objected to their going out.[18] For example, al-Abbasi ruled that a married woman who worked as a bathhouse attendant forfeited her right to maintenance even though she returned to the marital home each day.[19] Conversely, a woman who stayed at home could petition a Sharia Court judge to determine the amount of maintenance she was owed and even to garnish her husband's wages or property for payment.[20] Thus the maintenance-obedience relationship was not a simple matter of the entitlement of the husband to the submission and obedience of the wife after paying the advance dower. He was also obliged to provide maintenance. A disobedient wife forfeited her entitlement to maintenance but she could not be restrained in the marital domicile.

The typical form of disobedience (*nushuz*) was abandonment of the marital domicile, and it was commonplace. To judge from latter-day ethnographies, young married women often returned to their natal families to air their grievances. Many if not most of these situations were resolved by the intervention of mediators.[21] Precolonial writings strongly emphasized the obligation of the wife to stay in her husband's house and not to go out without his permission, which indicates how often women violated that norm. Ibn Hajar al-Haythami discussed wifely disobedience in his book of major transgressions, and other writers invoked hadiths that said the angels would curse a disobedient wife until she returned to the obedience of her husband.[22] These rhetorical exhortations and threats in the precolonial writings, together with declarations of conditional divorce, are suggestive of the limited coercive power available to men when it came to controlling the mobility of their wives.

The Grand Mufti al-Abbasi heard numerous obedience cases, all of them involving women who left their husbands.[23] A contract of marriage and payment of the advance dower entitled a man to the obedience of his wife, including her residence with him, provided she was old enough for sexual relations. If she refused to join him or left him, he had a number of recourses. A disobedient wife might ask her husband to divorce her, though by doing so he would incur the obligation of paying her the delayed portion of her dower and temporary maintenance. Alternatively, the couple could bargain for a *khul'* or *mubara'a* divorce, in which she released him from most or all of his obligations as an inducement to divorce her.

Of course, men had the option of polygyny, and they did not have to divorce a disobedient wife to be free of responsibility for her. A man whose wife refused to live with him could petition a judge to affirm her disobedience and thereby relieve him of the obligation to provide her with maintenance. The mufti heard this case in 1849:

> Question: In the case of a woman who departed from the obedience of her husband, and he entreated her in the presence of the Sharia Court judge, so [the judge] set such-and-such an amount daily for her as maintenance and ordered her to reside with [her husband] in the place of his obedience, and he requested her to do that but she refused to obey him in the presence of Muslim witnesses: shall she be considered disobedient and [shall] the husband not be obligated to provide her with maintenance nor with clothing as long as she is disobedient? Answer: Yes, she shall be considered disobedient by that, whereas he provided her with the advance dower and the domicile was appropriate, and she is not due maintenance as long as she is like that, and God the Exalted is most knowing![24]

The same principle applied if a woman refused when her husband summoned her to reside in his house. In one such case, after a woman repeatedly refused to join her husband, the mufti ruled that she was disobedient and had no claim to maintenance as long as she persisted in her refusal.[25]

A third situation arose when the aggrieved husband declined to accept an affirmation of his wife's disobedience and persisted in demanding that she return to him. After quarreling with her mother-in-law and being struck by her husband, a woman went to stay with her mother. When asked to return she refused, requesting instead to remain in a state of disobedience—that is, to remain in her mother's house and to forfeit maintenance from her husband. But her husband refused to accept that. "And so," the mufti was asked, "if he was providing what she was legally due, shall her request be refused and shall she be obligated to obey him and to remain in his domicile by compulsion (*jabran alayha*), he having the right to domicile her in a place free of his family or of her family?" The mufti answered in the affirmative.[26] In this and similar cases in which the husband refused to accept an affirmation of his wife's disobedience, the mufti would rule that she should be "ordered" (*tu'mar*) to return to him or "compelled" (*tujabbar*) to do so. But the execution of these decisions was impossible if her family was willing to support and protect her.

Several cases illustrate the absence of means to enforce orders of obedience. Consider this fatwa from 1856:

> Question: In the case of a man who married a woman and [consummated the marriage] in the house of her father, and then after that he desired to move her to another house that was appropriate as their residence, free of his family and of her family, in the town in which he married her, but she refused to do that: whereas the husband paid her what was agreed upon as the prompt dower and he was providing what she was due legally, shall she be compelled to obey him, and if she refuses to do that shall she be disobedient so he shall not be required to provide her with maintenance and clothing? Answer: Yes, the wife shall be compelled to obey her husband, the situation being as was mentioned, and if she refuses to move with him to his legally appropriate domicile she shall be disobedient and shall have no maintenance as long as she is like that, and God the Exalted is most knowing![27]

Both the question and the answer anticipated the refusal of the woman to comply with the order of obedience. In this and similar cases it appears that so long as the family of a disobedient wife was willing to harbor her, the authorities would not enforce an order of obedience by removing her from their house.

The limited ability of the judicial and civil authorities to enforce orders of obedience was illustrated vividly in this case heard by the mufti in 1852:

> Question: In the case of a man whose wife became disobedient from him [by staying] in the house of her father for a period of two years, and the husband summoned her to his obedience in [the court], but she refused, saying, "I detest him and I do not agree to join myself and him"; and so the judge threatened her and put her in fear of a harsh beating and the civil official (*al-hakim al-siyasi*) gave her brother a harsh beating so that he would induce his sister to [return to] the obedience of the husband, but she did not agree, saying, "I will kill myself but I will not return to him," and she remained in the house of her father. And so, as the situation is this, shall she be recorded as disobedient and undeserving of maintenance, while it is not permitted to cause her pain by beating at any time until God shall unite them? Answer: There is no maintenance

due the wife as long as she is disobedient and outside of the obedience of the husband without a legal justification; she shall be ordered to obedience, and the disobedience shall not be affirmed because it is an act of insubordination. [The jurists] have explained that in every act of insubordination there is no divinely ordained punishment (*hadd*) determined, but in it there is a discretionary punishment, and it mentions in *al-Tanwir* and its explication in the chapter of discretionary punishment, "the master shall chastise his slave, and the husband his wife for her neglect of the legally prescribed adornment of which she is capable, her neglect of cleansing [herself of] impurity, upon going out of the house if she is not entitled to do so, and neglecting to answer to the bed if she is not menstruating." And God the Exalted is most knowing![28]

The authority cited in the answer was the compendium of Hanafi law by Shams al-Din Muhammad al-Timurtashi titled *Tanwir al-Absar wa Jami' al-Bihar*, which was completed in 1587. The explication mentioned was al-Haskafi's *al-Durr al-Mukhtar*, which in turn was the subject of Ibn Abdin's influential commentary, *Radd al-Muhtar*.[29] The passage quoted makes clear the view of the jurists that a husband was entitled to chastise his wife for a variety of misdeeds, including leaving the house without his permission or a legally sanctioned reason, but that a painful beating was not permitted, as the question in the fatwa stated. The obvious and therefore unmentioned reference was the commentary on the Qur'anic verse (4:34), which was interpreted as authorizing a husband to induce his wife to obedience by admonishing her, then depriving her of affection, and finally by striking her. But that was not to be done with excessive force and not on the face or another sensitive part of the body.[30]

Thus in spite of the judge's order of obedience, his attempt to frighten the woman, and the beating of her brother, she could not be coerced to join her husband. Neither the husband nor the authorities were authorized to violate the authority of a household head over his or her dependents, even if they were harboring a disobedient wife. In another case the mufti mentioned that an appropriate discretionary punishment could be prescribed by the judge to bring an end to the insubordination of a disobedient wife. But again there was no suggestion of how the punishment could be meted out, nor that the woman could be returned to her husband by force.[31]

It should be emphasized that the maintenance-obedience relationship was the context in which the jurists carried on these discussions. Al-Abbasi's fatwas on this subject all appeared in his chapter on maintenance (*nafaqa*). In his commentary on the passage quoted above from al-Haskafi's chapter on discretionary punishment, Ibn Abdin directed the reader to his own chapter on maintenance, where the discussion concerned the denial of maintenance to a disobedient wife, and no other form of coercion. The forcible return of runaway wives was not sanctioned either in jurisprudence or in Egyptian judicial practice before 1897. Article 93 of the procedural law of that year introduced a significant change by authorizing the police to enforce orders of obedience by entering houses and using force.

French and Algerian Precedents

The earliest instance of the use of state power to return runaway wives to their husbands was not in a Muslim country but in France. Articles 213 and 214 of the Napoleonic code of 1804 stated that a married woman owed obedience to her husband and that she was required to live with him wherever he chose to reside.[32] A woman might be granted a legal separation for cruelty or injury, but divorce was not available to French women between 1816 and 1884. Women who left their husbands without legal justification were deprived of financial support at first, but in 1827 the Court of Cassation of Paris ruled that "[w]hen a wife has been directed by court order to return to the conjugal domicile" and refuses to comply, "police force [may] be used to return the wife to the home and to the conjugal bed."[33] The police continued to be called upon to enforce the duty of cohabitation of French wives until late in the century.[34]

The idea that a wife should obey her husband had deep roots in French culture, but the categorical requirement of obedience and cohabitation in the civil code and the sanctioning of the use of police to enforce the law were modern innovations. The involvement of the state in the return of runaway wives reflected concern for the integrity of the conjugal family, which, in the view of the French authorities, required the upholding of the husband's marital authority. Coincidentally a similar situation prevailed in Britain after the Divorce Act of 1857, in which a runaway wife could be subject to a court order of "restitution of conjugal rights," or in other words an order to return to the conjugal home. However, Britain decriminalized abandonment of the marital domicile in 1884, and in France, the Naquet law of the same year reintroduced divorce, which tended to mitigate the marital authority of men, though the relevant sections of the civil code were not revised until 1938.[35] By then the forcible return of runaway wives had migrated into Algerian jurisprudence, and it had become associated exclusively with Muslim culture.

French studies of Algerian Muslim law permit us to identify the approximate moment of that migration. In a study published in 1860, Charles Gillotte asserted that although a Muslim married woman owed "absolute submission to her husband's orders," her husband could not force her to change the location of her residence (that is, to move a great distance from her family) nor to accompany him on a trip of more than three days.[36] Evidently Gillotte found this remarkable because French law required women to accompany their husbands wherever they chose to reside. Gillotte's discussion, which followed precolonial Muslim writings similar to those in use in Egypt, exposed additional limits to the marital authority of the husband. It began by stating that a husband should use kindness to encourage his wife to fulfill her duties. While mentioning his right to enforce her obedience by denying her affection and even striking her, Gillotte devoted most of that passage to the procedure recommended when a woman complained to the Sharia Court about her treatment by her husband. It was the responsibility of the judge to hear marital disputes and to appoint mediators between the spouses.[37] Gillotte made no mention of the forcible return of runaway wives because it did not occur.

The later study by Sautayra and Cherbonneau shows how quickly things changed. They cited, for example, a decision by the Sharia Court of Constantine in 1861 that a married woman who left her husband must be returned immediately to the conjugal domicile regardless of any lawsuit she had initiated to the contrary. An 1866 decision by the Sharia Court of Mostaganem held that a married woman who refused to reside with her husband could be compelled to do so by force. Another 1866 decision by the Sharia Court in Constantine, upheld by the Court of Algiers, determined that a married woman was required "to live with her husband and to follow him wherever he decides to reside."[38] The last decision, which echoed Article 214 of the French civil code and not historical Muslim jurisprudence, clearly shows the infiltration of French legal doctrine into Muslim Algerian jurisprudence. In Ottoman-era Muslim jurisprudence a man could not compel his wife to move a great distance from her hometown or natal family, something accurately reported by Gillotte less than a decade earlier.

These and other decisions cited by Sautayra and Cherbonneau indicate that a more coercive attitude toward married women entered Muslim Algerian jurisprudence in the 1860s at about the time of the reorganization of the Sharia Court system.[39] The use of police to enforce a married woman's duty to live with her husband continued in Algeria long after the practice ceased in France. Recalcitrant wives reportedly would attempt to face down their husbands by declaring, "Even the superintendent of police will not make me return to you!"[40] French colonial officials became reluctant to use the gendarmerie to execute orders of obedience in the 1920s, fearing public scandal. The solution of the procurer-general was to have the orders enforced by local agents.[41] By then, the practice was thoroughly identified with Muslim culture, its French origin erased from memory. The French made use of the knowledge of Muslim family law they had developed in Algeria when establishing Sharia Court systems in Sudanic Africa, and the practice of forcibly returning runaway wives migrated there along with French expertise.[42] It was that knowledge of Muslim family law that the French consular court of Alexandria applied in its interpretation of Qadri's personal status code as requiring Nafisa Dhuhni to return to the house of her husband.

Enforcement of House of Obedience in Egypt

Why did the officials who drafted the 1897 procedural law include a provision authorizing the police to enforce orders of obedience? To begin with, it was consistent with social norms. The term *bayt al-ta'a* or "house of obedience," which referred to the maintenance-obedience relationship, came from Muslim jurisprudence. The juridical literature and fatwa collections are replete with references to the wife's duty of obedience (*ta'a*) and the marital domicile as the "place" or the "house" of obedience to the husband (*mahall* or *bayt ta'atihi*). This was also an era of growing anxiety over the presence of women in public space, which seems to have correlated with the redesign and expansion of cities following European models, and the creation of new and unfamiliar kinds of public space.[43] The explication of Qadri's code by al-Ibyani might be read as one response to these changes. Al-Ibyani preferred the view of Ibn al-Humam, namely that women should not be permitted to go out often, and that those who did so should do their utmost to avoid attracting attention. That conservative ideal could only be realized in practice by the wealthy, but it was a widespread ideal nevertheless. It was evident, for example, in press coverage of the infamous Raya and Sakina murders in Alexandria, which were discovered in 1920. The victims were women whom the two sisters lured to their apartment to be robbed and killed. According to Shaun Lopez, editorialists blamed the victims for venturing into public space without a chaperone, which they attributed to the loss of traditional mores, including women's modesty. One writer made the confused claim that "our religion forbids [the] Muslim [woman] from being visible outside the home unless she is with a close family member strong enough to protect her if an assailant attacked her, to keep away from her suspicion and the suspicious, to order her to stay in her house and not to display her beauty out of ignorance, [to] order her to veil or seclude herself for fear of *fitna*, sin, and the forbidden."[44] Muslim jurisprudence required that a close relative accompany a woman when she traveled, not when she went out of her home, but the writer conveyed the idea that women should remain at home and not appear in public. The concern of late-nineteenth-century male reformers over easy divorce and the nonpayment of maintenance was also expressed in terms of the moral peril that impoverished and unsupervised women supposedly posed.[45] Thus while the maintenance-obedience relationship had a basis in jurisprudence, in the public mind it was strongly connected with morality.

It is likely that the new family ideology had some influence on the officials who drafted the 1897 law and that they intended Article 93 to protect the integrity of the conjugal family. The preamble to the law mentioned that it was drafted in the Ministry of Justice and reviewed by the prime minister in consultation with certain members of the parliament before the khedive issued it.[46] The future Grand Mufti Muhammad Abduh participated in a committee the previous year that suggested a number of reforms, some of which were included in this law,[47] but it was mainly the work of civil servants trained in French law, not religious scholars. The exposure of civil servants to Muslim family law was largely through the study of Qadri's code and al-Ibyani's teaching in the School of Law.

Disobedient wives were not a new phenomenon, as evidenced by Ibn Hajar al-Haythami's discussion of it in the sixteenth century, nor is there any indication of an outbreak of disobedience toward the end of the nineteenth century. The difference between the time of Ibn Hajar al-Haythami and the late nineteenth century was twofold. First, there was the reimagining of the family and its role in society, or in other words the new family ideology. Disobedient—in the sense of runaway—wives disrupted and potentially broke up the conjugal family, which was now identified as the elemental unit in a modern society. Second, and given the importance of the family, there was the idea that the state ought to enforce the wife's obligation of obedience just as it enforced the husband's obligation to pay maintenance. Thus at a time in which European governments were abandoning coercion and adopting other, less direct measures to keep women at home, such as labor laws restricting their employment, Egyptian civil servants decided that the state should enforce the duty of a married woman to remain at home. Though couched in the juridical language of "obedience," this was a hybridization of former French legal practice with Muslim jurisprudence.

It was also consistent with the goal of making the judicial system more effective, as Ron Shaham has argued.[48] One of the criticisms Abduh leveled at the operation of the Sharia court system in his report of 1900 had to do with the haphazard implementation of court orders, including orders of obedience. Men used multiple tricks to avoid the garnishment of their wages to pay arrears of maintenance, divorcées were routinely prevented from visiting children in the custody of their ex-husbands, and when the police returned a disobedient wife to her husband there was nothing to stop her from leaving him again the next day.[49] Abduh viewed the misbehavior of husbands and ex-husbands as a bigger problem than the disobedience of wives, but he clearly thought that orders of obedience should be enforced.

Abduh's report, based on an investigation carried out in 1899, incidentally confirms that orders of obedience were being enforced shortly after the 1897 law was issued. Additional confirmation appears in the memoirs of Huda al-Sha'rawi, who separated from her husband in 1894. He withheld financial support but she was able to make do with her own income. Some seven years later a family friend pressured her to reconcile, mentioning that her husband had the right to force her to return to him—a reference to the enforcement of house of obedience that her readers would have understood. In the end it was pressure from her brother that induced her to rejoin her husband.[50] A year or two later the case of Shaykh Ahmad Sulayman Basha and Nafisa Dhuhni was aired before the public, and the indignant response in *al-Ahkam al-Shar'iyya* referred to the possibility of the police escorting her back to the house of her husband. Ahmad Amin, who served as a Sharia Court judge in the early 1920s, also mentioned the use of police in these cases:

> There were wives asking for financial support from their husbands, and husbands asking for obedience from their wives. About eighty percent of the cases were of this sort. Husbands were sentenced to pay financial support, and if they did not they were sentenced to a term of imprisonment. Wives were sentenced to obey. I continued to rule obedience although I did not deem it proper and felt it was unthinkable. How could a woman be taken from her own home by the police and placed in her husband's by the police too? How could this be marital life? I could understand the use of police force in implementing material affairs, such as the restoration of a plot of land to its owner, the placing of a sentenced man in prison, the execution of the death sentence, and similar financial and criminal matters. But I could never understand the implementation of marital life by the police unless I understood love by force or affection by the sword. For this reason, I used to pass these sentences in accordance with traditions not conscience, and in agreement with books, laws and regulations, not the heart.[51]

As Abduh had observed, a man could not prevent his wife from leaving again after she was returned, and the husband had to petition the court for an order of obedience each time his wife left him. In France critics raised this point to show how impractical the forcible return of runaway wives was.[52] But in Egypt the law was amended in 1910 to allow the repeated enforcement of an order of obedience.[53] That provision was retained in the procedural law of 1931,[54] and it remained in effect until set aside by the ministerial order in 1967.

Despite the enactment of house of obedience in 1897 and the strengthening of the enforcement regime in 1910, opposition to it was slow to appear. Abduh supported it, and Qasim Amin did not mention it. Nor did Malak Hifni Nasif, even though she took up writing a decade after the procedural law was issued. Margot Badran has suggested that the early feminists were slow to oppose the law because it mainly affected lower-class women,[55] but Nafisa Dhuhni and Huda al-Sha'rawi were certainly not from the lower class. Opposition to the enforcement of house of obedience began to appear in the 1920s, especially after the formation of the Egyptian Feminist Union (EFU, 1925), which gave activist women a platform from which they could articulate multiple demands for reform to improve the lot of women and their families. The EFU characterized house of obedience in speeches and in articles as a barbaric practice inconsistent with Islam.[56] But by then it was so thoroughly identified with Muslim culture that liberals assumed it to be one of a number of erroneous interpretations and backward traditions that were not condoned by the true faith. The EFU was correct in labeling house of obedience un-Islamic but they and others failed to recognize its roots in colonial modernity.

Obedience cases were prosecuted well into the middle of the twentieth century,[57] and denunciations of the enforcement of obedience continued.[58] But house of obedience was defended by socially conservative writers who argued—much like French conservatives had argued a century earlier—that its abolition would result in social chaos. According to one of those writers the obligation of women to reside with their husbands in return for their husbands' support was not unique to Islam:

[I]t is the established principle in most laws of civilized nations. For example the French civil code in articles 213 and 214 states that a man is responsible for providing all of his wife's needs and that in return a woman is required to obey her husband and live with him wherever he resides and to accompany him to wherever he decides to reside. It is as if these two articles are translations of the Qur'anic verse, "Men are in charge of women in that God has favored one over the other and in that they spend of their wealth."[59]

The author had no inkling that the similarity between the French code and Egyptian legal practice was more than coincidental. However, his use of a Qur'anic verse in defense of the enforcement of house of obedience is an example of how that practice became indigenized and sacralized.

The order of the Ministry of Justice instructing the police not to enforce orders of obedience, issued in February 1967, indicates the extent to which sentiments had changed since the early twentieth century. It cited widespread complaints about the enforcement of obedience and explained that it was not based on any Islamic text, nor was it called for in other religious laws. Moreover, it taxed the honor of women and caused instability and hatred in the family, undoubtedly with negative effects on the children.[60] Ninety years earlier the unstated reason for enforcing orders of obedience had been the effectiveness of Sharia Court decisions that upheld the integrity of the conjugal family. Now the welfare of the family was invoked to cancel the policy of enforcing orders of obedience.[61]

Thereafter the situation reverted to something like what it had been before the procedural law of 1897, in which women who deserted the marital home were regarded as disobedient and lost their entitlement to maintenance. Their husbands had to petition the court for an order of obedience, and the disobedient wife would be notified by the court that noncompliance with the order would result in the forfeiture of maintenance.[62]

The curious history of house of obedience contradicts the commonplace notion that processes of "modernization" invariably produce improvements in the human condition. It also complicates the question of the impact of Western-inspired reforms on the status of women. Legal modernization—that is, the reorganization of the judicial system along European lines—produced a hybridized system in which the flexibility of the old Sharia court system was replaced by rigidity, and formerly normative legal rules that were not always enforced became positive law enforced by the state. Nineteenth-century legal modernization produced at least two significant setbacks for the welfare of women that required subsequent amelioration. Hanafization disadvantaged married women by making it more difficult for them to collect arrears of maintenance or to escape marriages in which they were unsupported, deserted, or abused, and the enforcement of house of obedience ironically gave new meaning to the concept of married women as captives or prisoners of their husbands.

Conclusion and Epilogue

Egypt's marriage system, its family ideology, and its family law originated in the late nineteenth and early twentieth centuries. A century later the foundations of modern family life established in that era continued to affect behavior and influence debates, and certain features of family law persisted nearly unchanged.

One of the purposes of this book has been to document and narrate those beginnings and observe how family life changed from what it had been in the precolonial era. The reconstruction of this history has debunked the idea that no significant changes occurred in family life before World War I and also showed that the causes of change were complex. The modernization of marriage was not solely due to European influence, as older theories of modernization would have predicted, nor was it entirely due to internal socioeconomic factors. In any event, the internal-external dichotomy is meaningless, for the construction of a family ideology involved the hybridization of post-Enlightenment European and precolonial Muslim ideas and their alteration in the process. Nor do contingent political developments that profoundly affected ruling- and upper-class family culture conform to an internal—external dichotomy. In the 1870s the khedival family abandoned slave concubinage in favor of royal endogamy and, necessarily, monogamy, following the establishment of primogeniture in succession to the khedivate. Monogamy and polygyny were not considered to be mutually exclusive opposites in Ottoman Egyptian culture, which may be why only Westerners found the change remarkable. Nevertheless, the khedival family were trendsetters and their monogamy was on public display. This change coincided with the publication of modernist works and, in the following decades, periodicals that promoted the virtues of companionate marriage, including monogamy. The demise of household government and the suppression of slave trafficking occurred in the same decade. The last generation of harem women (slaves trained to become upper-class consorts) was married off in the final decades of the century, leaving upper-class families without the option of reproducing through slave concubines. With the end of the slave trade, also, men in the lower strata were no longer able to substitute slave women for contractual wives. Anecdotal evidence suggests a decline in ruling- and upper-class polygyny in the last quarter of the nineteenth century, and Khedive Abbas II's clandestine polygyny is a sure sign that public opinion had turned against that practice—a change of attitude to which the example of the khedival family contributed. Census data show a steady decline in polygyny from the beginning of the twentieth century, even though it was unrestricted until 1979.[1]

There was a dramatic rise in the age of marriage between the mid-nineteenth century and the early twentieth century, especially in urban society. It began well before the enactment of a minimum age requirement in 1923, and since it occurred society-wide it cannot have been purely an effect of "enlightenment" (the beneficial effects of modern education) at that early date.[2] However, among the *effendiyya* men delayed marriage to finish their education and start a career, and that may have contributed to the demise of large joint households in the urban upper class after World War I.

If before the war political events and economic and demographic trends had the greatest influence on the system of marriage and family formation, the family ideology articulated by modernist intellectuals and popularized in the periodical press, and later in school textbooks, films, and television serials, became dominant afterward. Egyptian family ideology was a hybrid of post-Enlightenment French social thought and precolonial Muslim writings on marriage. Modernist intellectuals like al-Tahtawi and Mubarak and their counterparts elsewhere in the Ottoman Empire drew upon Islamic sources and the literary heritage to valorize women's education and companionate, monogamous marriage. They drew more directly on European ideas of social progress for a domestic ideology, joining it with the maintenance-obedience relationship. Family ideology, including domesticity, aimed at social improvement through the proper education of children, including the formation of their character. Domesticity was not an antimodern idea invented to keep women in the domestic sphere. Rather, it constructed a domestic sphere to serve as the married woman's domain as part of the modernist project. At a time when popular writings still asserted that women were deficient in intellect and faith, describing married women as captives in the house of their husbands, modernist domesticity affirmed the ability of women to acquire an education, manage a household, and rear children, activities upon which the improvement of the nation depended. Early feminist-modernist writers joined their male counterparts in valorizing women's domestic vocation but differed from them in asserting that women should also have the option of pursuing a higher education and working outside of the home.

Today secular nationalists and religious conservatives alike uphold the conjugal family and companionate marriage as normative, projecting them into the distant past as authentically Egyptian and Islamic and as a foil to modern times, in which family values have supposedly weakened. The main difference between religious and nonreligious supporters of the conjugal family ideal, as Lila Abu-Lughod has written, is the degree to which they accept the participation of women in the paid workforce.[3] Tension between the two modern ideals of women's domesticity and women's emancipation, which was noticeable in the contrasting attitudes of male modernists and feminist-modernists toward women's work, found expression later in the republican constitutions, each of which has committed the state to enabling women to balance family obligations with work.

Another aim of this book was to assess the validity of the idea that as societies urbanize and industrialize they will develop similar family patterns. Here it is useful to recall Talal Asad's point that Egyptian modernity has not replicated European culture, due to a different starting point and because there is no single European or Western modernity. The trend has not been one of convergence in the sense that William Goode predicted, not only because of the persistence of important differences but also because the Western family pattern, which Goode took as the exemplary modern one, has changed from what it was in the mid-twentieth century.

The differences between Egyptian and Euro-American family patterns are numerous. Marriage in Egypt continues to be relatively early and nearly universal, while Northwestern Europe and North America seem to have reverted to historical patterns of relatively late and nonuniversal marriage. In Egypt the urban middle and upper classes no longer form joint family households, but extended families prefer to reside in adjacent or nearby apartments, often within the same building, which they may own. This contrasts with the Northwestern European system, in which historically the joint family household was rare and has left no vestiges. In today's Egypt the young are able to meet and get to know potential spouses, but arranged and negotiated marriages are still the norm. Family are often involved in the choice of a spouse, and the regime of separate property in marriage requires the negotiation of financial arrangements as a hedge against divorce. Films and television serials idealize love matches, but families discourage autonomous choice in marriage and passionate feelings are distrusted when it comes to such an important decision.[4] Historically in the Northwestern European system, the young chose their spouses at a later age and more autonomously, and that is especially true today. In Egypt the rate of divorce declined dramatically in the second half of the twentieth century, reducing the chance that a married woman would be divorced by two-thirds. Most Egyptians are unaware of this since the media emphasize the *number* of divorces and not the declining *rate* of divorce in relation to the population. In the West the trend has been in the opposite direction, with divorce rates rising since the mid-twentieth century.[5]

Egyptian family ideology is both a cause and a reflection of what may be called the familialist features of their marriage system. Both the constitutional commitment to preserve the cohesion and stability of the family and the mistaken alarm over a nonexistent upsurge in divorce show the extent to which the conjugal family has become ideologically normative. While the Egyptian conjugal family ideal approximates that of the early-twentieth-century West, in today's West the growing acceptance of same-sex marriage along with a trend of informal cohabitation and single parenthood out of choice raises the question of whether any family pattern can be identified as modern.

This study has also examined the transformation of Muslim family law in application that preceded and influenced its codification. That transformation was an effect of state centralization and the transnational flow of ideas about legal modernization, including colonial knowledge of Islamic law. The Muhammad Ali dynasty enforced the application of Hanafi law in the Sharia Courts, bringing an end to pluralism and forum shopping, which had given the system flexibility. Hanafization disadvantaged married women who were owed arrears of maintenance or whose husbands deserted or abused them. Successive procedural laws enhanced the importance of documents in legal proceedings, making the effects of Hanafization inescapable. Women adapted to the changing legal environment with strategies such as lawsuits to establish the maintenance they were due, but those who were in difficult marriages had fewer legal options than before the beginning of judicial "reform."

The legal difficulties faced by married women gave rise to several reform proposals, including the use of Maliki and Shafiʿi jurisprudence to make it easier for them to collect arrears of maintenance or to escape marriage to a man who failed to support them or who abused them. These proposals, advanced by Muhammad Abduh and his circle, influenced the drafting of the family law codes of 1920 and 1929. However, they embedded their proposals in a discourse of family crisis, raising the specter of unsupported and unsupervised women resorting to immoral activity. Their emphasis on the irresponsibility of men who failed to fulfill their obligations in the maintenance-obedience relationship constructed normative women as obedient and dependent. Eliding respectable working women, they construed women who were unsupported and unsupervised as a threat to morality.

The officials who undertook the reorganization of the judicial system were trained in French law and influenced by the Algerian model in which the Sharia Courts were incorporated into a civil law system. European scholars believed that Islamic law was not suitable for a modern legal system, and in Egypt political conditions closed off discussion of the composition of a civil law based on Islamic jurisprudence like the Ottoman *Mecelle*. Muslim family law became a personal status law, in Muhammad Qadri's informal but influential code. Codification interrupted the historical process of discussion that had produced Muslim jurisprudence and encouraged an understanding of the Sharia as a set of positive rules. The restriction of the jurisdiction of the Sharia Courts to family matters also gave birth to the association of the family with religion and religious law.

The enforcement of orders of obedience, beginning in 1897, was one of the consequences of legal modernization. The practice migrated to Egypt from France via Algeria, where it became associated with Muslim culture. Other than its apparent Islamic pedigree, its social acceptance in Egypt was perhaps explainable in light of the incorporation of the maintenance-obedience relationship in the new family ideology. In Qadri's code and especially in al-Ibyani's explication of it, the wife's duty of obedience appeared to be more absolute than it was in the historical jurisprudence.

The 1920s and Later

The family law codes enacted in the 1920s ameliorated the direst consequences of Hanafization, restoring to married women nearly all of the legal options they had lost a century earlier. Subsequent efforts to revise the family law were stalemated, however, due to the politicization of the family and the disruptive effects of revolutions and wars. A new phase of family law reform began in 1979, after a fifty-year hiatus.

The early-twentieth-century reforms were the work of men. They reflected the concerns elite men had voiced over the breakdown of the maintenance-obedience relationship in the preceding decades, they were drafted by male officials, and they embodied many of the ideas of Muhammad Abduh. Women, as scholars, lawyers, and activists, were much more involved in the second phase of reform. The close association of religion and family life persists, as it does in nearly every Muslim society, obliging women activists to draw upon historical Muslim jurisprudence and juridical practices. Working within that frame they "chipped away" at the asymmetrical authority of husbands.[6] By mining the indigenous historical culture to reclaim rights that, arguably, had fallen in abeyance, they were largely successful in warding off the predictable criticism that their proposals were foreign-inspired and un-Islamic.

Law No. 25 of 1920 Concerning the Legal Rules of Maintenance and Some Questions of Personal Status was the first Egyptian code governing marriage, and as the title indicates it mainly reflected concerns over the enforcement of maintenance payments. Its drafters drew on Maliki jurisprudence in providing for unpaid maintenance to accumulate automatically as a debt against the husband. This could result in the garnishment of his property or wages, as before, but if he was unable to pay or absent the judge was authorized to annul the marriage. The judge could also declare a man who went missing for four years to be deceased. In either case the woman was free to remarry after her waiting period.[7]

Legal historians have stressed the innovativeness of the legislators' use of *takhayyur* (the selection of legal rules from diverse schools of Sunni jurisprudence) and *talfiq* (the combining of legal rules from different schools) as methods of arriving at the desired result in this and subsequent laws. Abduh had recommended the use of those methods, which to some extent recovered the flexibility of pluralism and forum shopping. The memory of the old system may have inspired Abduh's recommendation, and there was the more recent example of the Ottoman Law of Family Rights, which selectively incorporated Maliki jurisprudence.[8] Legal experts declared these methods to be in keeping with "the spirit of the age,"[9] but the law it produced was socially conservative. The legislators' intent was to preserve the normative conjugal family and the maintenance-obedience relationship.

The law of 1920 embodied several recommendations made by a committee of senior ulama convened in 1915 to draft a family law. According to Muhammad Abu Zahra the draft was circulated widely among judges, lawyers, and ulama and received much commentary before its approval,[10] indicating that it represented a consensus of the legal and religious establishment. Law No. 56 of 1923, which set the minimum age of marriage for women and men at sixteen and eighteen, respectively, was more controversial. This law instructed judges not to hear cases involving marriage in which either of the spouses was younger than the minimum age at the time of the contract. One effect of it was to outlaw the forced marriage of minors, like Zaynab Ibrahim Sulayman in Alexandria a decade earlier, since the consent of someone fifteen or older was required in marriage. Those who drafted the 1923 law could find no justification in the opinions of the four schools of law and cited instead individual jurists of the early Islamic period. Its enforcement became stricter in 1926, when the Ministry of Justice ordered the forwarding of cases of false testimony about the age of marriage to the public prosecutor.[11]

The next (and for fifty years the last) step in codifying the law of marriage was Law No. 25 of 1929 Concerning Certain Rules of Personal Status, which introduced important changes in the rules of divorce. It declared all conditional repudiations as well as those pronounced by men accidentally, while inebriated, and in anger to be without effect. Declarations of triple repudiation at one time would now count only as single, revocable divorces. The only final dissolutions were repudiations pronounced three times with intervals, those negotiated in exchange for a financial settlement (*khul'* and *mubara'a*), and annulments specified in the laws of 1920 and 1929 as final. This law too drew on Maliki jurisprudence in expanding women's access to divorce by permitting them to petition a judge for an annulment on the ground of marital difficulties (*al-shiqaq*) and that they suffered harm or injury (*al-darar*) in the marriage. If the wife established that she suffered harm to an extent that reconciliation was impossible, the judge was to annul the marriage. If she could not convince the judge of that but brought repeated complaints, the judge was to appoint arbiters, and if they could not reconcile the couple they were to recommend an annulment. In addition, the wives of absent and imprisoned husbands were now permitted to request an annulment on the ground that they suffered harm due to the absence of their husband even if he had assets that could be used to pay their maintenance.[12]

This law too incorporated the recommendations of a committee that reflected the ideas of Abduh. However, the parliament omitted two recommendations restricting polygyny and enabling women to insert stipulations in the marriage contract. The first recommended measure would have required a man wishing to marry an additional wife to establish in court his ability to provide maintenance and a good family life for her as well as for his existing wife and children. The second would have permitted women to stipulate, as a condition of their marriage, that their husband would not take an additional wife, or remove her to another town, and so on. The violation of any stipulation would have been a cause of divorce.[13] The first recommendation originated in Abduh's reinterpretation of the Qur'anic verses on polygyny, and it was adopted in the Syrian and Iraqi personal status laws of 1953 and 1959.[14] The second recommendation was consistent with Hanbali jurisprudence and it was adopted in the Iraqi personal status law of 1959.[15]

The second phase of family law reform in Egypt began with Law No. 44 of 1979, derided by its opponents as "Jihan's law" due to the role of the wife of President Anwar al-Sadat in supporting it. The Supreme Constitutional Court ruled it unconstitutional in 1985 because Sadat had implemented it in an emergency decree although there was no genuine state of emergency. The most controversial feature of that law was the provision allowing a divorcée to keep possession of the marital home, usually owned by the husband, as long as she had custody of the children. Law No. 100 of 1985, enacted after the Supreme Constitutional Court's decision, omitted that provision but largely preserved two other features of the 1979 law concerning polygyny and obedience. The 1979 law defined polygyny as harmful to the first wife, enabling her to demand an annulment under the terms of the 1929 law within twelve months of learning of her husband's additional marriage. The 1985 law modified this provision by requiring the wife to prove she suffered harm due to her husband's polygyny, provided she took action within twelve months of learning of it. That proviso in both laws acknowledged a well-known abuse in which men concealed polygynous marriages from their wives, sometimes for years.[16]

Orders of obedience had gone unenforced for several years by the time Sadat decreed Law No. 44, but the relevant law had not been revised. The 1979 law foreclosed the possibility of enforcement by allowing a woman served with an order of obedience thirty days to present her reasons for not complying with it. If the court accepted her reasons as justified her husband was obligated to continue maintenance payments, and if not he was relieved of that obligation and was not required to pay temporary maintenance if they divorced. The 1985 law retained this provision, which is slightly more advantageous to women than the jurisprudence of the nineteenth century, in which defiance of an order of obedience, regardless of the justification, resulted in the loss of maintenance. However, because married women are still legally obligated to obey their husbands, men are able to use orders of obedience to deter their wives from seeking divorce or to delay divorce proceedings once they have begun, both to inflict humiliation on the wife and to avoid paying temporary maintenance.[17]

Following the passage of the 1985 law a group of women activists proposed a redesign of the printed fill-in-the-blank marriage contract form in use since 1931 to include a checklist of ten stipulations, which if accepted by a couple in their entirety would have made the marital relationship much less asymmetric. The "new marriage contract project," as they called it, was consistent with Hanbali jurisprudence, which permitted the inclusion of enforceable stipulations in the marriage contract. The activists' proposal was similar in intent to the recommendation omitted from the 1929 law. However, a checklist of stipulations would have informed the bride and groom of their legal options on the spot. The new marriage contract project ran into strong resistance, especially from the Shaykh al-Azhar, and so the redesigned marriage contract form issued in late 2000 merely had a blank space added where stipulations could be written if agreed to by the couple. Reportedly very few couples have taken advantage of it.[13] One of the stipulations in the proposed checklist was that the wife would have the ability to divorce herself from her husband if he took an additional wife without her consent, mistreated her, or left her for at least eight months, or simply if she determined she could not live with him. This was a version of the delegated divorce entirely consistent with Hanafi jurisprudence. It is reportedly in use among the upper class, but unknown to most of the population.[19]

Some of the same activists involved in the new marriage contract project promoted what became Law No. 1 of 2000, popularly known as the "*khul'* law." In the past *khul'* had involved a pronouncement of divorce by the husband in exchange for his wife surrendering her right to the delayed dower, temporary maintenance, and even any arrears of maintenance she was owed. However the 2000 law made it possible for a woman to petition for a *khul'* divorce unilaterally, and for a judge to grant it without the husband's agreement. The law offered relief to a large number of women seeking divorces whose cases were stalled due to uncooperative husbands.

Opponents warned of a surge in divorce and damage to the family,[20] but a decade later the results were ambiguous. The crude divorce rate rose from 1.1 per thousand population to 1.9 per thousand, which may reflect the processing of the stalled cases as well as the creation of Family Courts in 2004, which facilitated the hearing of divorce cases.[21]

After the January 2011 Revolution and the election of a government dominated by the Muslim Brotherhood, the advances in women's rights of the past century seemed to some observers to be threatened. Women's rights advocates expressed concern over wording in the draft constitution of 2012 that seemed to invoke Islamic law to restrict women's equality in public life,[22] and they denounced radicals who criticized the 2000 law and questioned the legitimacy of the minimum marriage age.[23] Those skirmishes ended with the removal of Mursi's Islamist government in July 2013. Whether a new government will pursue further substantive change in family law is uncertain, though experience suggests that bold departures are unlikely so long as there is political instability and economic uncertainty.

The 2014 constitution not only reaffirmed that the family is "founded on religion, morality and patriotism," it also left intact the close association of family life and religion. While women have a constitutional guarantee of equality in public life, the domestic sphere continues to be the domain of religious law. In spite of some success in "chipping away" at it, inequality is at the core of Muslim family law as presently constructed, and especially in the maintenance-obedience relationship. In past time the maintenance-obedience ideal influenced elite behavior but bore little relationship to life in the majority of families, where married women contributed to the household income. It bears even less resemblance to present-day reality.

NOTES

SELECT BIBLIOGRAPHY

INDEX

Notes

Introduction

1. Mariam Rizk and Osman El Sharnoubi, "Egypt's Constitution 2013 vs. 2012: A Comparison," *Ahram Online*, Dec. 12, 2013. http://english.ahram.org.eg/News/88644.aspx.

2. Egypt's first constitution of 1923 made no direct reference to the family or to women. This and the next paragraph reference the constitutions of 1923 and 1956 in Yusuf Qazmakhuri, *Al-Dasatir fi al-Alam al-Arabi* (Beirut: Dar al-Hamra, 1989); The Constitution of the Arab Republic of Egypt, 1971 (as amended to 2007), www.constitutionnet.org/files/Egypt%20Constitution.pdf; the 2012 constitution in https://archive.org/details/dostor-misr-2012.pdf; 2014 constitution in Dustur Misr http://dostour.eg/; and Ellen McLarney, "Women's Rights in the Egyptian Constitution: (Neo)Liberalism's Family Values," *Jadaliyya*, May 22, 2013, http://www.jadaliyya.com/pages/index/11852/womens-rights-in-the-egyptian-constitution_(neo)li.

3. Non-Muslims are subject to their own religious laws (Article 3).

4. Amira El-Azhary Sonbol, "A History of Marriage Contracts in Egypt," in Asifa Quraishi and Frank E. Vogel, *The Islamic Marriage Contract: Case Studies in Islamic Family Law* (Cambridge, MA: Harvard University Press, 2008), 113, 117n3. On family terminology see Kenneth M. Cuno, "Joint Family Households and Rural Notables in Nineteenth-Century Egypt," *International Journal of Middle East Studies* 27, no. 4 (Nov. 1995): 489; and cf. Talal Asad, *Formations of the Secular: Christianity, Islam, Modernity* (Stanford: Stanford University Press, 2003), 231. The term *usra* (conjugal family) became common in book titles in the 1940s. See Aida Nosseir (Ayda Ibrahim Nusayr), *Dalil al-Matbu'at al-Misriyya 1940–1956* (Cairo: The American University in Cairo Press, 1975); Nosseir, *al-Kutub al-Arabiyya allati Nushirat fi Misr bayn Amay 1926–1940* (Cairo: The American University in Cairo Press, 1980); Nosseir, *al-Kutub al-Arabiyya allati Nushirat fi Misr bayn Amay 1900-1925* (Cairo: The American University in Cairo Press, 1983); and Nosseir, *al-Kutub al-Arabiyya allati Nushirat fi Misr fi al-Qarn al-Tasi' Ashar* (Cairo: The American University in Cairo Press, 1990).

5. Mounira Charrad, *States and Women's Rights: The Making of Postcolonial Tunisia, Algeria, and Morocco* (Berkeley and Los Angeles: University of California Press, 2001), 28–50.

6. See, e.g., Cissie Fairchilds, "Women and the Family," in Samia I. Spencer, ed., *French Women and the Age of Enlightenment* (Bloomington: Indiana University Press, 1984), 97–110.

7. Kecia Ali, *Marriage and Slavery in Early Islam* (Cambridge, MA: Harvard University Press, 2010), 6.

8. See chapter 3.

9. Nadia Sonneveld, *Khul' Divorce in Egypt: Public Debates, Judicial Practices, and Everyday Life* (Cairo: The American University in Cairo Press, 2012), 17–34.

10. This is discussed in detail in chapter 3.

11. Alan Duben and Cem Behar, *Istanbul Households: Marriage, Family and Fertility, 1880–1940* (Cambridge: Cambridge University Press, 1991), chap. 4; Lisa Pollard, *Nurturing the Nation: The Family Politics of Modernizing, Colonizing, and Liberating Egypt, 1805–1923* (Berkeley and Los Angeles: University of California Press, 2005), 5; Hanan Kholoussy, *For Better, For Worse: The Marriage Crisis That Made Egypt* (Stanford: Stanford University Press, 2010), 1–2.

12. Stephanie Coontz, *The Way We Never Were: American Families and the Nostalgia Trap* (New York: Basic Books, 1992); and *Marriage, a History: How Love Conquered Marriage* (New York: Penguin, 2006).

13. Iris Agmon, *Family and Court: Legal Culture and Modernity in Late Ottoman Palestine* (Syracuse: Syracuse University Press, 2006), 28–30.

14. Louise A. Tilly, "Women's History and Family History: Fruitful Collaboration or Missed Connection?" *Journal of Family History* 12, nos. 1–3 (1987): 309.

15. Megan Doolittle, "Close Relations? Bringing Together Gender and Family in English History," *Gender & History* 11, no. 3 (Nov. 1999): 547, 548.

16. See, e.g., Dipesh Chakrabarty, "The Difference—Deferral of Colonial Modernity: Public Debates on Domesticity in British Bengal," in Frederick Cooper and Ann Laura Stoler, eds., *Tensions of Empire: Colonial Cultures in a Bourgeois World* (Berkeley and Los Angeles: University of California Press, 1997), 373–74. For Egypt see Samira Haj, *Reconfiguring Islamic Tradition: Reform, Rationality, and Modernity* (Stanford: Stanford University Press, 2009); Hiba Abugideiri, "Colonizing Mother Egypt, Domesticating Egyptian Mothers," in Poonam Bala, ed., *Biomedicine as a Contested Site: Some Revelations in Imperial Contexts* (New York: Lexington Books, 2000), 9–28; the several contributions in Lila Abu-Lughod, ed., *Remaking Women: Feminism and Modernity in the Middle East* (Princeton: Princeton University Press, 1998); and Mervat Hatem, "Egyptian Discourses on Gender and Political Liberalization: Do Secularist and Islamist Views Really Differ?" *Middle East Journal* 48, no. 4 (1994): 661–76.

17. On the pervasive influence of modernization theory in family history see Doolittle, "Close Relations?" 546–47.

18. William J. Goode, *World Revolution and Family Patterns* (New York: Free Press, 1963), 1.

19. This important scholarship was especially associated with the Cambridge Group for the History of Population and Social Structure, and is discussed in Michael Anderson, *Approaches to the History of the Western Family, 1500–1914*, 2d ed. (Cambridge: Cambridge University Press, 1995), 10–13.

20. John Bongaarts, "Household Size and Composition in the Developing World in the 1990s," *Population Studies* 55 (2001): 263–79; "The Changing American Family," a report issued by the Pew Research Center, Nov. 18, 2010, http://www.pewsocialtrends.org/2010/11/18/five-decades-of-marriage-trends/.

21. Arland Thornton, *Reading History Sideways: The Fallacy and Enduring Impact of the Developmental Paradigm on Family Life* (Chicago: University of Chicago Press, 2005), 21.

22. Thornton, *Reading History Sideways*, 56–57, 62.

23. Patrick Kay Bidelman, *Pariahs Stand Up! The Founding of the Liberal Feminist Movement in France, 1858–1889* (Westport, CT: Greenwood Press, 1982), 10.

24. Chakrabarty, "The Difference—Deferral of Colonial Modernity," 373.

25. The term "semicolonized" refers to the permeation and constraint of local sovereignty by multiple and contending foreign powers. See Tani E. Barlow, "Introduction: On 'Colonial Modernity,'" in Barlow, ed., *Formations of Colonial Modernity in East Asia* (Durham: Duke University Press, 1997), 1–20.

26. Asad, *Formations*, 217.

27. Duben and Behar, *Istanbul Households*, 200.

28. Ibid., 5.

29. This issue is addressed throughout chapters 4–6. On the colonial origins of Muslim family law in other societies see Michael R. Anderson, "Legal Scholarship and the Politics of Islam in British India," in R. S. Khare, *Perspectives on Islamic Law, Justice, and Society* (London: Rowman & Littlefield, 1999), 65–91; Daniel Lev, "Colonial Law and the Genesis of the Indonesian State," *Indonesia* 40 (1985): 57–74; Robert D. Crews, *For Prophet and Tsar: Islam and Empire in Russia and Central Asia* (Cambridge, MA: Harvard University Press, 2006); and Jean-Robert Henry and François Balique, *La Doctrine Coloniale du Droit Musulman Algérien. Bibliographie Systématique et Introduction Critique* (Paris: CNRS, 1979).

30. Kholoussy, *For Better, For Worse*; Agmon, *Family and Court*; Pollard, *Nurturing the Nation*; Beshara Doumani, ed., *Family History in the Middle East: Household, Property, and Gender* (Albany: State University of New York Press, 2003); Margaret Meriwether, *The Kin Who Count: Family and Society in Ottoman Aleppo, 1770–1840* (Austin: University of Texas Press, 1999); Amira Sonbol, ed., *Women, the Family, and Divorce Laws in Islamic History* (Syracuse: Syracuse University Press, 1996); Colette Establet and Jean-Paul Pascual, *Familles et Fortunes à Damas: 450 Foyers Damascains en 1700* (Damascus: Institut Français des Études Arabes, 1994); and Alan Duben and Cem Behar, *Istanbul Households: Marriage, Family and Fertility, 1880–1940* (Cambridge: Cambridge University Press, 1991).

31. Mervat F. Hatem, *Literature, Gender, and Nation-Building in Nineteenth-Century Egypt: The Life and Works of 'A'isha Taymur* (New York: Palgrave Macmillan, 2011); Liat Kozma, *Policing Egyptian Women: Sex, Law, and Medicine in Khedival Egypt* (Syracuse: Syracuse University Press, 2011); Beth Baron, *Egypt as a Woman: Nationalism, Gender, and Politics* (Berkeley and Los Angeles: University of California Press, 2005); Mona L. Russell, *Creating the New Egyptian Woman: Consumerism, Education , and National Identity, 1863–1922* (New York: Palgrave Macmillan, 2004); Marilyn L. Booth, *May Her Likes Be Multiplied: Biography and Gender Politics in Egypt* (Berkeley and Los Angeles: University of California Press, 2001); Margot Badran, *Feminists, Islam, and Nation: Gender and the Making of Modern Egypt* (Princeton: Princeton University Press, 1995); Beth Baron, *The Women's Awakening in Egypt: Culture, Society, and the Press* (New Haven: Yale University Press, 1994); Judith Tucker, *Women in Nineteenth-Century Egypt* (Cambridge: Cambridge University Press, 1984).

32. Mary Ann Fay, *Unveiling the Harem: Elite Women and the Paradox of Seclusion in Eighteenth-Century Cairo* (Syracuse: Syracuse University Press, 2012); Pascale Ghazaleh, *Fortunes Urbaines et Stratégies Sociales: Généalogies Patrimoniales au Caire, 1780–1830* (Cairo Institut Français d'Achéologie Orientale, 2010); Nelly Hanna, *Making Big Money in 1600: The Life and Times of Isma'il Abu Taqiyya, Egyptian Merchant* (Syracuse: Syracuse University Press, 1998); Jane Hathaway, *The Politics of Households in Ottoman Egypt: The Rise of the Qazdağlıs* (Cambridge: Cambridge University Press, 1997); Afaf Marsot, *Women and Men in Late Eighteenth-Century Egypt* (Austin: University of Texas Press, 1995); Kenneth M. Cuno, *The Pasha's Peasants: Land, Society, and Economy in Lower Egypt 1740–1858* (Cambridge: Cambridge University Press, 1992).

33. Avi Rubin, *Ottoman Nizamiye Courts: Law and Modernity* (New York: Palgrave Macmillan, 2011); Wael Hallaq, *Shari'a: Theory, Practice, Transformations* (Cambridge: Cambridge University Press, 2009); Judith Tucker, *Women, Family, and Gender in Islamic Law* (Cambridge: Cambridge University Press, 2008); John Esposito with Natana J. Delong-Bas, *Women in Muslim Family Law*, 2d ed. (Syracuse: Syracuse University Press, 2001); Judith Tucker, *In the House of the Law: Gender and Islamic Law in Ottoman Syria and Palestine* (Berkeley and Los Angeles: University of California Press, 1998); Nathan J. Brown, *The Rule of Law in the Arab World: Courts in Egypt and the Gulf* (Cambridge: Cambridge University Press, 1997); Ron Shaham, *Family and the Courts in Modern Egypt* (Leiden: Brill, 1997); Allan Christelow, *Muslim Law Courts and the French Colonial State in Algeria* (Princeton: Princeton University Press, 1985).

34. Gabriel Baer attributed lack of change in the family to the absence of industrialization in "Summary and Conclusion: Social Change in Egypt, 1800–1914," in *Studies in the Social History of Egypt* (Chicago: University of Chicago Press, 1969), 210–12. Others in the no-change-before-1914 camp are Esposito with Delong-Bas, *Women in Muslim Family Law*, 48; and Shaham, *Family and the Courts*, 5. Ehud R. Toledano restated Baer's point about the family but qualified it by noting changes in the status of women: "Social and Economic Change in the 'Long Nineteenth Century,'" in M. W. Daly, ed., *The Cambridge*

History of Egypt, vol. 2, *Modern Egypt from 1517 to the End of the Twentieth Century* (Cambridge: Cambridge University Press, 1998), 277.

35. This group includes Hatem, *Literature, Gender, and Nation-Building*, 115–16; Haj, *Reconfiguring Islamic Tradition*, 155; Pollard, *Nurturing the Nation*, 5; Baron, *Egypt as a Women*, 17–22; Russell, *Creating the New Egyptian Woman*, 2–5; Booth, *May Her Likes*, 37–38; Kozma, *Policing Egyptian Women*, xvi, 117; Badran, *Feminists, Islam, and Nation*, 6; Baron, *The Women's Awakening*, 145; and Tucker, *Women in Nineteenth-Century Egypt*, throughout.

36. A useful overview of how these factors affected family structure in early modern Europe is in the Introduction to David I. Kertzer and Marzio Barbagli, eds., *The History of the European Family*, 3 vols. (New Haven: Yale University Press, 2001), vol. 1, *Family Life in Early Modern Times 1500–1789*, ix–xxxii. For a discussion of how household structure in Egypt was influenced by economic, demographic, and legal factors in the nineteenth century see Cuno, "Joint Family Households."

37. Tucker, *Women in Nineteenth-Century Egypt*, 194–96; and Tucker, "Decline of the Family Economy in Mid-Nineteenth-Century Egypt," *Arab Studies Quarterly* 1, no. 3 (1979): 245–71.

38. Khaled Fahmy, *All the Pasha's Men: Mehmed Ali, his Army and the Making of Modern Egypt* (Cambridge: Cambridge University Press, 1997), 229.

39. Baron, *The Women's Awakening*, 145, 155, 158, and *Egypt as a Woman*, 17–18, 32; Margot Badran, "Introduction," in Huda Shaarawi, *Harem Years: The Memoirs of an Egyptian Feminist* (New York: Feminist Press, 1986), 10 ff.; and *Feminists, Islam, and Nation*, 4 ff.

40. Pollard, *Nurturing the Nation*, 5.

41. Kholoussy, *For Better, For Worse*, 5–6.

42. Janet Thomas, "Women and Capitalism: Oppression or Emancipation?" *Comparative Studies in Society and History* 30, no. 3 (1988): 534–49.

43. The first in that genre was Timothy Mitchell's *Colonising Egypt* (Cambridge: Cambridge University Press, 1988).

44. Baron, *Egypt as a Women*, 17–33; Badran, *Feminists, Islam, and Nation*, 6–11; Pollard, *Nurturing the Nation*, chaps. 1–3.

45. See Dror Ze'evi, "The Use of Ottoman Sharia Court Records as a Source for Middle Eastern Social History: A Reappraisal," *Islamic Law and Society* 5, no. 1 (1998): 35–56.

46. Duben and Behar noted that Ottoman writing on the family was often at variance with the statistical reality, e.g., *Istanbul Households*, 103–4; and Kholoussy concluded that the Egyptian "marriage crisis" was an expression of anxiety, not reality: *For Better, For Worse*, 8.

47. Dror Ze'evi, *Producing Desire: Changing Sexual Discourse in the Ottoman Middle East, 1500–1900* (Berkeley and Los Angeles: University of California Press, 2006); Khaled El-Rouayheb, *Before Homosexuality in the Arab-Islamic world, 1500–1800* (Chicago: University of Chicago Press, 2005).

48. See Duben and Behar on trendsetting social elements in Istanbul, in *Istanbul Households*, 25.

49. I have borrowed the term "political work" from Tamara Loos, *Subject Siam: Family, Law, and Colonial Modernity in Thailand* (Ithaca: Cornell University Press, 2006), 7.

50. Timothy Mitchell, "Introduction," in Timothy Mitchell, ed., *Questions of Modernity* (Minneapolis and London: University of Minnesota Press, 2000), xi.

51. I have discussed the influence of family ideology on behavior in "Divorce and the Fate of the Family in Modern Egypt," in *Family in the Middle East: Ideational Change in Egypt, Iran, and Tunisia*, ed. Kathryn Yount and Hoda Rashad (New York: Routledge, 2008), 196–216.

52. Yossef Rapoport argued that flexibility was the intent in the appointment of chief judges from the four schools of law in Mamluk Cairo. See "Legal Diversity in the Age of Taqlid: The Four Chief Qadis under the Mamluks," *Islamic Law and Society* 10, no. 2 (2003): 210–28.

53. Hussein Ali Agrama, *Questioning Secularism: Islam, Sovereignty, and the Rule of Law in Modern Egypt* (Chicago: University of Chicago Press, 2012), 98.

54. On the census registers see Ghislaine Alleaume and Philippe Fargues, "La Naissance d'une Statistique d'État," *Histoire et Mesure* 13, no. 1 (1988): 147–93; and Kenneth M. Curo and Michael J. Reimer, "The Census Registers of Nineteenth-Century Egypt: A New Source for Social Historians," *British Journal of Middle Eastern Studies* 24, no. 2 (1997): 193–216.

55. T. H. Hollingsworth, *Historical Demography* (London: n.p., 1969), 76.

56. Justin A. McCarthy, "Nineteenth-Century Egyptian Population," *Middle Eastern Studies* 12, no. 3 (Oct. 1976): 1–39; Daniel Panzac, "The Population of Egypt in the Nineteenth Century," *Asian and African Studies* 21 (1987): 11–32.

57. Hollingsworth, *Historical Demography*, 29.

58. R. El-Shanawany, "The First National Life Tables for Egypt," *L'Egypte Contemporaine* 27 (1936): 214.

59. El-Shanawany, "The First National Life Tables for Egypt," 224–25.

60. On these distinctions see E. A. Hammel and Peter Laslett, "Comparing Household Structure over Time and between Cultures," *Comparative Studies in Society and History* 16, no. 1 (1974): 75–78.

61. Rudolph Peters, "Muhammad al-Abbasi al-Mahdi (d. 1897), Grand Mufti of Egypt, and his *al-Fatawa al-Mahdiyya*," *Islamic Law and Society* 1, no. 1 (1994): 66–82.

1. Marriage in Politics

1. *Al-Waqa'i' al-Misriyya*, 491–93 (Jan. 21, Jan. 28, and Feb. 4, 1873). This is the same Qadri who published a manual of personal status law in 1875 (see chapter 5). I found no information on Ali Abu al-Nasr.

2. In 1841 Egypt, a province of the Ottoman Empire, became the hereditary viceroyalty of Muhammad Ali Pasha (r. 1805–48) and his descendants. He and his immediate successors used the Persian title *khedive* informally; it was officially conferred on Ismail in 1867.

3. The four weddings were called *afrah al-anjal* or "the weddings of the children" at the time.

4. The debate over women's rights and roles emerged in the young periodical press in the 1880s. See Booth, *May Her Likes*, xxi, ff.

5. Pollard, *Nurturing the Nation*, chaps. 2 and 3.

6. Seclusion is hardly an adequate interpretation of *ihtijab*, which might better be rendered as "concealment" or "covering." *Ihtijab* did not necessarily mean the segregation of women from public spaces or activities, but rather their separation and/or concealment from unrelated men in those spaces.

7. Well before the nineteenth century European scholars had begun to map geographical differences in family practices and to associate difference from the Northwestern European family pattern with backwardness: Thornton, *Reading History Sideways*, 22–43.

8. Earl of Cromer, *Modern Egypt*, 2 vols. (New York: Macmillan, 1908), 2:158.

9. Pollard, *Nurturing the Nation*, 85–97; Julia Clancey-Smith, "La Femme Arabe: Women and Sexuality in France's North African Empire," in Sonbol, ed., *Women, the Family, and Divorce Laws*, 52–63.

10. A. D. Alderson, *The Structure of the Ottoman Dynasty* (Oxford: Clarendon Press, 1956), 176–77.

11. Leslie P. Peirce, *The Imperial Harem: Women and Sovereignty in the Ottoman Empire* (Oxford: Oxford University Press, 1993), 69.

12. The terms "political work" and "politics of kinship" are borrowed, respectively, from Tamara Loos, *Subject Siam*, 7, and Mytheli Sreenivas, *Wives, Widows, Concubines: The Conjugal Family Ideal in Colonial India* (Bloomington: Indiana University Press, 2008), 25.

13. E.g., James Augustus St. John, *Egypt and Mohammed Ali*, 2 vols. (London: Longman, Rees, Orme, Brown, Green & Longman, 1834), 2:181; and *The Times*, Jan. 8, 1877, Dec. 18, 1880, Apr. 19, 1881, Apr. 23, 1881, Apr. 26, 1882.

14. Edward Dicey, *The Story of the Khedivate* (London: Rivingtons, 1902), 62.

15. Fanny Davis, *The Ottoman Lady: A Social History from 1718 to 1918* (Westport, CT: Greenwood Press, 1986), 7–8; Sophia Lane Poole, *The Englishwoman in Egypt* (London: C. Cox, 1851–53), 74; Lucie Duff Gordon, *Letters from Egypt* (London: Virago, 1983/1865), 112.

16. Terence Walz, "Sudanese, Habasha, Takarna, and Barabira: Trans-Saharan Africans in Cairo as Shown in the 1848 Census," in Terence Walz and Kenneth M. Cuno, eds., *Race and Slavery in the Middle East: Histories of Trans-Saharan Africans in*

Nineteenth-Century Egypt, Sudan, and the Ottoman Mediterranean (Cairo: The American University in Cairo Press, 2010), 58.

17. Billie Melman, *Women's Orients: English Women and the Middle East, 1718–1918* (Ann Arbor: University of Michigan Press, 1995), 145–47.

18. Melman, *Women's Orients*, 106.

19. E.g., Poole, *The Englishwoman in Egypt*; and Ellen Chennells, *Recollections of an Egyptian Princess by Her English Governess, Being a Record of Five Years' Residence at the Court of Ismael Pasha, Khédive*, 2 vols. (London: William Blackwood & Sons, 1893).

20. George Michael LaRue, "'My Ninth Master Was a European': Enslaved Blacks in European Households in Egypt, 1798–1848," in Walz and Cuno, eds., *Race and Slavery in the Middle East*, 100–101.

21. *The Times*, Jan. 12, 1884; Apr. 1, 1884 (text of 1877 decree); Apr. 7, 1884. The Egyptian official gazette, *Al-Waqa'i' al-Misriyya*, published regular accounts of the slaves freed at each of the bureaus. On the problems faced by the former slaves, most of whom were women, see the contributions by Liat Kozma and Eve M. Troutt Powell in Walz and Cuno, *Race and Slavery*.

22. Davis, *Ottoman Lady*, 87; Melman, *Women's Orients*, 142.

23. Quotation from J. C. McCoan, *Egypt as It Is* (London: Cassell, Petter & Galpin, 1877), 319; J. Lewis Farley, *Modern Turkey* (London: Hurst and Blackett, 1872), 114–15; Melman, *Women's Orients*, 143. The Egyptian feminist writer Malak Hifni Nasif, who wrote under the pen name Bahithat al-Badiya, also believed that polygyny had declined. See Bahithat al-Badiya, "Ta'addud al-Zawjat, aw al-Dara'ir," in *al-Nisa'iyyat: Majmu'a Maqalat Nushirat fi al-Jarida fi Madwu' al-Mar'a al-Misriyya* (Cairo: Matba'at al-Jarida, 1910), 30.

24. Rifaat 'Ali Abou-el-Haj, "The Ottoman Vezir and Pasa Households, 1683–1703: A Preliminary Report," *Journal of the American Oriental Society* 94, no. 4 (1974): 438; I. Metin Kunt, *The Sultan's Servants: The Transformation of Ottoman Provincial Government, 1550–1650* (New York: Columbia University Press, 1983), 65–67.

25. F. Robert Hunter, *Egypt under the Khedives, 1805–1879: From Household Government to Modern Bureaucracy* (Pittsburgh: University of Pittsburgh Press, 1984), 23.

26. Imad Ahmad Hilal, *Al-Raqiq fi Misr fi al-Qarn al-Tasi' Ashar* (Cairo: Al-Arabi li-l-Nasr wa al-Tawzi', 1999), 409–12.

27. P. N. Hamont, *L'Égypte sous Méhémet-Ali*, 2 vols. (Paris: Leautey & Lecointe, 1843), 1:422.

28. Poole, *The Englishwoman in Egypt*, 2:21–23.

29. Cuno, *The Pasha's Peasants*, 163.

30. Hilal, *Al-Raqiq*, 412–13. His list omits former household slaves and government-owned slaves, who, at best, were married off to lower-class men. My thanks to Terry Walz for pointing this out. The earliest report I found of the Pasha marrying off his harem en masse was a notice of a report by Harriet Martnieau that the Pasha, in "a singular and

whimsical caprice" "has broken up his *harem*, retaining only such of his women as are mothers of children": *The Age*, Nov. 12, 1837, 364.

31. Hamont, *L'Égypte*, 1:422; and Constantine Tischendorff, *Travels in the East* (London: Longman, Brown, Green, and Longmans, 1847), 23.

32. Loos, *Subject Siam*, 110–15.

33. Ruby Lal, *Domesticity and Power in the Early Mughal World* (Cambridge: Cambridge University Press, 2005), 166–73.

34. Peirce, *The Imperial Harem*, 30.

35. Ibid., 28–39, 57–63.

36. Daniel Crecelius, *The Roots of Modern Egypt: A Study of the Regimes of Ali Bey al-Kabir and Muhammad Bey Abu al-Dhahab, 1760–1775* (Minneapolis: Bibliotheca Islamica, 1981), 115; Hilal, *Al-Raqiq*, 93–94.

37. Terri DeYoung, "Mahmud Sami al-Barudi," in Roger Allen, ed., *Essays in Arabic Literary Biography 1850–1950* (Wiesbaden: Harrassowitz, 2010), 62; Ardern Hulme Beaman, *The Dethronement of the Khedive* (London: G. Allen & Unwin, 1929), 27; and Ahmad Shafiq, *Mudhakkirati fi nisf qarn*, 3 vols. (Cairo: Matba'at Misr, 1934), 2:155.

38. Baron Karl de Malortie, *Egypt: Native Rulers and Foreign Interference*, 2d ed. (London: William Ridgway, 1883), 210–11. Similar comments were made in the time of Muhammad Ali by Hamont, *L'Égypte*, 1:422, and Tischendorff, *Travels*, 23.

39. Hamont, *L'Égypte sous Méhémet-Ali*, 1:422–23.

40. Poole, *The Englishwoman in Egypt*, 2:23.

41. Hunter, *Egypt under the Khedives*, 153, 158; personal communication from Terry Walz.

42. See chapter 3.

43. Davis, *Ottoman Lady*, 18; Peirce, *The Imperial Harem*, 69.

44. Hunter, *Egypt under the Khedives*, 26; Aziz Khanki, "Zawjat Hukkam Misr min Muhammad Ali Basha al-Kabir ila Jalalat al-Malik Faruq al-Awwal," special issue of *al-Musawwar* on the occasion of the wedding of King Faruq and Farida, 1938. Reprinted in Khanki, *Nafahat Tarikhiyya* (Cairo: al-Matba'a al-Asriyya, n.d.), 45, 47. Page references are to the latter source.

45. Shafiq, *Mudhakkirati*, 1:80.

46. Alfred J. Butler, *Court Life in Egypt* (London: Chapman and Hall, 1888), 110; and Harriot Georgina Blackwood, the Dowager Marchioness of Dufferin and Ava, *My Russian and Turkish Journals* (New York: C. Scribner's Sons, 1917), 248.

47. Khanki, "Zawjat Hukkam Misr," 44; Emine Foat Tugay, *Three Centuries: Family Chronicles of Turkey and Egypt* (Oxford: Oxford University Press, 1963), 76; *Burke's Royal Families of the World*, 2 vols. (London: Burke's Peerage, 1977–80), 2:27–28; Hanafi al-Mahallawi, *Harim Muluk Misr min Muhammad Ali ila Faruq* (Cairo: Dar al-Amin, 1993), 53.

48. Khanki, "Zawjat Hukkam Misr," 44–45; http://www.royalark.net/Egypt/egypt3.htm.

49. Tugay, *Three Centuries*, 114–15.

50. Peirce, *The Imperial Harem*, 23.

51. Khanki, "Zawjat Hukkam Misr," 44.

52. The most complete list is in the Royal Ark web site, http://www.royalark.net/Egypt/egypt3.htm; see also Khanki, "Zawjat Hukkam Misr," 45–47; Hilal, *Al-Raqiq*, table after 415. Al-Mahallawi cites sources saying that the Pasha had twenty-nine consorts: *Harim Muluk Misr*, 48. Peirce, *The Imperial Harem*, 42.

53. Peirce, *The Imperial Harem*.

54. Muhammad Ali reportedly learned to read at the age of 45, in about 1814: A.-B. Clot Bey, *Aperçu Général sur l'Égypte*, 2 vols. (Paris: Fortin, Masson et Cie., 1840), 1:lxxx. De Malortie reported that the slave woman who taught him to read died two years prior to the writing of his book, which would correspond to the year of Mahduran's death: De Malortie, *Egypt*, 65.

55. Ottoman princes: Alderson, *Structure*, 34–35; khedival wives: Khanki, "Zawjat Hukkam Misr," 45–47, and Hilal, *Al-Raqiq*, table after 415; http://www.royalark.net/Egypt/egypt5.htm ff.

56. Inji Hamin: Blanchard Jerrold, *Egypt under Ismail Pacha: Being Some Chapters of Contemporary History* (London: S. Tinsley & Co., 1879), 16; Edwin De Leon, *The Khedive's Egypt; or, The Old House of Bondage under New Masters* (New York: Harper & Brothers, 1878), 60; Edwin De Leon, *Thirty Years of My Life on Three Continents. With a Chapter on the Life of Women in the East, by Mrs. De Leon*, 2 vols. (London: Ward and Downey, 1890), 174, 202–11, 214–15; Melekber Hanim: Khanki, "Zawjat Hukkam Misr," 45–47, and Hilal, *Al-Raqiq*, table after 415; "publicity:" De Leon, *The Khedive's Egypt*, 61; "diplomatic wives": Davis, *Ottoman Lady*, 93–94.

57. Ismail's consorts: Khanki, "Zawjat Hukkam Misr," 45–47, and Hilal, *Al-Raqiq*, table after 415; Shafiq Nur Hanim: Shafiq, *Mudhakkirati*, 1:81. Ismail married twice more after his deposition: http://www.royalark.net/Egypt/egypt9.htm.

58. Pollard, *Nurturing the Nation*, 88 ff.

59. Mabel Caillard, *A Lifetime in Egypt, 1876–1935* (London: Grant Richards, 1935), 102–3.

60. Rachel G. Fuchs, Contested *Paternity: Constructing Families in Modern France* (Baltimore: Johns Hopkins University Press, 2008), 65 ff.

61. Al-Mahallawi, *Harim Muluk Misr*, 92; http://www.royalark.net/Egypt/egypt9.htm

62. Shafiq, *Mudhakkirati*, 1:81.

63. Aziz Zand, *Al-Qawl al-Haqiq fi Ritha' wa-Tarikh al-Khidiwi Muhammad Basha Tawfiq* (Cairo: Matba'at al-Mahrusa, 1892), 183–85.

64. Alderson, *Structure*, 12.

65. Peirce, *The Imperial Harem*, 21–22.

66. See Mikha'il Sharubim, *Al-Kafi fi Tarikh Misr al-Qadim wa al-Hadith*, 4 vols. (Bulaq: al-Matba'at al-Kubra al-Amiriyya, 1900), 99; P. M. Holt, *Egypt and the Fertile Crescent 1517–1922* (Ithaca: Cornell University Press, 1966), 196; and especially Ehud R. Toledano, *State and Society in Mid-Nineteenth-Century Egypt* (Cambridge: Cambridge University Press, 1990), 108–48.

67. Samir Raafat, "The Much Debated Royal Death on the Nile," *Egyptian Mail*, 11 June 1994. http://www.egy.com/historica.

68. Stanford J. Shaw, *History of the Ottoman Empire and Modern Turkey*, 2 vols. (Cambridge: Cambridge University Press, 1977), 2:130, 500; Holt, *Egypt and the Fertile Crescent*, 196–97.

69. Tugay, *Three Centuries*, 142.

70. Ibrahim Abduh, *Abu Nazzara: Imam al-Sihafa al-Fukahiyya al-Musawwara wa Za'im al-Masrah fi Misr 1839-1912* (Cairo: Maktabat al-Adab, 1953), 27; Irene Gendzier, *The Practical Visions of Yaqub Sanu* (Cambridge, MA: Harvard University Press, 1966), 35–36. The phrase was literally, "If your kidneys aren't up to pleasing more than one woman." To have "the kidneys" is to have the fortitude or to be man enough.

71. Chennells, *Recollections of an Egyptian Princess*, 1:222.

72. *Al-Waqa'i' al-Misriyya* 27, no. 4 (June 1866). An independent press arose in subsequent decades.

73. Two authors claim without evidence that monogamy increased and divorce decreased among the educated: Abd al-Rahman al-Rafi'i, *Asr Isma'il*, 2 vols. (Cairo: Maktabat al-Nahda al-Misriyya, 1948/1932), 2:274; and Angelo Sammarco, *Précis de l'Histoire d'Égypte*, 4 vols. (Rome: l'Imprimerie de l'Institut français d'archéologie orientale du Caire, 1932-35), vol. 4, *Les Règnes de 'Abbas, de Sa'id et d'Isma'il (1848-1879)*, 4:315.

74. *Al-Musawwar*, August 1938. A commemorative stamp was also issued.

75. De Malortie, *Egypt*, 203, quoting an article he published earlier: "Egyptian Sketches, I. The Khedive and His Views," *Pall Mall Gazette*, Oct. 7, 1881.

76. De Malortie, "Egyptian Sketches, I."

77. De Malortie, *Egypt*, 204. On the modernists' views see chapter 3.

78. On Tawfiq's views and his household see Alfred J. Butler, *Court Life in Egypt* (London: Chapman and Hall, 1888), 35, 151, 153–54, 193; Blackwood, *My Russian and Turkish Journals*, 248; Caillard, *A Lifetime in Egypt*, 107; and Princess Djavidan Hanum, *Harem Life* (New York: L. MacVeagh, Dial Press, 1931), 103. None of these authors mentioned whether the slaves were formally manumitted.

79. See chapter 3.

80. Avriel Butovsky, "Images of Monarchy: The Khedivate of Tawfiq Pasha and Reform," in *The Languages of History: Selected Writings on the Middle East* (Cambridge, MA: Center for Middle Eastern Studies, Harvard University, 1995); Yunan Labib Rizq, "Al-Ahram: A Diwan of Contemporary Life," *Al-Ahram Weekly*, Sept. 22–28, 1994;

summary translation of "Al-Ahram Diwan al-Haya al-Mu'asira," no. 61, *al-Ahram*, Sept. 22, 1994.

81. Pollard, *Nurturing the Nation*, 142–49.

82. A. D. Comanos-Pacha, *Mémoires du Dr. Comanos Pacha publiés à l'occasion de son jubilé de 40 ans d'exercise médical* (Cairo: Imprimerie de la Société Orientale de Publicité, 1920), 48–52, 60–62; Shafiq, *Mudhakkirati*, 2:155–57, 177–78, 186–87.

83. *Al-Waqa'i' al-Misriyya* 19 (Feb. 13, 1895); 21 (Feb. 18, 1895).

84. Caillard, *A Lifetime in Egypt*, 110; Djavidan, *Harem Life*, 103, 110.

85. *Al-Ahram*, June 26, 1931.

86. Comanos, *Mémoires*, 50–52; Shafiq, *Mudhakkirati*, 2:155.

87. Djavidan, *Harem Life*, 279; for an extensive account of this marriage see Samir Raafat, "Queen for a Day," *Ahram Weekly*, Oct. 6, 1994. http://www.egy.com/historica.

88. The first Arabic publications to mention it were Shafiq, *Mudhakkirati*, in 1934, and Khanki, "Zawjat Hukkam Misr," in 1938.

89. Dicey, *The Story of the Khedivate*, 468; Cromer, *Modern Egypt*, 2:158, and Cromer, *Abbas II* (London: Macmillan, 1915). Also "Khedive Opposes Polygamy. Has Only One Wife—How He Is Rearing Children," *Egyptian Gazette*, Sept. 15, 1909; and Raafat, "Queen for a Day."

90. Juan R. I. Cole, *Colonialism and Revolution in the Middle East: Social and Cultural Origins of Egypt's 'Urabi Movement* (Princeton: Princeton University Press, 1993), 110 ff.

91. See Beth Baron, "The Making and Breaking of Marital Bonds in Modern Egypt," in Nikki Keddie and Beth Baron, eds., *Women in Middle Eastern History: Shifting Boundaries in Sex and Gender* (New Haven: Yale University Press, 1991), 278; and Baron, *The Women's Awakening in Egypt*, 165. The new family ideology is discussed in chapter 3.

2. Marriage in Practice

1. Ahmad Shafiq, *Mudhakkirati fi Nisf Qarn*, 3 vols. (Cairo: Matba'at Misr, 1934), 1:90.

2. The domestic slaves and concubines of the middle strata were not always treated with the same consideration. See Liat Kozma, *Policing Egyptian Women*, chap. 3; and George Michael La Rue, "'My Ninth Master Was a European,'" 99–124.

3. The changing legal aspects of marriage in this period are discussed in chapters 4–6.

4. Badran, *Feminists, Islam, and Nation*, 127.

5. That discourse is discussed in the following chapter.

6. See the views of Muhammad Ali Allouba below; and Ahmad Hasan al-Baquri, *Al-Usra fi al-Islam* (Cairo: Akhbar al-Yawm, 1983), 26–28.

7. Shafiq, *Mudhakkirati*, 1:73.

8. Ibid., 2:part 1, 172.

9. Ibid., 2:part 3, 501.

10. Personal communication from Hassan Kamel-Kelisli-Morali; see also http://www.flickr.com/photos/kelisli/3966858385/in/set-72157600222898328.

11. Shafiq, *Mudhakkirati*, 2:part 1, 172.

12. Marilyn Booth, "Disruptions of the Local, Eruptions of the Feminine: Local Reportage and National Anxieties in Egypt's 1890s," in Anthony Gorman and Didier Monciaud, eds., *Between Politics, Society and Culture: The Press in the Middle East before Independence*, forthcoming.

13. Kozma, *Policing Egyptian Women*, 87–91.

14. He felt free to mention Isabelle Contal's name because there was no inhibition about naming women publicly in Europe.

15. Salama Musa, *The Education of Salama Musa*, trans. S. O. Schuman (Leiden: Brill, 1961), 7. By the 1930s women who were active in public as professionals, intellectuals, or activists necessarily permitted their names to be printed, and leading women's rights advocates like Huda Al-Sha'rawi and Safiya Zaghlul allowed their unveiled photos to be published. Yet even nowadays men are not likely to know the names of the wives and sisters of male friends, and one does not inquire.

16. Bahithat al-Badiya, "A Lecture in the Club of the Umma Party, 1909," in *Opening the Gates: An Anthology of Arab Feminist Writing*, ed. Margot Badran and miriam cooke, 2d. ed. (Bloomington: Indiana University Press, 2004), 234.

17. This issue is discussed in chapter 5.

18. Ibrahim al-Hilbawi, *Mudhakkirat Ibrahim al-Hilbawi (Tarikh Hayat Ibrahim al-Hilbawi Bayk) 1858–1940* (Cairo: General Egyptian Book Organization, 1995), 102–3.

19. Identified by al-Hilbawi without naming her as the consort of Ilhami Pasha, son of Abbas Hilmi I, and the mother of Princess Amina Ilhami, who married Khedive Tawfiq. She was in reality a concubine: see Prince Mohamed Ali (Tawfiq), *De Ma Naissance à 1882* (Cairo : n.p., 1950), 43.

20. Al-Hilbawi, *Mudhakkirat*, 103.

21. Ibid., 104.

22. Ibid., 150–51.

23. Hunter, *Egypt under the Khedives*, 141.

24. Sania Sharawi Lanfranchi, *Casting Off the Veil: The Life of Huda Shaarawi Egypt's First Feminist* (London: I. B. Tauris, 2012), 15–16.

25. Shaarawi, *Harem Years*, 18, 52–55. Her memoirs were published in Arabic as *Mudhakkirati* (Cairo: Dar al-Hilal, 1981). *Harem Years* and *Mudhakkirati* are the result of different editorial processes; the former is not a translation of the latter, and in a number of places the two texts diverge. See Mohja Kahf, "Packaging 'Huda': Sha'rawi's Memoirs in the United States Reception Environment," in *Going Global: The Transnational Reception of Third World Women Writers*, ed. Amal Amireh and Lisa Suhair Majaj (New York: Garland, 2000), 148–72.

26. These legal devices are discussed in chapter 4.

27. Shaarawi, *Harem Years*, 60–61; and Shaarawi, *Mudhakkirati*, 83. The Arabic text states: "It became clear that the meaning of the declaration (*iqrar*) [by Ali] was that I would be the sole wife, and that if he took back (*raja'a*) the mother of his children she would be divorced." To "take back" was the phrase used when a man resumed a marriage after a revocable divorce. Huda did not identify the mother of Ali's children by name.

28. Shaarawi, *Harem Years*, 61–62.

29. Ibid., 60–61, 64, 82.

30. http://www.flickr.com/photos/kelisli/8607991460/in/photostream.

31. Muhammad Ali Allouba, *Dhikriyyat Ijtima'iyya wa Siyasiyya* (Cairo: General Egyptian Book Organization, 1988), 54–56.

32. Ahmad Amin, *My Life: The Autobiography of an Egyptian Scholar, Writer, and Cultural Leader*, trans. Issa J. Boullata (Leiden: Brill, 1978), 16, 194.

33. Amin, *My Life*, 120–22, 125.

34. Muhammad Lutfi Jum'a, *Shahid ala al-Asr: Mudhakkirat Muhammad Lutfi Jum'a* (Cairo: General Egyptian Book Organization, 2000), 498–513.

35. For accounts of this demonstration see Shaarawi, *Harem Years*, 112–17; Badran, *Feminists, Islam, and Nation*, 75–76; and Abd al-Rahman al-Rafi'i, *Thawrat 1919: Tarikh Misr al-Qawmi min Sanat 1914 ila Sanat 1921*, 2 vols. (Cairo: Maktaba al-Nahda al-Misriyya, 1946), 1:137–41.

36. Abd al-Rahman al-Rafi'i, *Mudhakkirati 1889–1951* (Cairo: Dar al-Hilal, 1952), 37–38.

37. Musa, *The Education of Salama Musa*, 9, 20, 112–13.

38. Muhammad Abduh, "Wedding Customs," *Al-Waqa'i' al-Misriyya*, 1116 (May 19, 1881), in Muhammad Amara, ed., *Al-A'mal al-Kamila li-l-Imam Muhammad Abduh*, 6 vols. (Beirut: Al-Mu'assasa al-Arabiyya li-l-Dirasat wa al-Nashr, 1972), 2:100.

39. Michael Gaspier, *The Power of Representation: Publics, Peasants, and Islam in Egypt* (Stanford: Stanford University Press, 2009), 192–93.

40. Shafiq, *Mudhakkirati*, 1:73.

41. Amin, *My Life*, 121.

42. Jum'a's autobiography may not have been intended for the public; it was published nearly half a century after his death. But al-Rafi'i wrote his memoir for publication.

43. Ahmad b. Umar al-Dayrabi, *Kitab Gayat al-Maqsud li-Man Yata'ati al-Uqud* (Cairo: Matba't al-Wahbiyya, 1880), 34 ff.

44. See chapter 4.

45. Shaarawi, *Harem Years*, 55. These and other conditions agreed to at the time of marriage are discussed at length in chapter 4.

46. According to the Hanafi school of law, which was in force in the Sharia Courts. See chapter 4.

47. MM Murafa'at, 281:104–5, 22 Rajab 1274/March 8, 1858.

48. Karin van Nieuwkerk, *A Trade Like Any Other: Female Singers and Dancers in Egypt* (Austin: University of Texas Press, 1995), 24. See also the coverage of the four princely weddings in *al-Waqa'i' al-Misriyya* cited in chapter 1.

49. On marriage ceremonies in Cairo see Edward W. Lane, *An Account of the Manners and Customs of the Modern Egyptians: The Definitive 1860 Edition* (Cairo: American University in Cairo Press, 2003), 161–73; and on rural weddings a half-century later see Abduh, "Wedding Customs," 100–103.

50. FM 4:601, 21 Muharram 1273/September 21, 1856.

51. The famous case of the marriage of Safiyya Abd al-Khaliq al-Sadat and Ali Yusuf is discussed in chapter 4.

52. Shafiq, *Mudhakkirati*, 1:64; al-Hilbawi, *Mudhakkirat*, 141.

53. Lane, *Manners and Customs*, 173.

54. This paragraph and much of the following discussion is based largely on Walz and Cuno, eds., *Race and Slavery in the Middle East*, especially the introduction and the first three chapters.

55. Alleaume and Fargues, "La Naissance d'un Statistique d'État," 13, 1–2, 181–82.

56. Some women were also described as freed slave wives (*zawjat jariya ma'tuqa*). See Walz, "Sudanese, Habasha, Takarna, and Barabira," 56, 65–66.

57. Lane, *Manners and Customs*, quotation on 133.

58. Ibid., 155–56.

59. La Rue, "'My Ninth Master Was a European,'" quotation 112, 113.

60. See Kenneth M. Cuno, "Demography, Household Formation, and Marriage in Three Egyptian Villages during the Mid-Nineteenth Century," in *Sociétés Rurales Ottomanes/Ottoman Rural Societies*, ed. Mohammad Afifi, Rachida Chih, Brigitte Marino, Nicolas Michel and Isik Tamdogan (Cairo: IFAO, 2005), 109.

61. Kenneth M. Cuno, "African Slaves in Nineteenth-Century Rural Egypt: A Preliminary Assessment," in Walz and Cuno, *Race and Slavery*, 81–83, 90–92. On suitability see chapters 4 and 5.

62. Indeed, Fargues elsewhere contrasts the Cairo data with "the villages and rural areas still dominated by large, multinuclear households." See Philippe Fargues, "Family and Household in Mid-Nineteenth-Century Cairo," in Beshara Doumani, ed., *Family History in the Middle East: Household, Property, and Gender* (Albany: State University of New York Press, 2003), 38. Also Valentine M. Moghadam, *Modernizing Women: Gender and Change in the Middle East*, 2d ed. (Boulder: Lynne Rienner, 2003), 126; Daniel Bates and Amal Rassam, *Peoples and Cultures of the Middle East* (Englewood Cliffs, NJ: Prentice-Hall, 1983), 158–59, 162; Goode, *World Revolution*, 128–29; Judy Brink, "Changing Extended Family Relationships in an Egyptian Village," *Urban Anthropology* 16, no. 2 (1987): 136–37; and Lucie Wood Saunders, "Aspects of Family Organization in an Egyptian Delta Village," *Transactions of the New York Academy of Science*, ser. 2, 30, no. 5 (1968): 716.

63. Households are co-resident groups subsisting from the same set of resources—that is, they "eat from the same pot." For a discussions of household forms in the past see John Hajnal, "Two Kinds of Pre-Industrial Household Formation System"; and Peter Laslett, "Family and Household as Work Group and Kin Group: Areas of Traditional Europe Compared," in Richard Wall, Jean Robin, and Peter Laslett, eds., *Family Forms in Historic Europe* (Cambridge: Cambridge University Press, 1983), 65–104, and 513–63.

64. The multiple stages possible in a joint household cycle are discussed by James Lee and Jon Gjerde, "Comparative Household Morphology of Stem, Joint and Nuclear Household Systems: Norway, China, and the United States," *Continuity and Change* 1, no. 1 (1986): 92–95.

65. Cuno, "Joint Family Households," 485–502.

66. Deniz Kandiyoti, "Bargaining with Patriarchy," *Gender and Society* 2, no. 3 (1988): 278. David Ludden defines domestic patriarchy as "patriarchal power that is located historically inside institutions of kinship." See his "Patriarchy and History in South Asia: Interpretive Experiments," *Calcutta Historical Journal* 17, no. 2 (1995): 2.

67. Deniz Kandiyoti, "Gender, Power, and Contestation: 'Rethinking Bargaining with Patriarchy,'" in Cecile Jackson and Ruth Pearson, eds., *Feminist Visions of Development: Gender, Analysis and Policy* (London: Routledge, 1998), 135–51. See also Moghadam, *Modernizing Women*, 126.

68. Mary S. Hartman, *The Household and the Making of History: A Subversive View of the Western Past* (Cambridge: Cambridge University Press, 2004); Göran Therborn, *Between Sex and Power: Family in the World, 1900–2000* (London: Routledge, 2004), 13, 41, 65.

69. Duben and Behar, *Istanbul Households*, 200–201.

70. In Tables 2 and 3, "solitaries" are single-person households, and "no family households" have more than one inmate but no conjugal couple. Households with one couple may include their children and other relations, most often unmarried brothers and sisters. This rubric comprises two categories, the simple family household and the extended family household, in the terminology used by the Cambridge Group for the History of Population and Social Structure. See Hammel and Laslett, "Comparing Household Structure," 75–78.

71. Alleaume and Fargues, "La Naissance d'un Statistique d'État," 180 and 182, tables 11 and 12.

72. Kenneth M. Cuno, "A Tale of Two Villages: Family, Property, and Economic Activity in Rural Egypt in the 1840s," in Alan K. Bowman and Eugene Rogan, eds., *Agriculture in Egypt from Pharaonic to Modern Times* (Oxford: Oxford University Press, 1999), 320–24.

73. Andre Raymond, *Cairo* (Cambridge, MA: Harvard University Press, 2000), 206–7. The scholar-teachers should be distinguished from lesser religious functionaries such as Qur'an school teachers. The latter did not head joint family households, nor possess slaves or have live-in servants, in Alleaume and Fargues' sample.

74. On the changing relationship of the rulers with the large merchants and ulama see Pascale Ghazaleh, *Fortunes Urbaines et Stratégies Sociales: Généalogies Patrimoniales au Caire, 1780–1830* (Cairo: Institut Français d'Archéologie Orientale, 2010). On the control of trade see Cuno, *Pasha's Peasants*, chap. 7.

75. Alleaume and Fargues, "La Naissance d'un Statistique d'État," 181.

76. Cuno, "Joint Family Households."

77. NAE. Census register of Ikhtab, 1848.

78. Malak Zaalouk, *Al-Tarikh al-Ijtima'i li-Qarya Misriyya: Ikhtab Markaz Aja Muhafazat al-Daqahliyya* (Cairo: Markaz al-Qawmi li-l-Buhuth al-Ijtima'iyya wa al-Jina'iyya, 1995), 34.

79. NAE. Census register of Ikhtab, 1868.

80. Zaalouk, *Al-Tarikh al-Ijtima'i*, 40.

81. See Cuno, "Joint Family Households."

82. Alleaume and Fargues, "La Naissance d'un Statistique d'État," 180–81, Table 11.

83. Cuno, "A Tale of Two Villages," 322.

84. Al-Dayrabi, *Ghayat al-Maqsud*, 58.

85. Abduh, "Wedding Customs," 101.

86. El-Shanawany, "The First National Life Tables for Egypt," 256, Table 17.

87. Philippe Fargues, "The Stages of the Family Life Cycle in Cairo at the End of the Reign of Muhammad Ali, According to the 1848 Census," *Harvard Middle Eastern and Islamic Review* 8 (1999–2000): 9, 30, Table 6.

88. The village marriage data excludes slaves, who were not allowed to marry until later in life. Their inclusion would have exaggerated the urban-rural difference. See Cuno, "African Slaves in Nineteenth-Century Rural Egypt," 89. Fargues' data for men in Cairo in Table 4 and women in Old Cairo in Table 5 represents ever-married persons, i.e., it includes widows and divorcés. The village data represents currently married persons. This makes no difference in the early age groups but causes a misleading disparity in the higher ages.

89. Fargues, "Stages of the Family Life Cycle," 33, Table 10. In the registers for the districts of Cairo the ages of women were haphazardly entered depending on the census taker, but most of the time they were not listed. My thanks to Terry Walz for this clarification.

90. Lane, *Manners and Customs*, 156.

91. See Badran, *Feminists, Islam, and Nation*, 127–28.

92. Allouba's date of birth is given as either 1875 or 1878, making him either twenty-six or twenty-nine when he married.

93. William Wendell Cleland, *The Population Problem in Egypt* (Lancaster, PA: n.p., 1936), 41–44.

94. Kholoussy, *For Better, For Worse*.

95. See Afaf Lutfi al-Sayyid Marsot, "The Revolutionary Gentlewomen in Egypt," in Lois Beck and Nikki Keddie, eds., *Women in the Muslim World* (Cambridge, MA: Harvard

University Press, 1978), 265, 275n5. In Syria in the 1920s joint households with as many as forty or fifty inmates were still maintained by large merchants in Damascus and Aleppo, though they were becoming less common. See Goode, *World Revolution*, 124.

96. Shafiq, *Mudhakkirati*, 1:49–50.

97. Allouba, *Dhikriyyat*, 56.

98. Amin, *My Life*, 124.

99. Baron, "Making and Breaking of Marital Bonds"; Booth, *May Her Likes*, 172–73, 191, 207.

100. Cf. Kholoussy, *For Better, For Worse*, 36–38. In a representative case al-Abbasi ruled that a woman who lived in a house with the family of her husband had no cause for demanding to be lodged elsewhere so long as the part of the house in which she lived was separate, or it had a lock, and it included the normal appurtenances. For good measure the Mufti cited Ibn Abdin and Ahmad al-Tahtawi as his authorities. FM 1:379–80, 8 Jumada I 1265/April 1, 1849.

101. Orhan Pamuk, *Istanbul: Memories of the City* (New York: Knopf, 2005).

102. Duben and Behar, *Istanbul Households*, 55.

103. Al-Hilbawi, *Mudhakkirat*, 47, 140.

104. Arthur Goldschmidt Jr., *Biographical Dictionary of Modern Egypt* (Cairo: The American University in Cairo Press, 2000), 152; Badran and cooke, *Opening the Gates*, 134.

105. Lane, *Manners and Customs*, 182; Fargues, "Stages of the Family Life Cycle," 9.

106. Badran, *Feminists, Islam, and Nation*, 6, 128. In eighteenth- and nineteenth-century travel writing the Ottoman Balkans and Turkey were consistently said to have "a polygamous urban elite and a monogamous majority." See Melman, *Women's Orients*, 142.

107. NAE, Census of Sandub, 1847; Census of Sandub, 1848. The latter register is damaged and lacking pages, but it identifies the occupations of the men more often.

108. Not all of the census registers of al-Mansura have survived intact. In a sample of what survives, five of eleven large merchants (*tujjar*) were polygynous, with a lower proportion among retailers: one of three tobacco merchants, and one of five silk merchants. NAE, Census of al-Mansura, 1848. Unfortunately there is no comparable disaggregated data available for Cairo.

109. Cuno, *Pasha's Peasants*, 53, 129.

110. Lane, *Manners and Customs*, 82. In the same passage he asserted, incorrectly, that polygyny was more widespread "among the lower orders."

111. Goode, *World Revolution*, 104. See also Philippe Fargues, "Terminating Marriage," in *The New Arab Family*, ed. Nicholas S. Hopkins, *Cairo Papers in Social Science* 24, nos. 1–2 (2001): 255.

112. Lane, *Manners and Customs*, 183. Maintenance and obedience are discussed extensively in chapters 4–6.

113. Homa Hoodfar, *Between Marriage and the Market: Intimate Politics and Survival in Cairo* (Berkeley: University of California Press, 1997), 74.

114. Personal communication from Terence Walz.

115. MD Tarikat wa Aylulat, 3:120–24, no. 216, 28 Safar 1278/September 4, 1861; Census registers of Ikhtab, 1848 and 1868. The 1868 census of Ikhtab listed a woman named Nafisa who gave her age as twenty, and was the wife of Ahmad b. Abd Allah Shahata, twenty-five, a landholder.

116. MM Muba'iyat, 118:126–28, 14 Jumada I 1292/June 16, 1875; 187:8–9, 28 Jumada I 1303/Mar. 3, 1886; Tarikat 61:46–57, 25 Shawwal-10 al-Qa'da 1282/Mar. 13–27, 1866; 61:84–87, 16 Rabi' I 1283/Aug. 3, 1866; 119:15–17, 17 Rajab 1291/Aug. 30, 1874; 119:19–25, 6 al-Hijja 1291/Jan. 14, 1875; 120:1–2, 4 al-Hijja 1291/Jan. 12, 1875; MD Tarikat wa Aylulat, 3:84, no. 139, 17 Jumada II 1277/Dec. 31, 1860; 3:99–102, no. 175, 18 Shawwal 1277/April 29, 1861; 7:13–14, no. 65, 14 Muharram 1284/May 18, 1867; 20:27–29, no. 8, 22 Muharram 1299/Dec. 14, 1881; 20:29–30, no. 9, 10 Safar 1299/Jan. 4, 1882.

117. Bahithat al-Badiya, "Ya li-l-Nisa' min al-Rijal wa Ya li-l-Rijal minhinna," *al-Nisa'iyyat*, 24; and "A Lecture in the Club of the Umma Party," 234–35.

118. Personal communication from Marilyn Booth.

119. In the late 1980s 80 percent of women surveyed said that their marriages had been arranged. In rural and lower-income urban communities, the bride's or groom's family searched for a suitable match on the basis of "certain ascribed characteristics . . . [that took] precedence over personality and individual choice." Then the two families negotiated the terms of marriage, including financial arrangements. See Diane Singerman and Barbara Ibrahim, "The Costs of Marriage in Egypt: A Hidden Dimension in the New Arab Demography," in Nicholas S. Hopkins, ed., *The New Arab Family*; Cairo Papers in Social Science 24, nos. 1–2 (2001): 88–89; and Hoodfar, *Between Marriage and the Market*, 51 ff.

3. Marriage Reformed

1. Jean-Louis Flandrin, *Families in Former Times* (Cambridge: Cambridge University Press, 1979), 4–8.

2. See the issue devoted to "family law exceptionalism" of the *American Journal of Comparative Law* 58, no. 4 (Fall 2010): 753–1054.

3. On the transmission of those ideas see Thornton, *Reading History Sideways*, esp. chaps. 8, 11, and 12. Omnia (El) Shakry detected hybridization in the production of "anticolonial national discourses on motherhood," which were a feature of the new family ideology, in "Schooled Mothers and Structured Play: Child Rearing in Turn-of-The-Century Egypt," in Lughod, ed., *Remaking Women*, 127–28 and 157–58.

4. Omnia El Shakry, *The Great Social Laboratory: Subjects of Knowledge in Colonial and Postcolonial Egypt* (Stanford: Stanford University Press, 2007), 5, 6. A similar point about the medical profession was advanced by Hiba Abugideiri, in "Colonizing Mother

Egypt, Domesticating Egyptian Mothers," in Poonam Bala, ed., *Biomedicine as a Contested Site: Some Revelations in Imperial Contexts* (New York: Lexington Books, 2009).

5. See Pollard, *Nurturing the Nation*, chap. 3.

6. See Mitchell, *Colonising Egypt*, 108–11.

7. Sonneveld, *Khul' Divorce in Egypt*, 17 ff.

8. Hasan al-Idwi al-Hamzawi, *Ahkam Uqud al-Nikah*, published at the end of his *Kitab Tabsirat al-Qudat wa al-Ikhwan fi Wad' al-Yad wa Ma Yashhad la-hu Min al-Burhan* (Bulaq: al-Matba'a al-Amiriyya, 1859). For his biography see Gilbert Delanoue, *Moralistes et politiques musulmans dans l'Égypte du XIXe siècle (1798–1882)*, 2 vols. (Cairo: Institut Français d'Archéologie Orientale du Caire, 1982), 1:261–84.

9. Al-Dayrabi, *Gayat al-Maqsud*, republished as *Ahkam al-Zawaj ala al-Madhahib al-Arba'a al-Musamma Ghayat al-Maqsud li-Man Yata'ati al-Uqud* (Beirut: Dar al-Kutub al-Ilmiyya, 1986). See the short biography in the 1986 edition.

10. Abd al-Majid Ali al-Hanafi b. Shaykh Ali Ismail al-Idwi, *Matla' al-Badrayn fima Yata'allaq bi-l-Zawjayn* (Cairo: n.p., 1278/1862), 2, 13. There are no biographies of him that I know of.

11. Muhammad b. Umar al-Nawawi, *Sharh Uqud al-Lujayn fi Bayan Huquq al-Zawjayn*, 2d ed. (Cairo: al-Matba'at al-Wahbiyya, 1879), 29. See C. Brockelmann, "Al-Nawawi," *Encyclopaedia of Islam*, 2d ed., Brill Online.

12. See, for example, the introduction by Yahya Cheikh to his translation of al-Tahtawi's *Murshid, L'Emancipation de la Femme Musulmane: Le Guide Honnête pour l'Éducation des Filles et des Garçons* (Beirut: Les Éditions Al-Bouraq, 2000), 19–21, 23; Imad Abu Ghazi's introduction to Rifa'a Rafi'i al-Tahtawi, *Al-Murshid al-Amin li-l-Banat wa al-Banin*, ed. Imad Abu Ghazi (Cairo: al-Majlis al-A'la li-l-Thiqafa, 2002), b–j; Muhammad Imara, *Rifa'a al-Tahtawi Ra'id al-Tanwir fi al-Asr al-Hadith* (Cairo: Dar al-Shuruq, 1988), 333–68; and Rif'at Sa'id, *Tarikh al-Fikr al-Ishtiraki fi Misr* (Cairo: Matabi' Kustatsumas wa Sharikihi, 1969), 33–34.

13. See Fig. 5 for the text of Al-Tahtawi's declaration of conditional divorce. Sa'id wrote that it was an expression of al-Tahtawi's belief in a woman's right to equality (*Tarikh al-Fikr al-Ishtiraki*, 34–35), though it was no such thing. Leila Ahmed mistakenly compared it to John Stuart Mill's famous promise not to exercise the control that English law accorded him over his wife and her property (Leila Ahmed, *Women and Gender in Islam: Historical Roots of a Modern Debate* [New Haven: Yale University Press, 1992], 137, and 267n23). Al-Tahtawi is said to have had a Circassian concubine, but presumably that was after the death of his wife. See F. Robert Hunter, *Egypt under the Khedives, 1805–1879: From Household Government to Modern Bureaucracy* (Pittsburgh: University of Pittsburgh Press, 1984), 102.

14. All references are to the 2002 edition of the *Murshid* edited by Imad Abu Ghazi, which is a reproduction of the original edition.

15. See James Heyworth-Dunne, *An Introduction to the History of Education in Modern Egypt* (London: Luzac, 1938), 362–74, 380–81.

16. On al-Tahtawi's life and work see Albert Hourani, *Arabic Thought in the Liberal Age* (Cambridge: Cambridge University Press, 1983), 69; Imara, *Rifa'a al-Tahtawi Ra'id al-Tanwir*; Delanoue, *Moralistes*, 2:384–487; and the Introduction to Rifa'a Rafi' al-Tahtawi, *An Imam in Paris: Account of a Stay in France by an Egyptian Cleric (1826–1831)*, trans. Daniel L. Newman (London: Saqi Books, 2004). On al-Attar see Peter Gran, *Islamic Roots of Capitalism: Egypt 1760–1840* (Austin: University of Texas Press, 1979); and Delanoue, *Moralistes*, 2:344–56.

17. Ali Mubarak, *Al-Khitat al-Tawfiqiyya al-Jadida li-Misr al-Qahira*, 20 vols. (Bulaq: al-Matba'at al-Amiriyya, 1887–89).

18. Ali Mubarak, *Tariq al-Hija wa al-Tamrin ala al-Qira'a fi al-Lugha al-Arabiyya*, 2 vols. (Cairo: Matba'at Wadi al-Nil, 1868), quotation 2:4.

19. All references herein are to vols. 1–2 of Muhammad Imara, ed., *Ali Mubarak al-A'mal al-Kamila*, 3 vols. (Beirut: al-Mu'assasa al-Arabiyya li-l-dirasat wa al-Nashr, 1979). On the date of its composition see Darrell Dykstra, "A Biographical Study in Egyptian Modernization: 'Ali Mubarak (1823/4–1893)," unpublished Ph.D. dissertation, University of Michigan (1977), 401–5; and cf. Imara, *Ali Mubarak al-A'mal al-Kamila*, 1:84 ff.

20. Mubarak mentioned his marriages in his autobiography (*Khitat*, 9:43, 46, 48). On *Alam al-Din* see Dykstra, "Biographical Study," 400–18; Wadad al-Qadi, "East and West in 'Ali Mubarak's *'Alamuddin*," in Marwan Buheiry, ed., *Intellectual Life in the Arab East, 1890–1939* (Beirut: American University of Beirut, 1981), 21–37. On Mubarak's life and works, Delanoue, *Moralistes*, 2:488–559.

21. Hourani, *Arabic Thought*, 108, 132.

22. Mark Sedgwick, *Muhammad Abduh* (Oxford: Oneworld, 2010), 2, 4, 59–60; Amin Osman, *Muhammad Abduh* (Washington, DC: American Council of Learned Societies, 1953), 2, 5, 68, 71.

23. Kassem-Amin, *Les Égyptiens: Réponse a M. le Duc d'Harcourt* (Cairo: Jules Barbier, 1894).

24. Muhammad Imara, ed., *Qasim Amin: Al-A'mal al-Kamila* (Cairo: Dar al-Shuruq, 1989), 26; Margot Badran, "From Consciousness to Activism: Feminist Politics in Early Twentieth Century Egypt," in John P. Spagnolo, ed., *Problems of the Middle East in Historical Perspective* (Reading: Ithaca Press, 1996), 39n45; Joseph T. Zeidan, *Arab Women Novelists: The Formative Years and Beyond* (Albany: State University of New York Press, 1995), 123n19. There is a photograph of Zaynab Amin Tawfiq, uncovered, in Imara's edited volume. Their daughters did not cover.

25. Charles C. Adams, *Islam and Modernism in Egypt: A Study of the Modern Reform Movement Inaugurated by Muhammad Abduh* (New York: Russell & Russell, 1933), 231, citing an undated third edition of *Tahrir al-Mar'a* that appeared as a supplement in

al-Siyasa, in which Huda Sha'rawi lauded Amin as "the hero of the feminist awakening and its founder." "Luther of the East": Badran, *Feminists, Islam, and Nation*, 258n75.

26. E.g., Thomas Philipp, "Feminism and Nationalist Politics in Egypt," in Lois Beck and Nikki Keddie, eds., *Women in the Muslim World* (Cambridge, MA: Harvard University Press, 1978), 277–94; Baron, *The Women's Awakening*; Badran, *Feminists, Islam, and Nation*; Booth, *May Her Likes*; and Hatem, *Literature, Gender, and Nation-Building*.

27. On al-Taymur's life and writings see Marilyn Booth, "'A'ishah al-Taymuriyyah," in Allen, ed., *Essays in Arabic Literary Biography*, 366–76; and Hatem, *Literature, Gender, and Nation-Building*.

28. On Fawwaz's life and writings see Marilyn Booth, "Zaynab Fawwaz al-'Amili," in Allen, ed., *Essays in Arabic Literary Biography*, 93–98.

29. On Nasif's life and writings see Goldschmidt, *Biographical Dictionary*, 152; Badran and cooke, *Opening the Gates*, 134; and Badran, "From Consciousness to Activism," 32.

30. Imam al-Ghazali, *The Proper Conduct of Marriage in Islam (Adab an-Nikah): Book Twelve of Ihya' Ulum al-Din*, trans. Muhtar Holland (Hollywood, FL: al-Baz, 1998), 14–41.

31. Muhammad Amin b. Umar, known as Ibn Abdin, *Radd al-Muhtar ala al-Durr al-Mukhtar Sharh Tanwir al-Absar*, 3d ed., 5 vols. (Bulaq: n.p., 1905–8), 2:265; al-Idwi, *Ahkam Uqud al-Nikah*, 120–21, 179–80.

32. Ibn Abdin, *Radd al-Muhtar*, 2:325; al-Ghazali, *The Proper Conduct of Marriage*, 89. In different versions of this hadith, Asma' bt. Abi Bakr or Aisha bt. Abi Bakr or both of them say, "Marriage is slavery and so let each of you consider where he places his daughter [in marriage]" or "Marriage is slavery and so let each of you consider where he consigns to slavery his freewoman." Author's translation. From al-Bayhaqi's *Sunan al-Kubra*, al-Iraqi's *Takhrij Ahadith al-Ihya'*, Ibn Abi al-Dunya's *Al-Nafaqa ala al-Ayyal*, and Sa'id b. Mansur's *Al-Tafsir Sunan Sa'id b. Mansur*, accessed via the Complete Reference of Islamic Hadeeth CD ROM.

33. Yossef Rapoport, *Marriage, Money and Divorce in Medieval Islamic Society* (Cambridge: Cambridge University Press, 2005), 52.

34. Ali, *Marriage and Slavery in Early Islam*, 164. Examples of the use of the term *milk* occur later in this chapter.

35. Al-Idwi, *Ahkam Uqud al-Nikah*, 178, 184; Ibn Abdin, *Radd al-Muhtar*, 2:265.

36. Author's translation, using the version of the farewell sermon in *Sunan al-Tirmidhi*, 5 vols. (Beirut: Dar al-Kutub al-Ilmiyya, 1994), 4:256, no. 1159, accessed via the Complete Reference of Islamic Hadeeth CD ROM.

37. A young daughter, *bint shabba*, was a girl as young as twelve to fifteen years old; an elderly man or *shaykh kabir* was no younger than his late thirties. On that and "looking at" one's fiancée see al-Idwi, *Ahkam Uqud al-Nikah*, 185; and Ibn Abdin, *Radd al-Muhtar*, 2:269. In Yahya b. Sharaf al-Nawawi's (1233–77) *Kitab al-Adhkar* the preference for seeing a fiancée before the wedding was attributed to all four Sunni schools of law and

legitimized with a hadith related by Abu Hurayra. See *Al-Majmu': Sharh al-Madhhab*, 22 vols. (Beirut: Dar al-Fikr, 1996), 17:289.

38. Chaps. 1 and 8 in *Matla' al-Badrayn* and chaps. 1 and 2 in *Uqud al-Lujayn*. These phrases are often translated as "the rights of the wife against the husband" and "the rights of the husband against the wife."

39. Author's translation of both texts.

40. Al-Nawawi, *Uqud al-Lujayn*, 4–5, 10; Abd al-Majid Ali, *Matla' al-Badrayn*, 13, 14–15, 53.

41. Al-Nawawi, *Uqud al-Lujayn*, 5.

42. Abd al-Majid Ali, *Matla' al-Badrayn*, 14.

43. Al-Nawawi, *Uqud al-Lujayn*, 7; Abd al-Majid Ali, *Matla' al-Badrayn*, 11. Nearly identical versions of this hadith were reported by Abd Allah b. Umar, Abu Hurayra, and Abu Sa'id al-Khudari. See, e.g., *Sahih Muslim*, 2 vols. (Beirut: Dar al-Kitab al-Ilmiyya, 1992), 2:56, no. 203, accessed via the Complete Reference of Islamic Hadeeth CD ROM.

44. Fatima Mernissi, *The Veil and the Male Elite: A Feminist Interpretation of Women's Rights in Islam* (New York: Basic Books, 1991), 70–76. Joseph Zeidan noted that the Prophet's wife Aisha was considered a more accurate source of hadith than Abu Hurayra, in *Arab Women Novelists*, 12.

45. Barbara Freyer Stowasser, "Women and Citizenship in the Qur'an," in Sonbol, ed., *Women, the Family, and Divorce Laws*, 23–38; Leila Ahmed, *Women and Gender in Islam*, chaps. 4 and 5.

46. Al-Nawawi, *Uqud al-Lujayn*, 7–8. The hadith was transmited by Ibn Umar. See *Sahih al-Bukhari*, 9 vols. (Beirut: Dar Ihya' al-Turath al-Arabi, 1981), 1:303, no. 882, accessed via the Complete Reference of Islamic Hadeeth CD ROM.

47. Author's translation. Al-Nawawi,*Uqud al-Lujayn*, 8. Abd al-Majid Ali also references Q 4:34 indirectly: *Matla' al-Badrayn*, 54.

48. Stowasser, "Women and Citizenship in the Qur'an," 32.

49. Al-Nawawi, *Uqud al-Lujayn*, 8.

50. Abd al-Majid Ali, *Matla' al-Badrayn*, 4–5. See *Sunan al-Tirmidhi*, 4:253, no. 1155, accessed via the Complete Reference of Islamic Hadeeth CD ROM.

51. Al-Nawawi, *Uqud al-Lujayn*, 10.

52. Ibid., 9; Abd al-Majid Ali, *Matla' al-Badrayn*, 5–6. See, e.g., *Sahih al-Bukhari*, 3:1181, no. 3167, accessed via the Complete Reference of Islamic Hadeeth CD ROM. Related by Abu Hurayra.

53. Al-Nawawi, *Uqud al-Lujayn*, 11; Abd al-Majid Ali, *Matla' al-Badrayn*, 6. See *Musnad al-Tayalisi* (Beirut: Dar al-Ma'rifa, 1988), 447, no. 1952, accessed via the Complete Reference of Islamic Hadeeth CD ROM. Related by Ibn Umar.

54. Abd al-Majid Ali, *Matla' al-Badrayn*, 11–12.

55. Abd al-Rahman b. Hasan al-Jabarti, *Aja'ib al-Athar fi al-Tarajim wa al-Akhbar*, 4 vols. (Bulaq: n.p., 1880), 2:204.

56. See chapter 4.

57. Tucker, *Women, Family, and Gender in Islamic Law*, 183–95.

58. See the discussion in Ibn Abdin, *Radd al-Muhtar*, 2:665, of tradeswomen who attended to their affairs during the day and were with their husbands at night. Female vendors who had access to upper-class harems and other tradeswomen are mentioned in Lane, *Manners and Customs*, 187, 191, and 193. See also Tucker's discussion of women practicing crafts and trades in *Women in Nineteenth-Century Egypt*, 81–88, 91–93; and on rural women, Cuno, *The Pasha's Peasants*, 53, 129. For an earlier period see Yossef Rapoport, *Marriage, Money and Divorce*, 33–35.

59. Hatem, *Literature, Gender, and Nation-Building*, 125; Bahithat al-Badiya, "Al-Hijab wa al-Sufur," in *al-Nisa'iyyat*, 8–9.

60. Ibn Abdin, *Radd al-Muhtar*, 2:663.

61. Lane, *Manners and Customs*, 187.

62. DeYoung, "Mahmud Sami al-Barudi," 62.

63. Stefan Reichmuth, *The World of Murtada al-Zabidi (1732–91): Life, Networks and Writings* (Oxford: Gibb Memorial Trust, 2009), 75.

64. Mitchell, *Colonising Egypt*, 64–65, 68–69.

65. Pollard, *Nurturing the Nation*, 26, 28. Conrad Malte-Brun, *Universal Geography: or A Description of All the Parts of the World on a New Plan, According to the Great Natural Divisions of the Globe; Accompanied with Analytical, Synoptical, and Elementary Tables*, 6 vols. (Philadelphia: A. Finley, 1827–32), 1:261–62, 281–82. First published in 1812. G(eorges)-B(ernard) Depping, *Aperçu Historique sur les Moeurs et Coutumes des Nations, Contenant le Tableau Comparé Chez les Divers Peuples Anciens et Modernes, des Usages et des Cérémonies Concernant l'Habitation, la Nourriture, l'Habillement, les Mariages, les Funèrailles, les Jeux, les Fêtes, les Guerres, les Superstitions, les Castes, etc., etc.* (Paris: Mariet et Fournier, 1842), 54–55, 57–67 (quotation, 57). First published in 1826. On Enlightenment-era connections between the stages of civilization, family practices, and the status of women see Thornton, *Reading History Sideways*, 21–43, 55–57. Mubarak, *Khitat*, 9:42. Translations: Newman, *An Imam in Paris*, 40, 44.

66. Al-Tahtawi, *al-Murshid*, 8, 16–17, 19, 90 ff. Timothy Mitchell discussed the influence of Depping on al-Tahtawi's study of politics, *Manahij al-Albab al-Misriyya fi Mabahij al-Adab al-Asriyya* (1869) in *Colonising Egypt*, 107.

67. Al-Tahtawi, *al-Murshid*, 62–64.

68. Ibid., 56.

69. Depping, *Aperçu Historique*, 60–61; Bidelman, *Pariahs Stand Up!*, 17.

70. Al-Tahtawi, *al-Murshid*, 54.

71. Depping, *Aperçu Historique*, 68–69.

72. Al-Tahtawi, *al-Murshid*, 66.

73. See, e.g., Nadine Bérenguier, *Conduct Books for Girls in Enlightenment France* (Surrey: Ashgate, 2011), 90–91; on education to prepare women for a domestic role,

Patricia Mainardi, *Husbands, Wives, and Lovers: Marriage and Its Discontents in Nineteenth Century France* (New Haven: Yale University Press, 2003), 52.

74. Butrus al-Bustani, speech on "The Education of Women" (1849), in Fu'ad Afram al-Bustani, *Al-Muʻallim Butrus al-Bustani: Taʻlim al-Nisa' wa Adab al-Arab, Dars wa Muntakabat*, 2d ed. (Beirut: al-Matbaʻat al-Kathulikiyya, 1966), 97; and Namık Kemal's essay "On the Education of Women: a Draft" (1867), as discussed by Emel Sönmez, "Turkish Women in Turkish Literature of the 19th Century," *Die Welt des Islams* 12, nos. 1–3 (1969): 8–11.

75. Al-Tahtawi, *al-Murshid*, 66–68.

76. Mubarak, *Tariq al-Hija*, 2:81–82.

77. *Ali Mubarak al-Aʻmal al-Kamila*, 1:341–42.

78. Mainardi, *Husbands, Wives, and Lovers*, 104–6. On this shift see also Bidelman, *Pariahs Stand Up!* 21–30.

79. Mitchell, *Colonising Egypt*, 88. Al-Tahtawi's contemporary al-Bustani used the term *taʻlim*, "instruction," in advocating women's education.

80. Mubarak, *Tariq al-Hija*, 2:79–80.

81. Al-Tahtawi, *al-Murshid*, 134, 138 139.

82. Mainardi, *Husbands, Wives, and Lovers*, 3.

83. See chapter 4.

84. Al-Tahtawi, *al-Murshid*, 138.

85. Ibid., 148. My thanks to Marilyn Booth for her help in translating these lines. On al-Dirini (1215–95) and his better-known writings see Clément Huart, *A History of Arabic Literature* (New York: D. Appleton and Co., 1903), 279.

86. El-Said Badawi and Martin Hinds, eds., *A Dictionary of Egyptian Arabic* (Beirut: Librarie du Liban, 1986), 247. Thanks, again, to Marilyn Booth for pointing this out.

87. Al-Tahtawi, *al-Murshid*, 150–73.

88. See chapter 1.

89. Al-Tahtawi, *al-Murshid*, 206–7.

90. Ibid., 215.

91. Ibid., 278–79, 282.

92. Ibid., 37.

93. Ibid., 55.

94. Ibid., 206–7, 215, 273–74, 276.

95. *Ali Mubarak al-Aʻmal al-Kamila*, 1:345–67; Dykstra, "Biographical Study," 537–47.

96. Delanoue, *Moralistes*, 2:546.

97. *Ali Mubarak al-Aʻmal al-Kamila*, 1:459–66; and later, 623–24.

98. Delanoue, *Moralistes*, 2:546–49.

99. Mubarak, *Tariq al-Hija*, 2:110–11.

100. *Ali Mubarak al-Aʻmal al-Kamila*, 1:463–70.

101. *Ibid.*, 1:564–65.

102. Bidelman, *Pariahs Stand Up!* 38.

103. *Ali Mubarak al-A'mal al-Kamila*, 2:242–43.

104. On divorce and women's option of *khul'* and *mubara'a* agreements see Cuno, "Divorce and the Fate of the Family in Modern Egypt."

105. Mubarak, *Tariq al-Hija*, 2:112. Slightly different versions of this hadith narrated by Ibn Umar are found in Sunan Abi Dawud, 6:227, no. 2182; and Sunan Ibn Majah, 1:650, no. 2076, accessed via the Complete Reference of Islamic Hadeeth CD ROM.

106. Imara, ed., *Qasim Amin al-A'mal al-Kamila*, 21–25; Hourani, *Arabic Thought*, 170; Zeidan, *Arab Women Novelists*, 273n20.

107. Muhammad Abduh, *Al-A'mal al-Kamila li-l-Imam Muhammad Abduh*, ed. Muhammad Imara, 6 vols. (Beirut: al-Mu'assasa al-Arabiyya li-l-Dirasat wa al-Nashr, 1972), 1:245–67.

108. Hourani, *Arabic Thought*, 135.

109. On the curriculum of the Law School see chapter 5.

110. Hourani, *Arabic Thought*, 114, 132.

111. François Guizot, *History of Civilization in Europe, from the Fall of the Roman Empire to the French Revolution* (1828; reprint, New York: John B. Alden, 1885), 72–74.

112. Malte-Brun, *Universal Geography*, 1:273; Depping, *Aperçu Historique*, 67.

113. Muhammad Abduh, "Hajat al-Insan ila al-Zawaj," in *al-A'mal al-Kamila*, 2:68–71. *Husn al-mu'ashara* was one of the duties of husbands listed in the precolonial writings, but "domestic society" was a European term. See Malte-Brun, *Universal Geography*, 1:273.

114. Muhammad Abduh, *Taqrir Fadilat Mufti al-Diyar al-Misriyya al-Usthadh al-Shaykh Muhammad Abduh fi Islah al-Mahakim al-Shar'iyya* (Cairo: Matba'at al-Manar, 1900), 3.

115. E.g., Abduh, "Al-Tarbiya," address given in 1900, in *al-A'mal al-Kamila*, 3:170.

116. Nikkie Keddie, *Sayyid Jamal ad-Din "al-Afghani:" A Political Biography* (Berkeley and Los Angeles: University of California Press, 1972), 110–11.

117. Amin, *Les Égyptiens*, 109–11.

118. Qasim Amin, *Tahrir al-Mar'a*, in Imara, ed., *Qasim Amin al-A'mal al-Kamila*, 330 (quotation), 345, 347–48. Hereafter cited as TM in *Al-A'mal al-Kamila*. In Qasim Amin, *The Liberation of Women and The New Woman: Two documents in the History of Egyptian Feminism*, trans. Samiha Sidhom Peterson (Cairo: The American University in Cairo Press, 2000), the equivalent passages are on 12 (quotation), 30, 31–33. This is a poor-quality translation and reliable for only a rough idea of the original text.

119. TM in *Al-A'mal al-Kamila*, 342–43, 344. *Liberation*, 26–28.

120. TM in *Al-A'mal al-Kamila*, 339. *Liberation*, 22–23.

121. On household management as a popular topic in the 1890s see Baron, *The Women's Awakening*, 155–58; and Booth, *May Her Likes*, 43. Russell discusses it as a topic in periodicals and textbooks after 1900 in *Creating the New Egyptian Woman*, 85–87, 144–54.

122. TM in *Al-A'mal al-Kamila*, 336–37. *Liberation*, 18–20
123. TM in *Al-A'mal al-Kamila*, 388–90. *Liberation*, 77–81.
124. TM in *Al-A'mal al-Kamila*, 330–31. *Liberation*, 12–13.
125. TM in *Al-A'mal al-Kamila*, 332. *Liberation*, 14.
126. TM in *Al-A'mal al-Kamila*, 331. *Liberation*, 13.

127. Amin also used the term *hijab* in reference to the "confinement" of women in the home (e.g., TM in *Al-A'mal al-Kamila*, 355). Since the advent of the "new veiling" circa 1970, the term *hijab* has referred to various styles of head covering, while the face veil is called *niqab*.

128. TM in *Al-A'mal al-Kamila*, 351–52. *Liberation*, 36–37.
129. TM in *Al-A'mal al-Kamila*, 350. *Liberation*, 35–36.

130. TM in *Al-A'mal al-Kamila*, 353. *Liberation*, 38. Curiously, Amin cited only Hanafi and Shafi'i texts, saying that to provide the Maliki and Hanbali sources would prolong the discussion unnecessarily. The haphazard source citation is a good indication that Abduh did not write that passage.

131. TM in *Al-A'mal al-Kamila*, 353–55. *Liberation*, 38–41.

132. TM in *Al-A'mal al-Kamila*, 361–62; *Liberation*, 47–49. Leila Ahmed misinterpreted Amin in this passage as saying that women must mix with men to be educated.

133. See Beth Baron, "Unveiling in Early Twentieth Century Egypt: Practical and Symbolic Considerations," *Middle Eastern Studies* 25, no. 3 (July 1989): 370–86.

134. Abduh, "Hukm al-Shari'a fi Ta'addud al-Zawjat," in *Al-A'mal al-Kamila*, 2:76–81.

135. Ibid., 2:71, 77, 78, 80, 83.

136. Translation of 4:129 by A. J. Arberry, *The Koran Interpreted*. Hanafi jurists required a man to perform at least one act of sexual intercourse with his wife but no more than that. See Ibn Abdin, *Radd al-Muhtar*, 2:608–9.

137. Here and in his earlier essay the word *al-'adl*, which I interpret contextually as "equal treatment," also means "balance" and "justice." Abduh, *Al-A'mal al-Kamila*, 5:169.

138. Abduh, *Al-A'mal al-Kamila*, 5:170. *Maslaha*, the public interest, is a principle that can override a normative legal rule or even a scriptural text. See Madjid Khadduri, "Maṣlaḥa," *Encyclopaedia of Islam*, 2d ed., Brill Online.

139. Abduh, *Al-A'mal al-Kamila*, 2:88–92.
140. TM in *Al-A'mal al-Kamila*, 393. *Liberation*, 81–82.
141. TM in *Al-A'mal al-Kamila*, 394–95. *Liberation*, 83–84.
142. TM in *Al-A'mal al-Kamila*, 395–96. *Liberation*, 85–86.

143. Most family issues were heard in the Sharia Courts, but judges in the National Courts heard suits involving the enforcement of family law in such areas as maintenance and child custody. Moreover, Abduh conducted a study of the Sharia Court system in 1899, and as mufti he regularly dealt with Muslim family law.

144. Booth, *May Her Likes*, 140; Baron, "Unveiling," 376–77; Bahithat al-Badiya, "Ya li-l-Nisa' min al-Rijal wa Ya li-l-Rijal minhinna," *al-Nisa'iyyat*, 23.

145. Abduh, *Al-Aʿmal al-Kamila*, 2:654 (quotation), 657–58.

146. Ibid., 2:655–56. On necessity in jurisprudence see Y. Linant de Bellefonds, "Darura," *Encyclopaedia of Islam*, 2d ed., Brill Online. Law No. 25 of 1920 is discussed in the conclusion.

147. TM in *Al-Aʿmal al-Kamila*, 408–10. *Liberation*, 99–100.

148. TM in *Al-Aʿmal al-Kamila*, 397–400. *Liberation*, 87–90.

149. TM in *Al-Aʿmal al-Kamila*, 400–406. *Liberation*, 90–97.

150. These laws are discussed in chapter 4.

151. TM in *Al-Aʿmal al-Kamila*, 407–8. *Liberation*, 98.

152. Cuno, "Divorce and the Fate of the Family," 201.

153. Zaynab Fawwaz, Essay No. 59, "Mujmal Hayat al-Nisa'" (1898), in *al-Rasa'il al-Zaynabiyya* (Cairo: al-Matbaʿat al-Mutawassita, 1905), 192.

154. Mitchell, *Colonising Egypt*, 112; Ahmad, in *Women and Gender*, 155; Lila Abu-Lughod, "The Marriage of Feminism and Islamism in Egypt," 258.

155. Cromer, *Modern Egypt*. Until then he kept his views on Egyptian family life private: see Roger Owen, *Lord Cromer: Victorian Imperialist, Edwardian Proconsul* (Oxford: Oxford University Press, 204), 246–48. The words "generation of mothers" appear in Clara Boyle, *Boyle of Cairo: A Diplomatist's Adventures in the Middle East* (Kendal: Titus Wilson & Son, 1965), 56.

156. Cromer, *Modern Egypt*, 2:155–57; compare with Amin, TM in *Al-Aʿmal al-Kamila*, 327, 361–62; *Liberation*, 9–10, 47–49.

157. The census of 1917 showed a 15 percent literacy rate for males and 2 percent for females.

158. Aisha al-Taymur, "Family Reform Comes Only through the Education of Girls," in Badran and cooke, *Opening the Gates*, 130–32; Zaynab Fawwaz, Essay No. 69 in *al-Rasa'il al-Zaynabiyya*, 214–16; Bahithat al-Badiya, "Madarisuna wa Fatayatuna," in *al-Nisa'iyyat*, 15–17.

159. Al-Taymur, "Family Reform," 129; Zaynab Fawwaz, "Fair and Equal Treatment," in Badran and cooke, *Opening the Gates*, 223; Bahithat al-Badiya, "Khutba fi al-Muqarana bayn al-Mar'a al-Misriyya wa al-Mar'a al-Gharbiyya," in *al-Nisa'iyyat*, 142.

160. Al-Taymur, "Family Reform," 132–33; Fawwaz, Essays No. 32 and 33 in *al-Rasa'il al-Zaynabiyya*, 109–10, 110–11; Bahithat al-Badiya, "The Evils of Men. Tyranny," in Badran and cooke, *Opening the Gates*, 228.

161. Fawwaz, "Fair and Equal Treatment," 223–25; Bahithat al-Badiya, "The Evils of Men," 228–31.

162. Booth, *May Her Likes*, 160.

163. Fawwaz, "Fair and Equal Treatment," 223–25; essay no. 51 in *al-Rasa'il al-Zaynabiyya*, 170.

164. Bahithat al-Badiya, "The Evils of Men," 228–30; and "Al-Hijab wa al-Sufur," in *al-Nisa'iyyat*, 8–9. Nasif's point about women and technology is consistent with the findings

of Judith Tucker, in *Women in Nineteenth-Century Egypt*, 88–91. Al-Taymur shared Nasif's disdain for working women: see Hatem, *Literature, Gender, and Nation-Building*, 125.

165. Hatem, *Literature, Gender, and Nation-Building*, 89.

166. Aisha al-Taymur, *Mir'at al-Ta'ammul fi al-Umur*, 2d ed. (Cairo: Women and Memory Forum, 2002), 29–30.

167. Al-Taymur, *Mir'at al-Ta'ammul*, 30–33; quotation 33.

168. Ibid., 34.

169. Hatem, *Literature, Gender, and Nation-Building*, 116 (quotation), 118. Unlike Hatem I read the discussion of *huquq* in terms of the maintenance-obedience relationship and not as evidence of a new conception of "rights."

170. See chapter 4.

171. Al-Taymur, *Mir'at al-Ta'ammul*, 32.

172. Fawwaz, unnumbered essay, "Ya Allah li-l-Mar'a min al-Rijal" (1900), in *al-Rasa'il al-Zaynabiyya*, 202.

173. Bahithat al-Badiya, "Ya li-l-Nisa' min al-Rijal wa Ya li-l-Rijal minhinna," *al-Nisa'iyyat*, 24.

174. Bahithat al-Badiya, "Ra'i fi al-Zawaj (wa Shakwa al-Nisa' minhi)," *al-Nisa'iyyat*, 4; and "Ya li-l-Nisa' min al-Rijal wa Ya li-l-Rijal minhinna," *al-Nisa'iyyat*, 26.

175. Hatem, *Literature, Gender, and Nation-Building*, 118, 120; and in a later context, Kholoussy, *For Better or Worse*,

176. Fawwaz, Essay No. 59, "Mujmal Hayat al-Nisa'," (1898), in *al-Rasa'il al-Zaynabiyya*, 122–23; Bahithat al-Badiya, "Ta'addud al-Zawjat, aw al-Dara'ir," in *al-Nisa'iyyat*, 27–31. See Hatem, *Literature, Gender, and Nation-Building*, 100–111, for a discussion of al-Taymur's portrayal of two plural marriages in *Nata'ij al-Ahwal*.

177. Badran, *Feminists, Islam, and Nation*, 62, 64; Baron, *The Women's Awakening*, 155, 158.

178. Baron, *The Women's Awakening*, 156, 158, and 234–35, nn. 33, 35, 44, 53, citing articles published in 1909 and 1915; and Malika Sa'd's *Rabbat al-Dar*, published in 1915 and 1917.

179. Afsaneh Najmabadi, *Women with Mustaches and Men without Beards: Gender and Sexual Anxieties of Iranian Modernity* (Berkeley and Los Angeles: University of California Press, 2005), 202 (quotation), 205.

180. El Shakry, "Schooled Mothers and Structured Play," 126; Abugideiri, "Colonizing Mother Egypt, Domesticating Egyptian Mothers," 19.

181. Najmabadi, *Women with Mustaches*, 202 and 203 (quotations), 206; Badran, *Feminists, Islam, and Nation*, 61–65.

4. Marriage in Law

1. These laws were: (1) *La'ihat al-Qudat*, 28 Rabi' II 1273/Dec. 26, 1856, in Filib Jallad, *Qamus al-Idara wa al-Qada'*, 4 vols. (Alexandria: al-Matba'a al-Bukhariyah, Yani

Lagudakis, 1890–92), 4:129–32; (2) *La'ihat al-Mahakim al-Shar'iyya*, 9 Rajab 1297/June 17, 1880, in Jallad, *Qamus*, 4:145–56; and (3) *La'ihat Tartib al-Mahakim al-Shar'iya wa al-Ijra'at al-Muta'alliqa bi-ha*, May 27, 1897, in *Majmu'a al-Awamir al-Ulya wa al-Dikritat al-Sadira fi Sanat 1897* (Bulaq: al-Matba'a al-Amiriyya, 1898), 155–75.

2. Cole, *Colonialism and Revolution*, 37. About 7 percent of the al-Abbasi's questions were identified as coming from government offices or the Sharia Courts: Peters, "Muḥammad al-Abbasi al-Mahdi," 69.

3. See Ido Shahar, "Legal Pluralism and the Study of the Shari'a Courts," *Islamic Law and Society* 15 (2008): 112–41; Rapoport, "Legal Diversity," 210–28; and James E. Baldwin, "Islamic Law in an Ottoman Context: Resolving Disputes in Late 17th/Early 18th-Century Cairo," Ph.D. dissertation, New York University, 2010, chap. 3, "Pluralism and Policy," 120–67. I am indebted to James Baldwin for his comments and willingness to share his knowledge of the Ottoman legal system.

4. *La'ihat Tartib al-Mahakim, 1897*, 163, Art. 31.

5. See, e.g., Latifa Muhammad Salim, *Al-Nizam al-Qada'i al-Misri al-Hadith 1875–1914* (Cairo: Markaz al-Dirasat al-Siyasiyya wa al-Istratijiyya bi-l-Ahram, 1984); and Farhat J. Ziadeh, *Lawyers, the Rule of Law and Liberalism in Modern Egypt* (Stanford: Hoover Institution, 1968), 24–43. For a critique of the secular-religious dichotomy in Ottoman legal history see Avi Rubin, "Ottoman Judicial Change in the Age of Modernity: A Reappraisal," *History Compass* 7, no. 1 (2009): 119–40.

6. On the judicial councils see Rudolph Peters, "Administrators and Magistrates: The Development of a Secular Judiciary in Egypt, 1842–1871," *Die Welt des Islams* 39, no. 3 (1999): 378–97; Kozma, *Policing Egyptian Women*, 6 ff.; and Aziz Khanki, "Al-Tashri' wa al-Qada' qabl Insha' al-Mahakim al-Ahliyya," in *Al-Kitab al-Dhahabi li-l-Mahakim al-Ahliyya, 1883–1933*, 2 vols. (Bulaq: al-Matba'at al-Amiriyya, 1937), 1:65. On the police see Khaled Fahmy, "The Police and the People in Nineteenth-Century Egypt," *Die Welt des Islams* 39, no. 3 (1999): 340–77.

7. See chapter 5.

8. See, e.g., Esposito with DeLong-Bas, *Women in Muslim Family Law*, 48.

9. Shahar, "Legal Pluralism," 138; Halil Inalcik, "i. The Earlier Centuries," in "Mahkama," Part 2, "The Ottoman Empire," *Encyclopaedia of Islam*, 2d ed., Brill Online; Wael B. Hallaq, *Shari'a: Theory, Practice, Transformations* (Cambridge: Cambridge University Press, 2009), 216–17; Knut Vikør, *Between God and the Sultan: A History of Islamic Law* (Oxford: Oxford University Press, 2005), 209, 217; Christelow, *Muslim Law Courts*, 86.

10. Nelly Hanna, "The Administration of Courts in Ottoman Cairo," in Nelly Hanna ed., *The State and Its Servants: Administration in Egypt from Ottoman Times to the Present* (Cairo: American University in Cairo Press, 1995), 45; Rapoport, "Legal Diversity," 210–28.

11. Rapoport, "Legal Diversity," 221.

12. Baldwin, "Islamic Law in an Ottoman Context," 146–52.

13. Khayr al-Din b. Ahmad al-Ramli, *Al-Fatawa al-Khayriyya li-Nafʿ al-Barriyya*, 2d ed., 2 vols. (Beirut: Dar al-Maʿrifa, 1974), 1:76.

14. Tucker, *In the House of the Law*, 83; Baldwin, "Islamic Law in an Ottoman Context," 138–39.

15. Al-Ramli, *Al-Fatawa al-Khayriyya*, 1:76; A. A. Fyzee, *Outlines of Muhammadan Law*, 3d ed. (London: Oxford University Press, 1964), 75–76; Seymour Vesey-Fitzgerald, *Muhammadan Law: An Abridgment According to Its Various Schools* (Oxford: Oxford University Press, 1931), 18.

16. Baldwin, "Islamic Law in an Ottoman Context," 157–59.

17. FM 1:162, 13 al-Qaʿda 1265/Oct. 12, 1849.

18. The views of Joseph Schacht and Noel Coulson on this point seem to have been influenced by what Jean-Robert Henry and François Balique call the "colonial school" of Muslim Algerian law. See Schacht, *Introduction to Islamic Law*, 61–62; Noel J. Coulson, *A History of Islamic Law* (Edinburgh: Edinburgh University Press, 1964), 142–48, and Henry and Balique, *La Doctrine Coloniale*, 11.

19. Hallaq, *Sharia*, 215; Vikor, *Between God and Sultan*, 209.

20. Hallaq, *Sharia*, 203; Cuno, *The Pasha's Peasants*, 89–96.

21. Zayn al-Abidin Ibrahim b. Muhammad, known as Ibn Nujaym, *Al-Ashbah wa al-Naza'ir* (Damascus: Dar al-Fikr, 1983), 108.

22. Ibn Nujaym, *Al-Ashbah wa al-Naza'ir*, 109.

23. Only the Shafiʿis did not require the presence of witnesses.

24. Al-Dayrabi, *Gayat al-Maqsud*, 51.

25. Ibid., 51.

26. In the absence of qualified agnates the Hanbalis allowed male maternal relations to stand in as guardians, and the Hanafis allowed maternal relations as well as women to stand in. See al-Dayrabi, *Gayat al-Maqsud*, 55–57; FM 1:36, 23 al-Hijja 1267/Oct. 19, 1851; 37, 12 Safar 1268/Dec. 7, 1851; 45–46, 22 Safar 1269/Dec. 6, 1852; 60–61, 5 Safar 1272/Oct. 17, 1855.

27. On the minimum age: FM 1:51, 20 Rabiʿ I 1270/Dec. 21, 1853; 63–64, 4 Ramadan 1272/May 10, 1856, and al-Dayrabi, *Ghayat al-Maqsud*, 64. On the maximum age: FM 1: 37–38, 7 Rabiʿ I 1268/Dec. 31, 1851; 5:95, 5 Muharram 1269/Oct. 20, 1852.

28. The distinction between adulthood and discretion arose in a fatwa by the Shafiʿi jurist Shams al-Din Muhammad b. Ahmad al-Ramli (1513–96), in which a boy was judged to have reached sexual maturity (*bulugh*) while not enough time had passed to ascertain his discretion (*rushd*): *Fatawa Shams al-Din Muhammad al-Ramli*, in the margin of Ahmad b. Muhammad Ibn Hajar al-Haythami, *al-Fatawa al-Kubra al-Fiqhiyya*, 4 vols. (Cairo: Matbaʿa Abd al-Hamid Ahmad Hanafi, 1938), 3:151.

29. FM 1:19, 24 Jumada II 1265/May 17, 1849. Tucker mistakenly claimed that a girl had an absolute right to refuse an arranged marriage, even one arranged by her father (*In the House of the Law*, 49). The fatwa she cited as support involved the right of an *adult*

woman to refuse, in Muhammad Amin, known as Ibn Abdin, *Al-Uqud al-Durriyya fi Taqih al-Fatawa al-Hamidiyya*, 2d ed., 2 vols. (Bulaq: al-Matba'at al-Miriyya, 1882–83), 1:31. See also Joseph Schacht, "Nikaḥ," I, "In Classical Islamic Law," *Encyclopaedia of Islam*, 2d ed., Brill Online.

30. Al-Dayrabi, *Ghayat al-Maqsud*, 62; al-Idwi, *Ahkam Uqud al-Nikah*, 222; Ibrahim al-Bajuri, *Sharh Minah al-Fattah ala Daw' al-Misbah fi Ahkam al-Nikah* (Cairo[?]: n.p., 1870), 18.

31. E.g., FM 1:27, 16 Shawwal 1266/August 25, 1850; 38, 13 Rabi' I 1268/Jan. 6, 1852; 30, 18 Sha'ban 1270/May 16, 1854; 89–90, 8 Jumada II 1297/May 19, 1880.

32. See chapter 2.

33. Al-Idwi, *Ahkam Uqud al-Nikah*, 222; al-Bajuri, *Sharh Minah al-Fattah*, 18.

34. Al-Dayrabi, *Ghayat al-Maqsud*, 39, 57; al-Idwi, *Ahkam Uqud al-Nikah*, 185.

35. Al-Dayrabi, *Ghayat al-Maqsud*, 51.

36. Nelly Hanna, "Marriage among Merchant Families in Seventeenth-Century Cairo," in Amira El Azhary Sonbol, ed., *Women, the Family, and Divorce Laws in Islamic History* (Syracuse: Syracuse University Press, 1996), 150.

37. Al-Dayrabi, *Ghayat al-Maqsud*, 51.

38. Hanna, "Marriage among Merchant Families," 150.

39. Ibid., 152–53.

40. This dislike is also evident in literary sources, e.g., Remke Kruk, "Click of Needles: Polygamy as an Issue in Arabic Popular Epic," in Manuela Marin and Randi Deguilhem, eds., *Writing the Feminine: Women in Arab Sources* (London: I. B. Tauris, 2002), 3–23.

41. On Maliki judicial practice see Henry Toledano, *Judicial Practice and Family Law in Morocco: The Chapter on Marriage from Sijilmasi's Al-Amal al-Mutlaq* (Boulder: Social Science Monographs, 1981). On a women's contractual options in practice see G. H. Bousquet, "Islamic Law and Customary Law in French North Africa," *Journal of Comparative Legislation and International Law*, 3d ser., 32, nos. 3–4 (1950), 60; J. Lapanne-Joinville, "Les Conventions Annexées au Contrat de Mariage (tatawwu'at) en Droit Musulman Malékite," *Revue Algérienne, Tunisienne et Marocaine de Législation et de Jurisprudence* 70, no. 4 (1954): 112–25; and Dalenda Largueche, "Monogamy in Islam: The Case of a Tunisian Marriage Contract," Institute of Advanced Studies, School of Social Science Occasional Papers, 39 (September 2010).

42. FM 1:160–61, 27 Sha'ban 1265/July 18, 1849.

43. NAE, Damietta divorce register of Muhammad al-Nahhas (*ma'dhun*/registrar), old no. 131, new no. 25, Aug. 8, 1911, case no. 45.

44. Delegated divorce is discussed by Ibn Abdin in *Radd al-Muhtar*, 2:494–505. The phrase *ismatuha fi yadiha* occurs, for example, in the divorce of Sharifa Umm Isa mentioned above. *Amruha fi yadiha* occurs in FM 1:160–61, 27 Sha'ban 1265/July 18, 1849 and 1:202, 1 Jumada I, 1271/Jan. 20, 1855.

45. Shafiq, *Mudhakkirati*, 2: part 3, 500; Jum'a, *Shahid ala al-Asr*, 513; Amin, TM in *Al-A'mal al-Kamila*, 410; *Liberation*, 100.

46. On delegated divorce in South Asia see Syed Ameer Ali, *Mahommedan Law. Containing the Law Relating to Succession and Status. Compiled from Authorities in the Original Arabic* (Lahore: Law Publishing, 1976/1880), 455–57; M. A. Abdur Rahim, *Principles of Muhammadan Jurisprudence According to the Hanafi, Maliki, Shafi'i and Hanbali Schools* (London: Luzac, 1911), 327, 338; Fyzee, *Outlines of Muhammadan Law*, 151; Lucy Carroll, "Talaq-i-Tafwid and Stipulations in a Muslim Marriage Contract: Important Means of Protecting the Position of the South Asian Muslim Wife," *Modern Asian Studies* 16, no. 2 (1982): 277–309; Farhat Hasan, *State and Locality in Mughal India: Power Relations in Western India, c. 1572–1730* (Cambridge: Cambridge University Press, 2004), 79–81; and Fareeha Khan, "Tafwid al-Talaq: Transferring the Right of Divorce to the Wife," *Muslim World* 99 (July 2009): 503–5.

47. Tucker, *In the House of the Law*, 101–8.

48. FM 1:174, 5 Muharram 1267/Nov. 11, 1850.

49. For example, FM 1:164–65, 2 Muharram 1266/Nov. 19, 1849.

50. For example, FM 1:160, 9 Sha'ban 1265/June 30, 1849; 240–41, 18 Rajab 1297/June 26, 1880; 234–35, 14 Jumada II 1290/Aug. 9, 1873.

51. FM 1:164, 14 al-Hijja 1265/Oct. 31, 1849.

52. Untitled document in the Tahtawi family archive dated 14 Shawwal 1255/December 21, 1839. My thanks to Archana Prakash for providing a copy and to Ali Rifaah for permission to use it. The agreement is quoted in Sa'id, *Tarikh al-Fikr al-Ishtiraki*, 24.

53. The text of Law No. 25 of 1929 and its explanatory memorandum appear in Ahmad Muhammad Ibrahim, *Majmu'a Qawanin al-Ahwal al-Shakhsiyya* (Alexandria: Al-Dar al-Misriyya li-l-Tiba'a wa al-Nashr, 1956[?]), 18, art. 2.

54. Text of the OLFR in Arabic, *Qarar Huquq al-A'ila*, in Bassam Abd al-Wahhab al-Jabi, *Al-Majalla: Majallat al-Ahkam al-Adiliyya; ma'ha Qarar Huquq al-A'ila fi al-Nikah al-Madani wa al-Talaq* (Limassol: Dar Ibn Hazm, 2004), 534: Art. 106. On the conditional divorce as a means of controlling the husband's behavior see Ronald C. Jennings, "Women in Early 17th Century Ottoman Judicial Records: The Sharia Court of Anatolian Kayseri," *Journal of the Economic and Social History of the Orient* 18, no. 1 (Jan. 1975): 87 ff., and "Divorce in the Ottoman Sharia Court of Cyprus, 1580–1640," *Studia Islamica* 78 (1993): 155–67; and Tucker, *In the House of the Law*, 103–5.

55. On South Asia see Fyzee, *Outlines of Muhammadan Law*, 152. On Southeast Asia see Elsbeth Locher-Scholten, *Women and the Colonial State: Essays on Gender and Modernity in the Netherlands Indies 1900–1942* (Amsterdam: Amsterdam University Press, 2000), chap. 6; and Hisako Nakamura, "Conditional Divorce in Indonesia," *Islamic Legal Studies Program Occasional Studies* 7, Harvard Law School (July 2006): 1–44.

56. La'ihat al-Qudat, 1856, 4:129, Art. 2.

57. Cole, *Colonialism and Revolution*, 37–38.

58. Mubarak, *Khitat*, 4:29–30. Hallaq noted a similar outcome in the Syrian provinces: *Sharia*, 217.

59. *La'ihat al-Mahakim al-Shar'iyya*, 1880, 4:146, Art. 10.

60. *La'ihat Tartib al-Mahakim al-Shar'iyya*, 1897, 159, Art. 16.

61. Abduh, *Taqrir*, 15.

62. Cuno, *The Pasha's Peasants*, 193–94.

63. *La'ihat al-Qudat, 1856*, 4:130, Art. 8.

64. *Ibid.*, Art. 9.

65. For example, in October 1797 Shaykh Ahmad b. Abd Allah al-Muzayyin, a *faqih* in the village of Sallant in al-Daqahliyya province, was appointed by the chief judge of al-Mansura for a period of two years to deal with marriage contracts and divorces, for a payment of 120 *nisf fidda* per year. MM 35:111, Rabi' II 1212/Sept.–Oct. 1797.

66. *La'ihat al-Qudat, 1856*, 4:130, Art. 12. Fees were set in an appendix to the law; see Surat Dhayl La'ihat al-Qudat, in Jallad, *Qamus al-Idara*, 4:132–34.

67. *La'ihat al-Mahakim al-Shar'iyya*, 1880, 4:146–47, Arts. 13, 14.

68. *La'ihat al-Mahakim al-Shar'iyya*, 1880, 4:155–56, Arts. 159–178.

69. *La'ihat Tartib al-Mahakim*, 1897, 163, Art. 31.

70. In January 1885 several members of a family testified that they had agreed to divide a landholding three months earlier in a "customary contract" (*aqd urfi*): MM Muba'iyat 181:9–10, 10 Rabi' II 1302/June 26, 1885. In June 1899 Shaykh Ahmad Jalabi and his freed slave Farida Hanim testified that they were married outside the court twenty years earlier, and that the marriage was still valid. MD al-Ahwal al-Shaksiyya, 86:49–50, no. 80, June 28, 1899.

71. Cleland, *Population Problem*, 43.

72. FM 1: 378, 24 al-Hijja 1264/Nov. 21, 1848.

73. Ibn Abdin, *Radd al-Muhtar*, 2: 676. FM 1:400, 30 al-Hijja 1267/Oct. 27, 1851; 408, 13 Rabi' I 1269/Dec. 25, 1852; 431–32, 30 al-Qa'da 1276/June 20, 1859; 442, 13 al-Qa'da 1283/Mar. 19, 1866.

74. FM 1:443, 21 Rabi' II 1285/Aug. 11, 1868.

75. FM 1: 384–85, 14 al-Hijja 1265/Oct. 31, 1849.

76. Ibn Abdin, *Radd al-Muhtar*, 2:665; FM 1: 416, 30 Shawwal 1270/July 26, 1854.

77. FM 1: 399, 1 al-Hijja 1267/Sept. 27, 1851.

78. FM 1:391, 9 al-Qa'da 1266/Sept. 16, 1850; 398–99, 11 al-Qa'da 1267/September 7, 1851; 393, 19 Muharram 1267Nov. 24, 1850; 418, 10 Rabi' II 1271/ Dec. 31, 1854; 429, 13 Safar 1275/Sept 22, 1858. Agmon found that courts in Palestine would allow a woman to borrow as much as she was owed in maintenance and the lenders would collect from her husband: *Family and Court*, 111, 212n20. I found no examples of that in nineteenth-century Egypt.

79. E.g., FM 1:423, 18 al-Hijja 1272/Aug. 21, 1856; 426, 15 al-Qa'da 1273/July 7, 1857; 436, 29 Rajab 1279/Jan. 20, 1863; 447–48, 8 Jumada I 1288/July 26, 1871.

80. The one-month rule is stated, e.g., in FM 1:418, 10 Rabiʿ II 1271/ Dec. 31, 1854.

81. FM 1:396, 7 Rajab 1267/May 8, 1851; 378, 9 Safar 1264/Jan. 16, 1848.

82. The chapter on maintenance has twenty-seven cases of preemptive judgments or agreements setting the amount due compared to handfuls of post-desertion cases. Quarrels: FM 1:405, 19 Shawwal 1268/Aug. 7, 1852; 410, 7 Shaʿban 1269/May 16, 1853; 419, 16 Jumada II 1271/Mar. 6, 1855.

83. Eighty-nine of 288 lawsuits recorded. MD Murafaʿat 44, 1899.

84. MD Murafaʿat 44:1, no. 2, Jan. 7, 1899.

85. MD Murafaʿat 44:38–39, no. 134, June 19, 1899. A *kayla* was about 15.33 liters or 16.25 quarts.

86. MD Murafaʿat 44: 47–48, no. 163, July 29, 1899.

87. FM 1:58, 20 Shaʿban 1271/May 8, 1855; 153, 8 Safar 1265/Jan. 4, 1849; and 162, 13 al-Qaʿda 1265/Oct. 12, 1849.

88. J. N. D. Anderson, "Recent Developments in Sharʿia Law II," *Muslim World* 41, no. 1 (1951): 37; Abduh, *Taqrir*, 15; *Qarar Huquq al-A'ila*, 538, Arts. 126, 127.

89. Kayseri: Jennings, "Women in Early 17th Century Ottoman Judicial Records," 92–96. Ankara: Başak Tuğ, "Politics of Honor: The Institutional and Social Frontiers of 'Illicit' Sex in Mid-Eighteenth-Century Ottoman Anatolia," Ph.D. dissertation, New York University, 2009, 352–58; quotation, 354. Syria: Tucker, *In the House of the Law*, 84.

90. Tucker, *In the House of the Law*, 84.

91. FM 1:17, 16 Rabiʿ II 1265/May 12, 1849; 35, 24 al-Qaʿda 1267/Sept. 20, 1851; 36, 9 Muharram 1268/Nov. 4, 1851; 40, 5 Rajab 1268/Apr. 26, 1852; 42, 3 al-Qaʿda 1268/Aug. 20, 1852; 44, 5 Muharram 1269/Oct. 20, 1852; 49, 16 Shaʿban 1269/May 26, 1853.

92. These cases are discussed in detail in Kenneth M. Cuno, "Women with Missing Husbands: Marriage in Nineteenth Century Egypt," in *Objectivity and Subjectivity in the Historiography of Egypt: In Honour of Nelly Hanna*, ed. Nasser Ahmed Ibrahim (Cairo: General Egyptian Book Organization, 2012), 156–70.

93. MD Murafaʿat 1:5, no. 27, 17 Jumada I 1273/Jan. 14, 1857.

94. FM 1:53, 9 Rajab 1270/April 7, 1854; 72–73, 12 Shaʿban 1277/Feb. 22, 1861.

95. E.g., FM 1:23, 23 al-Hijja 1265/Nov. 9, 1849; 61, 22 Safar 1272/Nov. 18, 1855; 79, 30 Shaʿban 1284/Dec. 27, 1867; 86, 30 Rajab 1293/Aug. 21, 1876.

96. E.g., FM 1:18, 30 Rabiʿ II 1265/Mar. 25, 1849; 51–52, 11 Jumada II 1270/Mar. 11, 1854, 79, 13 Rajab 1285/Oct. 29, 1868.

97. E.g., FM 1:56, 1 Jumada I 1271/Jan. 20, 1855; 76–77, 8 Shaʿban 1282/Dec. 27, 1865.

98. E.g., FM 1:20–21, 21 Shaʿban 1275/Mar. 26, 1859; 64–65, 13 Muharram 1273/Sept. 3, 1856.

99. Arguments made, respectively, by Baron, in "Making and Breaking," 275–91, and *Egypt as a Woman*, 34–35; Kholoussy, *For Better, For Worse*, 111–17; and Haj, *Reconfiguring Islamic Tradition*, 170–71.

100. Compare Haj, *Reconfiguring Islamic Tradition*, 170, with Muhammad b. Abd Allah al-Kharashi, *Al-Kharashi ala Mukhtasar Sidi Khalil wa bi-Hamishih Hashiyat al-Shaykh Ali al-Idwi*, 8 vols. (Cairo: Dar al-Kitab al-Islami, n.d.), 3:272; and Ahmad b. Muhammad al-Dardir in *Hashiyat al-Disuqi ala al-Sharh al-Kabir*, 4 vols. (Cairo: Isa al-Babi al-Halabi, n.d.), 2:226, who state that *malika li-amr nafsiha* is the equivalent of *rashida* (of discretion, legally capable).

101. Lynn Hunt, *The Family Romance of the French Revolution* (Berkeley and Los Angeles: University of California Press, 1992), 39–40; Duben and Behar, *Istanbul Households*, 194; Deniz Kandiyoti, "Some Awkward Questions on Women and Modernity in Turkey," in Abu-Lughod, ed., *Remaking Women*, 280; Najmabadi, *Women with Mustaches*, 114–26.

102. Booth, *May Her Likes*, 195, 207, 215, 255–57; Pollard, *Nurturing the Nation*, 7; Hatem, *Literature, Gender, and Nation-Building*, 90–92.

103. See chapter 3.

104. See chapter 3.

105. Hamont, *L'Égypte sous Méhémet-Ali*, 1:309–10.

106. St. John, *Egypt and Mohammed Ali*, 2:176.

107. Ibid., 2:375. The term almé or *alma* (learned woman) meant a "woman well-versed in the arts, especially music and poetry," but Westerners routinely used this term for dancers, and by implication prostitutes. See Wendy Buonaventura, *Serpent of the Nile: Women and Dance in the Arab World* (London: Saqi Books, 1989), 7, 48.

108. See S. V. Spilsbury, "St. John, James Augustus (1795–1875)," *Oxford Dictionary of National Biography* (Oxford: Oxford University Press, 2004), http://www.oxforddnb.com.proxy2.library.illinois.edu/view/article/24498.

109. Cf. Fahmy, *All the Pasha's Men*, 229.

110. "Zawjat al-Mafqud bi-Hukm al-Shari'a al-Islamiyya al-Ghara'," *Al-Adab* 3, no. 61 (Feb. 16, 1889): 201–2.

111. "Zawjat al-Mafqud," 202.

112. FM 1:440, 16 Safar 1287/May 17, 1870; *La'ihat al-Qudat, 1856*, 4:129, Art. 4.

113. Decree of the Ministry of Justice, May 27, 1884, in Jallad, *Qamus al-Idara*, 4:163.

114. Abduh, *Taqrir*, 67–69.

115. *Majallat al-Ahkam al-Shar'iyya* 2, no. 2 (April 13, 1903): 35–41.

116. Al-Damurdash (1853–1920) was the head of the Damurdashi Sufi order and one Abduh's circle; see Adams, *Islam and Modernism in Egypt*, 209.

117. NAE, Majlis al-Nuzzar wa-l-Wuzara', File no. 0075-016495, Iqtirahat al-Jam'iyya al-Umumiyya bi-Sha'n Islah al-Mahakim al-Shar'iyya wa Insha' Qalam fi Kull Mahkama Mudiriyya li-Tanfidh Ahkam al-Nafaqat wa Ghayrihi wa al-Nazar fi Amr Mahkamat al-Daqahliyya allati Ulghiyat, Feb. 1909.

118. NAE, Majlis al-Nuzzar wa-l-Wuzara', File no. 0075-016495, Iqtirahat al-Jam'iyya al-Umumiyya, Feb. 1909.

119. NAE, Majlis al-Nuzzar wa-l-Wuzara, File no. 0075-016689, Iqtirahat al-Jamʿiyya al-Umumiyya fi Ijtimaʿiha Sanata 1910. Iqtirah bi-Talab Takhwil al-Qadi al-Sharʿi Haqq al-Hubs fi Mawadd al-Nafaqat wa Takhwil al-Mahakim al-Sharʿiyya Haqq Tanfidh Ahkamiha, April 17, 1910.

120. Abduh, *Taqrir*, 37.

121. Ibid., 71. A decree of Feb. 26, 1890 set one-fourth as the maximum of a civil servant's salary that could be garnished: *Majmuʿa al-Awamir al-Ulya wa al-Dikritat* (Cairo: al-Matbaʿat al-Ahliyya, 1890), 52–53.

122. Abduh, *Taqrir*, 70–72.

123. *Al-Waqaʾiʿ al-Misriyya*, 2, 25 (Jan. 5, 1901). A *qirat* is one twelfth-fourth of a feddan, which is approximately an acre.

124. Amin, *My Life*, 135.

125. Baron, *The Women's Awakening*, 146–49.

5. Marriage Codified

1. Muhammad Rashid Rida, *Tarikh al-Ustadh al-Imam al-Shaykh Muhammad Abduh*, 3 vols. (Cairo: Matbaʿat al-Manar, 1931), 1:620–21. Al-Tahtawi was not opposed to the idea of composing a code based on "the ordinances of the Sharia" (*al-ahkam al-sharʿiyya*), which he called for in *Manahij al-Albab*, 392.

2. The criticism of the judicial councils was voiced in a memorandum submitted by the Minister of Justice Husayn Fakhri to the Council of Ministers in 1882, "Madhkarat Husayn Fakhri Basha Nazir al-Haqqaniyya li-Majlis al-Nuzzar," in *Al-Kitab al-Dhahabi li-l-Mahakim al-Ahliyya*, 2 vols. (Bulaq: al-Matbaʿat al-Amiriyya, 1937), 1:109–10. On the *Mecelle* see Rubin, *Ottoman Nizamiye Courts*, 30 ff.; and Carter V. Findley, "Medjelle," *Encyclopaedia of Islam*, 2d ed., Brill Online.

3. Heyworth-Dunne, *Introduction*, 268, 271, 353, 355. The Online Catalog of the Library of Congress lists translations of the municipal code, the code of criminal procedure, the penal code, the civil code, and the commercial code.

4. On the creation of the Mixed Courts see Byron Cannon, *Politics of Law and the Courts in Nineteenth-Century Egypt* (Salt Lake City: University of Utah Press, 1988), 45–61; and Jasper Yeates Brinton, *The Mixed Courts of Egypt*, 2d ed. (New Haven: Yale University Press, 1968), 1–24.

5. On unequal treaties as a world-historical phenomenon see Richard S. Horowitz, "International Law and State Transformation in China, Siam, and the Ottoman Empire during the Nineteenth Century," *Journal of World History* 15, no. 4 (2005): 445–86.

6. Separately, Ottoman mixed courts of commerce were organized in the 1840s and decades later were incorporated into the *Nizamiye* court system. See Rubin, *Ottoman Nizamiye Courts*, 26, 68.

7. "Madhkarat Husayn Fakhri Basha," 111–15. Talal Asad thought that Fakhri's memorandum, in rejecting the idea of a Sharia-based law, referred to Qadri's personal status code. Rather, the issue was whether to adopt a civil law based on the Sharia, like the *Mecelle*. See Asad, *Formations of the Secular*, 215n26. On creation of the National Courts see also Brown, *Rule of Law*, 29–31; and Ziadeh, *Lawyers, the Rule of Law, and Libralism*, 30–36.

8. In addition there were the Christian and Jewish courts applying religious law to family affairs, and consular courts still heard criminal and personal law cases involving foreign nationals.

9. Loos, *Subject Siam*, 64–65.

10. Brinkley Messick, *The Calligraphic State: Textual Domination and History in a Muslim Society* (Berkeley and Los Angeles: University of California Press, 1992), 61–62; Loos, *Subject Siam*, 5; M. B. Hooker, *Legal Pluralism: An Introduction to Colonial and Neo-Colonial Laws* (Oxford: Oxford University Press, 1976), 94–100, 119–89; and Martin Chanock, *Law, Custom and Social Order: The Colonial Experience in Malawi and Zambia* (Cambridge: Cambridge University Press, 1985), 3–6. Peter Knauss described how a patriarchal family regime became associated with Algerian nationalism in *The Persistence of Patriachy* (New York: Praeger, 1987); and Mehranguiz Kar and Homa Hoodfar discussed how in the Islamic Republic of Iran the protection of "the sanctity and stability of the institution of the Islamic family" is a political goal, in Homa Hoodfar, ed., *Shifting Boundaries in Marriage and Divorce in Muslim Countries* (Montpellier: Women Living Under Muslim Law, 1996), 9.

11. Édouard Sautayra and Eugène Cherbonneau, *Droit Musulman: Du Statut Personnel et des Successions* (Paris: Maisonneuve et Cie, 1873), ii–iii. See also Messick, *The Calligraphic State*, 58–63.

12. Sautayra and Cherbonneau, *Droit Musulman*, iii–iv. The translations they relied upon, in addition to the Qur'an and Sunna, were of the *Multaqa al-Abhur* of Ibrahim al-Halabi, by Mouradgea d'Ohsson; the *Mukhtasar* of Abu Shuja' al-Isfahani by Salomo Keyzer (Kreijzer); the *Hidaya* of al-Marghinani, by Charles Hamilton; and a treatise on marriage and inheritance by Muhammad b. Asim al-Andalusi, with a commentary by Muhammad al-Tawudi, probably the *Tuhhfat al-Hukkam*, in a manuscript translation by Bourdens Lasalle that evidently was not published.

13. Messick, *The Calligraphic State*, 56–57; Christelow, *Muslim Law Courts*, 133 (quotation 253).

14. Arnold H. Green, *The Tunisian Ulama 1873–1915: Social Structure and Response to Ideological Currents* (Leiden: Brill, 1978), 116–17.

15. Herbert J. Liebesny, *The Law of the Near and Middle East: Readings, Cases, and Materials* (Albany: State University of New York Press, 1975), 67–69. For the text in Arabic translation see *al-Majalla*, 75–84.

16. Muhmmad Qadri Pasha, *Al-Ahkam al-Shar'iyya fi al-Ahwal al-Shakhsiyya* (Bulaq: al-Matba'at al-Amiriyya, 1875); and, with no author attributed, *Du Statut Personnel et des*

Successions d'après le Rite Hanafite (Alexandria: Imprimerie Française A. Mourès, 1875), and *Diritto Musulmano: Statuto Personale e Successioni Secondo il Rito Anafita* (Alexandria: Stamperia Francese A. Mourès, 1875); Mohammed Kadri Pasha, *Code of Mohammedan Personal Law According to the Hanafi School* (London: Spottiswoode, 1914).

17. Civil law: *Murshid al-Hayran ila Ma'rifat Ahwal al-Insan* (Cairo: Wizarat al-Ma'arif, 1890); the law of endowments: *Qanun al-Adl wa al-Insaf li-l-Qada' ala Mushkilat al-Awqaf* (Cairo: Wizarat al-Ma'arif, 1893). For biographical information on Qadri see Tawfiq Abkaryus, "Muhammad Qadri Pasha," *al-Muqtataf* 48 (1916): 253–63; and Muhammad Husayn Haykal, *Tarajim Misriyya wa Gharbiyya* (Cairo: Dar al-Ma'arif, 1980), 96–103.

18. E.g., Ziadeh, *Lawyers, the Rule of Law, and Liberalism*, 19–20; and Jamal J. Nasir, *The Islamic Law of Personal Status* (The Hague: Kluwer Law, 2002), 34, who only mention it in passing.

19. According to the editors of a recent edition of Qadri's code it is cited often in the explanatory memoranda of the Arab personal status laws: Muhammad Qadri Pasha, *Al-Ahkam al-Shar'iyya fi al-Ahwal al-Shakhsiyya wa Sharhhu li-Muhammad Zayd al-Ibyani ma' Mulhaq Qawanin al-Ahwal-Shakhsiyya al-Arabiyya*, ed. Muhammad Ahmad Siraj and Ali Jum'a Muhammad, 4 vols. (Cairo: Dar al-Salam, 2006), 1:7. It is also referenced in court decisions in Egypt, Jordan, the Palestinian Authority, and Israel, according to Moussa Abou Ramadan and Daniel Monterescu, "Islamic Justice in a 'Jewish and Democratic' State: Cooptation and Islamization of the Shari'a Field," *Mishpat U-Mimshal* (*Law and Government*, the journal of the Law School of the University of Haifa) 11 (2008): 435–73 (in Hebrew). I am grateful to Iris Agmon for this reference. I compiled the publication data from Worldcat.

20. NAE, Majlis al-Nuzzar wa-l-Wuzara', File no. 0075-044839, Projet de Règlement de l'Ecole de Droit Modifié d'après les Observations de S.E. le Président du Conseil, July 11, 1886.

21. Donald M. Reid, "Educational and Career Choices of Egyptian Students, 1882–1922," *International Journal of Middle East Studies* 8, no. 3 (1977): 349–78.

22. See the text of Law No. 1 of 2000, introductory article 3, in the Siraj and Jum'a edition of Qadri's Code, 4:1712.

23. NAE, Majlis al-Nuzzar wa-l-Wuzara', File no. 0075-016495, Iqtirahat al-Jam'iyya al-Umumiyya, Feb. 1909. See also Rida, *Tarikh al-Ustadh al-Imam*, 1:626–27, on the public discussion at the time.

24. Abduh, *Taqrir*, h–w, 64–65; and Rida, *Tarikh al-Ustadh al-Imam*, 1:628, reproducing passages from an essay in *al-Manar* (June 1904) that made essentially the same points.

25. NAE, Majlis al-Nuzzar wa-l-Wuzara', File no. 075-04039, Mukatabat al-Haqqaniyya bi-Sha'n Islah al-Mahakim al-Shar'iyya. Sura ma Tuqarrir Nizarat al-Haqqaniyya li-Fadilat Shaykh Jami' al-Azhar bi-Tarikh 4 Yunyu 1904 wa li-Fadilat Mufti al-Diyar

al-Misriyya fi al-Tarikh al-Madhkur. The French version of this document rendered *al-ahkam al-shar'iyya* as *les dispositions du droit musulman*.

26. See chapters 3 and 4.

27. Abduh, *Taqrir*, 70–71; Rida, *Tarikh al-Ustadh al-Imam*, 1:628–29.

28. Indira Falk Gesink, *Islamic Reform and Conservatism: Al-Azhar and the Evolution of Modern Sunni Islam* (London: I. B. Tauris, 2010), 129–32, 165–95.

29. Rida, *Tarikh al-Ustadh al-Imam*, 1:623–24.

30. Wyndham A. Bewes, "The Theory of the Statutes," *Journal of Comparative Legislation and International Law* 4, no. 1 (1922): 97–103.

31. Michael Brett, "Legislating for Inequality in Algeria: The Senatus-Consulte of 14 July 1865," *Bulletin of the School of Oriental and African Studies, University of London* 51, no. 3 (1988): 441.

32. Oussama Arabi, "Orienting the Gaze: Marcel Morand and the Codification of le Droit Musulman Algérien," *Journal of Islamic Studies* 11, no. 1 (2000): 47–48; also Sautayra and Cherbonneau, *Droit Musulman*, i–ii.

33. Henry and Balique, *Doctrine Coloniale*, 19–21.

34. Brett, "Legislating for Inequality," 441.

35. Christelow, *Muslim Law Courts*, 132–33; and Henry and Balique, *Doctrine Coloniale*, 49, who report that adherence to Muslim personal status was the principal criterion for determining Algerian citizenship upon independence.

36. On *Droit Musulman Algérien* or Algerian Muslim Law see Messick, *Calligraphic State*, 65; Joseph Schacht, who likened it as a hybrid law to Anglo-Muhammadan Law, in *An Introduction to Islamic Law* (Oxford: Clarendon Press, 1964), 97–99; and Henry and Balique, *Doctrine Coloniale*, 11. Rubin has applied the concept of hybridity in his discussion of the Ottoman *Mecelle*: "Ottoman Judicial Change," 128.

37. Christelow, *Muslim Law Courts*, 9, 23.

38. Ibid., on the Conseil de Jurisprudence Musulmane (1854–59), 110; and the Conseil Supérieure de Droit (1866–75), 116. The "sleeping baby" rule in Maliki jurisprudence held that a child born to a widow or a divorcée up to four or five years after the end of her marriage was "asleep" in the womb and hence legitimate. On this and the marriage age, see 124–29.

39. Henry and Balique, *Doctrine Coloniale*, 34

40. *La'ihat Tartib al-Mahakim al-Mukhtissa bi-l-Fasl fi al-Qadaya al-Mukhtalata bi-l-Diyar al-Misriyya* (1876), Art. 9; and al-Qanun al-Madani (1876), Art. 4.

41. *La'ihat al-Mahakim al-Shar'iyya*, 1880, 4:149, Art. 53; *La'ihat Tartib al-Mahakim*, 1897, in *Majmu'a al-Awamir 1897*, 173, Art. 93.

42. Rudolph Peters, "From Jurists' Law to Statute Law or What Happens When the Shari'a Is Codified," *Mediterranean Politics* 7, no. 3 (2002): 84; also Messick, *Calligraphic State*, 56–57.

43. Messick, *Calligraphic State*, 234–37.

44. I am not claiming that these texts preserved a complete and unbiased record of previous discussions. Jurists exercised some discretion in including earlier discussions, as will be evident.

45. Peters, "From Jurists' Law to Statute Law," 89.

46. Abd al-Rahman b. al-Shaykh Muhammad, known as Damad Afandi and also as Shaykhzadeh, *Majma' al-Anhur fi Sharh Multaqa al-Abhur* (Beirut: Dar Ihya' al-Turath, 1980).

47. Peters, "From Jurists' Law to Statute Law," 84–85; Damad Afandi, *Majma' al-Anhur* 1:332–33.

48. Damad Afandi, *Majma' al-Anhur* 1:332–33.

49. Ibn Abdin, *Radd al-Muhtar*, 2:304–6.

50. Ibid., 2:305; Damad Afandi, *Majm'a al-Anhur*, 1:332.

51. FM 1:56, 1 Jumada I 1271/Jan. 20, 1855; 65–66, 10 Jumada I 1273/Jan. 7, 1857; 76–77, 7 Sha'ban 1282/Dec. 26, 1865.

52. FM 1:76–77, 7 Sha'ban 1282/Dec. 26, 1865. Eleventh- and twelfth-century Hanafi scholars invoked "the corruption of the times" to justify diverging from the authoritative doctrine. The phrase often appeared in quotations by Ottoman-era scholars and does not refer to the Ottoman period itself, though the implication was that things had not changed for the better.

53. Qadri, *Al-Ahkam al-Shar'iyya*, Arts. 51–52. Qadri's Code also mentions that if she married without the agreement of her guardian for less than the going dower, then the contract was valid but an agnatic guardian could contest it until the husband paid the going rate or the marriage was annulled. According to Ibn Abdin the difference between an inadequate dower and an unsuitable groom was that the dower could be made good: *Radd al-Muhtar*, 2:305.

54. Ibn Abdin, *Radd al-Muhtar*, 2:369–70.

55. Damad Afandi, *Majma' al-Anhur*, 1:355; Ala' al-Din Muhammad b. Ali , known as al-Haskafi, *al-Durr al-Mukhtar*, citing *Tanwir al-Absar* for the first and *al-Fatawa al-Tatarkhaniyya* for the second, in the margin of Ibn Abdin, *Radd al-Muhtar*, 2:370.

56. Ibn Abdin, *Radd al-Muhtar*, 2:370.

57. See also Iris Agmon, "Women, Class and Gender: Muslim Jaffa and Haifa at the Turn of the 20th Century," *International Journal of Middle East Studies* 30 (1998): 486.

58. Ibn Abdin, *Radd al-Muhtar*, 2:370, citing an opinion by Ibn Bazzaz al-Kurdari (d. 1424).

59. E.g., FM 1:94, 10 Jumada II 1265/May 3, 1849; 96, 25 al-Qa'da 1265/Oct. 12, 1849; 97, 30 Muharram 1266/Dec. 15, 1849; 98, 18 Rajab 1266/May 30, 1850; 100, 19 Safar 1267/Dec. 23, 1850; 122, 4 Muharram 1274/Aug. 24, 1857; 128–29, 5 Rabi' II 1277/Oct. 20, 1860; 137–38, 15 Rabi' I 1293/Apr. 10, 1876; 139, 14 Ramadan 1300/July 19, 1883.

60. Rudolph Peters, "Safar," *Encyclopaedia of Islam*, 2d ed., Brill Online.

61. Agmon, "Women, Class and Gender," 486.

62. According to a previous decision, FM 1:128–29, 5 Rabi' II 1277/ Oct. 20, 1860.
63. FM 1:123–24, 9 Rabi' II 1274/Nov. 26, 1857.
64. Qadri, *Al-Ahkam al-Shar'iyya*, Art. 208.
65. Title VI of the Civil Code, "Of Divorce," was abrogated under the Restoration and divorce remained inaccessible until 1884.
66. Qadri, *Al-Ahkam al-Shar'iyya*, Art. 190.
67. *Radd al-Muhtar*, 2:674. On the Ottoman policy see the previous chapter.
68. Qadri, *Al-Ahkam al-Shar'iyya*, Art. 206.
69. *Civil Code*, Arts. 213–220. See Konrad Zweigert and Heinz Kötz, *Introduction to Comparative Law* (Oxford: Clarendon Press, 1987), 88–96. Also H. D. Lewis, "The Legal Status of Women in Nineteenth-Century France," *Journal of European Studies* 10 (1980): 178–88; and Bidelman, *Pariahs Stand Up!*, 4. The law was changed in 1907 to enable married women to control their own property and wages: Charles Lefebvre, *La Famille en France dans le Droit et dans le Moeurs* (Paris: Marcel Giard & Cie., 1920), 108.
70. Abu Bakr b. Masud al-Kasani, *Bada'i' al-Sana'i' fi Tartib al-Shara'i'*, 7 vols. (Beirut, Dar al-Kitab al-Arabi, 1974), 2:493; and Ibrahim Ibn Nujaym, *Bahr al-Ra'iq Sharh Kanz al-Daqa'iq*, 9 vols. (Beirut: Dar al-Kutub al-Ilmiyya, 1997), 3:84, both accessed via the Complete Reference of Islamic Fiqh CD ROM; al-Idwi, *Ahkam Uqud al-Nikah*, 184.
71. Article 206 begins, "La puissance maritale est toute disciplinaire," in the French translation of Qadri's code, in Eugène Clavel, *Droit Musulman. Du Statut Personnel et des Successions d'après les Différents Rites et Plus Particulièrement d'après le Rite Hanafite*, 2 vols. (Paris: Librairie du Recueil Général des Lois et des Arrêts, 1895), 2:313, Art. 206.
72. Roderick Phillips, *Putting Asunder: A History of Divorce in Western Society* (Cambridge: Cambridge University Press, 1988), 323–44.
73. Qadri, *Al-Ahkam al-Shar'iyya*, Arts. 209, 211. In the Sharia Court system two witnesses would be necessary to prove a violent beating took place, and the lack of any cases of this type in the court registers sampled speaks to their rarity. But see FM 1:423, 28 al-Hijja 1272/Aug. 29, 1856 for a case of beating that came to the mufti.
74. Qadri, *Al-Ahkam al-Shar'iyya*, Art. 207.
75. For example, FM 2:388, 23 Jumada I 1266/Apr. 6, 1850 and 389, 6 Rajab 1266/May 18, 1850.
76. Qadri, *Al-Ahkam al-Shar'iyya*, Art. 207–8. I have omitted some details.
77. *Civil Code*, Art. 214; O. Masselin, *Dictionnaire Juridique de Législation et Jurisprudence au 15 Janiver 1888* (Paris: Dépôt central des ouvrages de l'auteur, 1898), 644.
78. Qadri, *Al-Ahkam al-Shar'iyya*, Art. 212.
79. Ibid., Arts. 213–216.
80. Muhammad Zayd al-Ibyani, *Sharh al-Ahkam al-Shar'iyya fi al-Ahwal al-Shakhsiyya*, 2d ed., 3 vols. (Cairo: Matba'at Ali Shukri, 1911), 1:a.
81. Ibid.

82. In the twenty-first century digital technology compensates for the absence of such training.
83. Al-Ibyani, *Sharh*, 1:282, explicating Art. 207.
84. The opinions of both scholars are presented by Ibn Abdin, *Radd al-Muhtar*, 2:682.
85. I found no court cases or fatwas referring to this issue.
86. Al-Ibyani, *Sharh*, 1:282–83. The translation of Qur'an 33:33 is from Arberry, *The Koran Interpreted*.
87. From Ibn al-Humam's *Fath al-Qadir*, as quoted by Ibn Abdin, *Radd al-Muhtar*, 2:683.
88. Bahithat al-Badiyya, "Ya li-l-Nisa' min al-Rijal wa Ya li-l-Rijal minhinna," *al-Nisa'iyyat*, 23.
89. Bahithat al-Badiyya, "Al-Hijab aw al-Sufur," in *al-Nisa'iyyat*, 12.
90. This is the 2006 edition edited by Siraj and Muhammad, referenced earlier.
91. Robert D. Crews, *For Prophet and Tsar: Islam and Empire in Russia and Central Asia* (Cambridge, MA: Harvard University Press, 2006), 24.
92. Esposito and Delong Bas, *Women in Muslim Family Law*, xiv.

6. Marriage Modernized?

1. See Mohamed al-Nowaihi, "Changing the Law on Personal Status in Egypt within a Liberal Interpretation of the Shari'a," in Michael Curtis, ed., *Religion and Politics in the Middle East* (Boulder: Westview Press, 1979), 109–24; Enid Hill, *Mahkama! Studies in the Egyptian Legal System* (London: Ithaca Press, 1979), 82–83; and Badran, *Feminists, Islam, and Nation*, 131–32.
2. *La'ihat Tartib al-Mahakim*, 1897, in *Majmu'a al-Awamir 1897*, 173.
3. A couple should be separated during a revocable divorce or if their marriage was discovered to be legally invalid.
4. Also spelled Zuhni in some sources.
5. MA Ahkam Juz'iyya 56:44, no. 597, June 1902.
6. A year after this incident Shaykh Ahmad's brother, Shaykh Mahmud, was appointed shaykh of all the ulama of Alexandria, and Shaykh Ahmad was made his agent and president of the administrative council of ulama. Their ancestors endowed the al-Umari Mosque in the Labban district, which is still in use. See *Al-Mu'ayyad*, April 20, 1902; June 5, 1902; and July 2, 1903.
7. I am grateful to Will Hanley for providing me with the text of this decision, which he found in the archives of the Ministère des Affaires Étrangères, Centre des Archives Diplomatiques de Nantes: Fonds Alexandrie: Jugements (hereafter MAE AJ), 532:37–42.
8. The decision of the consular court, in summarizing Shaykh Ahmad's request, used the Latin phrase *etiam manu militari*, "even by force."

9. In essence, *al-Mu'ayyad* supported the argument made in vain by Nafisa's lawyer, namely that the consulate had no jurisdiction in a personal status case such as this. Although Shaykh Ahmad and his brothers were protégés of France, their status did not extend to their wives or children. The couple were Muslim and Egyptian, and they had contracted their marriage in the very Sharia Court in Alexandria where her case was pending. *Al-Mu'ayyad*, April 8, 1902; April 9, 1902; and April 13, 1902.

10. This summary of Nafisa's account in the following two paragraphs is taken from *Al-Mu'ayyad*, June 5, 1902.

11. *Majallat al-Ahkam al-Shar'iyya* 1, no. 1 (Apr. 24, 1902): 22.

12. *Al-Mu'ayyad*, May 11, 1902, May 20, 1902, and June 29, 1903; National Appeals Court of Cairo, the case of al-Sitt Zaynab Hanim bt. Shaykh Ibrahim Sulayman Basha vs. Shaykh Bakri Mahmud et al., reported in *al-Huquq*, 13, 25 (1903), 193–95, No. 117; MA Madbatat Ishhadat, 704:41, No. 86, 8 al-Hijja 1320/Mar. 7, 1903.

13. On Qasim Amin's argument see chapter 3. Beth Baron argued that the ideal of companionate marriage was taking hold at the turn of the century, in "Making and Breaking," 278–82.

14. MAE AJ 532:27a, 28b.

15. MAE AJ 532:41a.

16. The consular court declined to say that she could be returned by the use of police (*la force publique*) as Shaykh Ahmad requested, noting that it was up to the Egyptian authorities to enforce the order. MAE AJ 532:41a.

17. *Majallat al-Ahkam al-Shar'iyya* 1, no. 1 (Apr. 24, 1902): 22. The author might have gotten that image from a French source. In any event Nafisa agreed to return to Shaykh Ahmad after losing her case, and there was no report that the police escorted her.

18. Ibn Abdin, *Radd al-Muhtar*, 2:665.

19. FM 1:416, 30 Shawwal 1270/July 26, 1854.

20. See chapter 4.

21. See Richard Antoun, "Litigant Strategies in an Islamic Court in Jordan," in Daisy Hilse Dwyer, ed., *Law and Islam in the Middle East* (New York: Bergin & Garvey, 1990), 35–60; and Lawrence Rosen, "Equity and Discretion in a Modern Islamic Legal System," *Law and Society Review* 15, no. 1 (1980/1981): 231.

22. Ahmad b. Muhammad, known as Ibn Hajar al-Haythami, *Al-Zawajir an Iqtiraf al-Kaba'ir*, 2 vols. (Beirut: Dar al-Kutub al-Ilmiyya, 1987), 2:72 ff., in addition to the sources cited in chapter 3.

23. Some twenty cases appeared in the chapter on maintenance (*nafaqa*) alone, and there are numerous references to married women taking refuge in their parents' or a relative's house in other chapters.

24. FM 1:379, 16 Rabi' II 1265/Mar. 11, 1849.

25. FM 1:403, 10 Jumada I 1268/Mar. 1, 1852.

26. FM 1:404, 21 Rajab 1268/May 11, 1862. The question explained that the husband struck his wife to discipline her (*ta'diban la-ha*), meaning that his action was legitimate. One of the conditions of a legally proper domicile was that it must not be amidst his or her family but apart from them, hence the formula "free of his family or of her family."

27. FM 1:421, 9 Jumada II 1272/Feb. 16, 1856.

28. FM 1:406, 4 al-Hijja 1268/Sept. 18, 1852.

29. See Ibn Abdin, *Radd al-Muhtar*, 3:194, with al-Haskafi's *al-Durr al-Mukhtar* in the margin.

30. Abd al-Majid Ali, *Matla' al-Badrayn*, 14; and al-Nawawi, *Uqud al-Lujayn*, 4–5, 9. We should not take this discussion as descriptive of the actual behavior of men, but here our concern is with the legal arguments.

31. FM 1:459, 23 Shawwal 1299/Sept. 6, 1882. This fatwa cited a similar case heard more than two centuries earlier by Khayr al-Din al-Ramli, with similar results.

32. On the legal disabilities imposed on French women by the code see Bidelman, *Pariahs Stand Up!*, 4.

33. Mainardi, *Husbands, Wives, and Lovers*, 29.

34. Ibid., 29–30; Nicole Arnaud-Duc, "The Law's Contradictions," in Geneviève Fraisse and Michelle Perrot, *A History of Women in the West*, vol. 4, *Emerging Feminism from Revolution to World War* (Cambridge, MA: Belknap Press, 1996), 100.

35. Shanley, *Feminism, Marriage, and the Law*, 158, 177–81; James F. McMillan, *France and Women 1789–1914: Gender, Society and Politics* (London: Routledge, 2000), 152–53.

36. Charles Gillotte, *Traité du Droit Musulman Précédé du Décret du 31 Décembre 1859* (Constantine: Alessi et Arnolet, 1860), 14.

37. Gillotte, *Traité du Droit Musulman*, 20–21. He used the French term *puissance maritale* for the marital authority of the husband.

38. Sautayra and Cherbonneau, *Droit Musulman*, 198.

39. See chapter 5.

40. Jean-Paul Charnay, *La Vie Musulmane en Algérie d'après la Jurisprudence de la Première Motié du xxe Siècle* (Paris: Presses Universitaires de France, 1965), 47.

41. Ibid.

42. Marie Rodet, "'Le délit d'abandon de domicile conjugal' ou l'invasion du pénal colonial dans les jugements des 'tribunaux indigènes' au Soudan français, 1900–1947," *French Colonial History* 10 (2009): 151–70.

43. Elizabeth Thompson, *Colonial Citizens: Republican Rights, Paternal Privilege, and Gender in French Syria and Lebanon* (New York: Columbia University Press, 2000), 175 ff.

44. Shaun T. Lopez, "Madams, Murders, and the Media: *Akhbar al-Hawadith* and the Emergence of a Mass Culture in 1920s Egypt," in Arthur Goldschmidt, Amy J. Johnson,

and Barak A. Salmoni, eds., *Re-Envisioning Egypt 1919–1952* (Cairo: The American University in Cairo Press, 2005), 185, quoting the periodical *al-Umma*, Nov. 21, 1920.

45. See chapter 4.

46. I have been unable to find detailed information on the individuals who drafted the law, and no explanatory memorandum accompanied the law.

47. Abduh, *Taqrir*, 4–5.

48. Ron Shaham, "Bayt al-taʿa," *Encyclopaedia of Islam*, 3d ed., Brill Online. Shaham disagreed with my suggestion in an earlier, unpublished paper of European origins. However, the two explanations are not mutually exclusive.

49. Abduh, *Taqrir*, 67–71.

50. Shaarawi, *Harem Years*, 64–76, 83.

51. Amin, *My Life*, 135–36.

52. Onésome Masselin, *Dictionnaire Juridique de Législation et Jurisprudence au 15 Janiver 1888* (Paris: Dépot central des ouvrages de l'auteur, 1898), 645.

53. Law No. 31 of 1910, in *Majallat al-Ahkam al-Sharʿiyya* 9, no. 9 (September 19, 1910): 229, Art. 342.

54. Law No. 78 of 1931, in Ahmad Nasr al-Jundi, *Al-Taʿliq ala Nusus Laʾihat al-Mahakim al-Sharʿiyya wa Qanun al-Ahwal al-Shakhsiyya* (Cairo: Alam al-Kutub, 1976), 113, Art. 346.

55. Badran, *Feminists, Islam, and Nation*, 126–27.

56. Ibid., 131–32.

57. Ahmad Nasr al-Jundi, *Mabadiʾ al-Qadaʾ al-Sharʿi fi Khamsin Aman* (Cairo: Dar al-Fikr al-Arabi, 1973), 624–47.

58. Adil Ahmad Sarkis, *Al-Zawaj wa Tatawwur al-Mujtamʿ* (Cairo: Dar al-Kitab al-Arabi, 1967), 132.

59. Ali Abd al-Wahid Wafi, *Bayt al-Taʿa wa Taʿaddud al-Zawjat wa al-Talaq fi al-Islam* (Cairo: Muʾassasat al-Matbuʿat al-Haditha, 1960), 5–6, citing Qurʾan 4:34.

60. Kamal Salih al-Banna, *Tashriʿat al-Ahwal al-Shakhsiyya fi Misr Muʿallaqan alayha bi-l-Mudhakkirat al-Idahiyya wa al-Mabadiʾ al-Qadaʾiyya wa Araʾ al-Shurrah* (Cairo: al-Sharika al-Misriyya li-l-Tibaʿa wa al-Nashr, 1976), 359.

61. This was part of a broader project to reform the family law that lost momentum after the June war with Israel.

62. Al-Banna, *Tashriʿat al-Ahwal al-Shakhsiyya fi Misr*, 359.

Conclusion and Epilogue

1. Using the "surplus wife" method (the excess of married women over married men), some 6.5 percent of married men appear to have been polygynous in 1907, and the censuses of 1927 through 1986 showed a decline in the proportion of polygynous married men from 4.8 percent to 1.92 percent. Polygynous marriage, which indicates the extent of

transitory polygyny leading to divorce, also fell from 11.4 percent during 1936–40 to 5.6 percent in the early 1990s. For polygyny in the census data in 1907–27 see Cleland, *Population Problem*, 48, Table IX; 1927–47, al-Bayyuni, *Al-Usra al-Misriyya*, 130, Table 113; and 1976–86, CAPMAS, *Census of Population, Housing and Establishments*. For polygynous marriage see Fargues, "Terminating Marriage," 271.

2. The proportion of women below the age of eighteen who were married fell from 4.8 percent in 1907 to 3.9 percent in 1917 and 3.5 percent in 1927. From 1935 to 1991 the mean age of first marriage rose from nineteen to twenty-two for women and from twenty-six to twenty-eight for men. See Fargues, "Terminating Marriage," 263–64, 272–73.

3. Abu-Lughod, "The Marriage of Feminism and Islamism," 251–54.

4. Zeinab Khedr and Laila El Zeini, "Families and Households: Headship and Co-residence," in *The New Arab Family*, 148; Singerman and Ibrahim, "The Costs of Marriage," 89; Homa Hoodfar, "Survival Strategies and the Political Economy of Low-Income Households in Cairo," in Diane Singennan and Homa Hoodfar, eds., *Development, Change and Gender in Cairo: A View from the Household* (Bloomington: Indiana University Press, 1996), 51.

5. Cuno, "Divorce and the Fate of the Family."

6. Lama Abu-Odeh, "Modernizing Muslim Family Law: The Case of Egypt," *Vanderbilt Journal of Transnational Law* 37 (2004): 1049.

7. The text of the law and its explanatory memorandum are in Ibrahim Ahmad Abd Allah, *Majmuʻa al-Awamir wa al-Manshurat wa al-Qawanin al-Mutaʻalliqa bi-Laʼihat Tartib al-Mahakim al-Sharʻiyya (al-Qanun Nimra 31 Sanat 1910) min Sanat 1910 ila Sanat 1926*, 2d ed. (Tanta: al-Matbaʻa al-Ahliyya al-Kubra, 1926), 166–79.

8. *Qarar Huquq al-Aʼila*, in al-Jabi, *Al-Majalla*, 514–16.

9. The phrase used by Egyptian authors, *ruh al-zaman*, may be a translation of *zeitgeist*: See Abd Allah, *Majmuʻa al-Awamir*, 4; Muhammad Abu Zahra, *Al-Ahwal al-Shakhsiyya: Qism al-Zawaj* (Cairo: n.p., 1950), 8–9; and Sarkis, *Al-Zawaj wa Tatawwur al-Mujtamʻ*, 153. The OLFR employed similar language, e.g., *Qarar Huquq al-Aʼila*, in al-Jabi, *Al-Majalla*, 515.

10. Abu Zahra, *Al-Ahwal al-Shakhsiyya*, 9.

11. Ibid., 11; Abd Allah, *Majmuʻa*, 188–89.

12. The text of the law and its explanatory memorandum appears in Ibrahim, *Majmuʻa Qawanin al-Ahwal al-Shakhsiyya*, 18–36.

13. Abu Zahra, *Al-Ahwal al-Shakhsiyya*, 12–13.

14. Abdullahi A. An-Naʼim, ed., *Islamic Family Law in a Changing World: A Global Resource Book* (London: Zed Books, 2002), 112, 140.

15. An-Naʼim, *Islamic Family Law in a Changing World*, 113.

16. In Alaa al Aswany's novel *Imarat Yaʻqubian* (*The Yacoubian Building*, 2002/2006), a corrupt businessman surreptitiously marries a younger woman to satisfy his lust, keeping his first wife in the dark.

17. Human Rights Watch, "Divorced from Justice: Women's Unequal Access to Divorce in Egypt," Report 16, 8(E) (Dec. 2004), 30–32; Esposito with Delong-Bas, *Women in Muslim Family Law*, 60.

18. See Hind Ahmed Zaki, "The New Marriage Contract in Egypt: Religious Reframing and the Hazards of Reform," paper prepared for the American Anthropological Association Annual Meeting, November 19, 2010, http://www.academia.edu/2132743/The_New_Marriage_Contract_in_Egypt_Religious_Reframing_and_the_Hazards_of_Reform; Mona Zulficar, "The Islamic Marriage Contract in Egypt," in Asifa Quraishi and Frank E. Vogel, eds., *The Islamic Marriage Contract: Case Studies in Islamic Family Law* (Cambridge, MA: Harvard University Press, 2008), 230–59; Diane Singerman, "Rewriting Divorce in Egypt: Reclaiming Islam, Legal Activism, and Coalition Politics," in Robert W. Hefner, ed., *Remaking Muslim Politics: Pluralism, Contestation, Democratization* (Princeton: Princeton University Press, 2005), 171–74; Dena Rashed, "Bound by the Blank," *al-Ahram Weekly*, 523 (March 1–7, 2001), http://weekly.ahram.org.eg/2001/523/sc5k.htm; Reem Leila, "The Terms of Engagement," *al-Ahram Weekly* 484 (June 1–7, 2000), http://weekly.ahram.org.eg/2000/484/li1.htm; and Ron Shaham, "State, Feminists and Islamists—The Debate over Stipulations in Marriage Contracts in Egypt," *Bulletin of the School of Oriental and African Studies* 62, no. 3 (1999): 462–83.

19. Amira Sonbol, "Modernity, Standardization, and Marriage Contracts in Nineteenth Century Egypt," in Daniel Panzac, ed., *Histoire Économic et Sociale de l'Empire Ottoman et de la Turquie (1326–1960)* (Paris: Peeters, 1995), 491.

20. Cuno, "Divorce and the Fate of the Family."

21. CAPMAS, Table "A'dad wa Ma'dalat Shihadat al-Zawaj wa al-Talaq," 1985–2011, http://www.capmas.gov.eg/pdf/Number_MD.pdf.

22. "Egypt Draft Constitution Article Raises Fears for Women's Rights," *Ahram Online*, Sept. 23, 2012, http://english.ahram.org.eg/News/53598.aspx; "Women's Equality Article Removed From Constitution," *Al-Masry al-Youm*, Nov. 12, 2012, http://www.egyptindependent.com/node/1236371.

23. "Controversy over 'Suzanne's laws,'" *Ahram Weekly* 1046, May 5–11, http://weekly.ahram.org.eg/2011/1046/eg14.htm; The New Woman Foundation, "Al-Munazzamat Ghayr al-Hukumiyya Tudin Mashru' Marsum Qanun al-Ahwal al-Shakhsiyya li-l-Mustashar Abd Allah Baja," July 21, 2011, http://nwrcegypt.org/?p=5210; "Al-Mustashar al-Baja: Qanun al-Mar'a al-Jadid Yuhallil al-Haram wa Yuharrim al-Halal, April 14, 2013, http://www.ikhwanonline.net/Article.aspx?ArtID=145938&SecID=323.

Select Bibliography

Archives

Egypt. National Archives (Dar al-Watha'iq)
    Census Registers (Ta'dad al-Nufus) of 1848 and 1868
    Council of Ministers Files (Majlis al-Nuzzar wa-l-Wuzara')
    Damietta Divorce Registers (Sijillat al-Talaq)
    Damietta Marriage Registers (Sijillat al-Jawaz)
    Registers of the Alexandria Sharia Court of First Instance (Mahkamat al-Iskandariyya)
    Registers of the Sharia Court of al-Daqahliyya Province (Mahkamat al-Daqahliyya)
    Registers of the al-Mansura Sharia Court of First Instance (Mahkamat al-Mansura)
Egypt. Public Record Office (Dar al-Mahfuzat).
    Land-Tax Records (Dafatir al-Mukallifat)

Periodicals

Al-Adab
Al-Ahkam al-Shar'iyya
Al-Ahram
Ahram Weekly
Daily News Egypt
The Egyptian Gazette
Al-Masry al-Yaum
Al-Mu'ayyad
The Times
Al-Waqa'i' al-Misriyya

Dissertations

Baldwin, James E. "Islamic Law in an Ottoman Context: Resolving Disputes in Late 17th/Early 18th-Century Cairo." Ph.D. dissertation, New York University, ProQuest, UMI Dissertations Publishing, 2010.

Dykstra, Darrell. "A Biographical Study in Egyptian Modernization: 'Ali Mubarak (1823/4–1893)." Ph.D. dissertation, University of Michigan, ProQuest, UMI Dissertations Publishing, 1977.

Tuğ, Başak "Politics of Honor: The Institutional and Social Frontiers of 'Illicit' Sex in Mid-Eighteenth-Century Ottoman Anatolia." Ph.D. dissertation, New York University, ProQuest, UMI Dissertations Publishing, 2009.

Electronic Resources

The Constitution of the Arab Republic of Egypt, 1971 (as amended to 2007). www.constitutionnet.org/files/Egypt%20Constitution.pdf.

Dustur Misr. http://dostour.eg/.

Encyclopaedia of Islam. 2d ed. Brill Online.

Al-Marja' al-Akbar fi al-Fiqh al-Islami/The Complete Reference of Islamic Fiqh Version 9. El Ariss Computer, Inc. CD ROM.

Al-Marja' al-Akbar fi al-Hadith al-Sharif/The Complete Reference of Islamic Hadeeth Version 10. El Ariss Computer, Inc. CD ROM.

The Royal Ark: Royal and Ruling Houses of Africa, Asia, Oceania, and the Americas. Egypt. http://www.royalark.net/Egypt/egypt3.htm.

Printed Books and Articles

Abd Allah, Ibrahim Ahmad. *Majmu'a al-Awamir wa al-Manshurat wa al-Qawanin al-Muta'alliqa bi-La'ihat Tartib al-Mahakim al-Shar'iyya (al-Qanun Nimra 31 Sanat 1910) min Sanat 1910 ila Sanat 1926.* 2d. ed. Tanta: al-Matba'a al-Ahliyya al-Kubra, 1926.

Abduh, Muhammad. *Taqrir Fadilat Mufti al-Diyar al-Misriyya al-Usthadh al-Shaykh Muhammad Abduh fi Islah al-Mahakim al-Shar'iyya.* Cairo: Matba'at al-Manar, 1900.

———. *Al-A'mal al-Kamila li-l-Imam Muhammad Abduh.* Edited by Muhammad Imara. 6 vols. Beirut: Al-Mu'assasa al-Arabiyya li-l-Dirasat wa al-Nashr, 1972.

Abdur Rahim, M. A. *Principles of Muhammadan Jurisprudence According to the Hanafi, Maliki, Shafi'i and Hanbali Schools*. London: Luzac, 1911.

Abkaryus, Tawfiq. "Muhammad Qadri Pasha." *Al-Muqtataf* 48 (1916).

Abugideiri, Hiba, "Colonizing Mother Egypt, Domesticating Egyptian Mothers." In Poonam Bala, ed., *Biomedicine as a Contested Site: Some Revelations in Imperial Contexts*. New York: Lexington Books, 2000, 9–28.

Abu-Lughod, Lila. "The Marriage of Feminism and Islamism in Egypt: Selective Repudiation as a Dynamic of Postcolonial Cultural Politics." In Abu-Lughod, ed., *Remaking Women*, 243–69.

———, ed. *Remaking Women: Feminism and Modernity in the Middle East*. Princeton: Princeton University Press, 1998.

Abu-Odeh, Lama. "Modernizing Muslim Family Law: The Case of Egypt." *Vanderbilt Journal of Transnational Law* 37 (2004): 1043–146.

Abu Zahra, Muhammad. *Al-Ahwal al-Shakhsiyya: Qism al-Zawaj*. Cairo: N.p., 1950.

Adams, Charles C. *Islam and Modernism in Egypt: A Study of the Modern Reform Movement Inaugurated by Muhammad Abduh*. New York: Russell & Russell, 1933.

Agmon, Iris. "Women, Class and Gender: Muslim Jaffa and Haifa at the Turn of the 20th Century." *International Journal of Middle East Studies* 30 (1998): 477–500.

———. *Family and Court: Legal Culture and Modernity in Late Ottoman Palestine*. New York: Syracuse University Press, 2006.

Agrama, Hussein Ali. *Questioning Secularism: Islam, Sovereignty, and the Rule of Law in Modern Egypt*. Chicago: University of Chicago Press, 2012.

Ahmed, Leila. *Women and Gender in Islam: Historical Roots of a Modern Debate*. New Haven: Yale University Press, 1992.

Ali al-Hanafi b. Shaykh Ali Ismail al-Idwi, Abd al-Majid. *Matla' al-Badrayn fima Yata'allaq bi-l-Zawjayn*. Cairo: N.p., 1278/1862.

Ali, Kecia. *Marriage and Slavery in Early Islam*. Cambridge, MA: Harvard University Press, 2010.

Ali, Syed Ameer. *Mahommedan Law. Containing the Law Relating to Succession and Status. Compiled from Authorities in the Original Arabic*. 1880. Reprint, Lahore: Law Publishing, 1976.

Alleaume, Ghislaine, and Philippe Fargues. "La Naissance d'une Statistique d'État." *Histoire et Mesure* 13, no. 1 (1988): 147–93.

Alluba, Muhammed Ali. *Dhikriyyat Ijtima'iyya wa Siyasiyya*. Cairo: General Egyptian Book Organization, 1988.

Amin, Ahmad. *My Life: The Autobiography of an Egyptian Scholar, Writer, and Cultural Leader.* Translated by Issa J. Boullata. Leiden: Brill, 1978.

Amin, Qasim. *Qasim Amin: Al-A'mal al-Kamila.* Edited by Muhammad Imara. Cairo: Dar al-Shuruq, 1989.

———. *The Liberation of Women and The New Woman: Two Documents in the History of Egyptian Feminism.* Translated by Samiha Sidhom Peterson. Cairo: The American University in Cairo Press, 2000.

Amin, Kassem. *Les Égyptiens: Réponse a M. le Duc d'Harcourt.* Cairo: Jules Barbier, 1894.

Anderson, J. N. D. "Recent Developments in Shar'ia Law II." *Muslim World* 41, no. 1 (1951): 34–48.

Anderson, Michael. *Approaches to the History of the Western Family, 1500–1914.* 2d ed. Cambridge: Cambridge University Press, 1995.

Anderson, Michael R. "Legal Scholarship and the Politics of Islam in British India." In *Perspectives on Islamic Law, Justice, and Society,* edited by R. S. Khare, 65–91. London: Rowman & Littlefield, 1999.

An-Na'im, Abdullahi A., ed. *Islamic Family Law in a Changing World: A Global Resource Book.* London: Zed Books, 2002.

Antoun, Richard. "Litigant Strategies in an Islamic Court in Jordan." In *Law and Islam in the Middle East,* edited by Daisy Hilse Dwyer, 35–60. New York: Bergin & Garvey, 1990.

Arabi, Oussama. "Orienting the Gaze: Marcel Morand and the Codification of le Droit Musulman Algérien." *Journal of Islamic Studies* 11, no. 1 (2000): 43–72.

Arberry, A. J. *The Koran Interpreted.* New York: Macmillan, 1955.

Arnaud-Duc, Nicole. "The Law's Contradictions." In *A History of Women in the West.* Vol. 4, *Emerging Feminism from Revolution to World War,* edited by Geneviève Fraisse and Michelle Perrot, 80–113. Cambridge, MA: Belknap Press, 1996.

Asad, Talal. *Formations of the Secular: Christianity, Islam, Modernity.* Stanford: Stanford University Press, 2003.

Badran, Margot. *Feminists, Islam, and Nation: Gender and the Making of Modern Egypt.* Princeton: Princeton University Press, 1995.

———. "From Consciousness to Activism: Feminist Politics in Early Twentieth Century Egypt." In *Problems of the Middle East in Historical Perspective,* edited by John P. Spagnolo, 27–48. Reading: Ithaca Press, 1996.

Badran, Margot, and miriam cooke, eds. *Opening the Gates: An Anthology of Arab Feminist Writing.* 2d ed. Bloomington: Indiana University Press, 2004.

Bahithat al-Badiya (Malak Hifni Nasif). *Al-Nisa'iyyat: Majmuʻa Maqalat Nushirat fi al-Jarida fi Madwuʻ al-Mar'a al-Misriyya*. Cairo: Matbaʻa al-Jarida, 1910.
Al-Bajuri, Ibrahim. *Sharh Minah al-Fattah ala Daw' al-Misbah fi Ahkam al-Nikah*. Cairo [?]: N.p., 1870.
Al-Banna, Kamal Salih. *Tashriʻat al-Ahwal al-Shakhsiyya fi Misr Muʻallaqan alayha bi-l-Mudhakkirat al-Idahiyya wa al-Mabadi' al-Qada'iyya wa Ara' al-Shurrah*. Cairo: al-Sharika al-Misriyya li-l-Tibaʻa wa al-Nashr, 1976.
Barlow, Tani E. "Introduction: On 'Colonial Modernity.'" In *Formations of Colonial Modernity in East Asia*, edited by Tani E. Barlow, 1–20. Durham: Duke University Press, 1997.
Baron, Beth. "Unveiling in Early Twentieth Century Egypt: Practical and Symbolic Considerations." *Middle Eastern Studies* 25, no. 3 (July 1989): 370–86.
———. "The Making and Breaking of Marital Bonds in Modern Egypt." In *Women in Middle Eastern History: Shifting Boundaries in Sex and Gender*, edited by Nikki Keddie and Beth Baron, 275–91. New Haven: Yale University Press, 1991.
———. *The Women's Awakening in Egypt: Culture, Society, and the Press*. New Haven: Yale University Press, 1994.
———. *Egypt as a Woman: Nationalism, Gender, and Politics*. Berkeley: University of California Press, 2005.
Al-Bayyuni, Amira Abd al-Munʻim. *Al-Usra al-Misriyya: Dirasa Mufassila an al-Zawaj wa al-Talaq fi al-Jumhuriyya al-Arabiyya al-Mutahhida*. Cairo: Dar al-Kitab al-Arabi, 1967.
Beck, Lois, and Nikki Keddie, eds. *Women in the Muslim World*. Cambridge, MA: Harvard University Press, 1978.
Bérenguier, Nadine. *Conduct Books for Girls in Enlightenment France*. Surrey, UK: Ashgate, 2011.
Bewes, Wyndham A. "The Theory of the Statutes." *Journal of Comparative Legislation and International Law* 4, no. 1 (1922): 97–103.
Bidelman, Patrick Kay. *Pariahs Stand Up! The Founding of the Liberal Feminist Movement in France, 1858–1889*. Westport, CT: Greenwood Press, 1982.
Bongaarts, John. "Household Size and Composition in the Developing World in the 1990s." *Population Studies* 55 (2001): 263–79.
Booth, Marilyn L. *May Her Likes Be Multiplied: Biography and Gender Politics in Egypt*. Berkeley and Los Angeles: University of California Press, 2001.
———. "'A'ishah al-Taymuriyyah." In *Essays in Arabic Literary Biography 1850–1950*, edited by Roger Allen, 366–76. Wiesbaden: Harrassowitz, 2010.

———. "Zaynab Fawwaz al-'Amili." In *Essays in Arabic Literary Biography 1850–1950*, edited by Roger Allen, 93–98. Wiesbaden: Harrassowitz, 2010.

———. "Disruptions of the Local, Eruptions of the Feminine: Local Reportage and National Anxieties in Egypt's 1890s." In *Between Politics, Society and Culture: The Press in the Middle East before Independence*, edited by Anthony Gorman and Didier Monciaud. Edinburgh: Edinburgh University Press, forthcoming.

Bousquet, G. H. "Islamic Law and Customary Law in French North Africa." *Journal of Comparative Legislation and International Law*, 3d series, 32, nos. 3–4 (1950): 57–65.

Brett, Michael. "Legislating for Inequality in Algeria: The Senatus-Consulte of 14 July 1865." *Bulletin of the School of Oriental and African Studies, University of London* 51, no. 3 (1988): 440–61.

Brinton, Jasper Yeates. *The Mixed Courts of Egypt*. 2d ed. New Haven: Yale University Press, 1968.

Brown, Nathan J. *The Rule of Law in the Arab World: Courts in Egypt and the Gulf*. Cambridge: Cambridge University Press, 1997.

Al-Bustani, Fu'ad Afram. *Al-Mu'allim Butrus al-Bustani: Ta'lim al-Nisa' wa Adab al-Arab, Dars wa Muntakabat*. 2d ed. Beirut: al-Matba'at al-Kathulikiyya, 1966.

Cannon, Byron. *Politics of Law and the Courts in Nineteenth-Century Egypt*. Salt Lake City: University of Utah Press, 1988.

Carroll, Lucy. "Talaq-i-Tafwid and Stipulations in a Muslim Marriage Contract: Important Means of Protecting the Position of the South Asian Muslim Wife." *Modern Asian Studies* 16, no. 2 (1982): 277–309.

Central Asia. Cambridge, MA: Harvard University Press, 2006.

Chakrabarty, Dipesh. "The Difference—Deferral of Colonial Modernity: Public Debates on Domesticity in British Bengal." In *Tensions of Empire: Colonial Cultures in a Bourgeois World*, edited by Frederick Cooper and Ann Laura Stoler, 373–405. Berkeley and Los Angeles: University of California Press, 1997.

Chanock, Martin. *Law, Custom and Social Order: The Colonial Experience in Malawi and Zambia*. Cambridge: Cambridge University Press, 1985.

Charnay, Jean-Paul. *La Vie Musulmane en Algérie d'après la Jurisprudence de la Première Motié du xxe Siècle*. Paris: Presses Universitaires de France, 1965.

Charrad, Mounira. *States and Women's Rights: The Making of Postcolonial Tunisia, Algeria, and Morocco*. Berkeley: University of California Press, 2001.

Chennells, Ellen. *Recollections of an Egyptian Princess by Her English Governess, Being a Record of Five Years' Residence at the Court of Ismael Pasha, Khédive*. 2 vols. London: William Blackwood, 1893.

Christelow, Allan. *Muslim Law Courts and the French Colonial State in Algeria*. Princeton: Princeton University Press, 1985.

Clancey-Smith, Julia. "La Femme Arabe: Women and Sexuality in France's North African Empire." In Sonbol, ed., *Women, the Family, and Divorce Laws in Islamic History*, 52–63.

Clavel, Eugène. *Droit Musulman. Du Statut Personnel et des Successions d'après les Différents Rites et Plus Particulièrement d'après le Rite Hanafite*. 2 vols. Paris: Librairie du Recueil Général des Lois et des Arrêts, 1895.

Cleland, William Wendell. *The Population Problem in Egypt*. Lancaster, PA: Science Press, 1936.

Clot, A.-B. *Aperçu Général sur l'Égypte*. 2 vols. Paris: Fortin, Masson, 1840.

The Code Napoleon; or the French Civil Code. Literally Translated from the Original and Official Edition, Published at Paris, in 1804, by a Barrister of the Inner Temple. New York: Halsted and Boorhies, 1841.

Cole, Juan R. I. *Colonialism and Revolution in the Middle East: Social and Cultural Origins of Egypt's 'Urabi Movement*. Princeton: Princeton University Press, 1992.

"Controversy over 'Suzanne's laws.'" *Ahram Weekly*, 1046 (May 5–11, 2011). http://weekly.ahram.org.eg/2011/1046/eg14.htm.

Coontz, Stephanie. *The Way We Never Were: American Families and the Nostalgia Trap*. New York: Basic Books, 1992.

———. *Marriage, a History: How Love Conquered Marriage*. New York: Penguin, 2006.

Crews, Robert D. *For Prophet and Tsar: Islam and Empire in Russia and*

Cromer, Earl of. *Modern Egypt*. 2 vols. New York: Macmillan, 1908.

———. *Abbas II*. London: Macmillan, 1915.

Cuno, Kenneth M. "African Slaves in Nineteenth-Century Rural Egypt: A Preliminary Assessment." In Walz and Cuno, eds., *Race and Slavery in the Middle East*, 77–98.

———. *The Pasha's Peasants: Land, Society, and Economy in Lower Egypt 1740–1858*. Cambridge: Cambridge University Press, 1992.

———. "Joint Family Households and Rural Notables in Nineteenth-Century Egypt." *International Journal of Middle East Studies* 27, no. 4 (Nov. 1995): 485–502.

———. "A Tale of Two Villages: Family, Property, and Economic Activity in Rural Egypt in the 1840s." In *Agriculture in Egypt from Pharaonic to Modern Times*, edited by Alan K. Bowman and Eugene Rogan, 301–29. Oxford: Oxford University Press, 1999.

———. "Demography, Household Formation, and Marriage in Three Egyptian Villages during the Mid-Nineteenth Century." In *Sociétés Rurales Ottomanes/Ottoman Rural Societies*, edited by Mohammad Afifi et al., 105–17. Cairo: Institut Française d'Archéologie Orientale, 2005.

———. "Divorce and the Fate of the Family in Modern Egypt." In *Family in the Middle East: Ideational Change in Egypt, Iran, and Tunisia*, edited by Kathryn Yount and Hoda Rashad, 196–216. New York: Routledge, 2008.

———. "Disobedient Wives and Neglectful Husbands: Marital Relations and the First Phase of Reform of Family Law in Egypt." In *Family, Gender and Law in a Globalizing Middle East and South Asia*, edited by Kenneth M. Cuno and Manisha Desai, 3–18. Syracuse: Syracuse University Press, 2009.

———. "Women with Missing Husbands: Marriage in Nineteenth Century Egypt." In *Objectivity and Subjectivity in the Historiography of Egypt: In Honour of Nelly Hanna*, edited by Nasser Ahmed Ibrahim, 158–72. Cairo: General Egyptian Book Organization, 2012.

Cuno, Kenneth M., and Michael J. Reimer. "The Census Registers of Nineteenth-Century Egypt: A New Source for Social Historians." *British Journal of Middle Eastern Studies* 24, no. 2 (1997): 193–216.

Damad Afandi. Abd al-Rahman b. al-Shaykh Muhammad, known as Damad Afandi and also as Shaykhzadeh. *Majmaʻ al-Anhur fi Sharh Multaqa al-Abhur*. Beirut: Dar Ihya' al-Turath, 1980.

Davis, Fanny. *The Ottoman Lady: A Social History from 1718 to 1918*. Westport, CT: Greenwood Press, 1986.

Al-Dayrabi, Ahmad b. Umar. *Kitab Gayat al-Maqsud li-Man Yataʻati al-Uqud*. Cairo: Matbaʻa al-Wahbiyya, 1880.

Delanoue, Gilbert. *Moralistes et politiques musulmans dans l'Égypte du XIXe siècle (1798–1882)*. 2 vols. Cairo: Institut Français d'Archéologie Orientale du Caire, 1982.

De Leon, Edwin. *The Khedive's Egypt; or, The Old House of Bondage under New Masters*. New York: Harper & Brothers, 1878.

———. *Thirty Years of My Life on Three Continents. With a Chapter on the Life of Women in the East, by Mrs. De Leon*. 2 vols. London: Ward and Downey, 1890.

De Malortie, Baron Karl. *Egypt: Native Rulers and Foreign Interference.* 2d. ed. London: William Ridgway, 1883.

Depping, G.-B. *Aperçu Historique sur les Moeurs et Coutumes des Nations, Contenant le Tableau Comparé Chez les Divers Peuples Anciens et Modernes, des Usages et des Cérémonies Concernant l'Habitation, la Nourriture, l'Habillement, les Mariages, les Funèrailles, les Jeux, les Fêtes, les Guerres, les Superstitions, les Castes, etc., etc.* Paris: Mariet et Fournier, 1842.

Dicey, Edward. *The Story of the Khedivate.* London: Rivingtons, 1902.

Doolittle, Megan. "Close Relations? Bringing Together Gender and Family in English History." *Gender & History* 11, no. 3 (Nov. 1999): 542–54.

Duben, Alan, and Cem Behar. *Istanbul Households: Marriage, Family and Fertility, 1880–1940.* Cambridge: Cambridge University Press, 1991.

Duff Gordon, Lucie. *Letters from Egypt.* 1865. Reprint, London: Virago, 1983.

Egypt. "A'dad wa Ma'dalat Shihadat al-Zawaj wa al-Talaq," 1985–2011. Central Agency for Public Mobilization and Statistics. http://www.capmas.gov.eg/pdf/Number_MD.pdf.

———. *Annuaire Statistique de l'Egypte, 1909.* Cairo: Ministry of Finance, 1909.

———. *Annuaire Statistique de l'Egypte, 1918.* Cairo: Ministry of Finance, 1919.

———. *Census of Population, Housing and Establishments, 1986. Final Results.* Cairo: Central Agency for Public Mobilization and Statistics, 1987.

———. *Demographic Analysis of 1976 Egyptian Population and Housing Census.* Cairo: Central Agency for Public Mobilization and Statistics, 1987.

———. *Al-Ta'dad al- Amm li-l-Sukkan wa-l-Iskan wa-l-Mansha'at fi Am 1996. Al-Nata'ij al-Niha'iyya li-l-Ta'dad.* Cairo: Central Agency for Public Mobilization and Statistics, 1998.

"Egypt Draft Constitution Article Raises Fears for Women's Rights." *Ahram Online,* Sept. 23, 2012, http://english.ahram.org.eg/News/53598.aspx.

El-Bahr, Sahar. "Loveless in Egypt." *Al-Ahram Weekly,* No. 908, July 31–August 6, 2008, http://weekly.ahram.org.eg/2008/908/li1.htm.

El Gaafari, Mahmoud. "Expert: A Divorce Occurs in Egypt Every 6 Mins." *Al-Masry al-Yaum,* Apr. 18, 2010. http://www.egyptindependent.com/node/35725.

El Masry, Sarah. "Under-Reported and Underage: Early Marriage in Egypt." *Daily News Egypt,* Dec. 5, 2012. http://www.dailynewsegypt.com/2012/12/05/under-reported-and-underage-early-marriage-in-egypt/.

El Shakry, Omnia. "Schooled Mothers and Structured Play: Child Rearing in Turn-of-the-Century Egypt." In Abu Lughod, ed., *Remaking Women,* 126–70.

———. *The Great Social Laboratory: Subjects of Knowledge in Colonial and Postcolonial Egypt*. Stanford: Stanford University Press, 2007.

El-Shanawany, R. "The First National Life Tables for Egypt." *L'Egypte Contemporaine* 27 (1936): 209–69.

Esposito, John, with Natana J. Delong-Bas. *Women in Muslim Family Law*. 2d ed. Syracuse: Syracuse University Press, 2001.

Fahmi, Hoda. *Divorcer en Egypte: Étude de l'application des lois du statut personnel*. Cairo: Centre d'Études et de Documentation Économiques, Juridiques et Sociales, 1986.

Fahmy, Khaled. *All the Pasha's Men: Mehmed Ali, His Army and the Making of Modern Egypt*. Cambridge: Cambridge University Press, 1997.

———. "The Police and the People in Nineteenth-Century Egypt." *Die Welt des Islams* 39, no. 3 (1999): 340–77.

Fairchilds, Cissie. "Women and the Family." *French Women and the Age of Enlightenment*, edited by Samia I. Spencer, 97–110. Bloomington: Indiana University Press, 1984.

Fargues, Philippe. "Terminating Marriage." In Hopkins, ed., *The New Arab Family*, 247–73.

———. "The Stages of the Family Life Cycle in Cairo at the End of the Reign of Muhammad Ali, According to the 1848 Census." *Harvard Middle Eastern and Islamic Review* 8 (1999–2000): 1–39.

———. "Family and Household in Mid-Nineteenth-Century Cairo." In *Family History in the Middle East: Household, Property, and Gender*, edited by Beshara Doumani, 23–50. Albany: State University of New York Press, 2003.

Farley, J. Lewis. *Modern Turkey*. London: Hurst and Blackett, 1872.

Fawwaz, Zaynab. *Al-Rasa'il al-Zaynabiyya*. Cairo: al-Matba'a al-Mutawassita, 1905.

Fay, Mary Ann. *Unveiling the Harem: Elite Women and the Paradox of Seclusion in Eighteenth-Century Cairo*. Syracuse: Syracuse University Press, 2012.

Flandrin, Jean-Louis. *Families in Former Times*. Cambridge: Cambridge University Press, 1979.

Fyzee, A. A. *Outlines of Muhammadan Law*. 3d ed. London: Oxford University Press, 1964.

Gesink, Indira Falk. *Islamic Reform and Conservatism: Al-Azhar and the Evolution of Modern Sunni Islam*. London: I. B. Tauris, 2010.

Ghazaleh, Pascale. *Fortunes Urbaines et Stratégies Sociales: Généalogies Patrimoniales au Caire, 1780–1830*. Cairo: Institut Français d'Achéologie Orientale, 2010.

Al-Ghazali, Imam. *The Proper Conduct of Marriage in Islam (Adab an-Nikah). Book Twelve of Ihya' 'Ulum al-Din*. Translated by Muhtar Holland. Hollywood, FL: al-Baz, 1998.

Gillotte, Charles. *Traité du Droit Musulman Précédé du Décret du 31 Décembre 1859*. Constantine: Alessi et Arnolet, 1860.

Goldschmidt, Arthur, Jr. *Biographical Dictionary of Modern Egypt*. Cairo: The American University in Cairo Press, 2000.

Goode, William J. *World Revolution and Family Patterns*. New York: Free Press, 1963.

Graham-Brown, Sarah. *Images of Women: The Portrayal of Women in Photography of the Middle East 1860–1950*. London: Quartet Books, 1988.

Gran, Peter. *Islamic Roots of Capitalism: Egypt 1760–1840*. Austin: University of Texas Press, 1979.

Guizot, François. *History of Civilization in Europe, from the Fall of the Roman Empire to the French Revolution*. New York: John B. Alden, 1885.

Haj, Samira. *Reconfiguring Islamic Tradition: Reform, Rationality, and Modernity*. Stanford: Stanford University Press, 2009.

Hallaq, Wael. *Shari'a: Theory, Practice, Transformations*. Cambridge: Cambridge University Press, 2009.

Hammel, E. A., and Peter Laslett. "Comparing Household Structure over Time and between Cultures." *Comparative Studies in Society and History* 16, no. 1 (1974): 73–109.

Hamont, P. N. *L'Égypte sous Méhémet-Ali*. 2 vols. Paris: Leautey & Lecointe, 1843.

Hanna, Nelly. "The Administration of Courts in Ottoman Cairo." In *The State and Its Servants: Administration in Egypt from Ottoman Times to the Present*, edited by Nelly Hanna, 44–59. Cairo: American University in Cairo Press, 1995.

———. "Marriage among Merchant Families in Seventeenth-Century Cairo." In Sonbol, ed., *Women, the Family, and Divorce Laws in Islamic History*, 143–54.

———. *Making Big Money in 1600: the Life and Times of Isma'il Abu Taqiyya, Egyptian Merchant*. Syracuse: Syracuse University Press, 1998.

Hasan, Farhat. *State and Locality in Mughal India: Power Relations in Western India, c. 1572–1730*. Cambridge: Cambridge University Press, 2004.

Al-Haskafi, Ala' al-Din Muhammad b. Ali. *Al-Durr al-Mukhtar Sharh Tanwir al-Absar*. In the margin of Ibn Abdin, *Radd al-Muhtar*. 5 vols. 3d. ed. Bulaq: al-Matba'a al-Amiriyya, 1905–8.

Hatem, Mervat F. "Egyptian Discourses on Gender and Political Liberalization: Do Secularist and Islamist Views Really Differ?" *Middle East Journal* 48, no. 4 (1994): 661–76.

———. *Literature, Gender, and Nation-Building in Nineteenth-Century Egypt: The Life and Works of 'A'isha Taymur*. New York: Palgrave Macmillan, 2011.

Hathaway, Jane. *The Politics of Households in Ottoman Egypt: the Rise of the Qazdağlıs*. Cambridge: Cambridge University Press, 1997.

Haykal, Muhammad Husayn. *Tarajim Misriyya wa Gharbiyya*. Cairo: Dar al-Ma'arif, 1980.

Henry, Jean-Robert, and François Balique, *La Doctrine Coloniale du Droit Musulman Algérien. Bibliographie Systématique et Introduction Critique*. Paris: Centre National de Recherche Scientifique, 1979.

Heyworth-Dunne, James. *An Introduction to the History of Education in Modern Egypt*. London: Luzac, 1938.

Al-Hifnawi, Iman. "One Divorce Case Every Six Minutes in Egypt." *Al-Musawwar* 14 (Apr. 1, 2005) (in Arabic). Translated by *Arab West Report*, July 28, 2008. http://www.arabwestreport.info/year-2005/week-14/34-one-divorce-case-every-six-minutes-egypt.

Hilal, Imad Ahmad. *Al-Raqiq fi Misr fi al-Qarn al-Tasi' Ashar*. Cairo: Al-Arabi li-l-Nashr wa al-Tawzi', 1999.

Al-Hilbawi, Ibrahim. *Mudhakkirat Ibrahim al-Hilbawi (Tarikh hayat Ibrahim al-Hilbawi Bayk) 1858–1940*. Cairo: General Egyptian Book Organization, 1995.

Hill, Enid. *Mahkama! Studies in the Egyptian Legal System*. London: Ithaca Press, 1979.

Hoodfar, Homa. "Survival Strategies and the Political Economy of Low-Income Households in Cairo." In *Development, Change and Gender in Cairo: A View from the Household*, edited by Diane Singerman and Homa Hoodfar, 1–26. Bloomington: Indiana University Press, 1996.

———. *Between Marriage and the Market: Intimate Politics and Survival in Cairo*. Berkeley: University of California Press, 1997.

———, ed. *Shifting Boundaries in Marriage and Divorce in Muslim Countries*. Montpellier: Women Living Under Muslim Law, 1996.

Hooker, M. B. *Legal Pluralism: An Introduction to Colonial and Neo-Colonial Laws*. Oxford: Oxford University Press, 1976.

Hopkins, Nicholas S., ed. *The New Arab Family*. Cairo Papers in Social Science 24, nos. 1–2 (2001).

Horowitz, Richard S. "International Law and State Transformation in China, Siam, and the Ottoman Empire during the Nineteenth Century." *Journal of World History* 15, no. 4 (2005): 445–86.

Hourani, Albert. *Arabic Thought in the Liberal Age*. Cambridge: Cambridge University Press, 1983.

Human Rights Watch. "Divorced from Justice: Women's Unequal Access to divorce in Egypt." Report 16, 8(E) (Dec. 2004). http://www.hrw.org/reports/2004/11/30/divorced-justice.

Hunt, Lynn. *The Family Romance of the French Revolution*. Berkeley: University of California Press, 1992.

Hunter, F. Robert. *Egypt under the Khedives, 1805–1879: From Household Government to Modern Bureaucracy*. Pittsburgh: University of Pittsburgh Press, 1984.

Ibn Abdin, Muhammad Amin b. Umar. *Radd al-Muhtar ala al-Durr al-Mukhtar Sharh Tanwir al-Absar*. 3d ed. 5 vols. Bulaq: al-Matba'a al-Amiriyya, 1905–8.

———, ed. *Al-Uqud al-Durriyya fi Taqih al-Fatawa al-Hamidiyya*. 2d ed. 2 vols. Bulaq: al-Matba'a al-Miriyya, 1882–83.

Ibn Hajar al-Haythami, Ahmad b. Muhammad. *Al-Zawajir an Iqtiraf al-Kaba'ir*. 2 vols. Beirut: Dar al-Kutub al-Ilmiyya, 1987.

Ibn Nujaym, Zayn al-Abidin Ibrahim b. Muhammad. *Al-Ashbah wa al-Naza'ir*. Damascus: Dar al-Fikr, 1983.

———. *Bahr al-Ra'iq Sharh Kanz al-Daqa'iq*. 9 vols. Beirut: Dar al-Kutub al-Ilmiyya, 1997. The Complete Reference of Islamic Fiqh CD ROM.

Al-Ibyani, Muhammad Zayd. *Sharh al-Ahkam al-Shar'iyya fi al-Ahwal al-Shakhsiyya*. 2d ed. Cairo: Matba'a Ali Shukri, 1911.

Al-Idwi al-Hamzawi, Hasan. *Ahkam Uqud al-Nikah*. Bulaq: al-Matba'a al-Amiriyya, 1276/1859.

Imara, Muhammad. *Rifa'a al-Tahtawi Ra'id al-Tanwir fi al-Asr al-Hadith*. Cairo: Dar al-Shuruq, 1988.

Al-Jabarti, Abd al-Rahman b. Hasan. *Aja'ib al-Athar fi al-Tarajim wa al-Akhbar*. 4 vols. Bulaq: Dar al-Tiba'a, 1880.

Al-Jabi, Bassam Abd al-Wahhab, ed. *Al-Majalla: Majalla al-Ahkam al-Adliyya. Ma'ha Qarar Huquq al-A'ila fi al-Nikah al-Madani wa al-Talaq*. Limassol: Dar Ibn Hazm, 2004.

Jallad, Filib. *Qamus al-Idara wa al-Qada'*. 4 vols. Alexandria: al-Matba'a al-Bukhariyah, Yani Lagudakis, 1890–92.

Jennings, Ronald C. "Women in Early 17th Century Ottoman Judicial Records: The Sharia Court of Anatolian Kayseri." *Journal of the Economic and Social History of the Orient* 18, no. 1 (1975): 53–114.

———. "Divorce in the Ottoman Sharia Court of Cyprus, 1580–1640." *Studia Islamica* 78 (1993): 155–67.

Jum'a, Muhammad Lutfi. *Shahid ala al-Asr: Mudhakkirat Muhammad Lutfi Jum'a*. Cairo: General Egyptian Book Organization, 2000.

Al-Jundi, Ahmad Nasr. *Mabadi' al-Qada' al-Shar'i fi Khamsin Aman*. Cairo: Dar al-Fikr al-Arabi, 1973.

Kandiyoti, Deniz. "Bargaining with Patriarchy." *Gender & Society* 2, no. 3 (1988): 274–90.

———. "Some Awkward Questions on Women and Modernity in Turkey." In Abu-Lughod, ed., *Remaking Women*, 270–87.

———. "Gender, Power, and Contestation: 'Rethinking Bargaining with Patriarchy.'" In *Feminist Visions of Development: Gender, Analysis and Policy*, edited by Cecile Jackson and Ruth Pearson, 135–51. London: Routledge, 1998.

Kahf, Mohja. "Packaging 'Huda': Sha'rawi's Memoirs in the United States Reception Environment." In *Going Global: The Transnational Reception of Third World Women Writers*, edited by Amal Amireh and Lisa Suhair Majaj, 148–72. New York: Garland, 2000.

Al-Kasani, Abu Bakr b. Mas'ud. *Bada'i' al-Sana'i' fi Tartib al-Shara'i'*. 7 vols. Beirut, Dar al-Kitab al-Arabi, 1974. The Complete Reference of Islamic Fiqh CD ROM.

Kertzer, David I., and Marzio Barbagli, eds. *The History of the European Family*. Vol. 1, *Family Life in Early Modern Times 1500–1789*. New Haven: Yale University Press, 2001.

Khan, Fareeha. "Tafwid al-Talaq: Transferring the Right of Divorce to the Wife." *Muslim World* 99 (July 2009): 502–20.

Khanki, Aziz. "Zawjat Hukkam Misr min Muhammad Ali Basha al-Kabir ila Jalalat al-Malik Faruq al-Awwal." In *Nafahat Tarikhiyya*, 43–55. Cairo: al-Matba'a al-Asriyya, n.d.

———. "Al-Tashri' wa al-Qada' qabl Insha' al-Mahakim al-Ahliyya." In *Al-Kitab al-Dhahabi li-l-Mahakim al-Ahliyya* 2 (n.d.): 62–96.

Khedr, Zeinab, and Laila El Zeini. "Families and Households: Headship and Co-Residence." In Hopkins, ed., *The New Arab Family*, 140–64.

Kholoussy, Hanan. *For Better, For Worse: The Marriage Crisis That Made Egypt*. Stanford: Stanford University Press, 2010.

Al-Kitab al-Dhahabi li-l-Mahakim al-Ahliyya, 1883–1933. 2 vols. Bulaq: al-Matbaʿat al-Amiriyya, 1937.

Knauss, Peter. *The Persistence of Patriachy.* New York: Praeger, 1987.

Kozma, Liat. *Policing Egyptian Women: Sex, Law, and Medicine in Khedival Egypt.* Syracuse: Syracuse University Press, 2011.

Lal, Ruby. *Domesticity and Power in the Early Mughal World.* Cambridge: Cambridge University Press, 2005.

Lane, Edward W. *An Account of the Manners and Customs of the Modern Egyptians: The Definitive 1860 Edition.* Cairo: American University in Cairo Press, 2003.

Lane Poole, Sophia. *The Englishwoman in Egypt.* London: C. Cox, 1851–53.

Lapanne-Joinville, J. "Les Conventions Annexées au Contrat de Mariage (tatawwuʾat) en Droit Musulman Malékite." *Revue Algérienne, Tunisienne et Marocaine de Législation et de Jurisprudence* 70, no. 4 (1954): 112–25.

Largueche, Dalenda. "Monogamy in Islam: The Case of a Tunisian Marriage Contract." Institute of Advanced Studies, School of Social Science Occasional Papers 39 (September 2010). http://www.sss.ias.edu/files/papers/paper39.pdf.

LaRue, George Michael. "'My Ninth Master Was a European': Enslaved Blacks in European Households in Egypt, 1798–1848." In Walz and Cuno, eds., *Race and Slavery in the Middle East*, 99–124.

Leila, Reem. "The Terms of Engagement." *Al-Ahram Weekly*, 484, June 1–7, 2000. http://weekly.ahram.org.eg/2000/484/li1.htm.

Lev, Daniel. "Colonial Law and the Genesis of the Indonesian State." *Indonesia* 40 (1985): 57–74.

Lewis, H. D. "The Legal Status of Women in Nineteenth-Century France." *Journal of European Studies* 10 (1980): 178–88.

Liebesny, Herbert J. *The Law of the Near and Middle East: Readings, Cases, & Materials.* Albany: State University of New York Press, 1975.

Locher-Scholten, Elsbeth. *Women and the Colonial State: Essays on Gender and Modernity in the Netherlands Indies 1900–1942.* Amsterdam: Amsterdam University Press, 2000.

Loos, Tamara. *Subject Siam: Family, Law, and Colonial Modernity in Thailand.* Ithaca: Cornell University Press, 2006.

Lopez, Shaun T. "Madams, Murders, and the Media: *Akhbar al-Hawadith* and the Emergence of a Mass Culture in 1920s Egypt." In *Re-Envisioning Egypt 1919–1952*, edited by Arthur Goldschmidt, Amy J. Johnson, and Barak A. Salmoni, 371–97. Cairo: The American University in Cairo Press, 2005.

Al-Mahallawi, Hanafi. *Harim Muluk Misr min Muhammad Ali ila Faruq*. Cairo: Dar al-Amin, 1993.

Al-Mahdi, Muhammad al-Abbasi. *Al-Fatawa al-Mahdiyya fi al-Waqa'i' al-Misriyya*. 7 vols. Cairo: al-Matba'a al-Azhariyya, 1883–86.

Mainardi, Patricia. *Husbands, Wives, and Lovers: Marriage and Its Discontents in Nineteenth Century France*. New Haven: Yale, 2003.

Majmu'a al-Awamir al-Ulya wa al-Dikritat al-Sadira min Awwal Shahr Yanayir Sanat 1890 ila 31 minhu [sic]. Cairo: al-Matba'a al-Ahliyya, 1890.

Majmu'a al-Awamir al-Ulya wa al-Dikritat al-Sadira fi Sanat 1897. Bulaq: al-Matba'a al-Amiriyya, 1898.

Al-Majmu': Sharh al-Madhhab. 22 vols. Beirut: Dar al-Fikr, 1996. The Complete Reference of Islamic Fiqh CD ROM.

Malte-Brun, Conrad. *Universal Geography: or A Description of All the Parts of the World on a New Plan, According to the Great Natural Divisions of the Globe; Accompanied with Analytical, Synoptical, and Elementary Tables*. 6 vols. Philadelphia: A. Finley, 1827–32.

Marsot, Afaf. "The Revolutionary Gentlewomen in Egypt." In Beck and Keddie, *Women in the Muslim World*, 261–76.

———. *Women and Men in Late Eighteenth-Century Egypt*. Austin: University of Texas Press, 1995.

McCarthy, Justin A. "Nineteenth-Century Egyptian Population." *Middle Eastern Studies* 12, no. 3 (Oct. 1976): 1–39.

McCoan, J. C. *Egypt as It Is*. London: Cassell, Petter & Galpin, 1877.

McMillan, James F. *France and Women 1789–1914: Gender, Society and Politics*. London: Routledge, 2000.

McLarney, Ellen. "Women's Rights in the Egyptian Constitution: (Neo)Liberalism's Family Values." *Jadaliyya*, May 22, 2013. http://www.jadaliyya.com/pages/index/11852/womens-rights-in-the-egyptian-constitution_(neo)li.

Melman, Billie. *Women's Orients: English Women and the Middle East, 1718–1918*. Ann Arbor: University of Michigan Press, 1995.

Mernissi, Fatima. *The Veil and the Male Elite: A Feminist Interpretation of Women's Rights in Islam*. New York: Basic Books, 1991.

Messick, Brinkley. *The Calligraphic State: Textual Domination and History in a Muslim Society*. Berkeley and Los Angeles: University of California Press, 1992.

Mitchell, Timothy. *Colonising Egypt*. Cambridge: Cambridge University Press, 1988.

———, ed. *Questions of Modernity*. Minneapolis and London: University of Minnesota Press, 2000.

Mohamed Ali (Tawfiq), Prince. *De Ma Naissance à 1882*. Cairo: N.p., 1950.

Mubarak, Ali. *Tariq al-Hija wa al-Tamrin ala al-Qira'a fi al-Lugha al-Arabiyya*. 2 vols. Cairo: Matba'a Wadi al-Nil, 1285/1868.

———. *Al-Khitat al-Tawfiqiyya al-Jadida li-Misr al-Qahira*. 20 vols. Bulaq: al-Matba'a al-Amiriyya, 1887–89.

———. *Ali Mubarak al-A'mal al-Kamila*. Edited by Muhammad Imara. 3 vols. Beirut: al-Mu'assasa al-Arabiyya li-l-Dirasat wa al-Nashr, 1979.

Muhammad, Ibrahim Ahmad. *Majmu'a Qawanin al-Ahwal al-Shakhsiyya*. Alexandria: Al-Dar al-Misriyya li-l-Tiba'a wa al-Nashr, 1956?

"Al-Munazzamat Ghayr al-Hukumiyya Tudin Mashru' Marsum Qanun al-Ahwal al-Shakhskyya li-l-Mustashar Abd Allah Baja." The New Woman Foundation. July 21, 2011. http://nwrcegypt.org/?p=5210.

Musa, Salama. *The Education of Salama Musa*. Translated by S. O. Schuman. Leiden: Brill, 1961.

Musnad al-Tayalisi. Beirut: Dar al-Ma'rifa, 1988. The Complete Reference of Islamic Hadeeth CD ROM.

"Al-Mustashar al-Baja: Qanun al-Mar'a al-Jadid Yuhallil al-Haram wa Yuharrim al-Halal." April 14, 2013. http://www.ikhwanonline.net/Article.aspx?ArtID=145938&SecID=323.

Najmabadi, Afsaneh. *Women with Mustaches and Men without Beards: Gender and Sexual Anxieties of Iranian Modernity*. Berkeley: University of California Press, 2005.

Nakamura, Hisako. "Conditional Divorce in Indonesia." *Islamic Legal Studies Program Occasional Studies*, No. 7, Harvard Law School (July 2006). http://www.law.harvard.edu/programs/ilsp/publications/nakamura2.pdf.

Al-Namnam, Hilmi. *Ali Yusuf wa Safiya al-Sadat: Rasa'il al-Hubb wa Ma'rakat al-Zawaj*. Cairo: Mirit, 2001.

Nasir, Jamal J. *The Islamic Law of Personal Status*. The Hague: Kluwer Law, 2002.

Al-Nawawi, Muhammad b. Umar. *Sharh Uqud al-Lujayn fi Bayan Huquq al-Zawjayn*. 2d ed. Cairo: al-Matba'a al-Wahbiyya, 1296/1879.

Nosseir, Aida (Ayda Ibrahim Nusayr). *Dalil al-Matbu'at al-Misriyya 1940–1956*. Cairo: The American University in Cairo Press, 1975.

———. *Al-Kutub al-Arabiyya allati Nushirat fi Misr bayn Amay 1926–1940*. Cairo: The American University in Cairo Press, 1980.

———. *Al-Kutub al-Arabiyya allati Nushirat fi Misr bayn Amay 1900–1925*. Cairo: The American University in Cairo Press, 1983.

———. *Al-Kutub al-Arabiyya allati Nushirat fi Misr fi al-Qarn al-Tasi' Ashar*. Cairo: The American University in Cairo Press, 1990.

Al-Nowaihi, Mohamed. "Changing the Law on Personal Status in Egypt within a Liberal Interpretation of the Shari'a." In *Religion and Politics in the Middle East*, edited by Michael Curtis, 109–23. Boulder: Westview Press, 1979.

Osman, Amin. *Muhammad Abduh*. Washington, DC: American Council of Learned Societies, 1953.

Osman, Magued, and Laila S. Shahd, "Age-Discrepant Marriage in Egypt." In Hopkins, ed., *The New Arab Family*, 51–61.

Panzac, Daniel. "The Population of Egypt in the Nineteenth Century." *Asian and African Studies* 21 (1987): 11–32.

Peirce, Leslie P. *The Imperial Harem: Women and Sovereignty in the Ottoman Empire*. Oxford: Oxford University Press, 1993.

Peters, Rudolph. "Muhammad al-Abbasi al-Mahdi (d. 1897), Grand Mufti of Egypt, and his *al-Fatawa al-Mahdiyya*." *Islamic Law and Society* 1, no. 1 (1994): 66–82.

———. "Administrators and Magistrates: The Development of a Secular Judiciary in Egpyt, 1842–1871." *Die Welt des Islams* 39, no. 3 (1999): 378–97.

———. "From Jurists' Law to Statute Law or What Happens When the Shari'a Is Codified." *Mediterranean Politics* 7, no. 3 (2002): 82–95.

The Pew Research Center. "The Changing American Family." Nov. 18, 2010. http://www.pewsocialtrends.org/2010/11/18/five-decades-of-marriage-trends/.

Philipp, Thomas. "Feminism and Nationalist Politics in Egypt." In Beck and Keddie, eds., *Women in the Muslim World*, 277–94.

Phillips, Roderick. *Putting Asunder: A History of Divorce in Western Society*. Cambridge: Cambridge University Press, 1988.

Pollard, Lisa. *Nurturing the Nation: The Family Politics of Modernizing, Colonizing, and Liberating Egypt, 1805–1923*. Berkeley: University of California Press, 2005.

Al-Qadi, Wadad. "East and West in 'Ali Mubarak's *'Alamuddin*." In Marwan Buheiry, ed., *Intellectual Life in the Arab East, 1890–1939*, 21–37. Beirut: American University of Beirut Press, 1981.

Qadri, Muhmmad. *Al-Ahkam al-Shar'iyya fi al-Ahwal al-Shakhsiyya*. 2d ed. Bulaq: al-Matba'a al-Amiriyya, 1881.

———. *Al-Ahkam al-Shar'iyya fi al-Ahwal al-Shakhsiyya wa Sharhhu li-Muhammad Zayd al-Ibyani ma' Mulhaq Qawanin al-Ahwal al-Shakhsiyya al-Arabiyya*. Edited by Muhammad Ahmad Siraj and Ali Jum'a Muhammad. 4 vols. Cairo: Dar al-Salam, 2006.

Qazmakhuri, Yusuf. *Al-Dasatir fi al-Alam al-Arabi*. Beirut: Dar al-Hamra, 1989.

Quraishi, Asifa, and Frank E. Vogel, eds. *The Islamic Marriage Contract: Case Studies in Islamic Family Law*. Cambridge, MA: Harvard University Press, 2008.

Al-Rafi'i, Abd al-Rahman. *Thawrat 1919: Tarikh Misr al-Qawmi min Sanat 1914 ila Sanat 1921*. 2 vols. Cairo: Maktaba al-Nahda al-Misriyya, 1946.

———. *Asr Isma'il*. 2d ed. 2 vols. Cairo: Maktaba al-Nahda al-Misriyya, 1948.

———. *Mudhakkirati 1889–1951*. Cairo: Dar al-Hilal, 1952.

Al-Ramli, Shams al-Din Muhammad b. Ahmad. *Fatawa Shams al-Din Muhammad al-Ramli*, in the margin of Ahmad b. Muhammad Ibn Hajar al-Haythami, *al-Fatawa al-Kubra al-Fiqhiyya*. 4 vols. Cairo: Matba'a Abd al-Hamid Ahmad Hanafi, 1938.

Al-Ramli, Khayr al-Din b. Ahmad. *Al-Fatawa al-Khayriyya li-Naf' al-Barriyya*. 2d ed. 2 vols. Beirut: Dar al-Ma'rifa, 1974.

Rapoport, Yossef. "Legal Diversity in the Age of Taqlid: The Four Chief Qadis under the Mamluks." *Islamic Law and Society* 10, no. 2 (2003): 210–28.

———. *Marriage, Money and Divorce in Medieval Islamic Society*. Cambridge: Cambridge University Press, 2005.

Rashad, Hoda, and Magued Osman. "Nuptiality in Arab Countries: Changes and Implications." In Hopkins, ed., *The New Arab Family*, 20–50.

Rashed, Dena. "Bound by the Blank," *Al-Ahram Weekly*, 523, March 1–7, 2001. http://weekly.ahram.org.eg/2001/523/sc5k.htm.

Reid, Donald M. "Educational and Career Choices of Egyptian Students, 1882–1922." *International Journal of Middle East Studies* 8, no. 3 (1977): 349–78.

Rida, Muhammad Rashid. *Tarikh al-Ustadh al-Imam al-Shaykh Muhammad Abduh*. 3 vols. Cairo: Matba'a al-Manar, 1931.

Rizk, Mariam, and Osman El Sharnoubi. "Egypt's Constitution 2013 vs. 2012: A Comparison." *Ahram Online*, Dec. 12, 2013. http://english.ahram.org.eg/News/88644.aspx.

Rosen, Lawrence. "Equity and Discretion in a Modern Islamic Legal System." *Law and Society Review* 15, no. 1 (1980/1981): 217–45.

Rubin, Avi. *Ottoman Nizamiye Courts: Law and Modernity*. New York: Palgrave Macmillan, 2011.

Russell, Mona L. *Creating the New Egyptian Woman: Consumerism, Education, and National Identity, 1863–1922*. New York: Palgrave Macmillan, 2004.
Sahih al-Bukhari. 9 vols. Beirut: Dar Ihya' al-Turath al-Arabi, 1981. The Complete Reference of Islamic Hadeeth CD ROM.
Sahih Muslim. 2 vols. Beirut: Dar al-Kitab al-Ilmiyya, 1992. The Complete Reference of Islamic Hadeeth CD ROM.
St. John, James Augustus. *Egypt and Mohammed Ali*. 2 vols. London: Longman, Rees, Orme, Brown, Green & Longman, 1834.
Sa'id, Rif'at. *Tarikh al-Fikr al-Ishtiraki fi Misr*. Cairo: Matabi' Kustatsumas wa Sharikihi, 1969.
Salim, Latifa Muhammad. *Al-Nizam al-Qada'i al-Misri al-Hadith 1875–1914*. Cairo: Markaz al-Dirasat al-Siyasiyya wa al-Istratijiyya bi-l-Ahram, 1984.
Sarkis, Adil Ahmad. *Al-Zawaj wa Tatawwur al-Mujtam'*. Cairo: Dar al-Kitab al-Arabi, 1967.
Sautayra, Édouard, and Eugène Cherbonneau. *Droit Musulman: Du Statut Personnel et des Successions*. Paris: Maisonneuve et Cie, 1873.
Schacht, Joseph. *An Introduction to Islamic Law*. Oxford: Clarendon Press, 1964.
Sedgwick, Mark. *Muhammad Abduh*. Oxford: Oneworld, 2010.
Shaarawi, Huda. *Harem Years: The Memoirs of an Egyptian Feminist*. Translated, edited, and introduced by Margot Badran. New York: Feminist Press, 1986.
Shafiq, Ahmad. *Mudhakkirati fi nisf qarn*. 3 vols. Cairo: Matba'a Misr, 1934.
Shaham, Ron. "Bayt al-ta'a," *Encyclopaedia of Islam*. 3d ed. Brill Online.
———. *Family and the Courts in Modern Egypt*. Leiden: Brill, 1997.
———. "State, Feminists and Islamists—The Debate over Stipulations in Marriage Contracts in Egypt." *Bulletin of the School of Oriental and African Studies* 62, no. 3 (1999): 462–80.
Shahine, Gihan. "Calling it Quits." *Al-Ahram Weekly*, No. 448, September 23–29, 1999. http://weekly.ahram.org.eg/1999/448/li2.htm.
Shanley, Mary Lyndon. *Feminism, Marriage, and the Law in Victorian England, 1850–1895*. Princeton: Princeton University Press, 1989.
Sha'rawi, Huda. *Mudhakkirati*. Cairo: Dar al-Hilal, 1981.
Singerman, Diane. "Rewriting Divorce in Egypt: Reclaiming Islam, Legal Activism, and Coalition Politics." In *Remaking Muslim Politics: Pluralism, Contestation, Democratization*, edited by Robert W. Hefner, 161–88. Princeton: Princeton University Press, 2005.

Singerman, Diane, and Barbara Ibrahim. "The Costs of Marriage in Egypt: A Hidden Dimension in the New Arab Demography." In Hopkins, ed., *The New Arab Family*, 80–116.

Sonbol, Amira El-Azhary. "A History of Marriage Contracts in Egypt." In Quraishi and Vogel, eds., *The Islamic Marriage Contract*, 87–122.

———. "Modernity, Standardization, and Marriage Contracts in Nineteenth Century Egypt." In *Histoire Économic et Sociale de l'Empire Ottoman et de la Turquie (1326–1960)*, edited by Daniel Panzac, 485–496. Paris: Peeters, 1995.

———, ed. *Women, the Family, and Divorce Laws in Islamic History*. New York: Syracuse University Press, 1996.

Sönmez, Emel. "Turkish Women in Turkish Literature of the 19th Century." *Die Welt des Islams*, 12, 1/3 (1969): 1–73.

Sonneveld, Nadia. *Khul' Divorce in Egypt: Public Debates, Judicial Practices, and Everyday Life*. Cairo: The American University in Cairo Press, 2012.

———. "Rethinking the Difference between Formal and Informal Marriages in Egypt." In *Family Law in Islam: Divorce, Marriage and Women in the Muslim World*, edited by Maaike Voorhoeve, 77–107. London: I. B. Tauris, 2012.

Sreenivas, Mytheli. *Wives, Widows, Concubines: The Conjugal Family Ideal in Colonial India*. Bloomington: Indiana University Press, 2008.

Stowasser, Barbara Freyer. "Women and Citizenship in the Qur'an." In Sonbol, ed., *Women, the Family, and Divorce Laws in Islamic History*, 23–38.

Sunan Abi Dawud. 2 vols. Beirut: Dar Ihya' al-Turath al-Arabi, 1974. The Complete Reference of Islamic Hadeeth CD ROM.

Sunan Ibn Majah. 2 vols. Beirut: Dar Ihya' al-Turath al-Arabi, 1975. The Complete Reference of Islamic Hadeeth CD ROM.

Sunan al-Tirmidhi. 5 vols. Beirut: Dar al-Kutub al-Ilmiyya, 1994. The Complete Reference of Islamic Hadeeth CD ROM.

Al-Tahtawi, Rifa'a Rafi'i. *Al-Murshid al-Amin li-l-Banat wa al-Banin*. Edited and introduced by Imad Abu Ghazi. Cairo: al-Majlis al-A'la li-l-Thiqafa, 2002.

———. *An Imam in Paris: Account of a Stay in France by an Egyptian Cleric (1826–1831)*. Translated and introduced by Daniel L. Newman. London: Saqi Books, 2004.

Al-Taymur, Aisha. *Mir'at al-Ta'ammul fi al-Umur*. 2d. ed. Cairo: Women and Memory Forum, 2002.

Thomas, Janet. "Women and Capitalism: Oppression or Emancipation?" *Comparative Studies in Society and History* 30, no. 3 (1988): 534–49.

Thompson, Elizabeth. *Colonial Citizens: Republican Rights, Paternal Privilege, and Gender in French Syria and Lebanon.* New York: Columbia University Press, 2000.

Thornton, Arland. *Reading History Sideways: The Fallacy and Enduring Impact of the Developmental Paradigm on Family Life.* Chicago: University of Chicago Press, 2005.

Tilly, Louise A. "Women's History and Family History: Fruitful Collaboration or Missed Connection?" *Journal of Family History* 12, nos. 1–3 (1987): 303–15.

Toledano, Henry. *Judicial Practice and Family Law in Morocco: The Chapter on Marriage from Sijilmasi's Al-Amal al-Mutlaq.* Boulder: Social Science Monographs, 1981.

Tucker, Judith. "Decline of the Family Economy in Mid-Nineteenth-Century Egypt." *Arab Studies Quarterly* 1, no. 3 (1979): 245–71.

———. *Women in Nineteenth-Century Egypt.* Cambridge: Cambridge University Press, 1984.

———. *In the House of the Law: Gender and Islamic Law in Ottoman Syria and Palestine.* Berkeley and Los Angeles: University of California Press, 1998.

———. *Women, Family, and Gender in Islamic Law.* Cambridge: Cambridge University Press, 2008.

Tugay, Emine Foat. *Three Centuries: Family Chronicles of Turkey and Egypt.* Oxford: Oxford University Press, 1963.

Vesey-Fitzgerald, Seymour. *Muhammadan Law: An Abridgment According to its Various Schools.* Oxford: Oxford University Press, 1931.

Vikør, Knut. *Between God and the Sultan: A History of Islamic Law.* Oxford: Oxford University Press, 2005.

Wafi, Ali Abd al-Wahid. *Bayt al-Ta'a wa Ta'addud al-Zawjat wa al-Talaq fi al-Islam.* Cairo: Mu'assasat al-Matbu'at al-Haditha, 1960.

Walz, Terence. "Sudanese, Habasha, Takarna, and Barabira: Trans-Saharan Africans in Cairo as Shown in the 1848 Census." In Walz and Cuno, eds., *Race and Slavery in the Middle East*, 43–76.

Walz, Terence, and Kenneth M. Cuno, eds. *Race and Slavery in the Middle East: Histories of Trans-Saharan Africans in Nineteenth-Century Egypt, Sudan, and the Ottoman Mediterranean.* Cairo: The American University in Cairo Press, 2010.

"Women's Equality Article Removed From Constitution." *Al-Masry al-Youm*, Nov. 12, 2012. http://www.egyptindependent.com/node/1236371.

Zaalouk, Malak. *Al-Tarikh al-Ijtima'i li-Qarya Misriyya: Ikhtab Markaz Aja Muhafazat al-Daqahliyya.* Cairo: Markaz al-Qawmi li-l-Buhuth al-Ijtima'iyya wa al-Jina'iyya, 1995.

Zaki, Hind Ahmed. "The New Marriage Contract in Egypt: Religious Reframing and the Hazards of Reform." Paper prepared for the American Anthropological Association Annual Meeting, November 19, 2010, http://www.academia.edu/2132743/The_New_Marriage_Contract_in_Egypt_Religious_Reframing_and_the_Hazards_of_Reform.

Ze'evi, Dror. "The Use of Ottoman Sharia Court Records as a Source for Middle Eastern Social History: A Reappraisal." *Islamic Law and Society* 5, no. 1 (1998): 35–56.

Zeidan, Joseph T. *Arab Women Novelists: The Formative Years and Beyond.* Albany: State University of New York Press, 1995.

Ziadeh, Farhat J. *Lawyers, the Rule of Law, and Liberalism in Modern Egypt.* Stanford: Hoover Institution, 1968.

Zulficar, Mona. "The Islamic Marriage Contract in Egypt." In Quraishi and Vogel, eds., *The Islamic Marriage Contract*, 231–55.

Index

Italic page number denotes illustration.

Abbas Hilmi I (viceroy of Egypt 1849–54), 19, 35, 36
Abbas Hilmi II (khedive of Egypt 1892–1914), xv, 20, 23; domestic life, 41–44, 47, 48, 206
al-Abbasi al-Mahdi, Muhammad (mufti of Egypt 1847–97), 18; his fatwas, 47, 130, 143, 145–49, 169, 172–76, 178, 192–96
Abduh, Muhammad (mufti of Egypt 1899–1905), xv, 14, 56, 81, 83–84, 92–93, 103–5, 109–115, 117, 120, 151–52, 157, 163–64, 200, 202, 209, 210–13; report on reform of Sharia Courts, 84, 104, 137, 153–56, 186, 200–201; *Tafsir al-Manar*, 84, 111
abortion, 101–2
absent (*gha'ib*) and missing (*mafqud*) husbands, 112, 127–28, 141–43, 145–47, 152–53, 204, 211, 212
Abugideiri, Hibba, 115, 122
Abu-Lughod, Lila, 115, 207
abuse, spousal, 14, 112; in France, 101–2. *See also* wives: striking of
Abu Zahra, Muhammad, 211
al-Adab (newspaper), 153
adultery, 34, 101

adulthood, legal (*bulugh*), 65, 130, 150, 249n28. *See also* age of discretion
al-Afghani, Jamal al-Din, 83, 104, 105, 116
age at marriage, 7, 11, 12, 46, 58–61, 64–68, 85, 97–98, 102, 140, 206, 211–12, 215, 265n2. *See also* marriage: of minors
agents, legal (*wakils*), 155, 177, 189, 261n6
age of discretion (*rushd*), 58, 130, 148, 171, 177, 249n28, 254n100
Agrama, Hussein Ali, 15
al-Ahkam al-Shar'iyya (legal journal), 154, 191, 201
Ahli Courts. *See* National Courts
Ahmed, Leila, 115, 238n13, 245n132
al-Ahram (newspaper), 43
Aisha bt. Abi Bakr, 95, 240n32, 241n44
Ali, Kecia, 2, 87
Ali al-Hanafi, Abd al-Majid, 80–81, 87–91, 94
Alleaume, Ghislaine, 59, 61
Allouba, Muhammad Ali, 53, 67, 68, 75, 148, 149
Amin, Ahmad, 53–54, 67–68, 201
Amin, Qasim, xv, 3, 13, 14, 81, 83–85, 103, 105–15, 114–16, 117, 120, 186, 202; authorship controversy, 103,

Amin, Qasim (*cont.*)
  245n130; *Les Égyptiens*, 84, 105; *Tahrir al-Mar'a* 3, 84, 105, 109, 113, 115, 116, 190
Amina Hanim (d. 1824; wife of Muhammad Ali), 31–32
Amina Ilhami (khediva 1879–92; khediva mother 1892–1914), xix, 19–20, 30, 41–42, 50–51
annulment, or judicial divorce (*tatliq*), 17, 112, 126–28, 132–33 146, 154, 171–72, 176, 211–13
anxieties and tensions, 9, 49, 67, 112, 153, 199. *See also* family: crisis of; morality and immorality; press, periodicals, and publishing; public space; women: public presence and in public
arbitration. *See* mediators and mediation between spouses; divorce: arbitration
Asad, Talal, 6, 207, 256n7
Asma' bt. Abi Bakr, 240n32
Atarbi family of Ikhtab, 63, 74
al-Attar, Hasan, 82
authority of husbands over wives, 86–87, 89–90, 132, 175–79; in French law, 177, 196–97; *qiwama*, 90, 99–100, 118, 203; *wilaya*, 177
autonomy of Egypt (1841), 35, 158, 225n2
al-Azhar and Azharis, 62, 137, 158, 161, 164

backwardness, 20, 79, 84, 109, 117, 165, 225n7. *See also* civilization, development, and progress
Badran, Margot, 8, 202
Bahithat al-Badiya. *See* Nasif, Malak Hifni
Baldwin, James, 127

bankruptcy of Egypt (1876), 10, 21, 22, 31
Baron, Beth, 8, 9, 262n13
al-Barudi, Mahmud Sami, 28, 30, 92
Basha, Ahmad Sulayman, and his family in Alexandria, 187–91, 201, 211, 261n6
bayt al-ta'a. *See* house of obedience
Behar, Cem, 3, 7, 10, 68, 151
Booth, Marilyn, 117, 151
British occupation of Egypt (1882–1914), 21–22, 31, 41, 159
bulugh. *See* adulthood, legal
al-Bustani, Butrus, 95, 121

capacity, legal, 130, 150, 171, 177, 254n100
Capitulations, 159
Charrad, Mounira, 2
chastisement. *See* wives: striking of
Chennells, Ellen, 38
Cherbonneau, Eugène, 161, 175, 183, 197–98
childcare, 2, 70, 80, 88, 95–96, 102
childhood, 2, 13, 97
child marriage. *See* marriage: of minors
childrearing, 2, 4, 13, 39, 77, 79, 80, 82, 85, 93–97, 102, 105–6, 114, 115–16, 121, 207. *See also tarbiya*
children, 5, 97, 101, 105–6, 110–12, 132–33, 155, 175, 203; of concubines, 24, 34; custody of, 132, 185–86, 200
child support, 130, 140, 143–45
civil code of France, 161, 165, 169, 175, 177, 196–98, 203
civilization, development, and progress, 9, 79, 93–94, 102, 104, 121. *See also* education: and civilization; Europe: civilization; family: and civilization;

Islam: as source of modern civilization; women: and civilization
civil service and civil servants, 6, 22, 28, 30, 45, 81, 93, 146, 155, 163, 187, 200; French, 28, 35
Cole, Juan, 44
colonialism, colonial knowledge, and colonial discourse, 20–21, 79, 115; colonial modernity, 16, 202; and law, 7, 9, 128, 160–61, 166, 185, 187, 191, 198, 209, 249n18; semi-colonization, 6, 160, 221n25. *See also* law and legal systems: colonial
concubines and concubinage, 12, 21–23, 51, 74–75, 82, 100, 132–34; khedival, 11, 19, 29–31, 33–34, 42, 42, 99; *mustawlada* (mother of her master's child), 24, 74–75; "one-mother-one-son," 31, 32 Ottoman, 21, 27; *umm walad* (mother of her master's child), 24
"confinement" of women in the home, 91–92, 109, 182, 186.
conjugal family ideal, xv, 39–41, 55, 77, 83, 111–12, 120, 207–8. *See also* family ideology
constitutions of Egypt, 1–3, 207, 215
consular courts, 159, 188–91, 198, 256n8, 262n9, n16
cooking, 80, 88, 96
Coontz, Stephanie, 4
correction. *See* wives: striking of
covering (veiling) and concealment (seclusion) of women, 3, 20, 23, 39, 47–50, 57, 72, 84, 91, 95, 100, 108–9, 115, 199, 225n6, 231n15, 245n127
Crews, Robert, 183
Cromer, Earl of (Sir Evelyn Baring; British consul-general in Egypt 1883–1907), 20, 114–15, 164

custody. *See* wives: custody of; children: custody of
customary contract (*aqd urfi*), 140, 252n70
customs, 18, 108, 185; un-Islamic, 109, 202

Damad Afandi, 171–73; *Majma' al-Anhur*, 171, 179
al-Damurdash, Abd al-Rahim, 154, 254n116
al-Dayrabi, Ahmad b. Umar, 64, 66, 80–81, 132
Dhuhni, Nafisa, and Dhunni family of Alexandria, 187–91, 198, 201, 202, 211
Depping, G.-B. (Georges-Bernard), 93–94, 95, 104
desertion: of wives by husbands, 14, 110, 119, 126–28, 134, 142–43, 145–46, 151, 156–57, 209; of husbands by wives (*see* domicile, marital: wife's abandonment of; wives: runaway). *See also* house of obedience
al-Dirini, Abd al-Aziz, 98–99
disobedience (of wives, *nushuz*), 74, 88, 91, 119, 142, 174, 176–78, 186, 192–96, 200–201
divorce, 2, 14, 109–10, 112–14, 129, 138–40; arbitration, 113, 212; in Britain, 197; capricious or unintentional, 113, 151, 212; causes of (*see* desertion; abuse, spousal; harm, as cause of divorce; maintenance: arrears of); conditional (*ta'liq al-talaq*), 51–52, 82, 113, 134–36, *136*, 141, 187–88, 212; defense of, 101–2; delegated (*tafwid al-talaq*), 51, 54, 113, 134–36, 214; disapproval and discouragement of, 13, 40, 78, 102, 113, 199;

divorce (cont.)
    in France, 101–2, 196–97, 260n65; *khul'* (divorce in exchange for cession of financial rights), 17–18, 101–2, 192, 212, 214–15; *mubara'a* (divorce by bargaining away financial rights), 17–18, 101–2, 192, 212; rate, 113–14, 208, 215, 229n73; repudiation, unilateral (*talaq*), 17, 102, 113–14, 212; restriction of, 113, 164; revocable, 17, 134, 212; Western views of, 20. *See also* annulment, or judicial divorce
divorcées, 3, 17, 59, 107, 110, 112, 117, 131, 132, 148, 200, 213
documents and documentation, 14, 15, 113, 124, 136, 138–40, 143, 167. *See also* notarization and registration
domesticity (domestic ideology), 1–4, 77–80, 84–85, 94–97, 102–3, 107, 109, 114, 116–17, 120–22, 206–7. *See also* childrearing; household management
domicile, marital: in French law, 178, 185, 196; removal of wife to, 129, 132, 135, 178, 189, 193–95; removal to distant locale, 50, 132, 173–75, 197–98; restriction of wife to, 90–91, 99, 109, 142, 178, 180–82, 187–88, 191–92, 197–200 (*see also* "confinement" of women in the home); stipulated in marriage, 58; wife's abandonment of, 74, 185, 188–89, 192–97
Doolittle, Megan, 4
dower (*mahr, sadaq*), 17–18, 58–59, 64, 88, 90, 129, 173–80, 259n53; going rate, 130, 132, 149, 173
droit Musulman Algérien. See family law, Muslim: Algerian Muslim law
Duben, Alan, 3, 7, 10, 68, 151

education, 7, 12, 44, 56, 79, 82–83, 93–97, 100, 102–3; and character formation, 13, 77, 97, 105, 106, 116, 121, 206; and civilization, 82, 93, 94, 116, 121; and family, 77, 95; French system of, 28, 81, 93, 94; governesses, 84, 116; government schools, 22, 28, 67, 81–83, 85, 93, 116; of men, 11, 39, 46, 56, 67, 94, 111, 246n157; religious, 54, 126, 165; of women, 3, 9, 13, 39, 77–79, 82–85, 94–97, 102, 105–9, 114–17, 121–22, 190, 206–7, 246n157
effendiyya, 67, 68, 206
Egyptian Feminist Union, 202
Enlightenment thought, xvi, 6, 78–79, 89; family in, 2, 96–97, 102, 115
Europe: civilization, 9, 21, 79, 116–17, 159–60; culture, 6, 9, 116; social thought, 5–6, 13, 81, 95–96, 115, 160, 205

Fahmy, Khaled, 8, 9, 10
family: basis or basic unit of society, 1–2, 4, 23, 77–78, 82, 89–90, 102, 104, 114, 150, 160, 186, 200; and civilization, 5–6, 11, 13, 20–21, 23, 44, 104, 114, 116, 203, 242n65; conjugal, 2, 3, 4, 9, 20, 23, 82, 104, 119, 186, 196, 199, 200, 203, 208; crisis of, 67, 151, 157, 209; Egyptian, 1, 3, 8, 20, 101, 108; European, 5, 208; extended, 68, 70, 78, 208; forms and formation patterns, 8, 10, 93, 207–8; historical development, 104; in Islamist discourse, 4, 207, 215; and nation, 1, 3, 4, 77, 104, 112, 121, 150–51, 186, 207; and politics, 4, 9, 20, 22, 41, 89, 150–51, 210, 225n12, 256n10; portraits

of, xviii, 40, 55, 69, 73; purpose of, 2, 4, 77, 102, 104; and religion, 1, 3, 7, 15, 117, 159–60, 166, 183–84, 210, 215; social construction of, 78, 89, 184, 215, 223n46; stability of, 1, 2, 8, 13, 77–78, 82, 97, 102–3, 110, 113–14, 121; Western views of, 3, 9, 13, 20–21, 23–25, 79, 100–102, 115, 225n7

family ideology, 1, 3, 23, 41, 44, 48, 68, 69, 77–80, 82–84, 102–5, 111–12, 114, 116, 120–22, 186, 199–200, 205, 206–8, 210. *See also* conjugal family ideal

family law, Muslim, 4, 7, 14, 15, 18, 68, 83, 107, 123–25, 146, 156, 159–64, 169, 185, 187, 190–91, 200, 205, 209, 215; Algerian Muslim law, 161, 165, 185, 197; Anglo-Muhammadan law, 258n36; codification of 3, 7, 14, 15, 114, 123, 125, 161, 163–64, 166, 183, 209–10 (*see also specific law*); and French scholarship, 160–61, 166, 187, 190, 197, 209; heart of Sharia, 15, 160, 184; reform and reform proposals, 14, 84, 110, 112–13, 114, 121, 137, 151, 153–57, 161, 163–64, 184, 200, 209–10. *See also* personal status; Qadri's code of personal status

farewell sermon of the Prophet, 87, 88

Fargues, Philippe, 59, 61, 65, 70

fathers, 11, 58–59, 64–65, 67, 68, 70, 87, 106, 118, 130, 132, 148–50, 190

Fawwaz, Zaynab, 81, 85, 114, 116–17, 119–20, 151; *al-Rasa'il al-Zaynabiyya*, 85

feminism and feminists, 13, 78, 81–82, 84, 102–3, 115–16, 120, 185, 202, 207

fiqh. *See* jurisprudence and juridical literature

fitna (temptation, discord), 108, 180–81, 199

France: sexual mores 34, 101; social thought, 81, 93, 94–98, 206. *See also* civil code of France; education: French system of; law and legal systems: French

French language, 6, 81, 160

garnishment of husband's property or wages, 153, 155–56, 186, 192, 211, 255n121

gender and gendering, 4, 8, 9, 84, 88–90, 95, 156. *See also* domesticity; hadiths: misogynist; historiography: of women and gender; jurisprudence and juridical literature: gendered discourse in; morality and immorality; public space; spheres: public and private; women

al-Ghazali, 86, 87

Gillotte, Charles, 197–98

Goode, William, 5, 207

Grand Mufti, office of, 18, 123

guardian (*wali*), 51–52, 60, 90, 107, 114, 175, 186, 189. *See also* marriage: of self, by women; marriage guardian

Guizot, François, 93, 104

hadiths (sayings and doings attributed to the Prophet Muhammad), 79, 92, 95, 97, 118, 120, 184, 192; misogynist, 89, 90, 91

Haj, Samira, 150

al-Halabi, Ibrahim, 171, 179

Hamont, P. N. (Pierre Nicolas), 26–27, 29

Hanafi school of law, 14, 18, 39, 86, 87, 98, 112–13, 123, 125–31, 132, 134, 137, 141, 146, 148, 150, 153–54, 158, 160, 161–64, 166–67, 169–77, 182–83, 187, 190, 214; authoritative doctrine (*zahir al-riwaya*), 171–74, 259 5n52; "corruption of the times," 173, 259n52

Hanafization, 15, 123–25, 128, 136–37, 140–41, 156, 204, 209–10

Hanbali school of law, 126–27, 129, 132–33, 141, 183, 213–14

Hanna, Nelly, 132–33

harems, 10–11, 25, 42, 84, 100, 114; gifting of daughters into, 27; "harem system," 20, 23–25, 39; khedival, 10, 22, 27, 23–29, 31, 38; marriage of women out of, 10, 22, 24, 26, 27–29, 31, 32, 45, 51, 206; Ottoman, 23–25, 27; and politics, 10, 22, 26, 28; Western views of, 23–25, 26–27, 33–34;

harm (*darar*), as cause of divorce, 212, 213

al-Haskafi, 81, 167, 179, 195–96

Hatem, Mervat, 117, 119–20, 151, 247n169

Helal, Emad, 26

hijab. *See* covering and concealment of women

al-Hilbawi, Ibrahim, 50–51, 59, 70, 72, 74

historiography: Egyptian, 8, 11, 28, 39, 120; of family, 4, 5, 7–10, 104, 150, 162, 205, 207; legal, 7, 15, 18, 125, 161–62, 211; sources, 10, 16, 18; of women and gender, 4, 7, 8, 15, 39, 120, 150, 162

Hourani, Albert, 104

household (a co-resident group of kin with or without slaves, servants, etc.), 4, 8, 17, 25, 47, 55, 78, 157, 234n63; conjugal (simple, nuclear), 5, 7, 11, 17, 46, 60–62, 67–68, 70, 97, 121; joint (multiple family, extended), 7, 11, 12, 17, 46, 60–68, 91, 155, 206, 208, 235–36n95

household, ruling class (a complex of kin, followers, slaves, and former slaves bound by ties of dependency and/or loyalty to ruling-class figure), 8, 22, 23, 25–27, 32, 45; as part of political system, 9, 26–28. *See also* khedives: households of; Ottoman imperial family: household

household government, 10–11, 26, 28, 45, 206

household management (*tadbir al-manzal*), 13, 41, 77, 85, 89, 96, 105–7, 116, 121–22, 207

house of obedience (*bayt al-ta'a*), 15–16, 185–87, 198–99, 202–3, 199; in Algeria, 197–98, 210; French origins, 15, 185, 196, 210. *See also* domicile, marital; obedience of wives; restitution of conjugal rights

housework, 2, 80, 88–89, 94–96, 102

Hunt, Lynn, 150–51

huquq al-nisa' ala al-rijal (what wives are due from their husbands), 87–89, 99, 104, 111, 118–19

huquq al-rijal ala al-nisa' (what husbands are due from their wives), 87–88, 90–91, 99, 118–19, 177–78

huquq al-zawjayn (what spouses are due) and *huquq al-zawjiyya* (marital obligations), 81, 87–92, 96, 99, 110, 118–19, 175–76, 247n169. *See also* farewell sermon of the Prophet

hybridity and hybridization: in ideas, 3, 12–15, 79, 102, 206, 237n3; in law,

14–16, 165, 200, 204, 205, 244n113, 258n36

Ibn Abdin, 86, 92, 172–75, 179; *Radd al-Muhtar*, 167, *168*, 169, 171, 176, 195–96
Ibn al-Humam, 181, 199
Ibn Hajar al-Haythami, 81, 192, 200
Ibn Nujaym, 128–29, 181
Ibrahim Pasha (regent viceroy of Egypt 1848), 31, 33, 35, 94
al-Ibyani, Muhammad Zayd, 179, 200. *See also* Qadri's code of personal status: explication by al-Ibyani
al-Idwi al-Hamzawi, Hasan, 80
Imara, Muhammad, 103
imprisonment of husbands, 112, 153, 186, 201, 212
indigenization: in ideas, 68, 95; in law, 166, 185–87, 197–98, 202, 210
infanticide, 101–2
inheritance, 2, 8, 90, 129, 138, 140, 189; probate inventories, 74, 75
Islam: as cause of backwardness, 84, 165; as source of modern civilization, 7, 79, 206, 210
Islamic law. *See* Sharia; jurisprudence
isma. *See* wives: custody of
Ismail (khedive of Egypt 1863–79), xv, 19, 21, 22, 28, 31, 33, 42, 45, 137, 158–59, 162; domestic life, 21, 33–39, 43, 82, 83, 99, 101

al-Jabarti, Abd al-Rahman, 91
al-Jarida (newspaper), 86
Javidan Hanim née Countess May Torok von Szendro, second wife of Abbas Hilmi II, 43, 44
"Jihan's law." *See* Law No. 44 of 1979

Jum'a, Muhammad Lutfi, 54, 56, 57, 59, 67, 75, 134
jurisprudence (*fiqh*) and juridical literature, 2, 78, 79, 81, 86, 103, 108, 125, 145, 165, 167, 180, 184, 191, 198–99, 210; Algerian, 161, 185, 191, 197, 198, 258n38; discussion, debate, and contending opinions within, 161–62, 164, 167, 169, 170–71, 173–75, 179–81, 183, 187, 210, 259n44, 259n52; gendered discourse in, 86, 88, 92; predominant or preferred opinions, 137, 162, 163, 167, 169, 172, 174–75, 179, 183

kafes. *See* Ottoman imperial family
Kandiyoti, Deniz, 61, 151
Kemal, Namık, 95, 121
Khalil b. Ishaq, 161; his *Mukhtasar*, 161, 165, 175, 183
Khatir family of Ikhtab, 63
khedives (title accorded Egyptian viceroys starting with Ismail), 36; autocracy, 10, 22, 28, 31, 44, 45; dynasty, 10, 21; households of, 22, 23–24, 26, 28–29, 31, 32, 33, 45; public image of, 21, 22, 23, 33, 38, 40–44; succession of, 21, 34, 35–39, 205
khedival family, 6, 11, 19–23, 26, 32, 85, 225n2; conflicts and rivalries within, 35–36; princes, 33, 35
khiyar al-bulugh, 131, 148. *See also* adulthood, legal; marriage: consent and choice in)
Kholoussy, Hanan, 3, 9, 10, 67
khul'. *See* divorce: *khul'*
"*khul'* law." *See* Law No. 1 of 2000
kifa'a (status suitability). *See* marriage: status suitability
Kozma, Liat, 49

Lane, Edward, 33, 59, 66, 70, 72, 74, 88–89
law and legal systems: Algerian, 160, 165–66, 209, 258n38; codes of law, 125; colonial, 160; and custom, 125, 128–29, 133, 165; Egyptian, 7, 13–16, 81, 125, 158–60, 165–66; English, 160; French, 81, 101, 125, 158–60, 163, 165–66, 209, 260n69; Mixed (*see* Mixed Courts); Ottoman, 125–29, 146, 160 (*see also* Mecelle; Ottoman Law of Family Rights); positive, 14, 166, 170, 187, 191, 204, 210; translations, 159, 161, 162, 165, 183, 190. *See also* civil code of France; family law, Muslim; jurisprudence and juridical literature; procedural laws; Sharia Courts
Law No. 1 of 2000, 214
Law No. 25 of 1920, 113, 124, 211
Law No. 25 of 1929, 113, 124, 135, 212, 214
Law No. 31 of 1910, 202
Law No. 44 of 1979, 213
Law No. 56 of 1923, 67, 140, 211–12
Law No. 78 of 1931, 202, 214
Law No. 100 of 1985, 213–14
Le Play, Frédéric, 5
Loos, Tamara, 160
Lopez, Shaun, 199
love and affection: in marriage, 12, 53, 54, 55, 56, 75–76, 87, 92–93, 97–99, 100, 101, 102, 107, 208; toward children, 97, 111
Ludden, David, 61

ma'dhuns. *See* marriage registrar
mahr. *See* dower
Mainardi, Patricia, 96

maintenance (*nafaqa*, due dependents such as wife, children, and aged parents), 3, 80, 87, 88, 89, 90, 92, 107, 109–10, 112, 114, 118–19, 124, 133, 140–45, 174, 176, 178, 182, 191–96, 200–201, 203, 213–14; arrears of, 14, 18, 119, 124, 141–43, 145, 153–57, 204, 209, 211 (*see also* garnishment of husband's property or wages; imprisonment of husbands); clothing allowance (*kiswa*), 88, 89; going rate, 141, 144; judicial orders setting rate of, 141–45, 153–54, 176, 192, 253n82; lodging (*maskan shar'i*), 68, 88, 236n100, 263n26; nonmaintenance, 14, 110, 111, 112, 120, 124, 126–28, 134–35, 145–46, 152, 154–55, 157, 164, 186, 199, 204, 209, 211; temporary maintenance (*nafaqa idda*, due a divorcée), 17–18, 129, 214
maintenance-obedience relationship, 3, 6, 15, 80, 88, 89, 95–96, 99, 102, 109, 112, 114, 117–21, 132, 141, 145, 151–53, 157, 184, 185–86, 192, 196, 198–99, 206, 209–11, 215
majority, legal. *See* adulthood, legal
Maliki school of law, 112–13, 126–27, 133, 137, 141, 146, 150, 153, 154, 157, 161, 164, 209–12
Malte-Brun, Conrad, 93–94, 104
al-Marghinani, 127
marital authority. *See* authority of husbands over wives
marital relations, 29, 90–91, 99–100
marriage, 3, 4, 46, 97, 175, 186; age difference in, 87, 92, 240n37; arrangement of, 11, 12, 46, 53, 56–60, 76, 87, 120, 130–31, 148, 208, 237n119; bachelors and delay of, 53–54, 56, 67, 120, 206; companionate, 3, 9, 13,

20, 23, 39, 44, 46–48, 61, 68, 75–76, 77–78, 84, 85–86, 95, 97, 99–100, 105, 107, 110, 114, 116, 117–18, 122, 190, 206; compulsion (*jabr*) in, 130; consent and choice in, 12, 29, 45–47, 50–51, 53, 56–57, 75–76, 98, 120, 107, 130–31, 150, 249n29; consummation of, 174, 176, 194, 245n136; contract of, 9, 17, 57, 67, 86, 91, 97, 129, 132–33, 138–40, 143, 176, 189–90, 192, 214; endogamous, 21, 36, 43, 50, 91, 189, 205; khedival, 11, 30, 36–38, 41; of minors, 46, 65–67, 85, 98, 127, 130–31, 148, 165, 189–90, 211; neolocal, 11, 67–68; Ottoman, 21, 22, 30; patrilocal, 61, 67; "pillars," in jurisprudence, 57–58, 129; and politics, 10, 22–23, 25–39, 45, 51, 72; in precolonial Muslim writings, 2, 3, 12, 13, 80–81, 89, 95, 96, 98, 99, 102, 118, 192, 205, 206; prenuptial meetings, 11–12, 46–48, 50, 53, 54, 56, 57, 75–76, 78, 87, 92, 97–98, 102, 107, 108, 182, 240n37; prenuptial negotiations, 12, 46–48, 56, 57–58, 67, 76; property regime, 2, 17, 208, 260n69; of self by women, 98, 127, 131, 141, 148–50, 171–73; of slaves, 59, 60, 148, 235n88 (*see also* harems: marriage of women out of); status suitability (*kifa'a*), 60, 86–87, 130, 149–50, 171–73, 259n53; stipulations in, 54, 58, 124, 132–33, 141, 212–14; virtues and purposes of, 2, 86, 92, 97, 104; Western views of, 24–25. *See also* domicile, marital; monogamy; polygyny; trousseau; weddings

marriage guardian (*wali nikah*), 11, 51–52, 58, 87, 97–98, 107, 130–31, 139, 148–49, 171–72; *jabbar*, 130, 148

marriage handbooks or manuals, precolonial, 78–81, 121, 176, 187, 197

marriage registrar (*ma'dhun*), 113, 124, 138–40, 143, 149

marriage systems: in Egypt, 3, 4, 6, 9, 10, 11, 26, 31, 38, 46, 51, 75, 79, 164, 205, 206, 208; in Europe, 75; in Turkey, 7, 68, 70

masafat al-qasr (travel distance justifying abbreviation of prayers), 174–75, 178

masculinity, xv, 27, 43, 120

Mecelle (Ottoman civil law based on Hanafi jurisprudence), 158, 161–62, 164, 209, 256n7

mediators and mediation between spouses, 192, 197. *See also* divorce: arbitration

Melman, Billie, 24

men's faults and irresponsibility, 110, 113, 118–20, 124, 141, 150–57, 186, 209

merchants, 61–62, 71–72, 74, 91, 92, 236n108

Mernissi, Fatima, 89

Messick, Brinkley, 160, 167

military and military officers, 8, 22, 26, 28, 30, 146–47, 152

milk (control or authority), 87, 134, 150, 254n100. *See also* authority of husbands over wives; wives: custody of

misalliance. *See* marriage: status suitability

missing (*mafqud*) men. *See* absent and missing husbands

Mitchell, Timothy, 13, 97, 114, 242n66

Mixed Courts, 14, 125, 159, 162, 165, 166

modernist intellectuals, xv, 4, 6, 12–13, 23, 79–86, 95, 107, 109–10, 114, 115–16, 120–22, 128, 186, 206;

modernist intellectuals (*cont.*)
  discourse on family, 6, 13, 40, 82–86, 115, 141, 150–51, 205–6; female, 81–82, 83–86, 115–17, 120, 157; male, 84, 151, 156–57, 199, 210
modernity and modernization, 5, 6, 13, 15, 49, 63, 78, 124–25, 156, 158, 186, 203–4, 205, 207–8, 210
modernization theory, 5, 205, 207
monogamy, xv, 6, 11, 10, 19–23, 29–31, 36, 38–40, 43–44, 51–52, 58, 78, 82, 84, 99, 114, 122, 135, *136*, 205, 206, 229n73
morality and immorality, 110, 151–53, 209; policing of, 49; women and, 49, 92, 108, 112, 117, 124, 145, 151–57, 199
mothers and motherhood, 2, 3, 13, 32, 34, 57, 70, 77, 97, 104–8, 114, 116, 118
al-Mu'ayyad (newspaper), 150, 188–91
mubara'a. *See* divorce: *mubara'a*
Mubarak, Ali, 81, 83, 93–94, 96–97, 100–103, 107, 110, 113, 212, 206; *Alam al-Din*, 83, 96, 100–102, 108; *Tariq al-Hija*, 83, 96–97, 100–102
Muhammad Ali (viceroy of Egypt 1805–48), 8, 10, 18, 26–33, 38, 62, 71, 82, 123, 152
mukhaddarat (highly secluded women), 91
Musa, Salama, 49, 55–56, 57, 59, 67, 75, 76
al-Musawwar (weekly magazine), xvii, xix
mustawlada. *See* concubines and concubinage

nafaqa. *See* maintenance
Najmabadi, Afsaneh, 121–22, 151

Nasif, Malak Hifni (Bahithat al-Badiya), 50, 56, 70, 75–76, 81, 85–86, 116–17, 119–20, 145, 151, 182, 202; *al-Nisa'iyyat*, 86
National Courts, 83, 125, 158–59, 162, 165, 190, 245n143
nationalism and nationalists, 4, 207; national identity, xvi, 165, 258n35; national narrative, 9, 28, 39, 49
Native Courts. *See* National Courts
al-Nawawi, Muhammad b. Umar, 80–81, 87–91, 94, 121, 187
necessity (*darura*), legal principle, 112
Nerval, Gérard de, 60, 88
nonsupport of wives. *See* maintenance: arrears of; maintenance: nonmaintenance
notarization and registration, 138–39; civil registration, 113, 124, 139–40, 156, 186. *See also* marriage registrar; Sharia Courts

obedience (*ta'a*) of wives, 3, 15, 80, 87, 88, 89–92, 114, 119, 129, 142, 145, 157, 178–79, 188–89, 191–204, 209; enforcement, 185–88, 191, 193–204, 210, 262nn16–17; in French law, 185, 187, 196, 202; judicial orders of obedience, 15, 185–86, 188, 193–95, 202, 203, 213–14; in precolonial jurisprudence, 80, 133, 186. *See also* house of obedience
officials. *See* civil service and civil servants
Ottoman imperial family, 10, 101; confinement of princes (*kafes*), 32–33, 35; household, 22, 23–24, 25–26, 32; reproduction, 25, 27; succession in, 35. *See also* concubines and

concubinage; harems; mothers and motherhood; slaves)
Ottoman Law of Family Rights (1917), 135–36, 146, 211
Ottoman ruling-class culture, 23, 25, 31–32, 34, 36, 38, 42, 43, 101, 205.

Pamuk, Orhan, 68
patriarchy: "classical," 61; domestic or family patriarchy, 11, 45, 61, 68, 89, 92, 148, 234n66
peasants, 9, 50, 58, *73*, 140; as authentic Egyptians, 57. *See also* rural society; women: peasant
Peirce, Leslie, 27, 32, 34
personal status (*statut personnel, al-ahwal al-shakysiyya*), 164–65, 166, 188
personal status law, 14–15, 183, 190, 209; Algerian, 160, 165; Egyptian, 1, 72, 78, 160. *See also* Qadri's code of personal status
Peters, Rudolph, 166, 169, 170–71
Pollard, Lisa, 3, 8, 20, 21, 34, 41, 93, 151
polygyny, xv, 2, 11, 12, 13, 19–23, 29–31, 36–38, 43–44, 46–47, 52, 70–75, 79, 84, 85–86, 109–12, 119, 132–35, 151, 155, 192, 205; clandestine, 43, 47, 72, 134, 213; decline of, 6, 7, 10, 12, 20, 25, 30–31, 44, 46, 61, 70, 111, 206; disapproval and discouragement of, 7, 11, 43, 78, 80, 94, 98–99; 100–103, 110, 213; and family discord, 98–99, 100, 101, 102, 110–11, 115, 120; rate of, 25, 70–72, 74, 101, 236n108, 264–65n1; restriction of, 80, 164, 212; Western views of, 20, 23, 25, 30, 43, 115; women's dislike of, 46, 52, 70, 99, 120
Poole, Sophia Lane, 26, 29, 33

population and demography, 4, 5, 8, 16, 94; censuses, xv, 12, 16, 47, 59, 61–66 tables 2–6, 68, 72, 74
postsexuality, 32
press, periodicals, and publishing, 8, 9, 13, 23, 41, 44, 49, 68, 76, 77, 84, 106, 110, 112, 114, 116, 121, 131, 150, 156, 164, 199, 205–6
primogeniture. *See* khedives: succession of
private sphere. *See* domesticity; spheres
procedural laws, 123, 136, 159, 186, 209; *La'ihat al-Mahakim al-Shar'iyya* of 1880, 137, 139, 143, 166; *La'ihat al-Qudat* of 1856, 137–39, 153; *La'ihat Tartib al-Mahakim al-Shar'iyya* of 1897, 15, 137, 140, 143, 166, 185–87, 191, 196, 198, 199–201, 203
public interest (*maslaha*), legal principle, 111, 112, 245n138
public opinion, 23, 44, 188–90, 206
public space, 49, 112, 199
puissance maritale. See authority of husbands over wives

Qadri Pasha, Muhammad, 14, 19, 161–62, 169
Qadri's code of personal status, 14–15, 161–64, 166–67, 169–71, 173, 175–84, 190–91, 200, 209–10; explication by al-Ibyani, 179–82, 183, 187, 199, 210; form and organization of, 162, 169, *170*, 175–77, 187; influence of, 162–63, 187, 257n19
qiwama. See authority of husbands over wives
Qur'an and Qur'anic verses, 79, 89, 92, 94, 96, 126, 133, 182, 184; verse 2:228, 88, 119; verse 2:233, 118; verse 2:282,

Qur'an and Qur'anic verses (*cont.*)
118; verse 4:3, 74, 98, 100, 110–11; verse 4:34, 90, 99–100, 118, 195, 203, 241n47; verse 4:129, 74, 110–11; verse 33:32, 182

al-Rafi'i, Abd al-Rahman, 54–55, 56, 57, 59, 67, 75
al-Ramli, Khayr al-Din, 126–27, 263n31
Rapoport, Yossef, 126
Raya and Sakina murders, 199
religion. *See* education: religious; family: and religion; family law, Muslim; spheres: and religion
residence. *See* domicile, marital
restitution of conjugal rights, 197
Rida, Muhammad Rashid, 158
Riyad, Mustafa, Pasha, 20, 30
El-Rouayheb, Khaled, 10
rural society, 12, 16, 60, 140; image of, 67, 106; landholding and landholders, 62, 63, 66, 71; notables in, 63, 71–72, 74–75, 131 (*see also* village headmen and shaykhs); slaves in, 60, 74

al-Sadat, Safiya, 150
Said Pasha (viceroy of Egypt 1854–63), 33, 34, 35
Sanu', Ya'qub, 36–37
Sautayra, Édouard, 161, 175, 183, 197–98
School of Administration and Languages, 158
School of Languages, 82, 158–59, 162
School of Law, 83, 103, 158, 162–63, 179, 200
schools. *See* education
schools of Islamic law (*madhhab*s), 18, 80, 123–24. *See also specific school*

seclusion. *See* covering and concealment of women
sexual relations, 2, 34, 41–42, 52, 59, 88, 89, 90, 97, 101, 110, 129, 176, 178–79, 192, 245n136. *See also* marriage: consummation of
Shafi'i school of law, 126–27, 131, 132, 134, 137, 141, 146, 153, 154, 157, 176, 209
Shafiq, Ahmad, 45, 47–50, 57, 59, 67, 68, 76, 134
Shafiq Nur Hanim (d. 1884; fourth wife of Khedive Ismail and mother of Khedive Tawfiq), 33–34, 42
Shaham, Ron, 200, 264n48
El Shakry, Omnia, 79, 115, 122
al-Shara'ibi family of Cairo, 91
al-Sha'rawi, Huda, 46, 51–52, 54, 58, 66, 70, 72, 131, 135, 201, 202; different versions of her memoirs, 231n25
Sharia (Islamic legal and social norms), 1, 8, 18, 101, 108, 165; codification of 158–62, 169, 183, 188 (*see also* family law, Muslim: codification); as jurists' law, 14, 125, 166–67; understandings of, 7, 14, 167, 183, 210
Sharia Courts, 18, 74, 80, 98, 112, 113, 119, 132, 137, 143, 147, 148, 156, 186, 187–90, 201, 204, 209; Algerian, 165, 184, 190, 197–98; enforcement of decisions, 153–57, 186, 200, 203; judicial procedure or practice (*amal*), 18, 133, 146–47, 165, 169; jurisdiction of, 159–60, 184, 210, 245n142; pluralism and forum shopping, 123–28, 146, 156, 183, 209, 211; records of, xv, 47, 138–39, 178, 189; reorganization of, 7, 14–15, 123–25, 159–60, 165–66, 183, 185, 198; social role, 124–25, 137–39, 156. *See also* Grand Mufti,

office of; Hanafization; law and legal systems; marriage registrar; notarization and registration; procedural laws

Sharif Pasha, Muhammad, 20, 30

al-Shurunbulali, 173

slavery: Anglo-Egyptian Convention for the Abolition of Slavery (1877), 11, 22, 25, 30, 42, 111; anti-slavery sentiment, 20, 39; Ottoman, 22–28; slave trade, 6, 9, 12, 45, 206; Western views of, 20, 23, 24–25

slaves, 47, 49, 62–63; African, 25, 59–60, 75; Circassian, 25, 41, 59, 75; domestics, 23, 24, 32, 42, 59, 89; eunuchs, 22, 28, 42, 49, 100; female, 24, 25–26, 32, 42, 59–60, 74, 99 226n21; harem women, 24–26, 27, 29, 30, 31, 32, 45, 50, 51, 92, 206; *kul*s (Ottoman imperial slaves), 22; male, 22, 25–26, 28, 59–60; mamluks (military slaves), 22, 26; manumission, 24, 25, 74, 226n21; marriage of (*see* marriage: of slaves); in military-administrative apparatus, 22, 25–25, 27–28; "slave wives," 12, 59–60, 74, 89, 206. *See also* concubines and concubinage; rural society: slaves in

sleeping baby, 165, 258n38

Sonneveld, Nadia, 3

spheres: public and private (domestic), 1, 95, 121, 207; and religion, 15, 159–60, 184, 215. *See also* domesticity

status suitability. *See* marriage: status suitability

St. John, James Augustus, 152–53

Stowasser, Barbara, 90

suicide, 101–2

Supreme Judicial Council (*Majlis al-Ahkam*), 125, 158

tabarruj. *See* women: modesty and immodesty of

tadbir al-manzal. *See* household management

al-Tahtawi, Rifaʻa Rafiʻi, 12, 81–83, 93–103, 105, 107, 110, 116, 212, 135, *136*, 158–59, 206, 238n13; *al-Murshid al-Amin*, 82, 83, 93, 94–95, 97–101; *Takhlis al-Ibriz*, 82

takhayyur (selection of rules from various schools of law), 163, 183, 211

talfiq (combining of legal rules from various schools of law), 211

tamlik. *See* milk

tarbiya (neologism for early educational formation), 97. *See also* childrearing

Tawfiq, Muhammad (khedive of Egypt 1879–92), xix, 19–21, 23, 30, 31, 33, 34, 36, 38, 39–41, 45, 162; as crown prince, 34–35; domestic life, 40, 101; views on women and family, 39–40

al-Taymur, Aisha, 66, 81, 85, 115–20, 131, 142, 145; *Mir'at al-Ta'ammul*, 85, 118–19, 151, 178; *Nata'ij al-Ahwal*, 85, 117, 151

Thornton, Arland, 5

Tilly, Louise, 4

al-Timurtashi, 167, 179, 195

travel: by men with their wife (*see* domicile, marital: removal to distant locale); by women, 199

trousseau (*jihaz*), 17, 24, 45, 58, 128–29

Tucker, Judith, 8, 9, 10, 127, 135, 242, 58, 249n29

ulama, 61–62, 161, 165, 186, 187, 200, 211. *See also* al-Azhar and Azharis

Umar b. Affan, Caliph, 88

*umda*s. *See* village headmen and shaykhs

umm walad. *See* concubines and concubinage
Urabi Revolution (1881–82), 22, 28–29, 31, 40, 159
urban society, 12, 25, 58, 67, 140, 145, 206; notables in, 74–75, 144
usra (term connoting conjugal family in twentieth-century Egypt), 2

veiling. *See* covering and concealment of women
village headmen and shaykhs, 62, 66, 71–72, 74, 75
villages. *See* rural society

waiting period (*idda*), 17, 127, 139, 149
al-Waqa'i' al-Misriyya (official gazette), 38, 42, 84, 104, 156
weddings: cost of, 45, 58–59; four princely weddings (*afrah al-anjal*), 19, 21, 38, 44; procession (*zifaf*), 19, 58, 91; public celebration of, 19, 30, 41. *See also* marriage
wilayat al-zawj. *See* authority of husbands over wives
witnesses, 58, 118, 137, 139, 188, 260n73. *See also* notarization and registration
wives: compared to captives or prisoners, 87, 88, 103, 121, 204, 207; compared to slaves, 86–87, 240n32; contractual, 12, 24, 59, 74, 107; co-wives, and their equitable treatment, 72, 74, 88, 98–99, 100, 110–11, 176, 189, 245n137; custody (*isma*) of, 134–35, 187; "diplomatic" wife, 33; duties and responsibilities of, 178–79; good treatment of, 86–89, 92, 99, 104, 176, 197; and property, 9, 51; runaway, 15, 185, 187, 192–98, 200–202; striking of, 88, 177, 195, 197, 263n26. *See also* "confinement" of women in the home; disobedience; *huquq al-nisa' ala al-rijal*; obedience
"woman question," 20, 84
women: abilities, agency, and autonomy of, 4, 9, 24, 45, 46, 68, 107, 156; activists, 210, 214; in Britain, 24; in business and legal affairs, 9, 107, 108, 177, 189–90; and civilization, 6, 93–94, 104; deceitfulness, 95, 103; deficient in intellect and faith, 89, 103, 118, 121, 153, 207; as dependents, 2, 3, 107, 151–53, 157, 209; disadvantages and difficulties of, 14, 83, 114, 115, 124, 140–41, 156, 204, 209; education (*see* education: of women); emancipation, 1, 9, 39, 49, 84, 109, 207; equality and inequality of, 1, 39, 61, 89, 90, 92, 94, 100, 215; ignorance of, 39, 95, 105–6, 115; legal strategies of, 144–45, 146–47, 209; middle class, 11, 92, 109, 117, 142, 145, 149, 109, 117, 142, 145, 149; modesty and immodesty (*al-tabarruj*) of, 49, 94, 95, 99, 119, 145, 181–82, 199; names of concealed, 49, 57 231n15; peasant, 56, 92, 106, 108, 117, 152, 191; poor, 145, 148, 154, 155; portraits of, xviii, 42, 48, 231n15; power of, 29–30, 32; public presence and in public space, 19–20, 22, 32, 41–42, 49, 54, 78, 84, 91, 94–95, 112, 119–20, 122, 181–82, 186, 191, 199; respectability, 49, 92, 119, 142, 145; rights of, 78, 150, 190, 210, 215; social life, 29, 58, 91, 133; status and role in society, 1, 6, 20, 28, 40, 79, 83, 93–94, 104–5, 107; unmarried, 2, 107, 117, 204; upper class, 9, 22, 49, 69, 91, 92,

109, 117, 133, 142, 145, 149; Western views of, 24–25, 79; widows, 3, 59, 60, 107, 117, 131, 148; and work, 2, 3, 6, 72, 92, 94, 95, 107, 108, 109, 114, 117, 119, 133, 145, 157, 191–92, 207, 242n58; working class, 92, 108, 133, 142, 145, 152, 191, 209. *See also* "confinement" of women in the home; covering and concealment of women; divorcées; domesticity; education: of women; household; marriage; morality and immorality; *mukhaddarat*

writers. *See* modernist intellectuals

Yakan family, 28, 30
Yusuf, Ali, 150, 188, 190

al-Zabidi, Murtada, 93
Ze'evi, Dror, 10